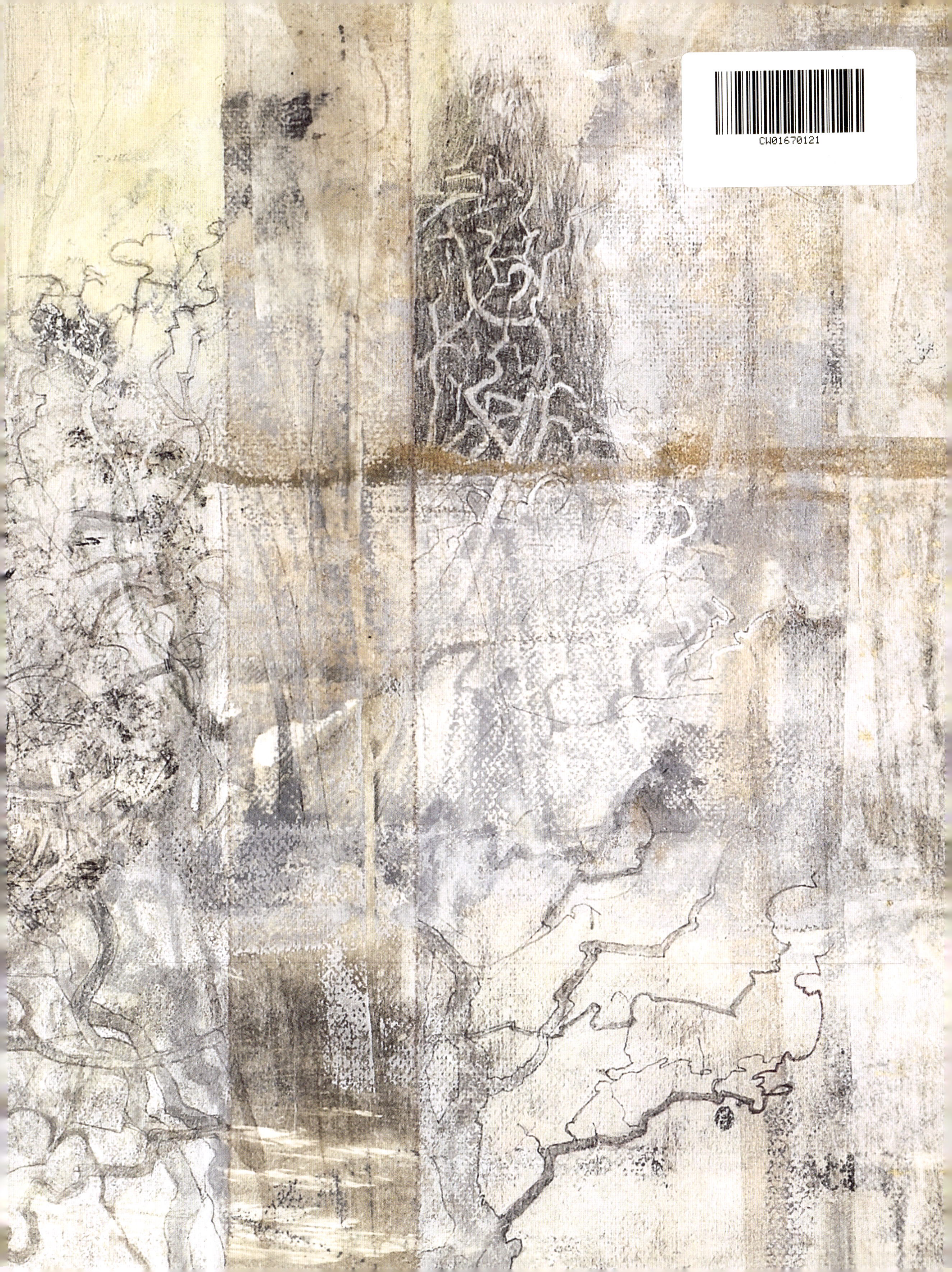

VICTORIA CROWE

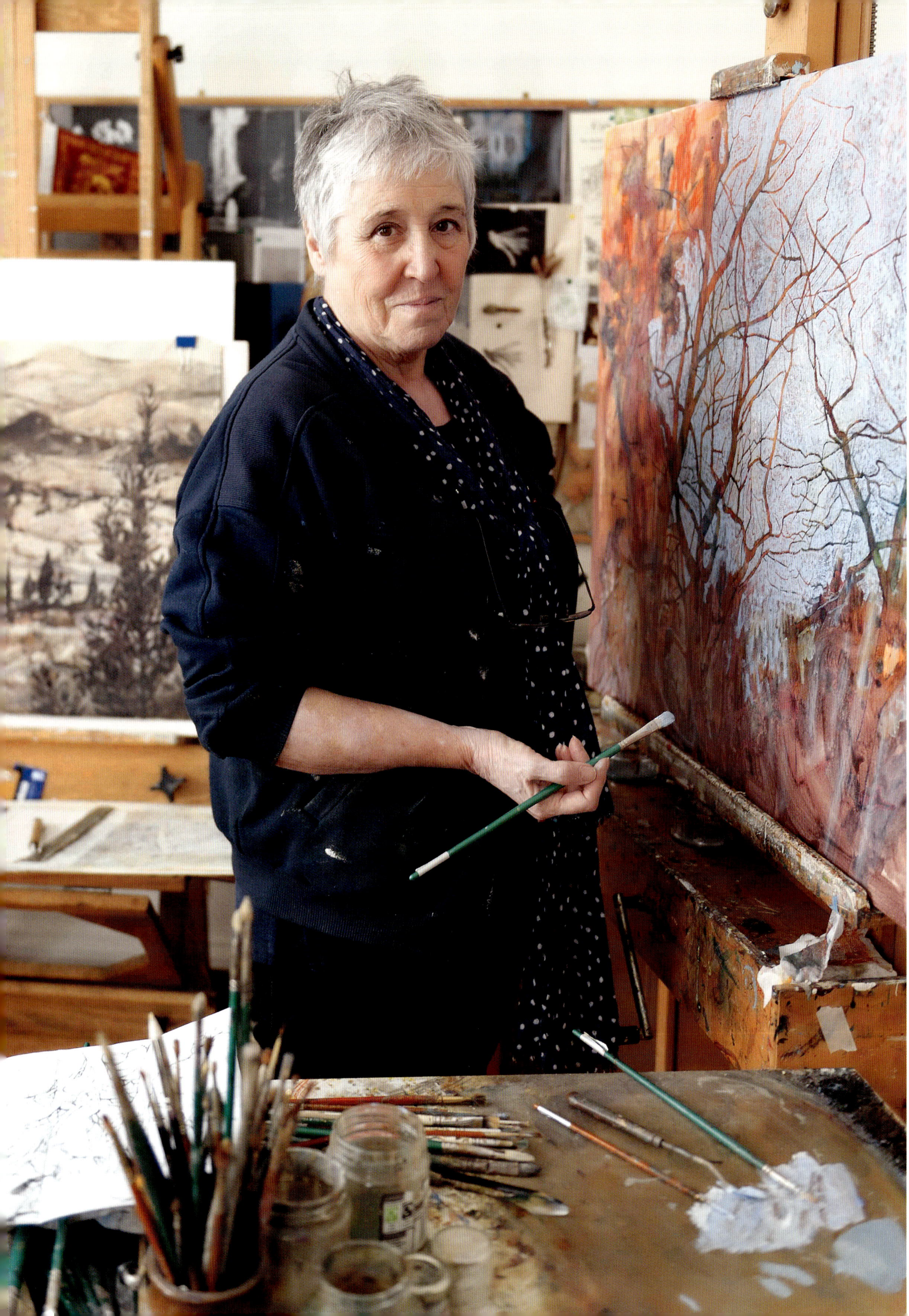

VICTORIA CROWE

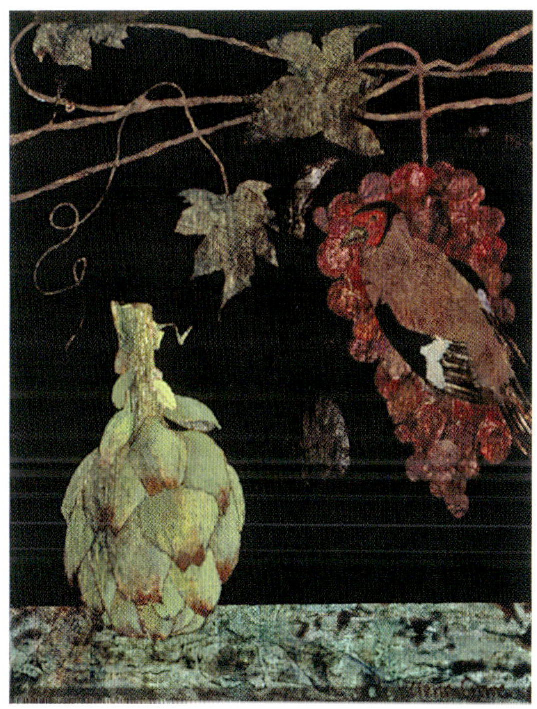

DUNCAN MACMILLAN

ANTIQUE COLLECTORS' CLUB

This book is dedicated to
The Family

First published 2012

ISBN 978-1-85149-714-0

British Library Cataloguing-in-Publication Data
A catalogue record for this book is available from the British Library

Frontispiece: Victoria Crowe in her studio
Title page: *Passionate Fruit*
Endpapers: *Contorta, Frost Sequence*

Printed in China
for the Antique Collectors' Club Ltd., Woodbridge, Suffolk

MIX
Paper from responsible sources
FSC® C104723

Contents

Acknowledgements	6
Foreword	6
Introduction	7
Early Years	8
The Move to Scotland	24
Kittleyknowe	34
Interiors, Monk's Cottage	50
First Portraits	62
West Linton	68
Venice	82
Plant Memories	104
New Departures	118
Recent Commissions	160
Chronology, Exhibitions, Collections, Publications	174
List of Illustrations	178
Notes	182

Acknowledgements

It was a pleasure to work with Duncan Macmillan on this project and I would like to thank him for his perceptive and original writing. I particularly like his attention to the early formative years, allowing the later work to flourish from clearly explained germinal roots.

My thanks also go to the editorial, design and publishing staff at ACC especially Diana Steel, Tom Conway, Stephen Mackinlay, Anna Morton and Sandra Pond.

Thanks to the many people who have encouraged, supported and been involved with this venture: Anne Thomson, Guy Peploe, Joshua Darby, Ken Gray, David Ingram, Helen Bell, Moira, John Sloss.

Thanks to the many friends and collectors who have continued to support my work and to those who have allowed access to their collections.

Photo credits: Ken Gray, John McKenzie, Chris Parks, Andy Phillipson, Antonia Reeve, Robin Scott, John Sherrin and Michael Walton.

Particular thanks to my husband, Michael Walton, who has shared the whole experience of these paintings over the 40-plus years of our life together. On this project he has contributed so much in terms of organising references, archives, images and the draft layout.

Victoria Crowe, West Linton, 2012

The author would like to thank the artist and her husband, Michael Walton, for being so generous with their time and assistance. Together they made the preparation for this book, not a labour, but a pleasure.

Duncan Macmillan, Edinburgh, 2012

Foreword

Victoria Crowe has quietly emerged into a preeminent position in Scottish painting. Her origins in London and time at the Royal College are important, and despite her thirty years as a tutor at Edinburgh College of Art from 1968–1998 and her continuing commitment to work in Scotland, she cannot be understood only in a Scottish context. Her work has always avoided the strident note which provides the 'catchiness' in much Scottish painting; it is instead contemplative, layered and stays in the mind's eye.

Her exhibitions here in December 2012 and for The Edinburgh Festival in 2014 will be her thirteenth and fourteenth with us since the first in 1970 and speak of a continuing relationship of which we are immensely proud.

Guy Peploe, The Scottish Gallery, Edinburgh

Browse & Darby has a long-standing tradition of exhibiting Scottish artists dating back to the era of Roland, Browse & Delbanco when Joan Eardley, Anne Redpath and latterly Robin Philipson, were regularly shown.

Today the gallery continues to exhibit contemporary Scottish painting by celebrated artists such as Dame Elizabeth Blackadder and John Houston. We are delighted to now include the highly regarded Victoria Crowe amongst them.

Victoria Crowe's unique and poetic approach to painting beautifully conveys her narrative subjects and bold use of colour. The unusual inclusion of gold leaf as a medium is testament to her creative and inventive style.

This extensively illustrated publication, which we are honoured to be launching in London, comes at an important stage in the artist's career and is sure to highlight her position as one of Scotland's leading figurative painters.

Joshua Darby, Browse and Darby, London

Introduction

I have shared and been party to Victoria's artistic development over the period covered by this book, almost 50 years.

Appealing to a broad range of people from different backgrounds, her work has an immediate aesthetic impact, recording the world around us, both external and internal. Her images continue to resonate in our minds long after being seen.

The word 'beautiful' is often used in description of her work. Being in a world where the immediate and the new demand attention, beauty is perhaps questioned as an outmoded form. The concepts of truth and beauty are dear to her, sometimes as an ephemeral beauty, but more often an enduring and common-to-all experience, an oceanic sense that has been tapped into by artists since time began. Perhaps as form follows function, beauty is a consequence of truth and truth the essence of beauty. Through seeing her work for what it is, a series of propositions and philosophical statements about the nature of existence, its validity and modernity can be understood.

Current theory on memory suggests that the brain only consciously processes and retains around 20% of what we experience; the other part is there, but less easily accessible. Victoria Crowe's work seems to hint at, and extemporise on, that other 80%. We intuitively sense that which we have known but missed – recollections on the edges of memory. This may explain why in her work, associations, while never seeming simple, appear to contain a truth, a gestalt – more than the sum of the parts. A glimpse not only into her mind, but also into ours, seen anew. Akin to a half-remembered piece of music, or the fragrance that unexpectedly reminds us of childhood, it is not only a memory but a distillation, and for that reason it is all the more potent.

In the book, the word 'industrious' is used about her work, demonstrated by the number of solo shows undertaken. Victoria's work demands time; she has never allowed the quality of work to be dictated by a deadline. She has always had a rich inner life and a strong conviction that her views on existence and meaning demand that they be brought to fruition.

While preparing for this book, two things came to light from early days at Kingston School of Art which explain another aspect of her work.

The first was a work sheet on the nature of colours. It describes the pigments, that with few changes, are those that she still uses, spread across her palette, today. It describes the density, the oil absorbency, drying time and nature of the skin formation on each of these paints. This thought and attention to detail goes some way towards explaining how she has such command of tonal range and colour, the physical handling of the pigment and the ability to produce sometimes startling colour combinations.

The second was a sketchbook note on the comments made at her student crit by Prunella Clough: 'The majority of students take a long time to find their feet and establishing a way of working – this is not your problem. You have the reverse, you have found your feet relatively quickly and now must strive to keep widening and broadening your experience – and never let a problem go untackled.' This is a suggestion that Victoria Crowe in her thoughtful, unassuming, but determined manner has not forgotten.

Michael Walton, West Linton, 2012

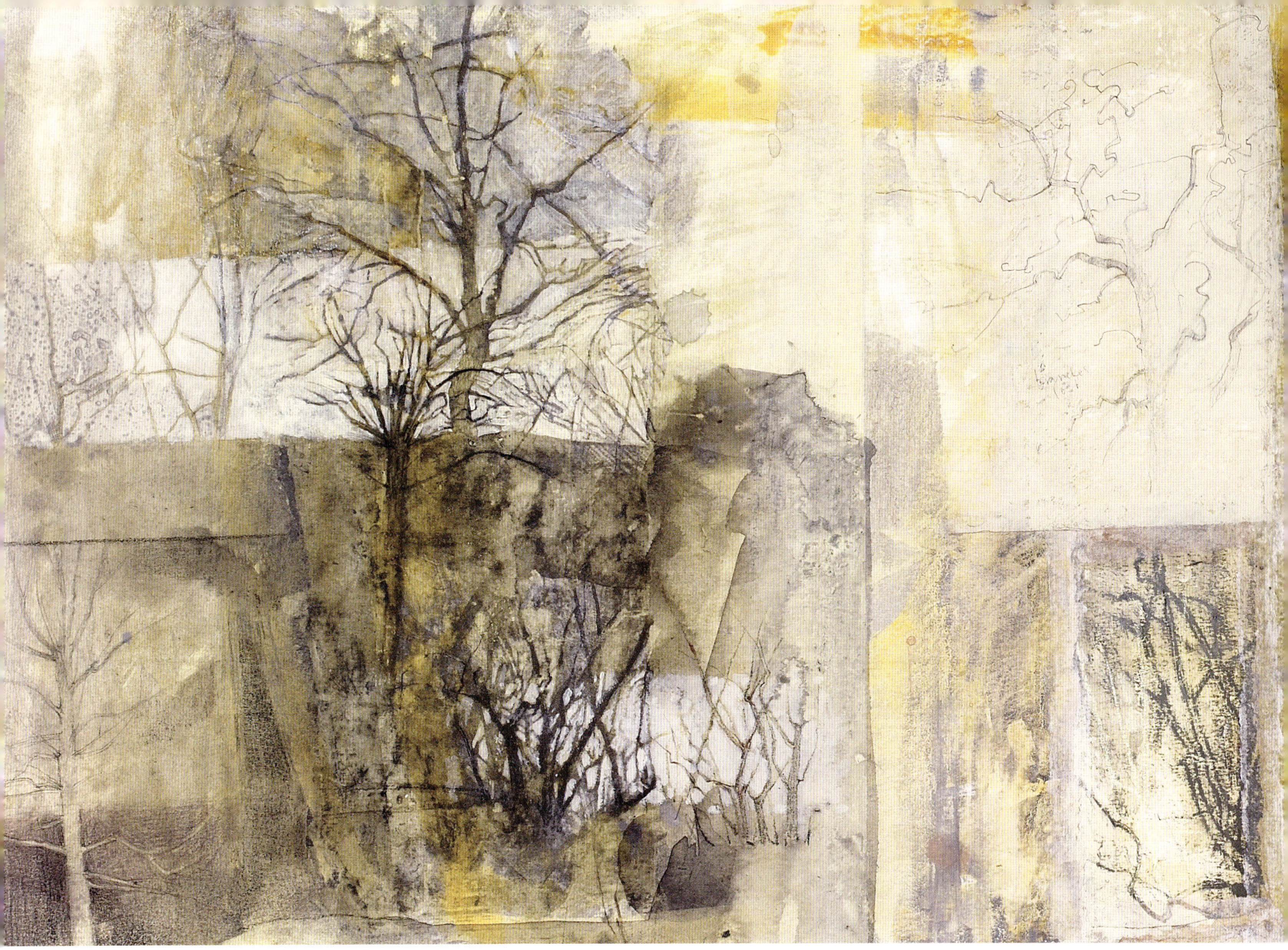

Early Years

When Victoria Crowe and her husband Michael Walton arrived in Edinburgh in the autumn of 1968, neither of them had ever been in Scotland before. On the strength of her degree show at the Royal College that summer, Victoria had been offered a post at Edinburgh College of Art by Robin Philipson, then Head of Painting, and John Hunter, who had recently succeeded William Gillies as Principal. The position in Edinburgh was originally just for one year, but she was to stay in the College of Art until her retirement thirty years later, and she and her husband have made Scotland their home.

Victoria was then just twenty-three years old. She was born on 8 May 1945. It was V.E. Day and so she was christened Victoria Elizabeth. Brought up in west London, she went to the Ursuline Convent Grammar School in Wimbledon and then in 1961, at the age of sixteen, to Kingston School of Art. After gaining her diploma in 1965 she won a place at the Royal College for a further three years study. Throughout this time she had always lived in west London, latterly in

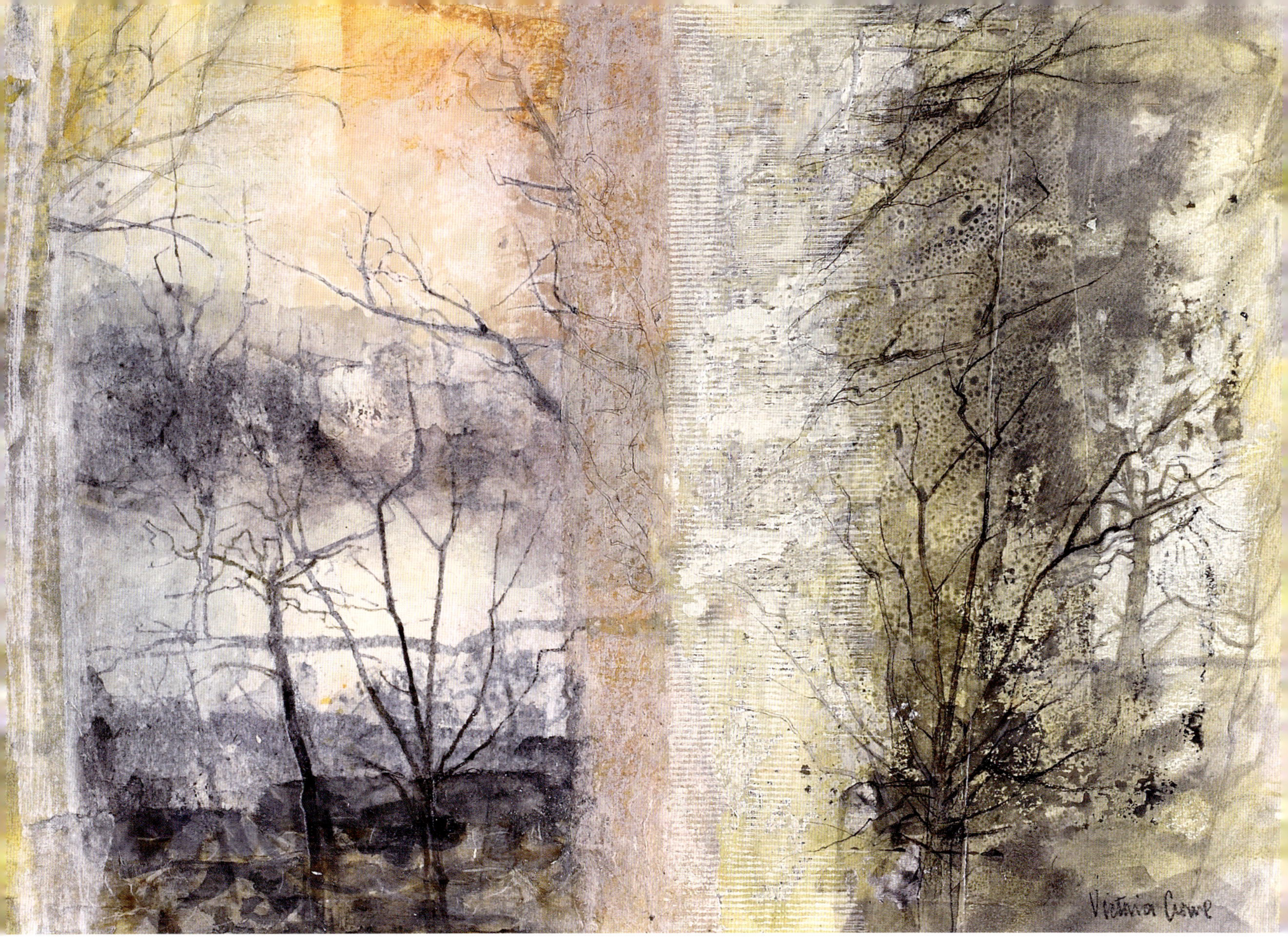

Luminous Winter

Hammersmith, and it was there that they were living in 1967 when she and Michael Walton were married, having met as students at Kingston.

During her childhood Victoria had been taken on family holidays to her mother's relations in Cornwall. She had also made a memorable trip to Russia while still a teenager, but otherwise she had travelled very little. The offer of a post in Edinburgh had been one of several options open to her, including a job as a studio assistant in New Mexico, and with her husband, she chose Scotland. John Bellany had been her contemporary at the Royal College, so the idea of Scotland was perhaps not altogether unfamiliar. The move was nevertheless a dramatic one. Even more so as, after many years in the city, they opted to live in the country outside Edinburgh. They chose the south west side because it was the most accessible. However, it was also the most immediately wild. Their first address was Marchwell, just at the top of the long hill that climbs up the side of the Pentland Hills on the road to Biggar. Later they moved to Kittleyknowe,

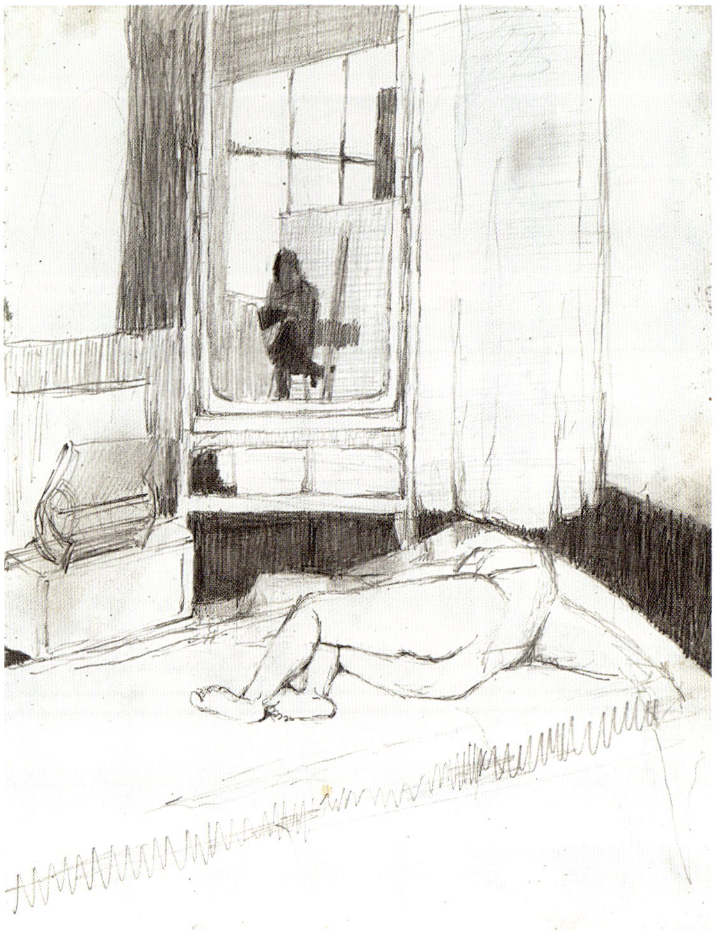

The Life Room, Kingston School of Art

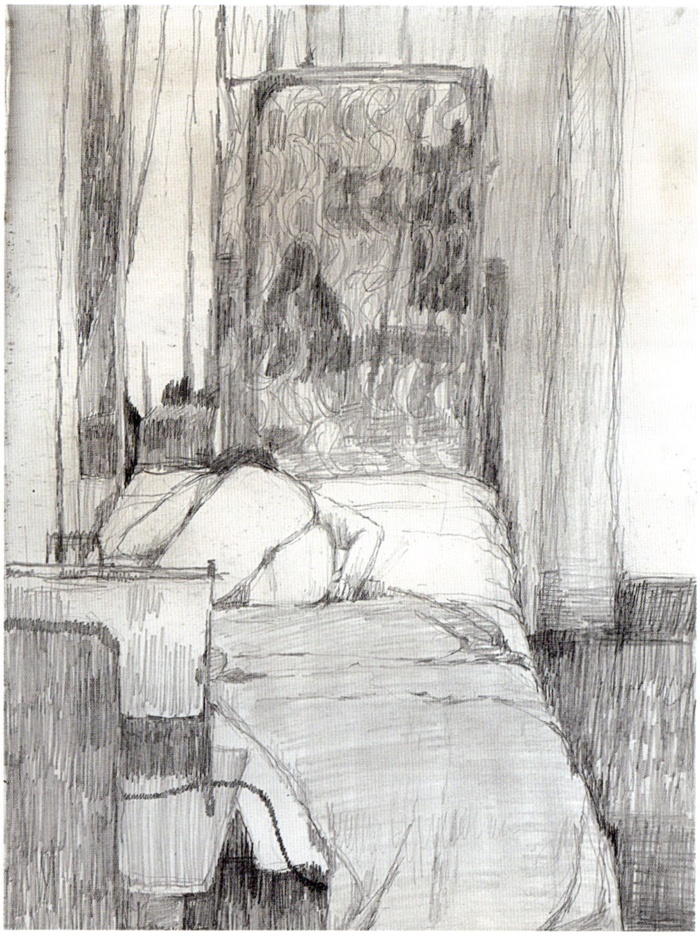

Pale Nude drawing

further out and deeper into the countryside. Then twenty years after that they moved to West Linton where they now live.

The wide spare landscape of the Pentlands was to enter Victoria's painting in many different ways, but looking back over the work that she had done in her student years before coming to Edinburgh, there are striking continuities. Especially in winter, the landscape of the Pentlands has within it a kind of stark drawing which, while it is clearly part of the scene and indeed defines it, is also independent of it, almost abstract. Later she turned such images into remarkable paintings. It was almost as though fate had brought her to the landscape that suited her best; certainly this was true during the first twenty years of her life in Scotland. Although it was later to become overlaid with much else, especially by the art and landscape of Italy, the Pentland landscape is often still visible in her work.

Victoria Crowe was an only child. Her father would have gone to art school, but there were not the funds. Surviving work by him suggests he could have done well. It was perhaps natural, therefore, that when she formed her own inclination to study art, she was encouraged in it. She had been brought up a Catholic and indeed at one point alarmed her parents by her piety. These things passed. One tangible legacy they did leave was a remarkable painting of the Crucifixion done by Victoria at school. The picture has an unusual iconography as it shows Christ in profile against the landscape and this shadowy profile recurs in her painting even now. Less tangibly though, her Catholic upbringing may still be reflected in the sense of mystery and of the transcendental in her work. One does not need to be a believer to feel the power of such things in the forms of religion and it is easy to forget that the real break with much older religions came with the Reformation. The Catholic Church carried on from earlier religions the idea of a priestly caste set apart from the laity, and of the sanctuary as the seat of a mystery to which lay people have no access. Even the use of music and ritual whose origins probably lie in the very remote past helps keep alive a more primitive sense of the divine, of a higher reality that humanity had first understood in the unchanging movement of the heavens and so is rooted in ideas far more ancient than Christianity.

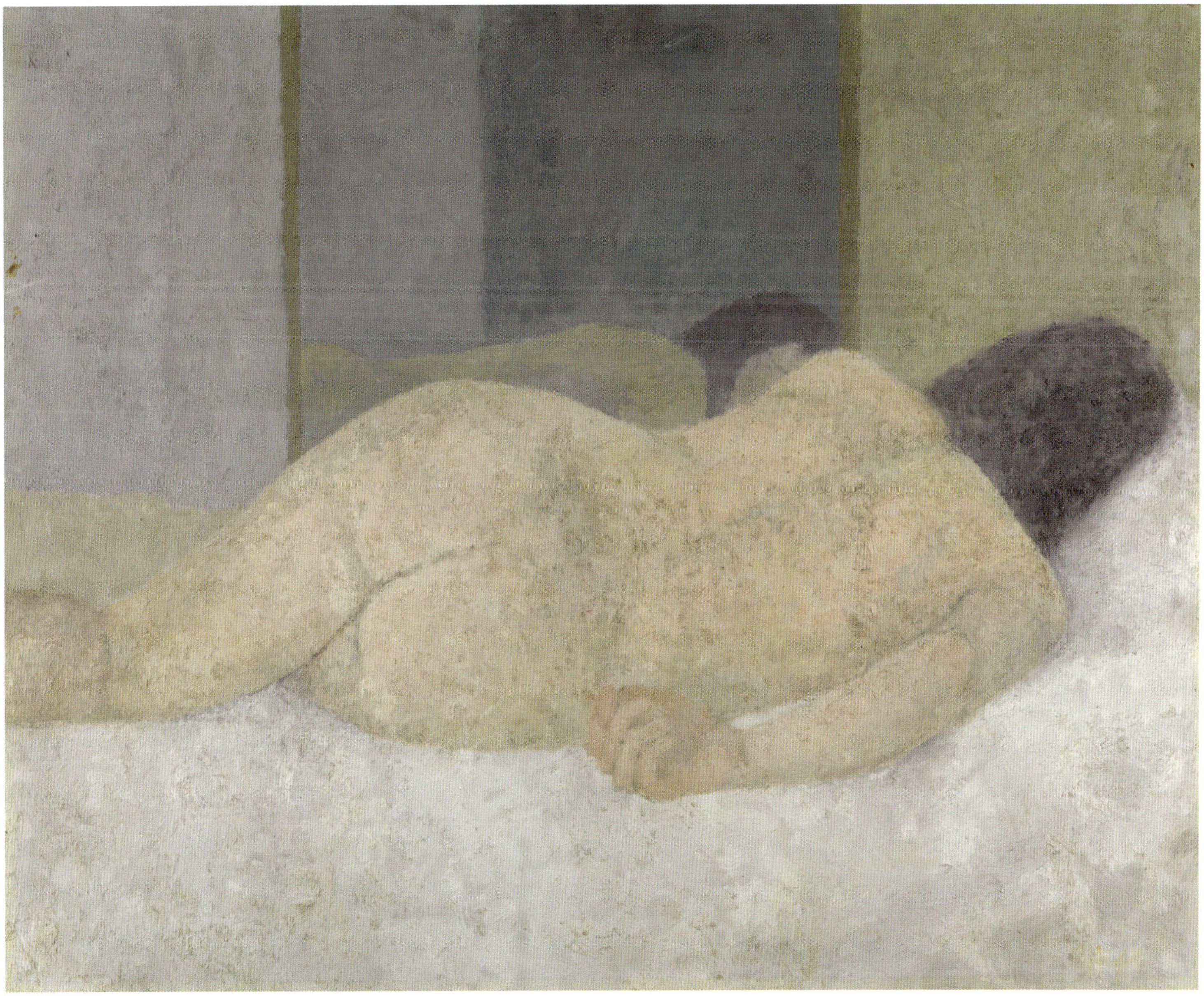

Pale Nude

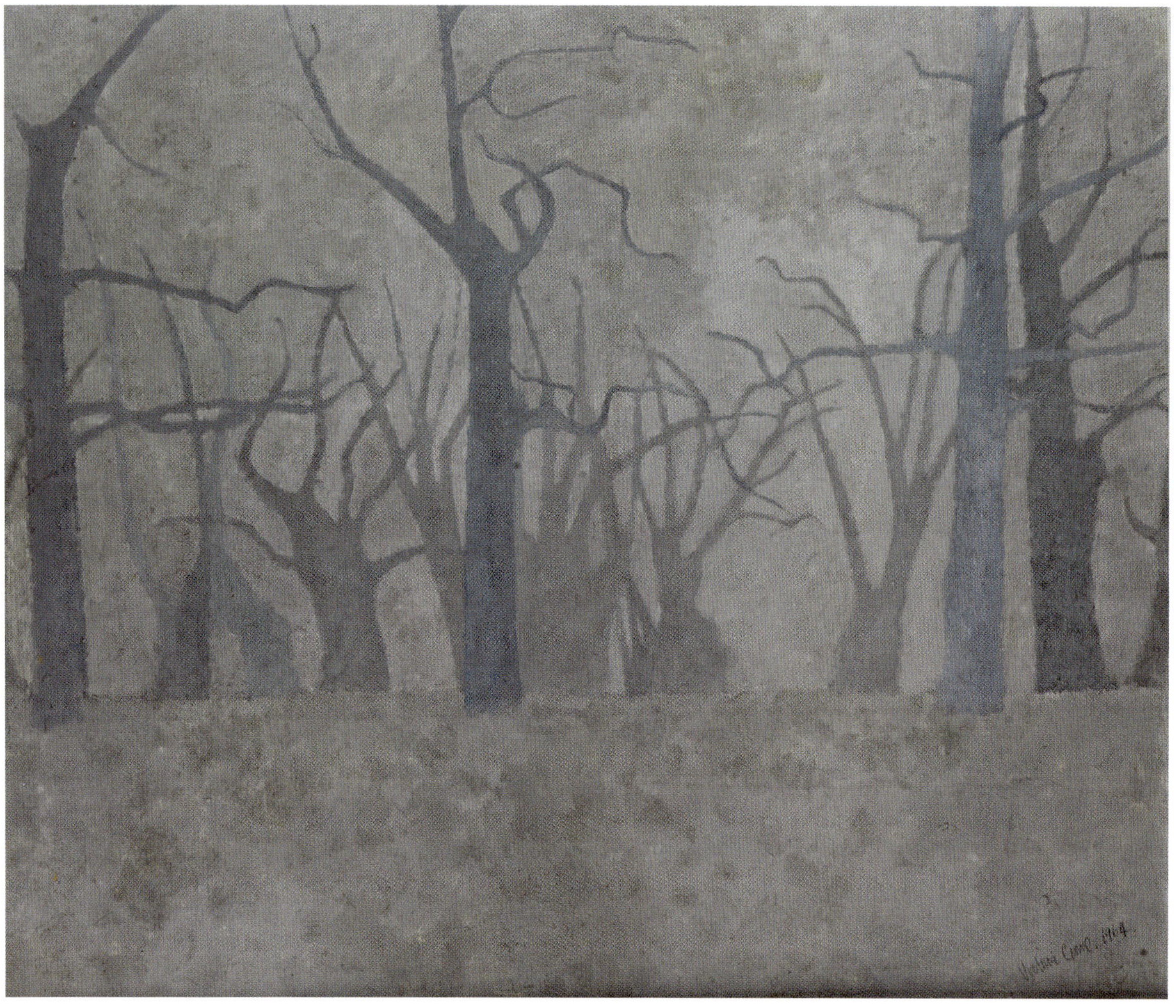

Trees in Richmond Park

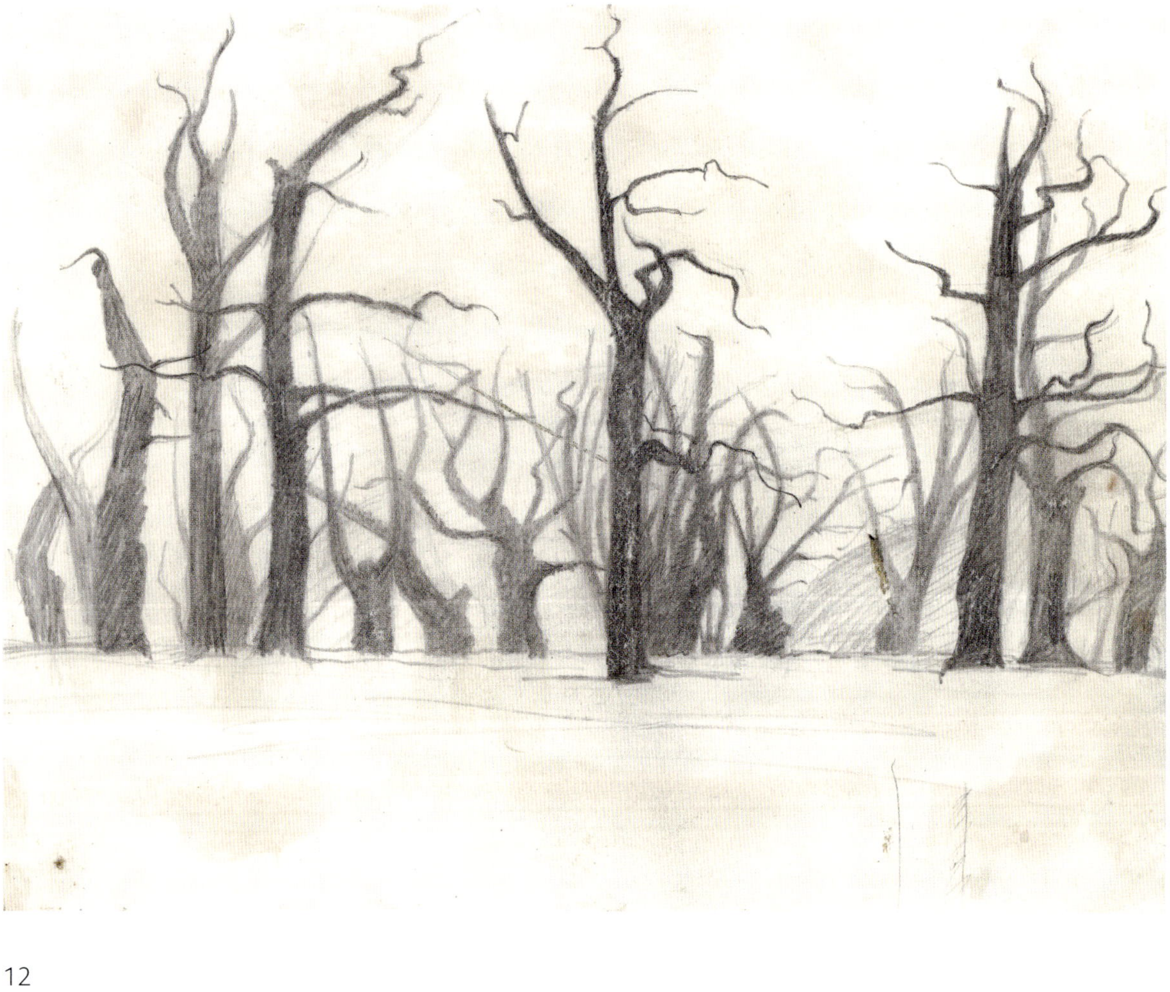

Trees in Richmond Park, study

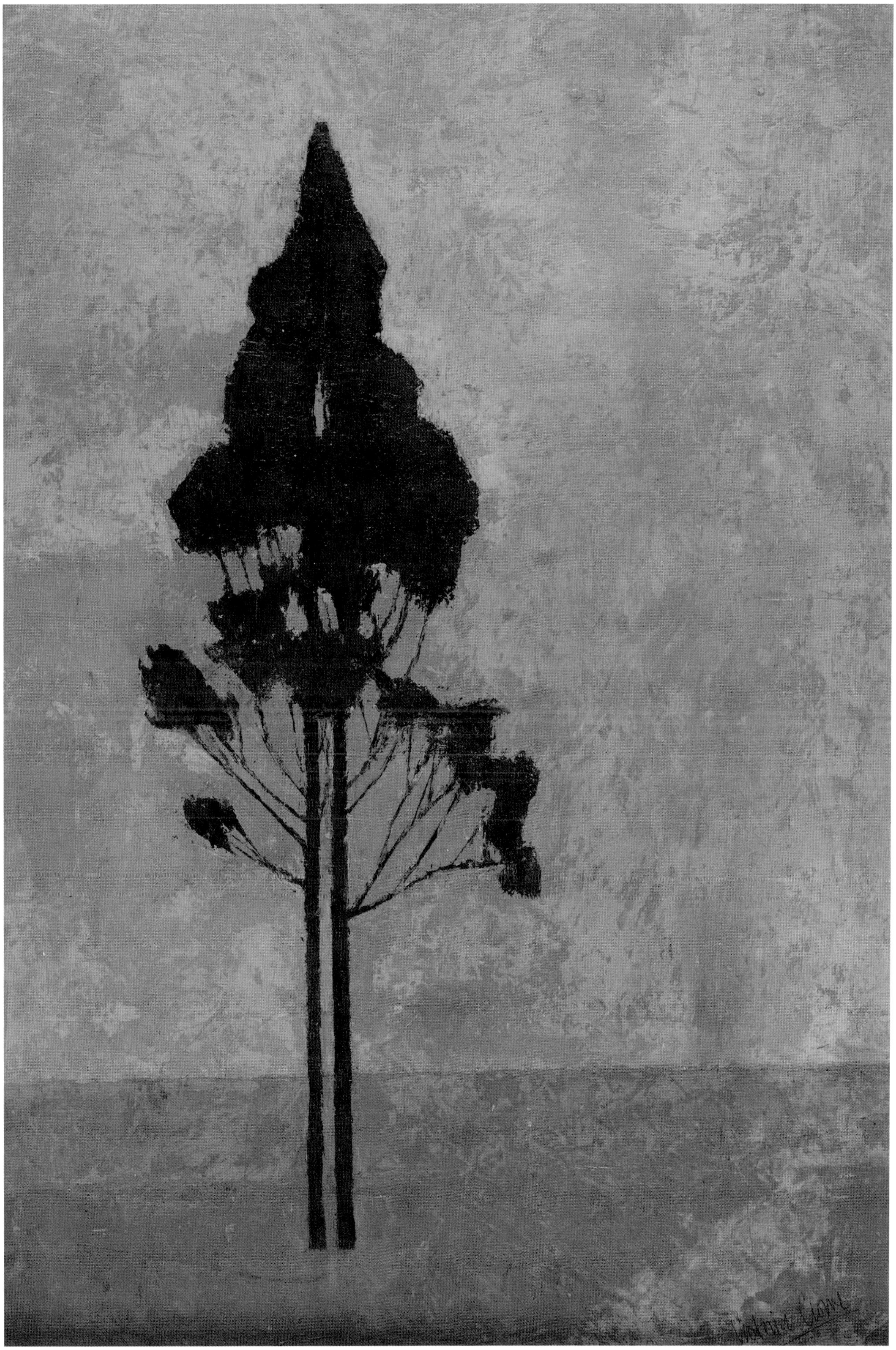

Lone Tree

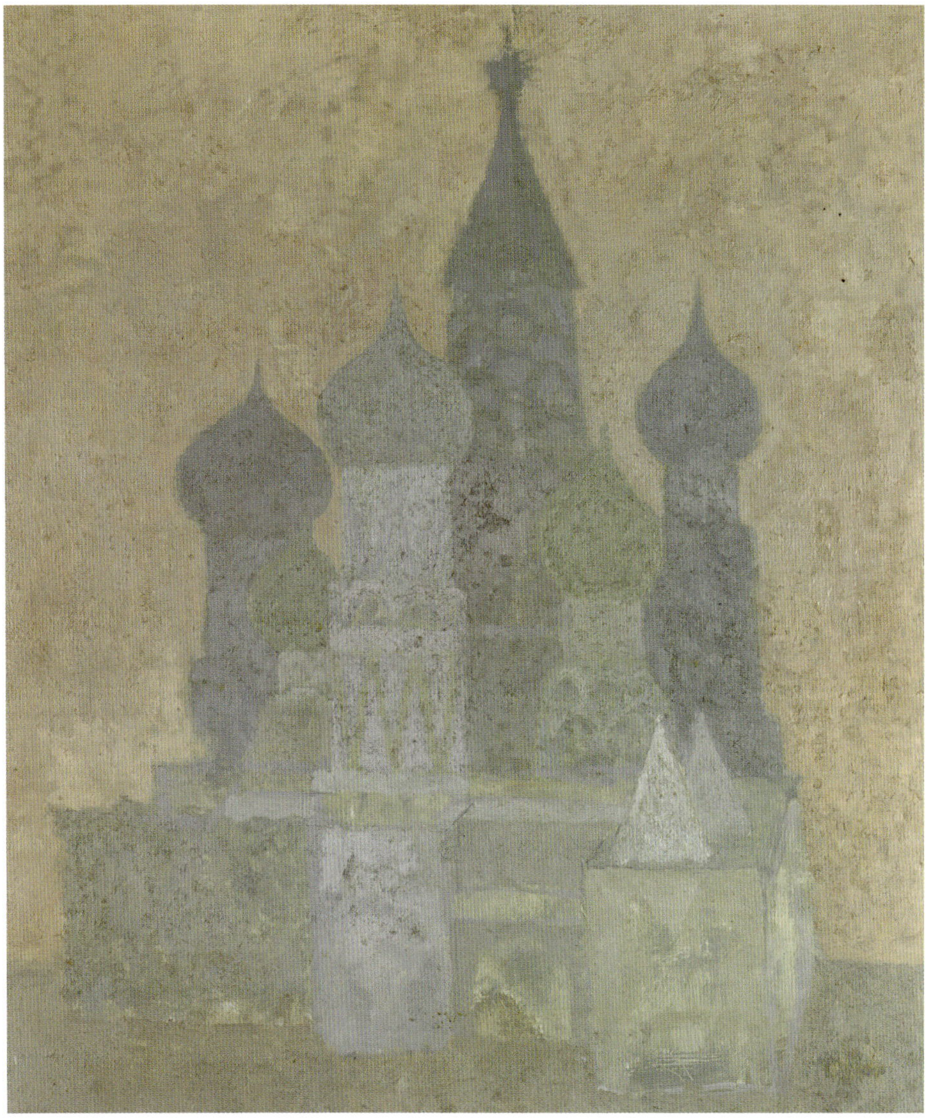

St. Basil's Cathedral, Moscow

Victoria seems to have been an introspective, rather serious child, but she remembers the move from school to art school as a moment of epiphany. Suddenly she was among people whose interests were the same as her own. At Kingston, the influence she still remembers with gratitude was that of Prunella Clough who was a visiting teacher. She remembers being taught by her such practical things as the construction of a composition and the significance of the choice of support. Prunella Clough's painting at the time was often engaged with urban and industrial landscapes and was painted in a low key. Victoria's interests were already rather different, but there is a group of works from these years in which she follows her teacher in her use of close-toned, low-key colours. These pictures are painted on board, a support she was to continue to use in preference to canvas for many years, and have a pronounced, rough texture that is not so much expressive as tactile. That effect is accentuated by the clear lines of drawing that demarcate the forms. One of the most successful of these pictures is *Pale Nude* painted in pink and white and several shades of grey. Strongly built, the woman is lying on a bed. She has her back to us, but her face is partly visible in a mirror beyond her. This reflected image and the strong vertical lines in the composition recur again much later. So, too, does the image of bare trees in Richmond Park silhouetted against a misty sky seen in a series of paintings from this time.

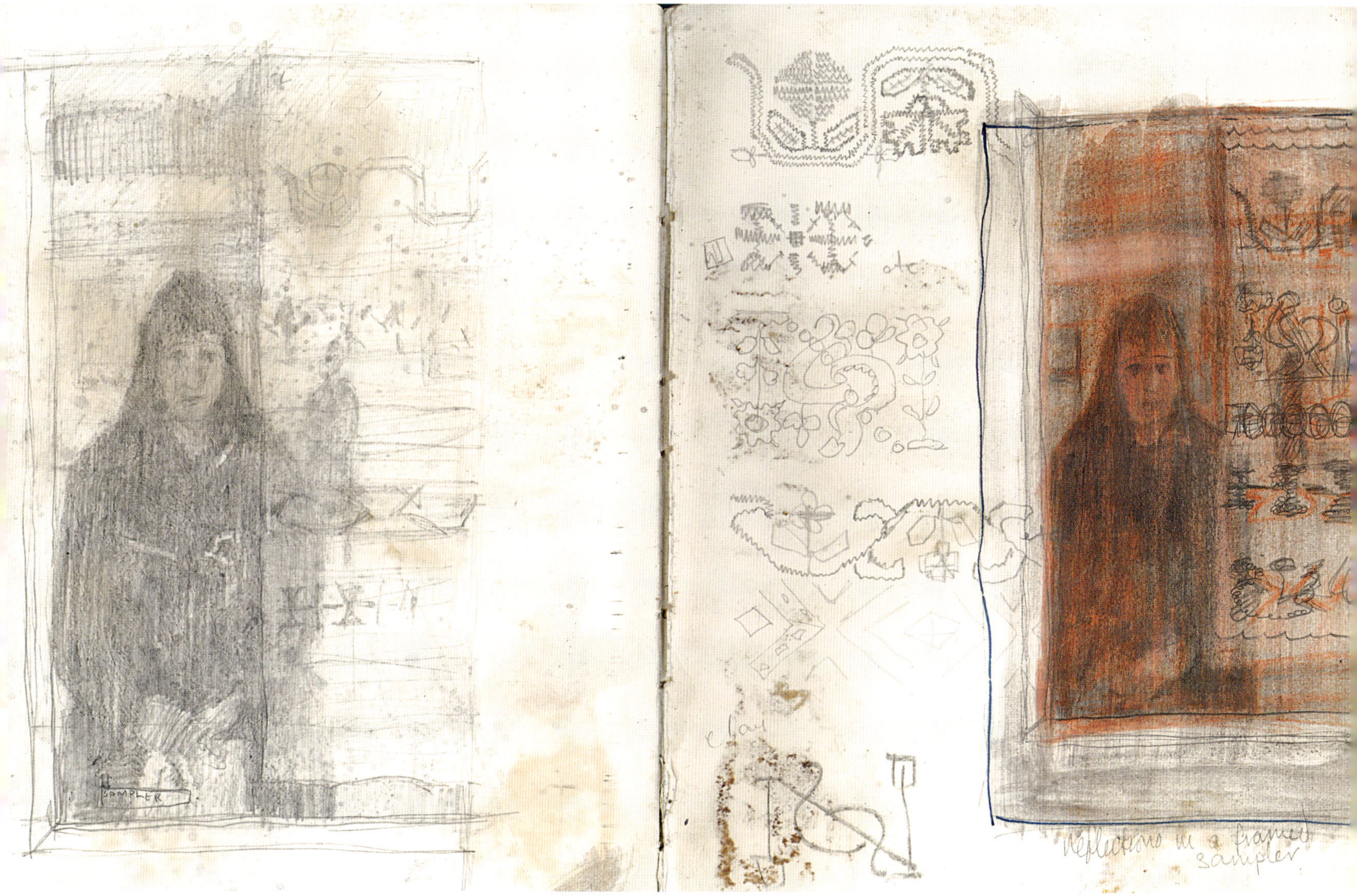

Self portrait sketch book studies

An interest in pattern and surface is a constant feature of Victoria's early work. It might not have been so fruitful if it were not for the way that she manages to convey that these things are not an end in themselves; that establishing the surface is a step that also enables us to go beyond it, perhaps from a physical surface to a mental space. The mirror behind the model reclining on a bed already hints at this. The world beyond is not an illusion, but is actually a different kind of place: the inner space of ideas and dreams that the model's hinted face suggests. The misty picture, *Trees in Richmond Park,* and indeed the equally misty *St Basil's Cathedral, Moscow* have a similar effect; what we see is both definite and indefinite; out there, but also in here. It is neither on the surface, as it might be, nor is it through the surface as ordinary picture-making would suggest it is. It does not lose resonance by this apparent indeterminacy, however. Rather it gains it. Somehow it is in the surface, suspended in a kind of force field between the two conventional possibilities, but beholden to neither.

It was perhaps partly in pursuit of this idea that the forms of religious art continued to play a significant part in Victoria's art even though at the age of twenty-one she formally abandoned the Church. The fact that she made a decision to do this, rather than simply drifting away as so many people do, indicates that the spiritual life it had represented continued to be important for her, even though the Church itself could no longer satisfy that need. Indeed she knew no church could. Nevertheless leaving the Church was, she said, like moving out of a relationship and having to start again. This was perhaps why Russian icons were to become a consuming interest. Her involvement with their forms was certainly linked to her artistic development, but it seems that they also offered a vehicle that could relate her continuing spiritual need to her artistic ambition, transmuting one into the other.

Icons and the Russian art which was their context were the subject that she chose for two dissertations that she had to write, the first at Kingston and the second at the Royal College. A self-portrait she painted in 1964/5 is a striking witness to her developing skills, but also explicitly to these same preoccupations. In the picture she paints her own head and shoulders seen frontally and very severely. Her face is framed by straight black hair, drawn back behind her ears to make an almost geometric shape, its formality echoed in the outline of her round-necked, black jumper. The composition is divided by a series of verticals. The right hand one seems to stand forward slightly and from behind it, painted on a much bigger scale than her own portrait, looms a head of Christ by Rublev. She had seen this painting, a fragment of a *Deesis*, or painting of Christ enthroned, in the Tretyakov Museum on the visit to Russia that she made in 1964. In her self-portrait she has carefully respected the appearance of this marvellous painting, precisely describing the damage the original had sustained to both the upper and lower parts of the figure. She also respects the suavity of Rublev's line, contrasting it with the starkness of the drawing of her own head and shoulders. This formal comparison, emphasised by the way the huge figure stands behind her, suggests the contrast between ancient and modern. But as this deeply introspective self-portrait was painted at just the time that the artist was undergoing the inner debate that was to lead to her leaving the Church a year later, the juxtaposition of her own figure with the figure of Christ surely also reflects her state of mind. Indeed the construction of the picture suggests that she was as much concerned with religion as with art, or perhaps that they were indivisible.

Looking back on this time much later, in the long, autobiographical recording Victoria made with Jenny Simmons for the British Library archival series *Artists' Lives*, she was to say of Rublev's icons, "These paintings ... produce images of a profound and lasting spirituality – transcendent of time and place, here and now – an eternal unchanging image of mankind."[1] Discussing the special characteristics of Russian icons in her RCA dissertation of 1968, however, she expresses it a little differently, but in terms that reveal how their example was helping her to formulate her own artistic ambitions:

> *Russian icon painters were not dealing with the real world. Whereas western artists have been obsessed by the visual aspects of the external world, the Russian painters were concerned exclusively with the inner vision which the contemplation of divine beings and sacred histories aroused in them. The imagery was not limited to the casual relationships of the western painters and consequently icons have no reality in the western sense at all. There is in fact in icon painting a constant removal of reality.*[2]

Later Victoria spoke of the way in which these paintings seem to gain power as they depart from the conventions of Western spatial picture making; how the painters reversed perspective as though to stop you entering the picture plane and so stepping into a world created by the illusion

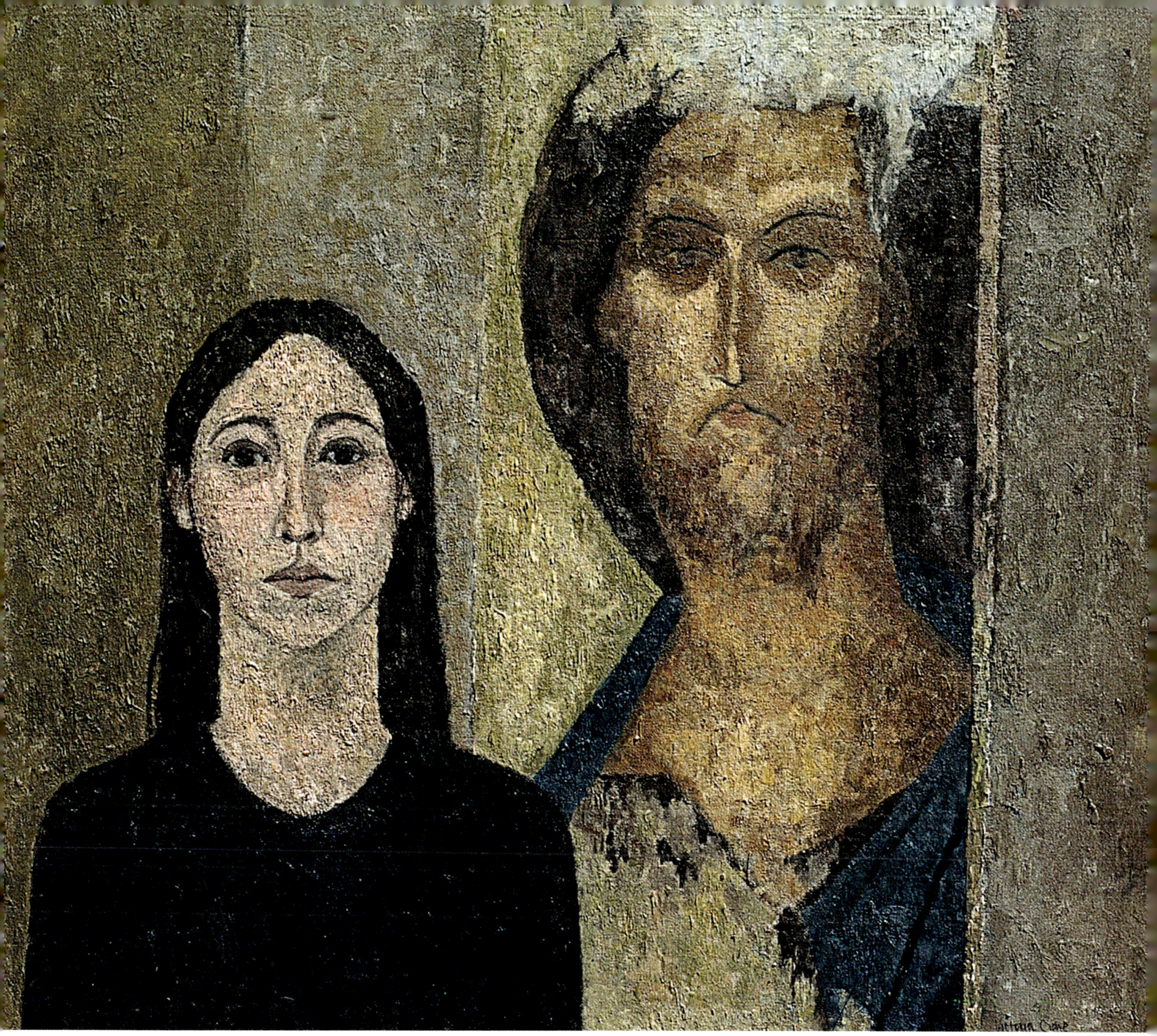

Self Portrait with Icon

of depth. Their impact was, she said, more like a sound, or a symbol, than a presentation of reality, or at least it was the presentation of a different, transcendent reality.[3] For her, therefore, the undoubted spiritual power of the icons depended on the way they defied representation. Indeed it seems she felt they achieved precisely the opposite of much Western religious art; rather than persuading us of the immediate reality of what is represented, they are effective in proportion to the degree they depart from representation. They create an independent pictorial reality by subordinating the figures to an overriding discipline of flatness and pattern. For this reason Victoria thought of her interest in icons as parallel with her interest in Matisse and Modigliani. She saw their art likewise as effective in proportion to its independence of representation. Icons, as

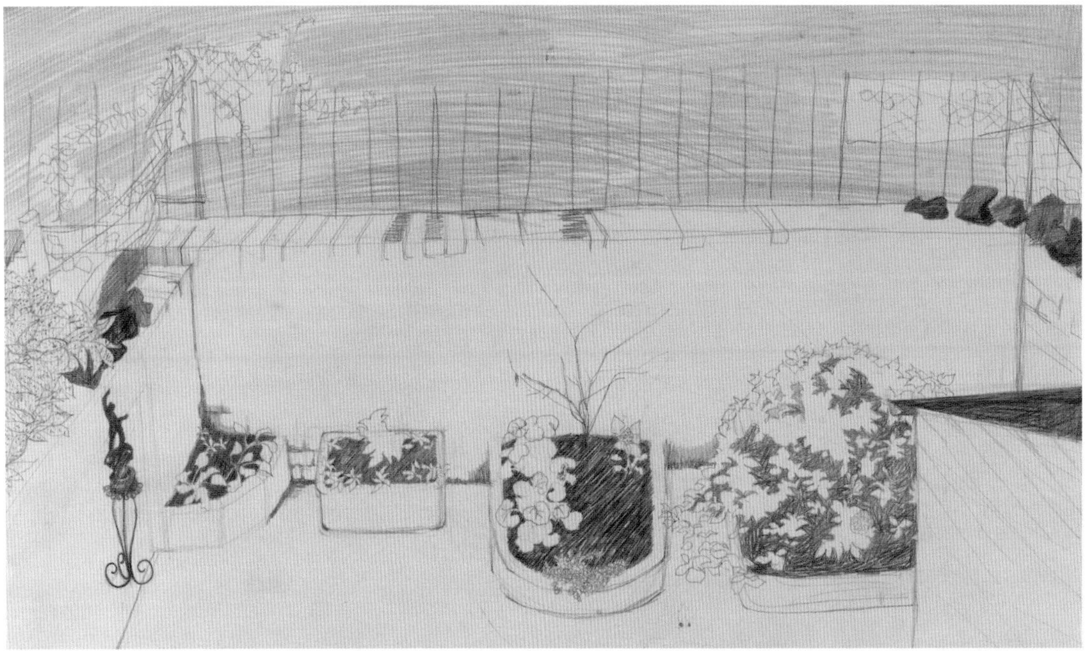

Study for Garden, W6

sacred objects, are essentially abstract in terms of paint and colour, which she also saw as akin to Malevich and the Suprematists and other painters of the Russian Revolution. Indeed, in her RCA thesis she describes how in Russia before the First War, Mikhail Larionov and Natalia Goncharova and the Donkey's Tail exhibitions made the link that she herself was trying to make between icon painting and modernism. She also noted the significance of Matisse's love of Russian icon painting; like his own art it is figurative painting without illusionism.

Victoria's interest in Russian art and history, but especially in icons, took her twice to the Soviet Union. The visit in 1964 was from Kingston with a party of students organised by the NUS. She went again in 1971 with her husband and a group of Edinburgh students. In 1964, her choice of destination was partly shaped simply by her determination to go somewhere quite different, she says, but Soviet film was also a key part of the curiosity which took her to the USSR before any nearer destination in Continental Europe. She is a great admirer of Eisenstein and indeed film has remained a passion. She also had a rather idealistic view of Communism. She was deeply impressed by the music of the Orthodox Church and in her thesis she wrote of the peasant soul of Russia. She felt the European character of Leningrad and even of the Russian ballet were not in tune with the true Russian spirit. Perhaps it was not just the icons alone, but the whole sense of the way that, in spite of Communism, the Orthodox Church appeared to be integrated into the life of the people who attracted her, and she felt the contrast with modern urban Catholicism which seemed to have joined the Protestants when it abandoned, along with Latin, so many of the ways of expressing the essential mystery at the heart of religion. She also found her romantic, rather Tolstoyan view of Russia and the myth of the land confirmed in the paintings of the 1890s that she saw during her first visit, although it was not until the next year that she actually read Tolstoy, and also Dostoevsky.

It was in Moscow at the Tretyakov Gallery that she saw for the first time, face to face, Rublev's icons. She also went to the Zagorsk Monastery where she saw icons in their proper context displayed on the iconostasis. Rather like a symbolic gateway, the iconostasis is laden with images and imbued

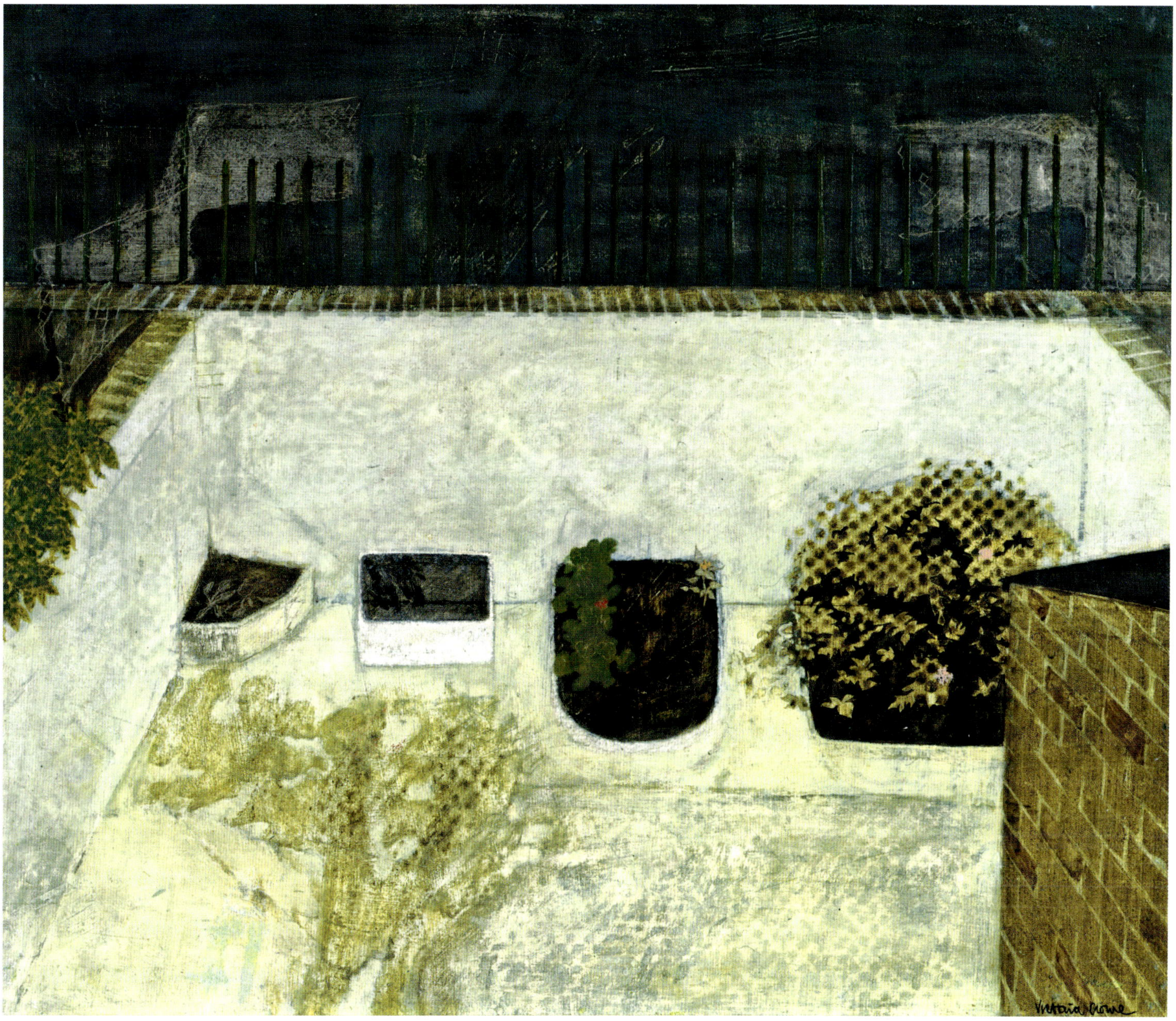

Garden, W6

with mystery, it is a deeply impressive sight and presents painting in a quite different way to anything with which she could have been familiar in the West, either in a church or an art gallery. This was a critical moment in Victoria's evolving career as her early spiritual inclination began to be transmuted into something visible and tangible in her art, and the direction in which she was moving began to become increasingly clear. In her degree show at the Royal College she included several paintings inspired directly by icons. One, for instance, was made after an icon of the Deposition. She began with a careful drawing of the original and then proceeded literally to abstract it, to turn a religious image into a formal one. In the finished painting she used the perforated back of an old radio to create a grid of dots and so unify the composition. In the final result the composition of the icon is still visible, but the picture is both abstract and colourful. In spite of its inspiration, it also seems very much of its time and to belong to what might be called the school of London. David Hockney and R.B. Kitaj, for instance, had only recently graduated from the Royal College.

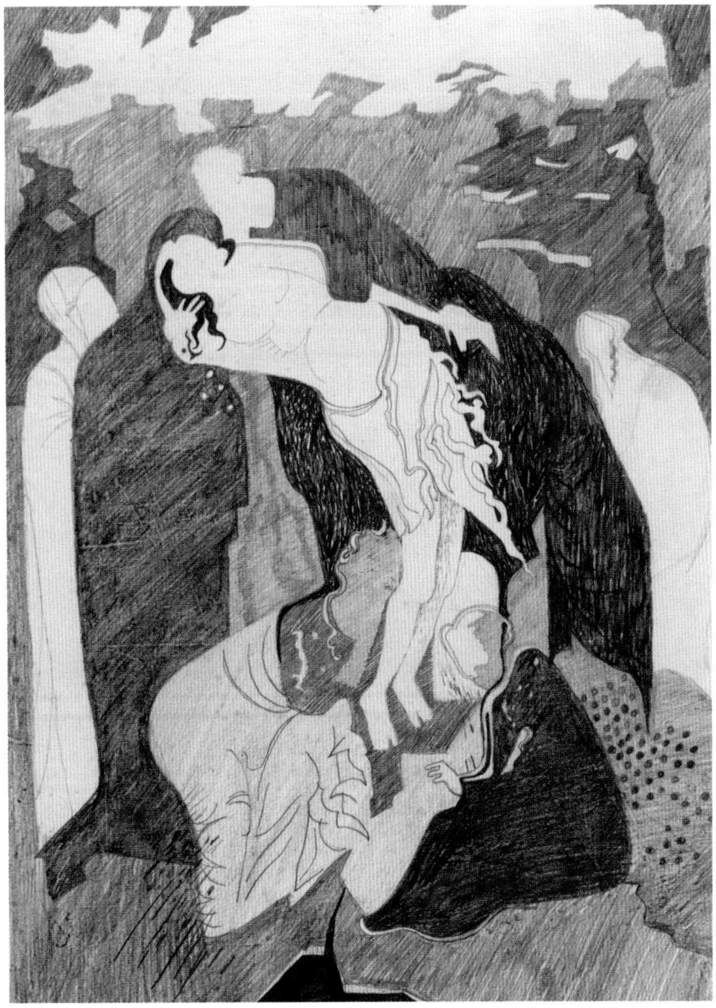

Study for Deposition I

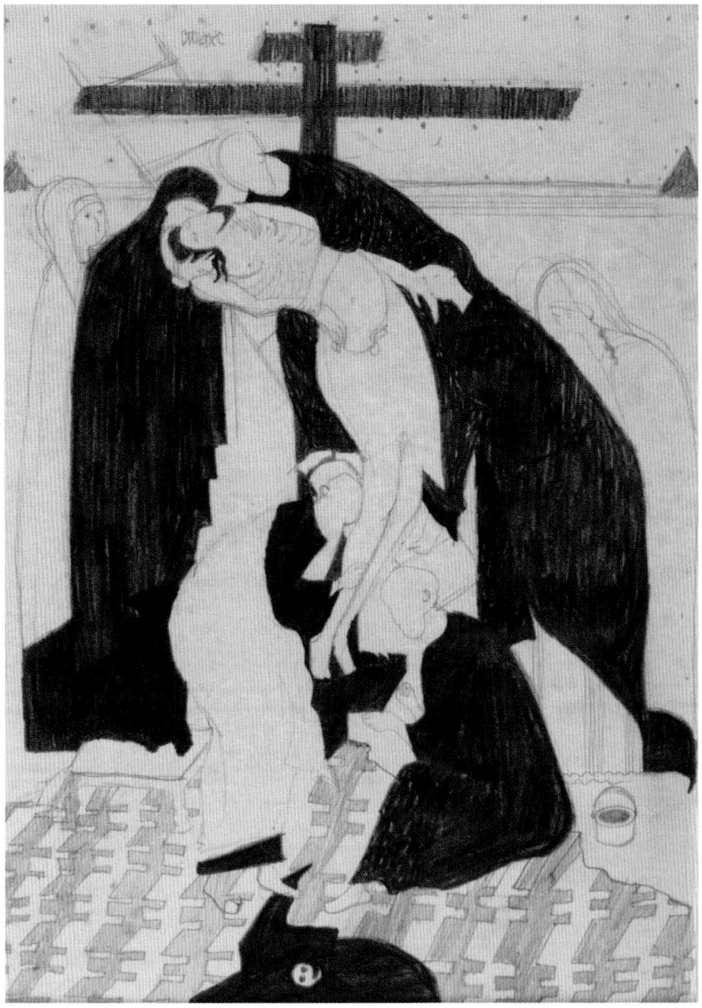

Study for Deposition II

Another striking, but rather different picture in her degree show, *Garden W6*, is of the narrow yard behind the flat in Hammersmith that was her first married home. We are looking down into the yard which is enclosed by a high wall topped by a fence. Beyond the landscape is dark. There are also several large pots filled with dark earth. She has again used a grid to unify the composition, linking the plants in the pots with the wall and the ground, thus bringing us back to the surface of the picture and so breaking the illusion. With echoes of Victor Pasmore's *Gardens of Hammersmith* of 1949, the picture is mostly in tones of grey and white, but in its austerity it also looks forward directly to the winter landscapes she was to paint in her new home beneath the Pentland Hills.

It seems to have been her pictures based on icons and perhaps especially their colourfulness which attracted Robin Philipson to Victoria Crowe's work when he and John Hunter visited her degree show. In his own painting, he liked to take an image and then work over it so that what tells is not the image itself, but the surface he has put onto it. This approach does suggest that there might be an affinity between his own work and her paintings based on icons, but the comparison also underlines the difference. Philipson's painting is very much about surface and display, focussing on what he liked to call 'the craft of painting', essentially his own dexterity as a picture maker. Victoria Crowe is never showy.

Deposition

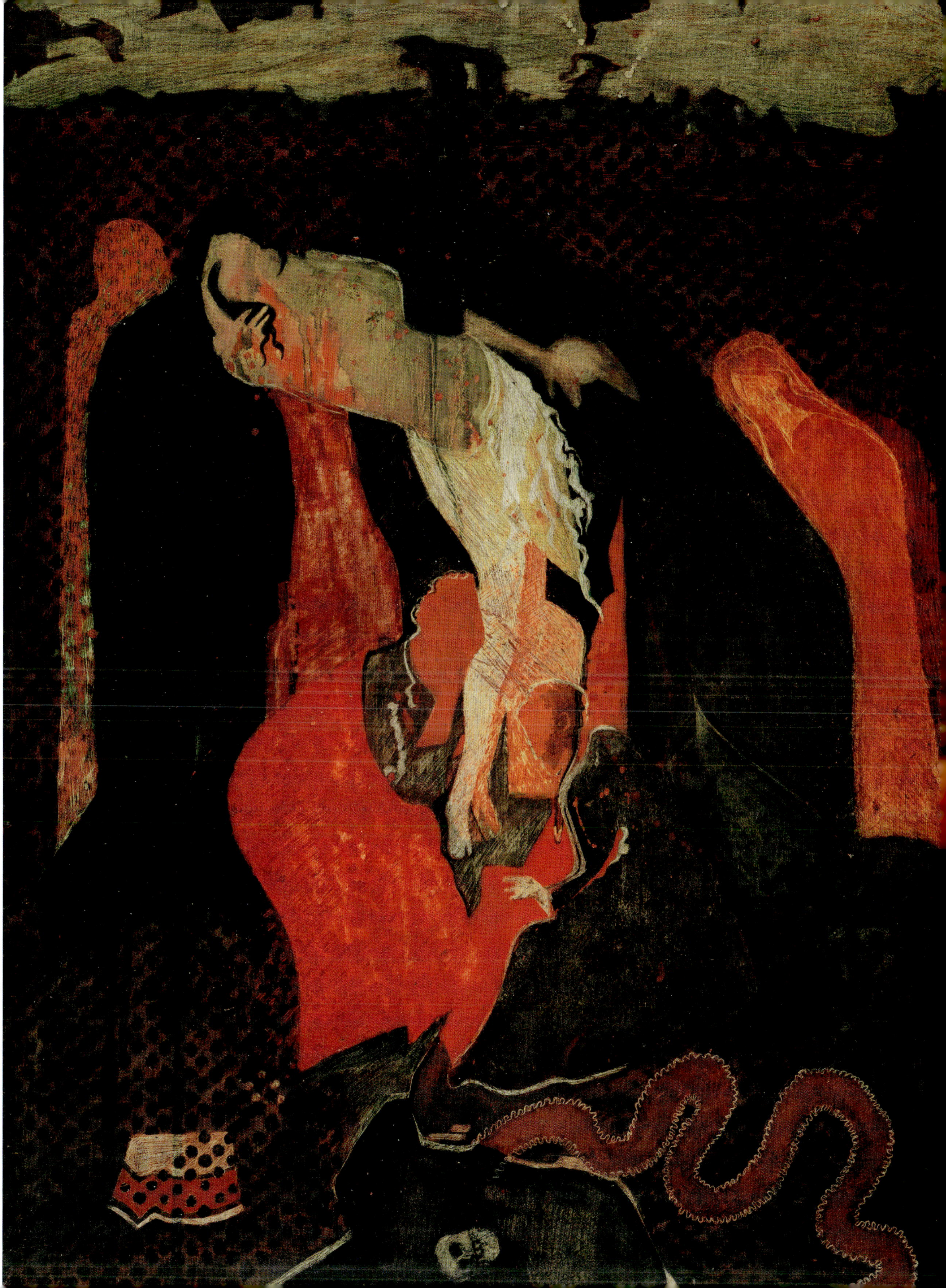

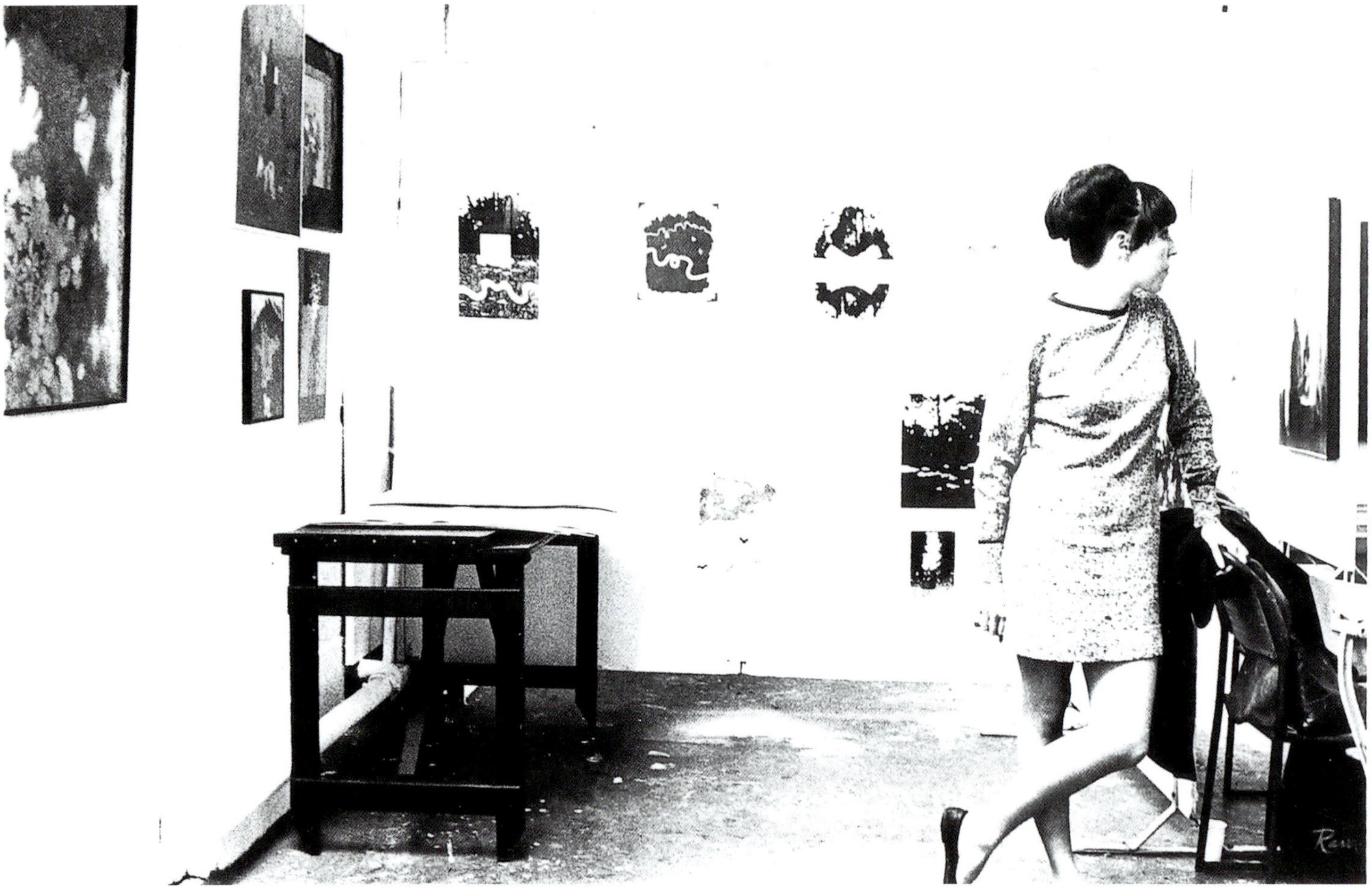

Postgraduate Degree Show, RCA, 1968

The Painting School at the RCA was situated in part of the V&A Museum. We worked in cubby-holes sectioned off in the studios, but also in the side corridors, screening off sunlight and passers-by with whatever we could. The three post-graduate years gave us that most valuable commodity – time. Time to think & question, time to develop, time to go in totally the wrong direction (!) and time to broaden our attitudes to our work. In the mornings I often met Carel Weight shambling up Exhibition Road from the tube. Carel was Head of the Painting School & had a studio there which doubled as a staff room and crit. room. He presided over the school with an assumption that we were all as committed to our work as he and his fellow artists/staff members were to theirs. Little formal teaching (but the crits were illuminating), more a kind of assimilation of attitudes and a seeking out of what we wanted to know and who we wanted to meet. Leonard Rossoman, Ruskin Spear, clunking along the corridor with his wooden leg, Peter Blake, Bateson Mason, Sandra Blow and fellow students all added to the Painting School dynamic.

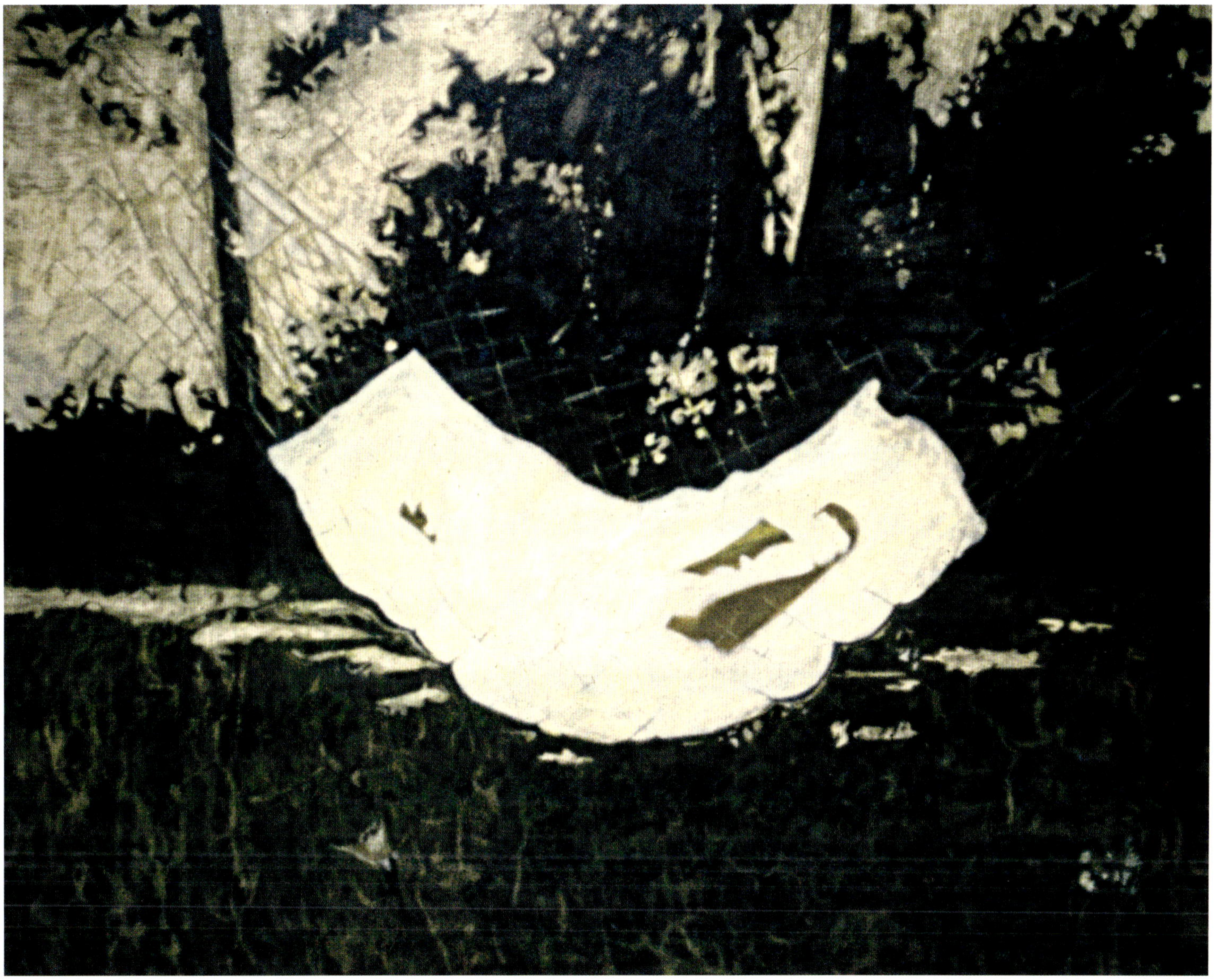

Svetlana Stalin in a Hammock

When asked if the religious imagery in her icon paintings signified anything to her at the time, Victoria replied that it did not. However, it is clear from the other things that were happening in her life that even if these were not intended to be religious images, they were inspired by her own interest in spirituality. It is also interesting that although she certainly admired abstract painters like Malevich or, closer to her own generation, Sergei Poliakoff, she seems never to have painted simply abstract pictures. Her later works suggest that it was not the abstract forms of the icons which attracted her, but the aura those forms create. It was in keeping with these concerns and through lectures at the Royal College that Victoria began to discover philosophy and so expand her own intellectual horizons. She found as she did so, that she was not alone in her search for a route from the actual to the transcendental outside the paths prescribed by formal religion.

Overleaf: *Rosa Proprina and the Pentland Hills*

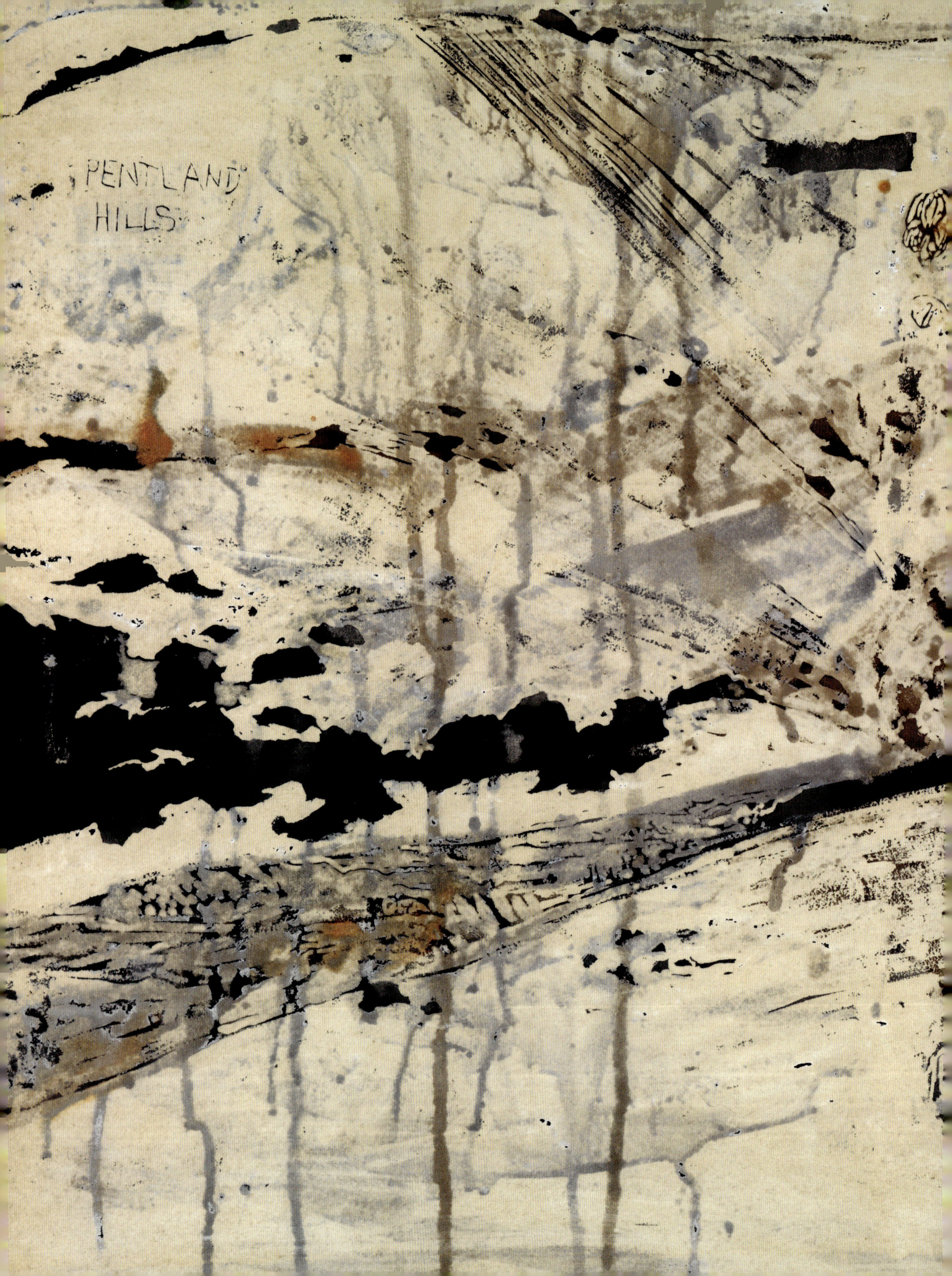
PENTLAND
HILLS

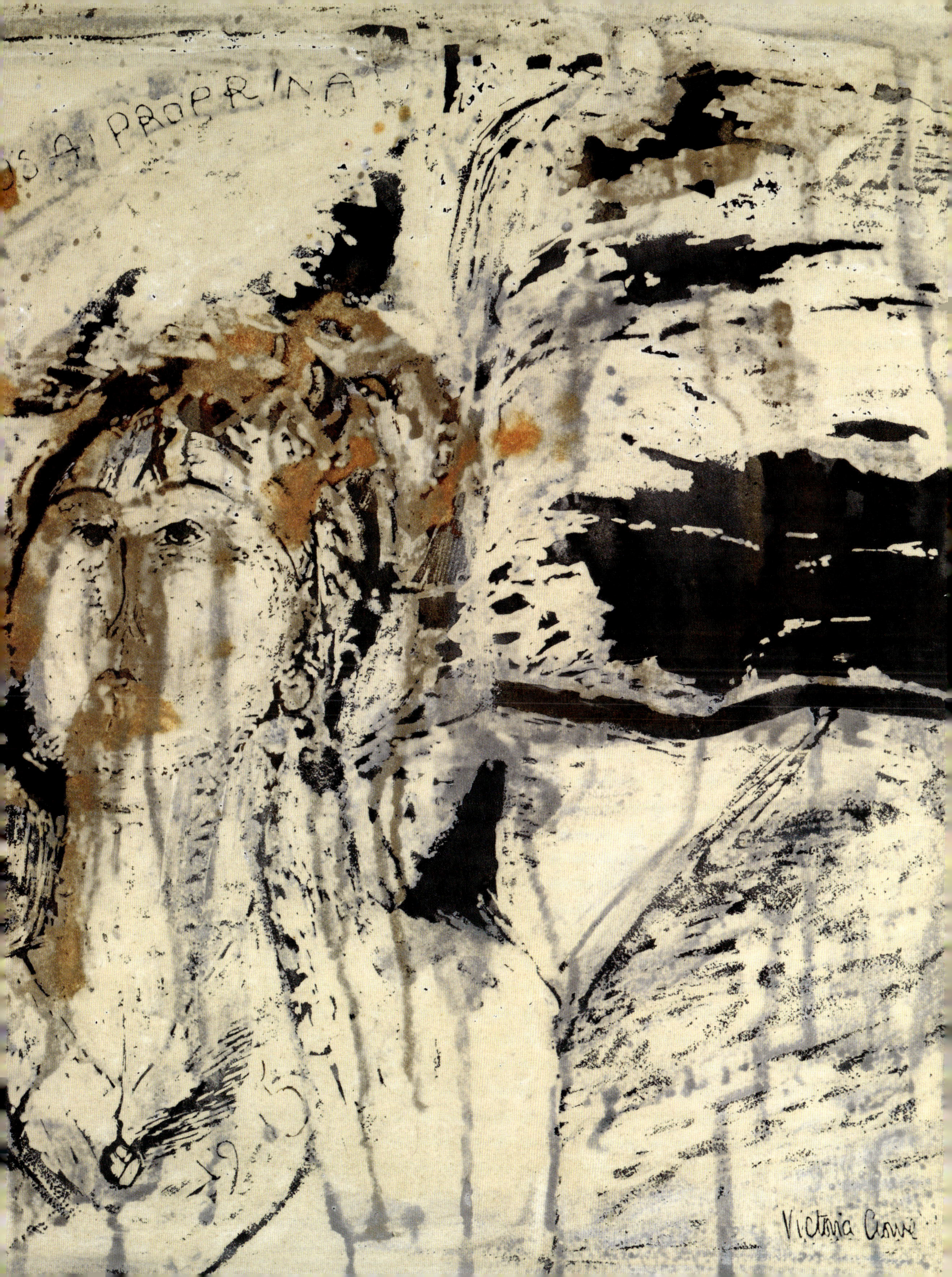
Victoria Crowe

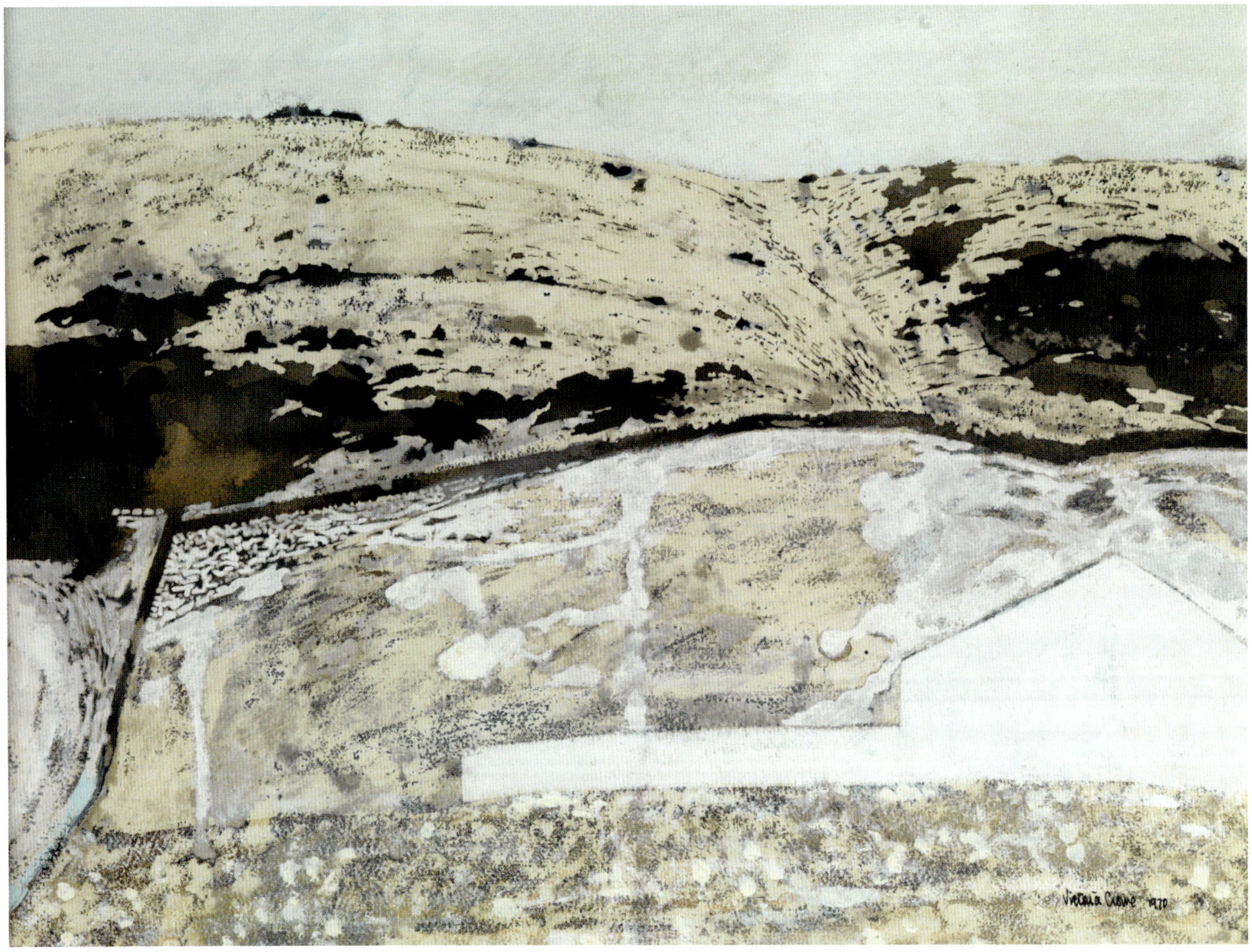

Pentland Hills, Marchwell (Winter)

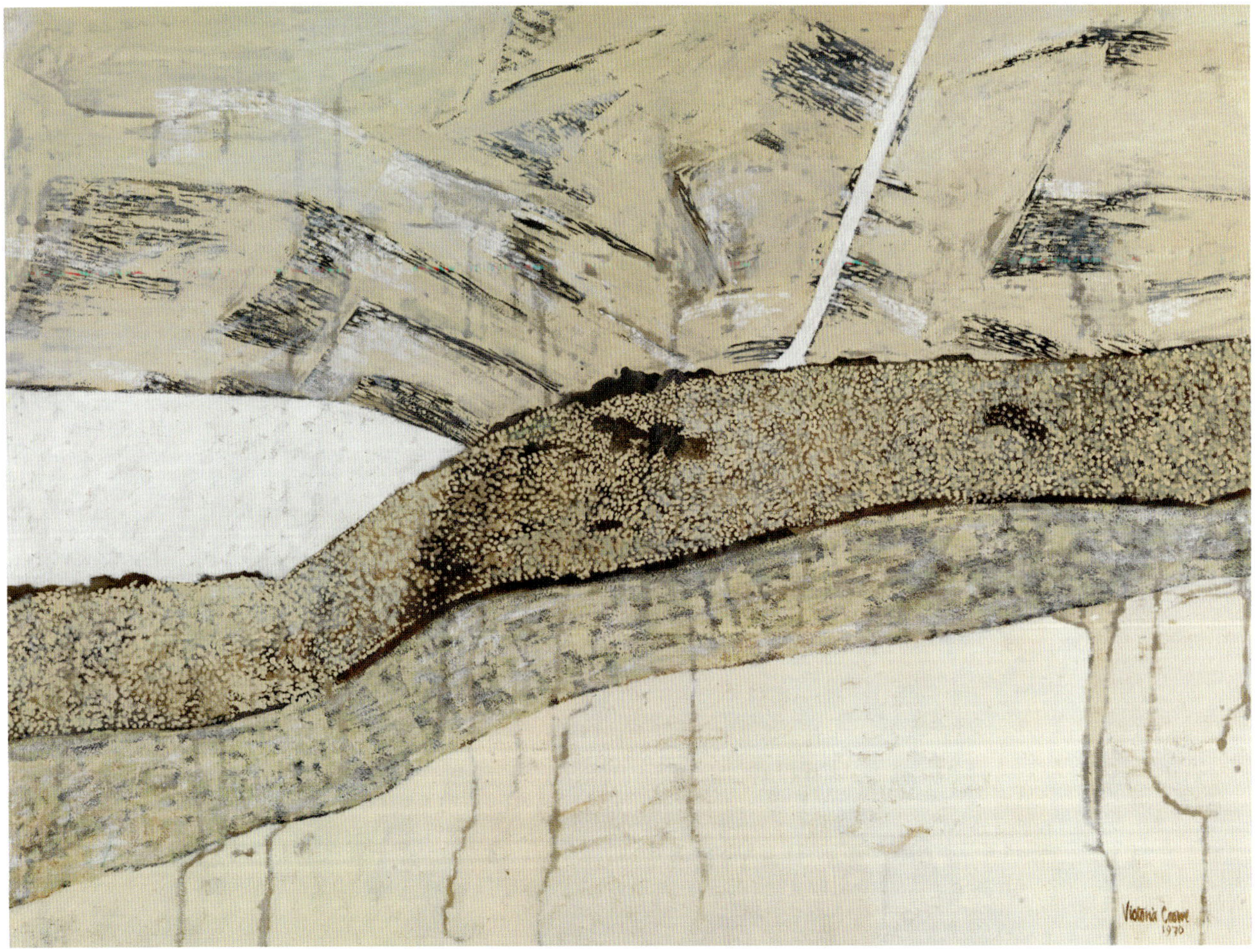

Pentland Landscape

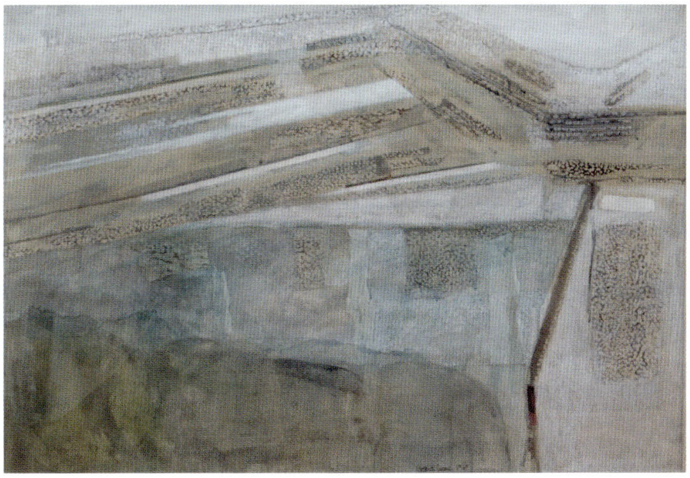

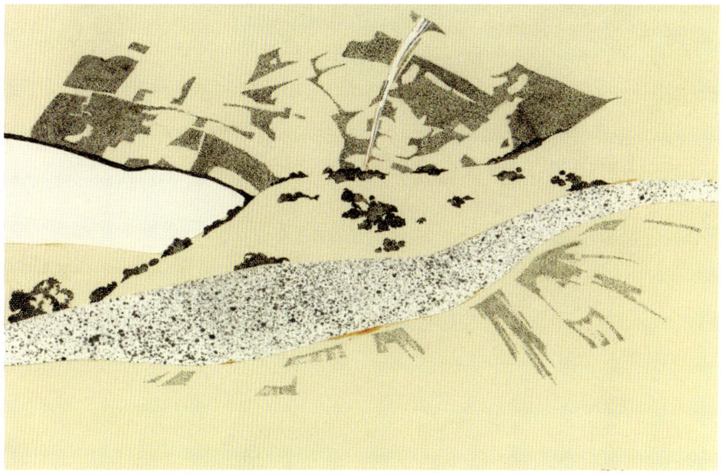

Study of the Pentlands

Landscape at Silverburn I

The Move to Scotland

When Victoria Crowe joined the staff at Edinburgh College of Art in 1968, William Gillies had only retired as Principal a couple of years before and the painting school was still very much dominated by his influence. It was rather an enclosed world, and one that was pretty hostile to any intellectualising about art. You did not speak about it, you just did it. In spite of the professionalism of colleagues like Elizabeth Blackadder, John Houston and Robin Philipson himself, Victoria was later to record that she scarcely talked about painting at all with her fellow artists in the school. Led at first by Eric Shilsky, the mood in the Sculpture School was very different and she found more sympathy there. Although she found the atmosphere difficult, she was nevertheless impressed by the dedication of her colleagues. Robin Philipson brought her into the professional circle, too, by introducing her to Bill Macaulay at the Scottish Gallery. She held her first show there in 1970 and has continued to exhibit her work with the gallery ever since. As so many artists have done at the beginning of their careers, she also enjoyed the support of Richard Demarco, however. Her first Scottish showing was in a group exhibition at his gallery in 1968.

When they arrived in Edinburgh and decided to live outside the town, Victoria and her husband found Marchwell Cottage within three days. A year and a half later they took a lease on Monksview at Kittleyknowe, a mile east of Carlops, one thousand feet above sea level and on the very edge of the cultivable land before the wide, boggy stretch of moor that lies above Penicuik. Later they were able to buy the house and then to add a studio to what was only a little more than a simple cottage. Immediately to the west, the bare Pentland Hills rise steeply above the house and its two or three neighbours. Nearby Newhall House stands among woods. The distant Moorfoot Hills close the view far to the east, but to north and south the skies are big and open. The only shelter is provided by belts of wiry, wind-bent beech trees. Like Victoria's decision to go to Russia, this was a move to somewhere entirely different and a startling contrast to anything she had experienced before. It was a world that Gillies had painted with great success, but she really had to find out how to paint it for herself.

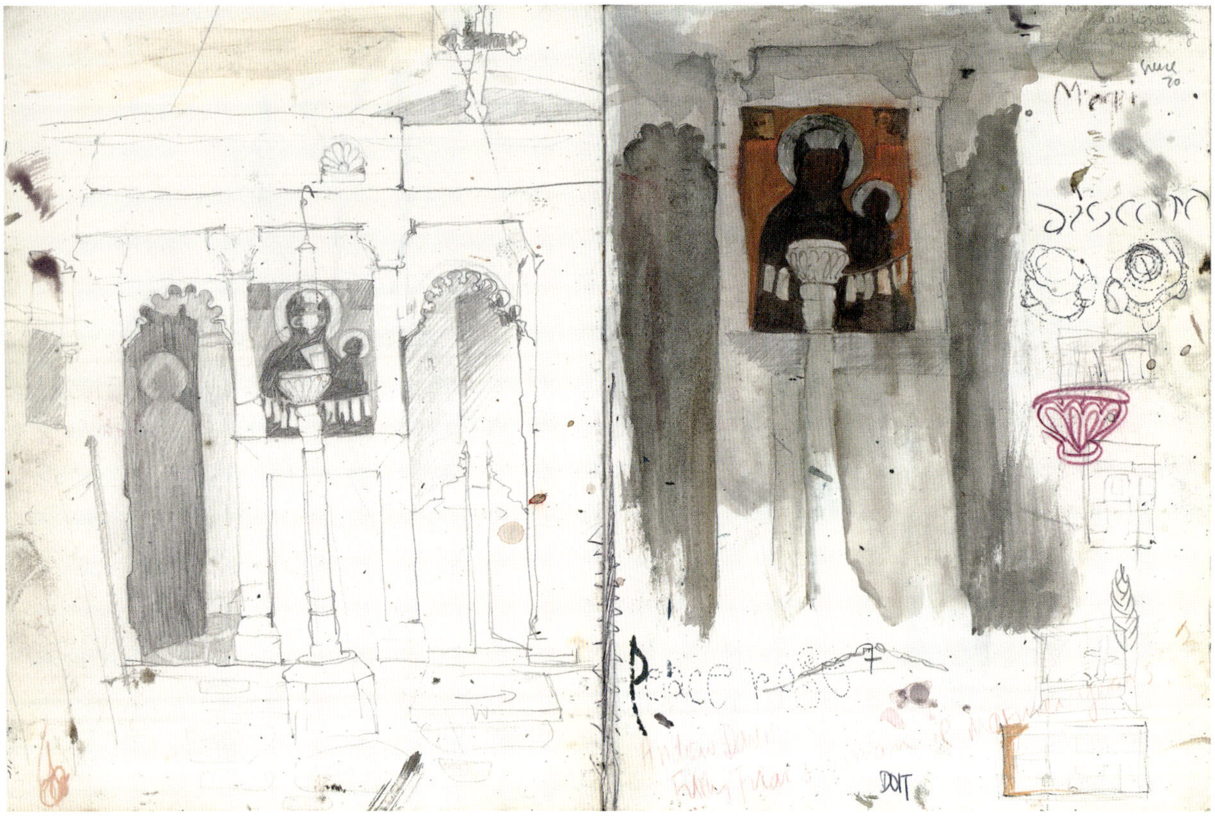

Greek sketch book

Iconastasis Fragment

Greek Orthodox Interior

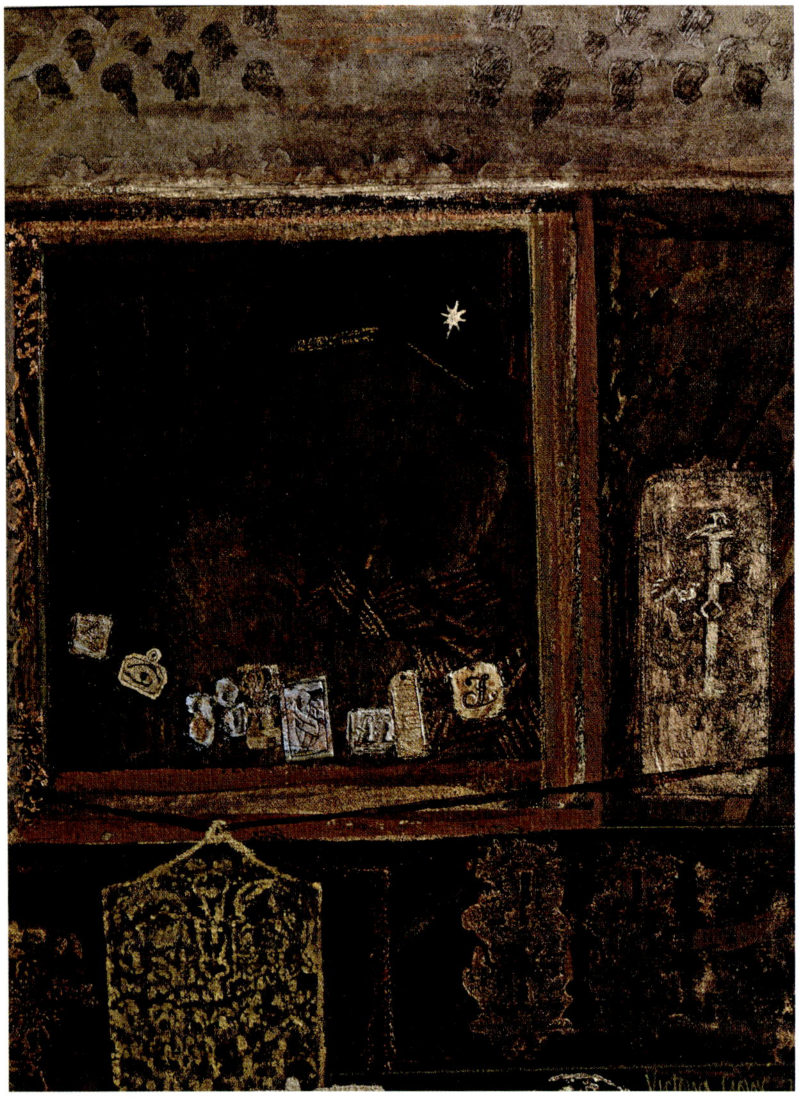

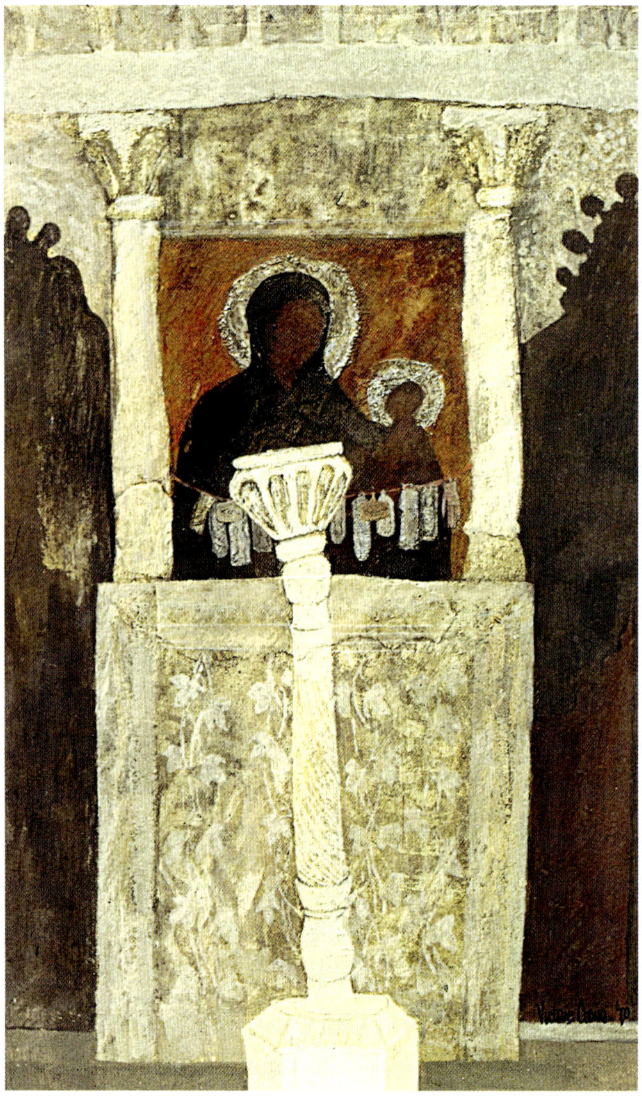

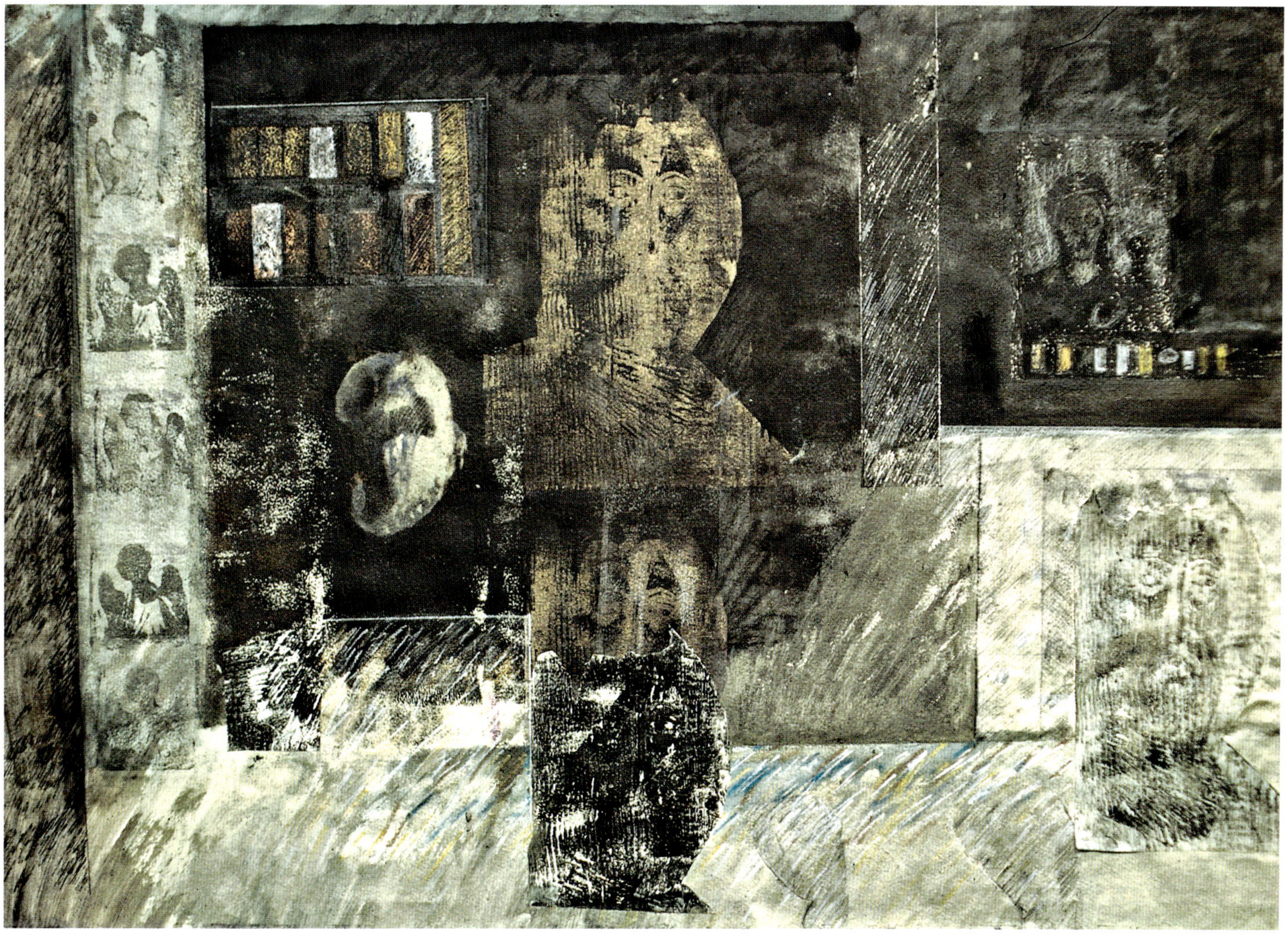

Black Icon

During those first winters she made drawings of the black and white patterns of snow melting on the hills. She then developed these drawings into a series of paintings. The subject matter was quite new, but the way she abstracted patterns and lines of drawing from the natural shapes of the geology, the order imposed upon it by the dikes and the shelter belts of the farmers, and on top of all that the random patterns of the melting snow, all in a palette of white, brown, black and grey, echoed work she had been doing while at the Royal College and so still perhaps the school of London. In some ways *Pentland Landscape* of 1969/70, for instance, again recalls Victor Pasmore. Like Pasmore, she has found in the landscape abstract patterns of dots and lines, of contrasted smooth and busy areas. The palette is like her own painting of a Hammersmith garden, but the abstracting lines and flat shapes work like those she found in the icons to block any shift into conventional representational space. As she had done before, she also used a mesh to lay a unifying grid over the image. She had found a landscape that suited her. It was dramatic certainly. It was spare and austere, too, as her painting had already often been, but the special quality that perhaps drew such a response from her was the way that it defied all the familiar tropes of representational landscape painting. She herself said of these pictures, "I liked the transforming nature of the snow – the commonplace becomes strangely different, the familiar contours of the field and hill become softened and unsure."[1]

Victoria has special affection for one particular picture done at this time, *Rosa Proprina*, a winter landscape in the Pentlands, dated 1970. The patches of melting snow on the hills are as black,

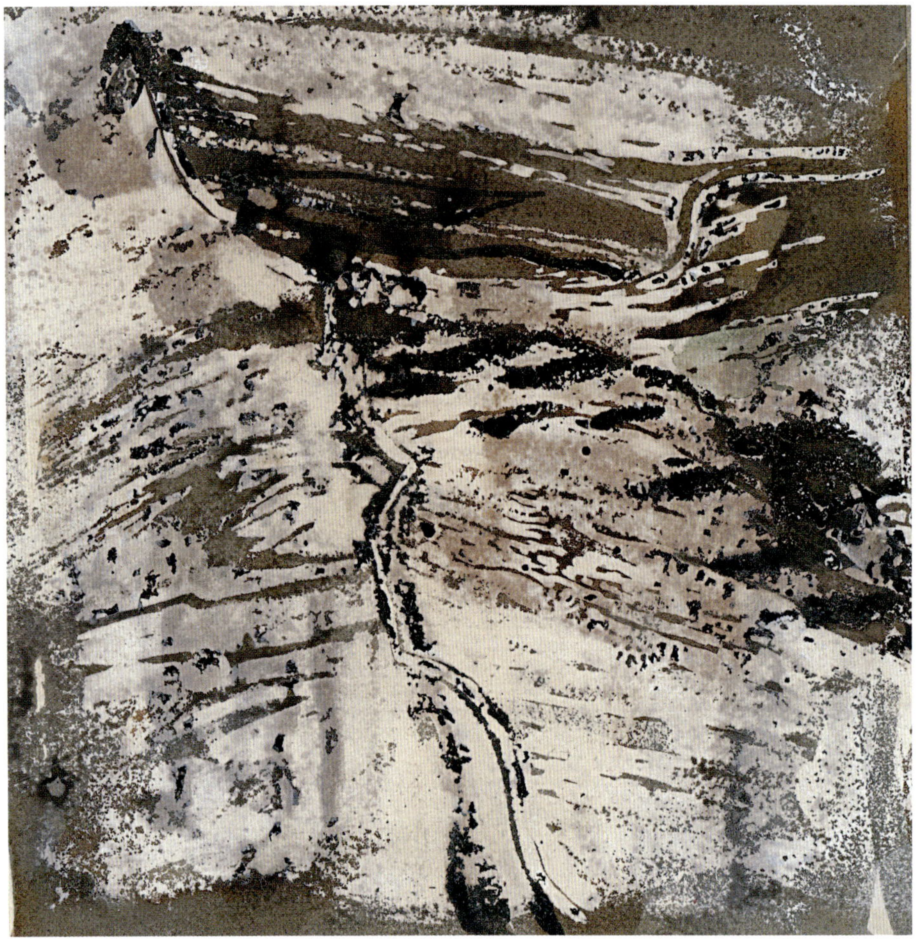

Greek Hillside I

Greek Hillside II

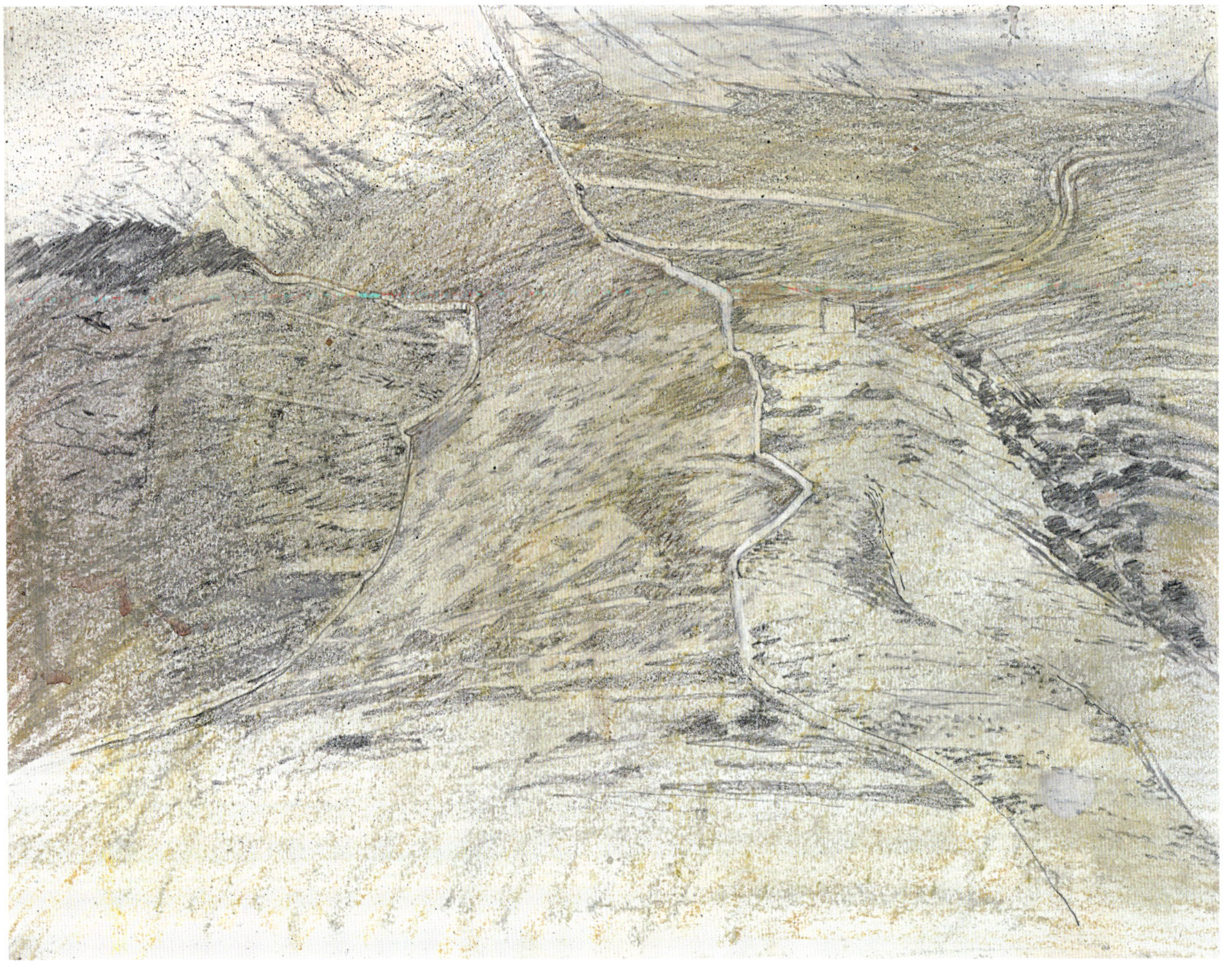

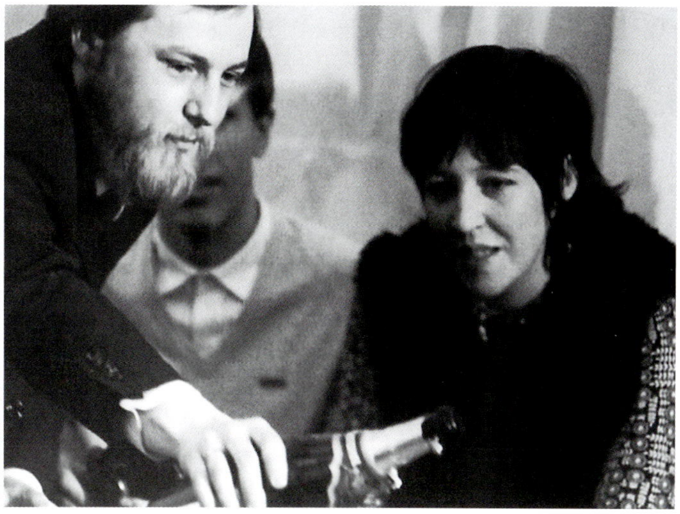

Victoria Crowe drinking Georgian champagne in Leningrad and diary entry

First day in Leningrad. Slept v. well in incredibly hot room (together luckily) & woke to breakfast (maccaroni, meat, bread, cheese, unsalted butter & sweet tea). M+I walked out for nearly an hour toward the centre of town & enjoyed the shops with bottled fruit, enormous cabbages and beautiful objects made from gingerbread – roundabouts and houses and baskets and animals – very Russian in character. We had a hectic tour of the city & I don't think many people could take in much that was hurled at us. We drove on to St Isaac's – the equestrian statue mounted on a soviet shaped rock in the middle of a slush and ice pool, which we trod over very gently! After St Isaac's – in the moving bus there was a strange peaceful atmosphere – maybe well-being at having warm feet after all that sloshing about to see the horse. We changed money at the Astoria Hotel, very faded salubrious type! Our cashier went to lunch just as we were about to be served so we had to queue all over again & then we bought papyrooski in the sterling shop (got a 10/- note & Yankee money back!)*

**Papyrooski - Russian cigarettes in long hollow paper tubes so you can still smoke while wearing heavy furry gloves.*

abstract, yet also imaginatively suggestive as Rorschach blots, and indeed she did use accident in these snow pictures. She laid layers of white poster paint over her drawing, then washed it with ink, allowed it to dry and then removed the poster paint so that the drawing was softened and an element of chance was introduced. In this particular picture, for instance, the ink has run across the paper. Its most striking feature, however, is the way that a drawing of a girl's head by Modigliani has been incorporated into the patterns of hills and snow. It is quite startling and reminiscent of the quality of the unexpected in Iris Murdoch's writing that Victoria admired. The words 'Rosa Proprina', the name written on the Modigliani drawing, are written across the hills behind her head. Iconographically, too, this image of a head suggested, but not fully described against the landscape, is something that was to recur often in her later work. This is perhaps one reason for her affection for this picture, but another may be that it marks how she had found, in her new environment, something that opened the way to realising the ambitions that she had earlier identified in her admiration for Modigliani, Matisse and indeed the Russian icon painters. The landscape and the Modigliani head are not contrasted; they are identified one with the other. In some important way they are the same.

Victoria was not completely taken over by her new environment, however. She won the David Murray Landscape Prize at the RCA in 1968 and this enabled her to make a trip to Greece in the summer of 1970. It was a journey that in some ways echoed her earlier Russian visit, particularly regarding her interest in the Orthodox Church. The drawings she did in Greece and indeed the paintings that followed

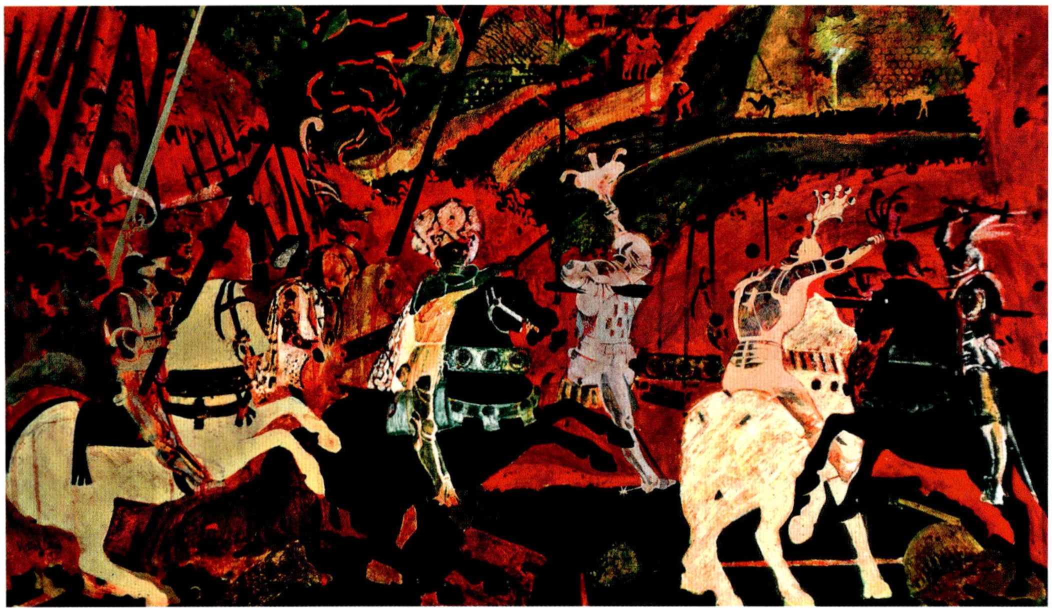

The Rout of San Romano

include church interiors, icons and votive tokens, as well as pictures of light glimmering on the mysterious gold and rich colours of an iconostasis. Looking back over a theme that had preoccupied her for almost ten years, in these pictures space is suggested simply by the presence of the objects and by the light. The icons in the background are dark, their subject matter mysterious and barely legible. Hanging in front of them are votive tokens, their gold and silver catching the light, suggesting their intricate detail, but not revealing it. Each one of these tokens represents a story of anxiety, of hope, of gratitude, or perhaps ultimately of sorrow, and despair. They are mute. Nevertheless each holds a key to memory as potent as Proust's madeleine which contained 'in the tiny and almost impalpable drop of [its] essence, the vast structure of recollection.'[2] Mysterious symbol is laid upon symbol to suggest there can be no simple answer; in its layers, truth is ultimately mysterious. This was how Victoria was to compose her paintings again much later, using objects whose significance is often hidden, but whose position is liminal, on the threshold of a deeper mystery.

In Greece, Victoria also made landscape drawings that are as spare as her Pentland pictures, but warmer in tone. For the first time, too, they include the cypress trees which were to appear so often in her later work, though there they are associated with Italy. It was years later that Italy began to become a primary inspiration, but her interest in Italian painting had begun much earlier. She had already raised eyebrows by writing about Piero della Francesca's *Baptism of Christ* when she was a student at the RCA. It was not the kind of picture that was expected to interest a young student at that time. In 1969 the major exhibition 'Frescos from Florence' at the Hayward Gallery, in the aftermath of the terrible Florence floods of 1966, was also something of a landmark in her evolving interest in Italian painting. She began to look more closely at it and to learn from it. In 1970, she made an ingenious copy of Uccello's *Rout of San Romano*, following the composition, but reversing the colour, an idea, she says, that was suggested by Richard Hamilton's experiments with reversed colour. In her first paintings of the Pentlands, too, there are clear echoes of the lines that define the hills in the background of Uccello's picture. After the move to Kittleyknowe, however, it seems to have been the winter landscapes of Peter Brueghel that were her ultimate inspiration, as she painted a series of pictures that clearly belong in the Northern tradition of winter painting which began with those great pictures.

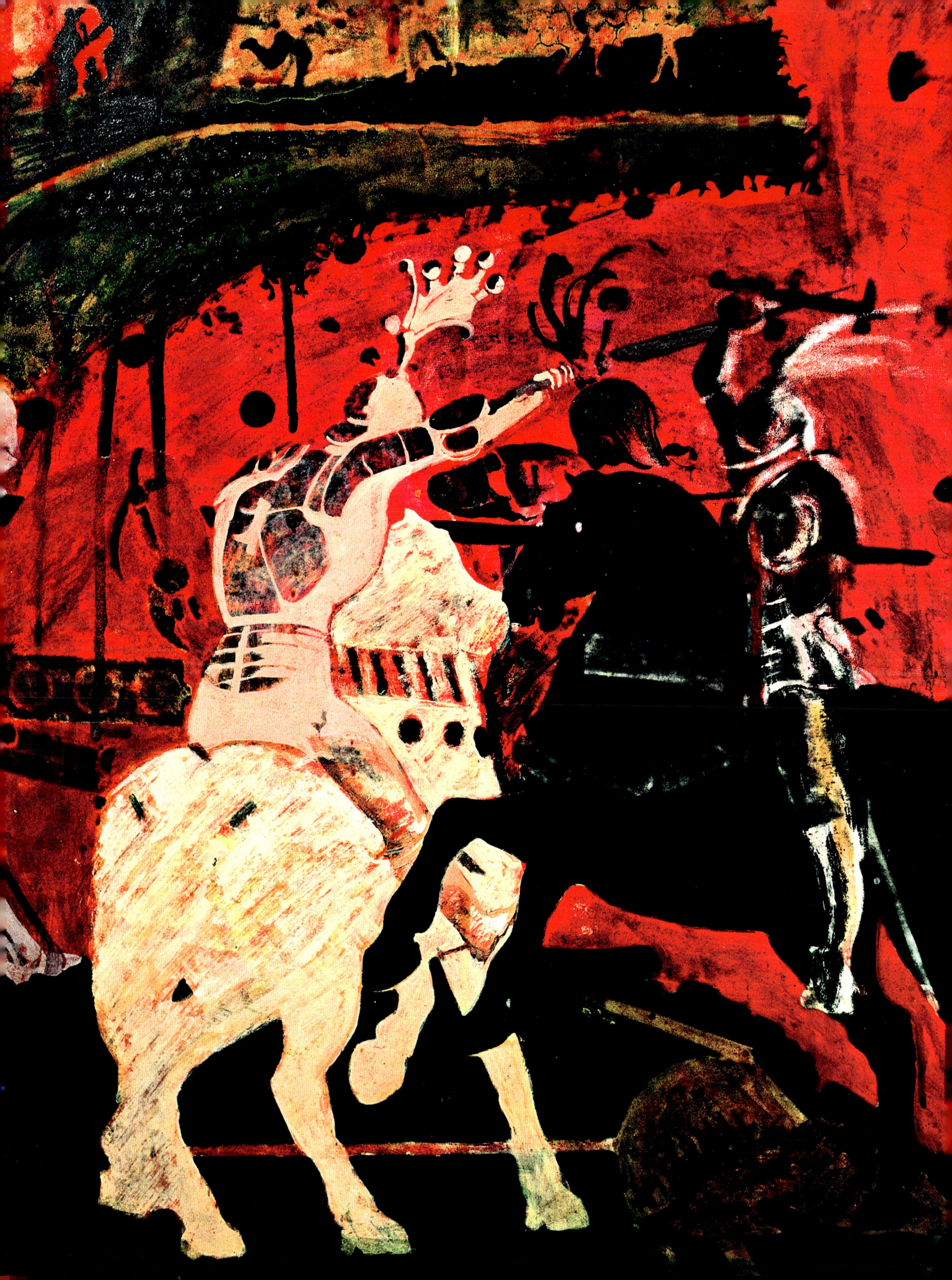

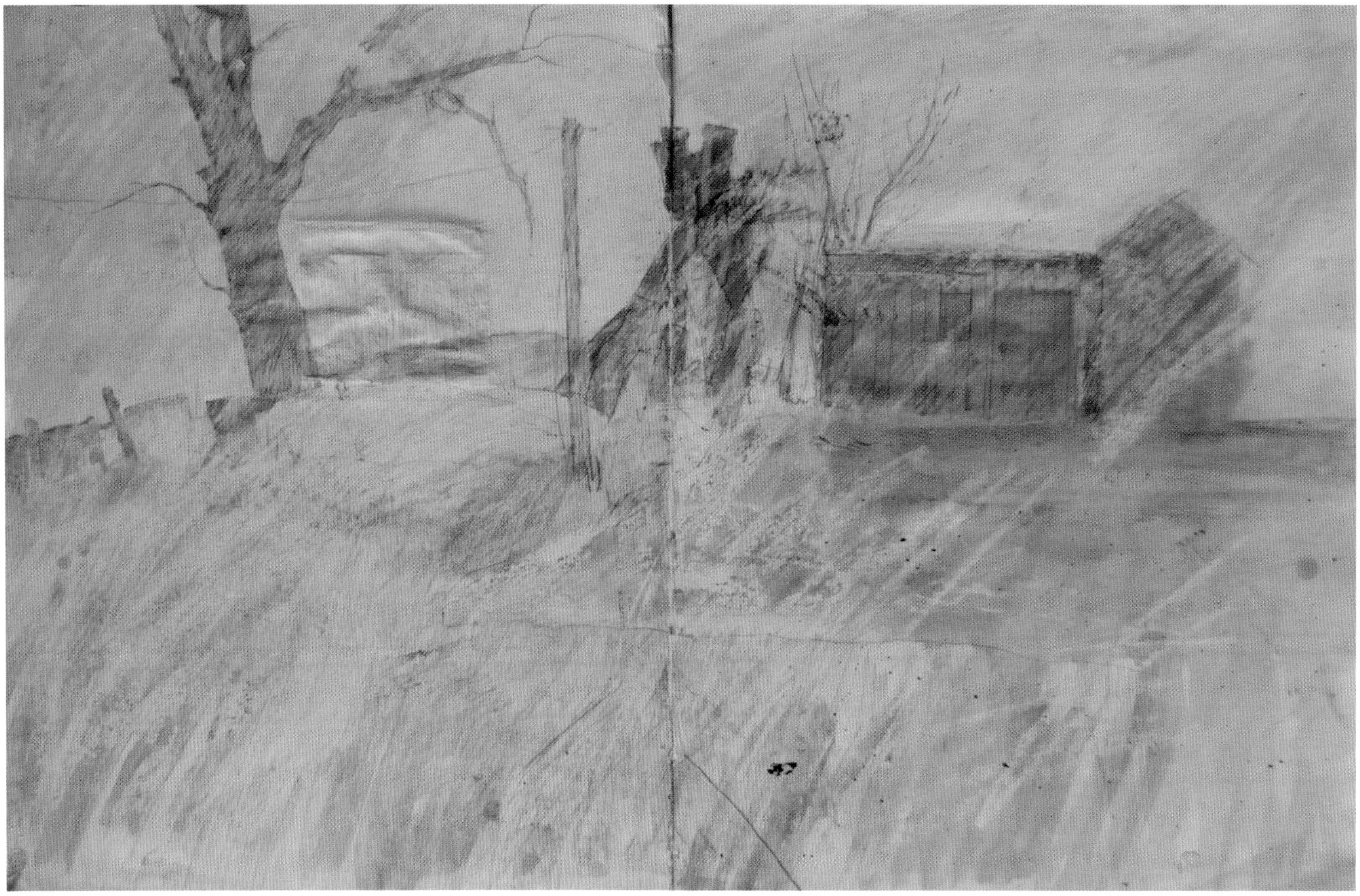

Drawing for Back Garden Monksview

Kittleyknowe

The views from Kittleyknowe and the light on the landscape were a constant in Victoria Crowe's new life, but her first drawing of it was modest enough. It is a pencil drawing of a stark winter tree, a washing line, a hut and the trunk of a dead tree, still standing, but its branches lopped. The drawing, which she also developed into a painting, is both under and over a white wash. This effect gives a sense of the layering of things in a way that is more mental than simply atmospheric. The surface suggests flux and so the picture combines the transience that we know is part of such a scene with the permanence that we feel it must have. As she finds a way to introduce such reflections into a humble scene like this, perhaps the artist was also freed from her earlier anxiety that she would slip back into representation; she does not need reverse perspective to keep us out. It is the quality she had sought in her even-toned pictures painted at Kingston. She has established an imaginative space even though in these pictures she is more direct in her approach to the landscape than she had been before, in her own words she was painting more objectively. Perhaps it helped her that this was more widely accepted in Edinburgh than it had been in London. A series of beautiful winter landscapes followed, such as

Back Garden with Snow (1973) and *Large Tree Group* (1975). *Winter at Kittleybrig* (1974) is a luminous view of the ancient gateposts on either side of the now disused drive that once led over the bridge visible in the picture and up to Newhall House.

It was around this time too that she painted the pictures of Greek icons, the iconostasis and hanging votives. They show the continuing spiritual concern underlying her art, not in order to put it in the service of some external spiritual ideal, but for the art itself to contain that dimension. These two things, the landscape and her search in it for a kind of meaningful imagery, then came

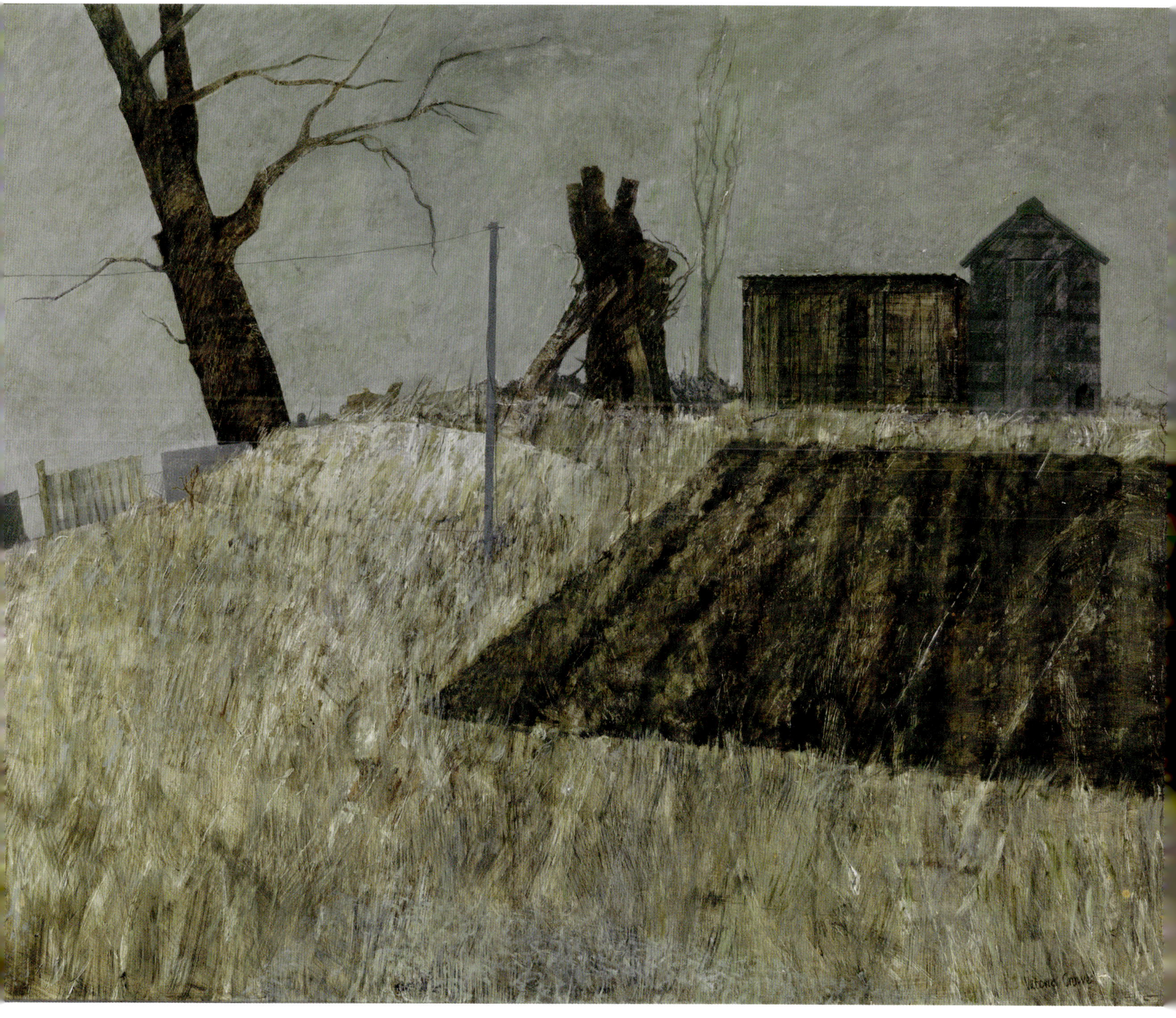

Back Garden Monksview

together in the life of her neighbour at Kittleyknowe, the shepherd, Jenny Armstrong. Their two adjacent homes as they then were – they have since much changed – are recorded in *Snowbound Cottages* from 1977. Beneath a dark grey sky, they sit on a low ridge beyond a snow-covered field. Across the lane from these two cottages an eccentric neighbour, Tom Wickham, lived in a tumbledown farmyard. This dwelling is also recorded in a number of drawings including a lovely, almost Pre-Raphaelite watercolour. A classic example of Diogenes syndrome, Tom Wickham could never throw anything away and so his immediate environment was pretty chaotic, but the delicacy of this drawing only celebrates that fact. Its Pre-Raphaelite quality is also seen in many of her other watercolour studies. Even something as simple as a roll of baler twine is rendered with exquisite delicacy. Coincidentally, it was in 1975 that in the south the Brotherhood of Ruralists returned to what they thought was a Pre-Raphaelite vision of the English countryside. One of their number, Graham Ovenden, had been a contemporary and friend of Victoria's at the RCA, but the comparison only points to the difference. Unlike their lushly sentimental landscapes, her work is austerely beautiful and is quite untouched by nostalgia.

Jenny Armstrong was in her sixties. The daughter and grand-daughter of shepherds, at one time she ran two thousand sheep on the Pentlands. Now she kept a little flock of foundlings in the nearby fields. She also kept hens in a run a little way away from her cottage. This was to be the subject of a number of studies and paintings. As she got to know her, Victoria found Jenny to be a woman at peace with herself, centred in what she did. Jenny was, she said, unlike anyone whom she had met before. The two women became close friends even though their lives were so different. Victoria was struggling in the brittle world of Edinburgh College of Art to the extent that she was not sure that she could continue. She and Mike had thought they might stay in Scotland only for three or four years, but then Mike enrolled at Moray House to get the qualification he needed to teach in a Scottish school. (Mike went on to teach in several schools and at Queen Margaret College before eventually joining Victoria on the staff of the College of Art.) It seemed they were beginning to put down roots, but Victoria nevertheless felt the isolation and lack of empathy at the College even more keenly when she became pregnant in 1972.

In contrast to her life at the College, even in the late twentieth century, Jenny Armstrong's life as a shepherd was in its essentials unchanged from the times of pastoral poetry. Dedicated and all absorbing, like an artist's, it was a life, not a job. It was, too, of necessity closely in tune with the weather, the seasons and the rhythms of nature, but also with the character and configuration of the landscape itself and the way the sheep themselves understood it. Jenny was wise in her way, but in keeping with Geddes's motto, *vivendo docemus* (by living we learn), her knowledge was intuitive, learnt neither from teaching, nor from books, but from experience. The landscape that she lived in was a hard one. It can snow any time between October and April, or even later, but, as Ian Hamilton Finlay, who lived nearby at Little Sparta, liked to point out, Arcadia, the ancient home of pastoral poetry, is also a hard landscape with cruel winters. It is a nice continuity, too, that, situated just on the edge of the Newhall estate, Kittleyknowe was also the very landscape that had inspired Allan Ramsay's pastoral play *The Gentle Shepherd*. Jenny Armstrong's language was, from Victoria's account of it, still very much the warm and pithy dialect of Ramsay's play.

Back Garden Under Snow

Kittleyknowe photographs

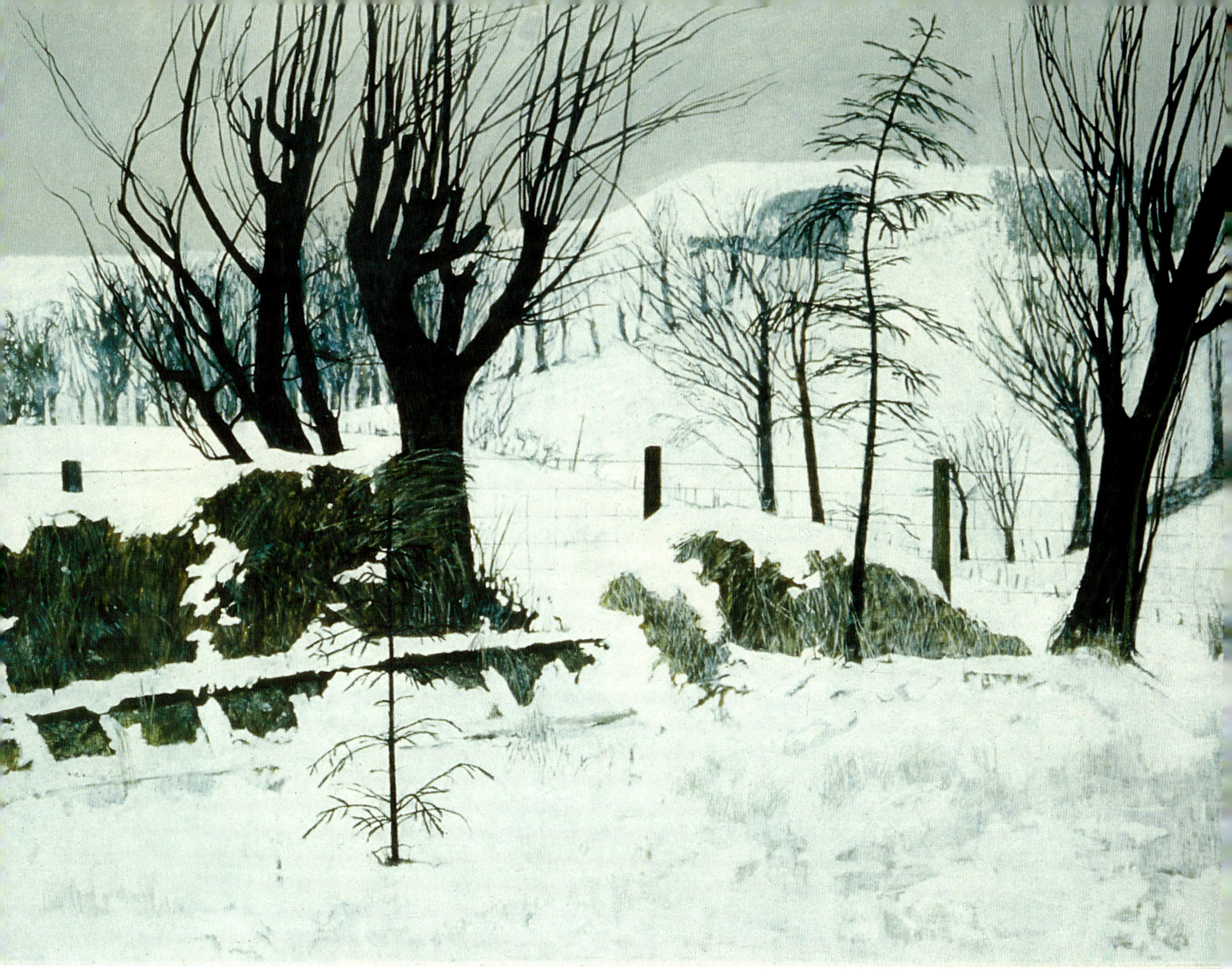

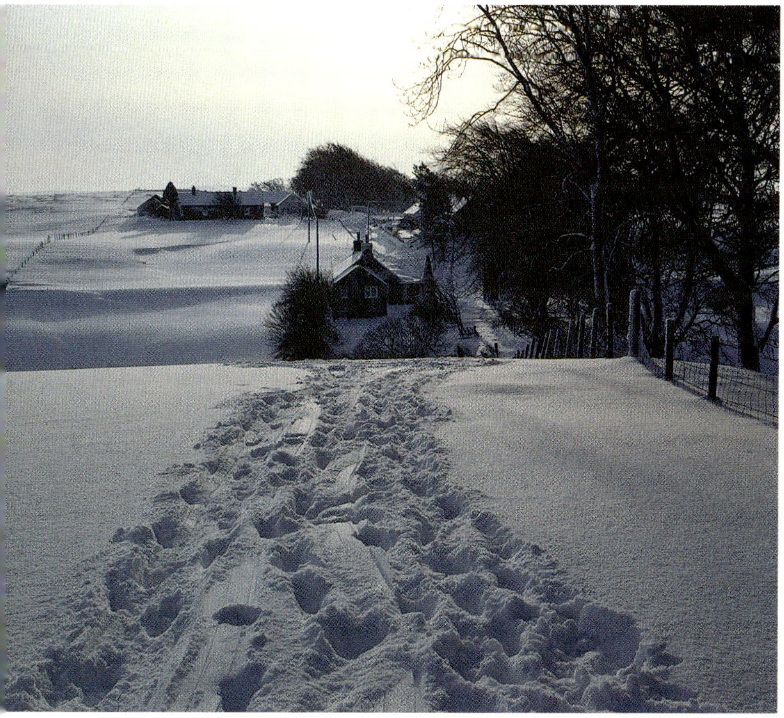

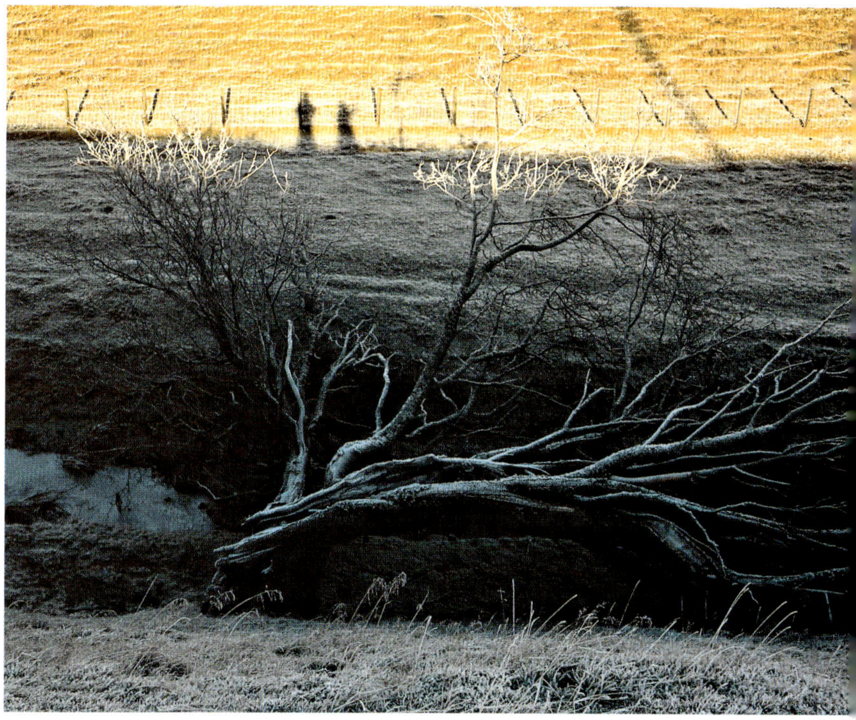

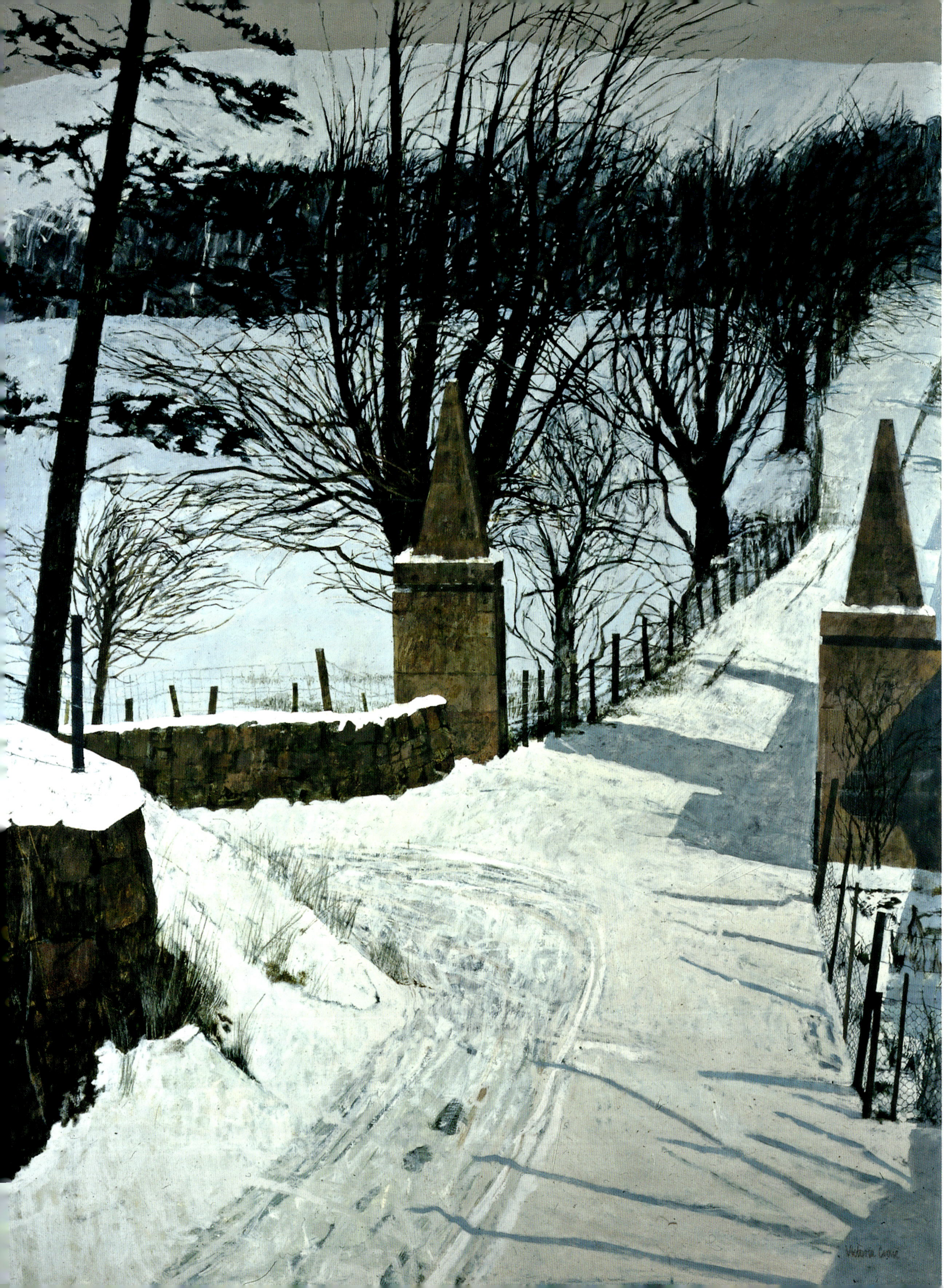

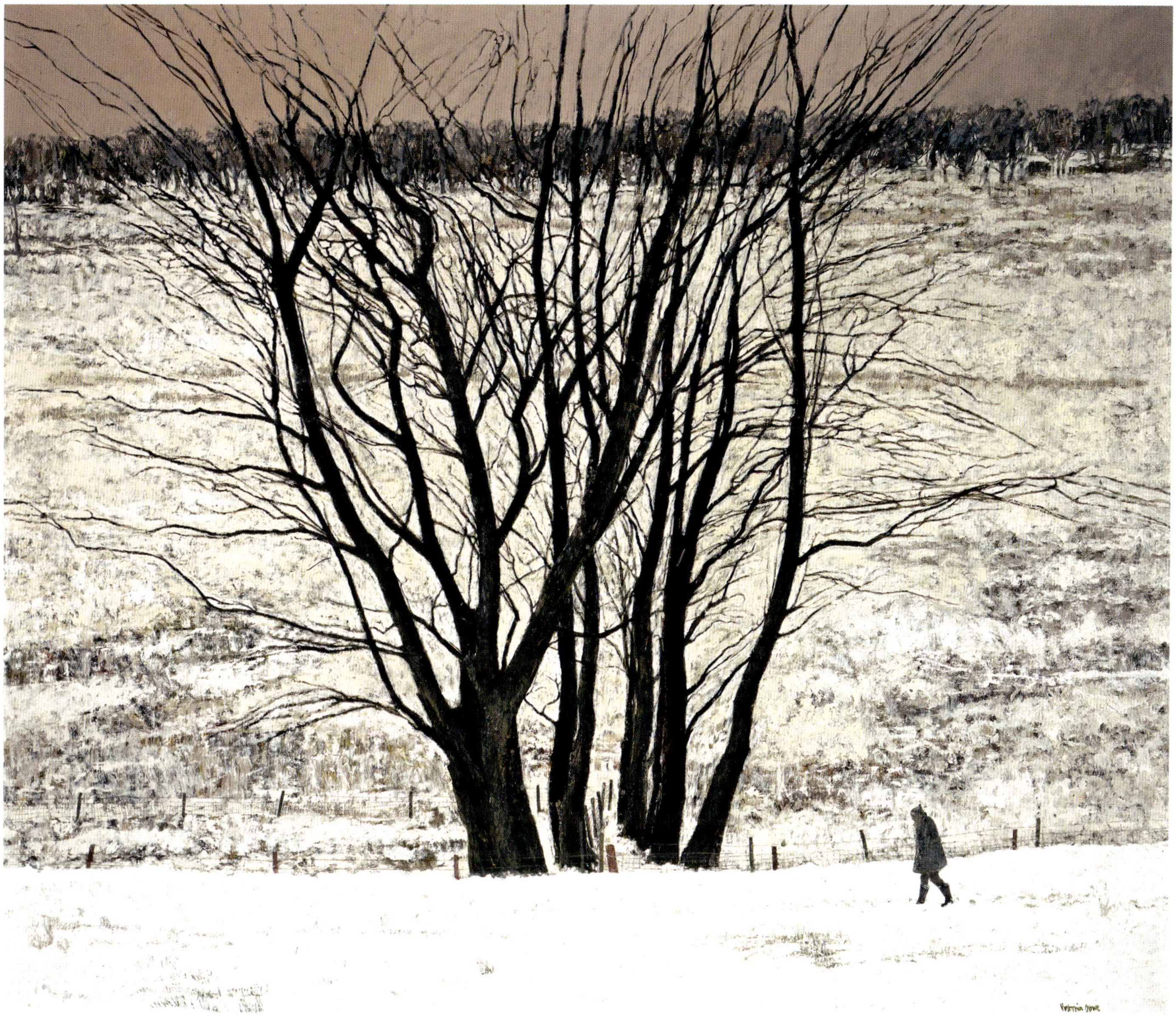

Large Tree Group

In its austerity and its poverty in material things, Jenny Armstrong's life was a little like that of a medieval saint or hermit. For her, however, this was simply practical and not a sacrifice made in the name of the doubtful rewards of religion, though she went to the kirk (at least in winter, in summer hers was the kirk o'the fields). It was balanced, too, by the richness of her engagement with practical things and the natural world that was their frame. It is easy to see how such a person could represent an echo for Victoria in both her own early religious experience and her romantic Tolstoyan ideas of the land, its people and the great continuities they shared. Indeed, perhaps, Jenny personified an idea about belief, not as a condition of the mind dependent on an external authority for its validation, but as the completion of self. William Blake saw it that way, too. In his engravings to the *Book of Job*, Job's revelation comes when he recognises that he – and indeed by extension all Christianity – has created a god, externalised it and then treated it as an independent authority to be obeyed, when in fact the divine was within himself.

Winter at Kittleybrig

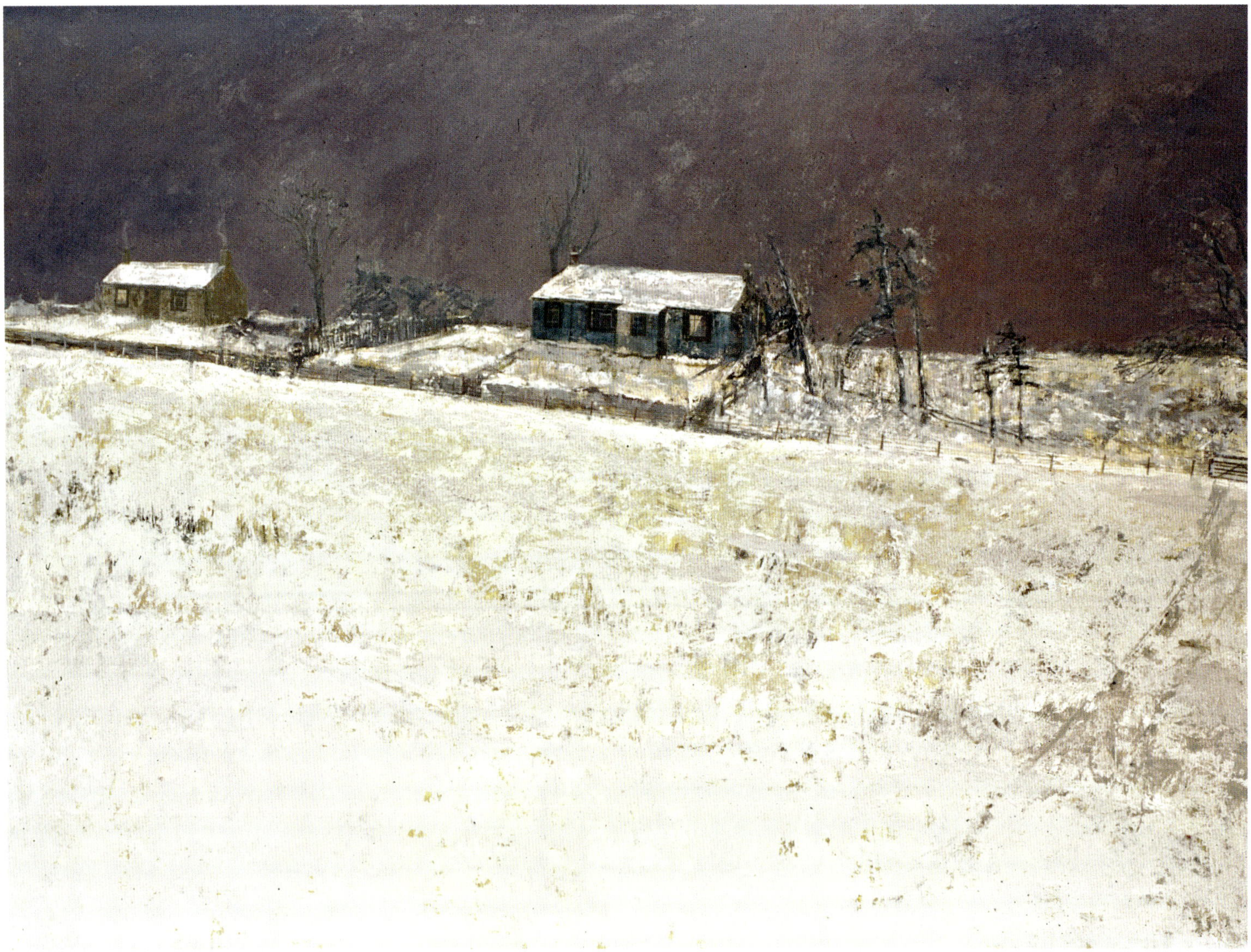

Snowbound Cottages

Nevertheless, such considerations would have been trivial beside the existential fact of Jenny Armstrong herself. A redoubtable figure, earthy, matter-of-fact, intimate with the land, Victoria introduced Jenny into her paintings after the birth of her first child, Ben, in 1973, although at this stage the shepherd simply served as an indicator of scale in a vast landscape. In *Large Tree Group* from 1975, for instance, she is a small black figure walking past a group of leafless trees, starkly silhouetted against the snow. The distant line of a wood marks the high horizon. Above it is a narrow band of pink sky, picking up the warm tints of grass showing through the snow and so softening a little the harshness of this wintry landscape. *Sheep, Shepherdess and Harbour Craig*, on the other hand, painted the same year, shows Jenny Armstrong feeding her sheep in the snow, and its subject seems to be the cold itself and the hardship that it brings. The picture is painted entirely in white, cool grey and black without a hint of warmth. (Harbour Craig is a ruined cottage visible at the top of the painting.)

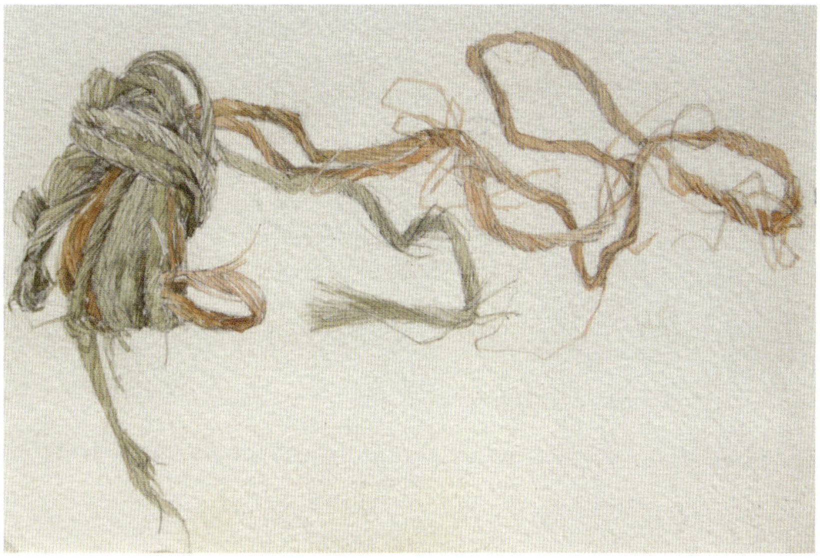

Baler Twine

Tom Wickham's Barns

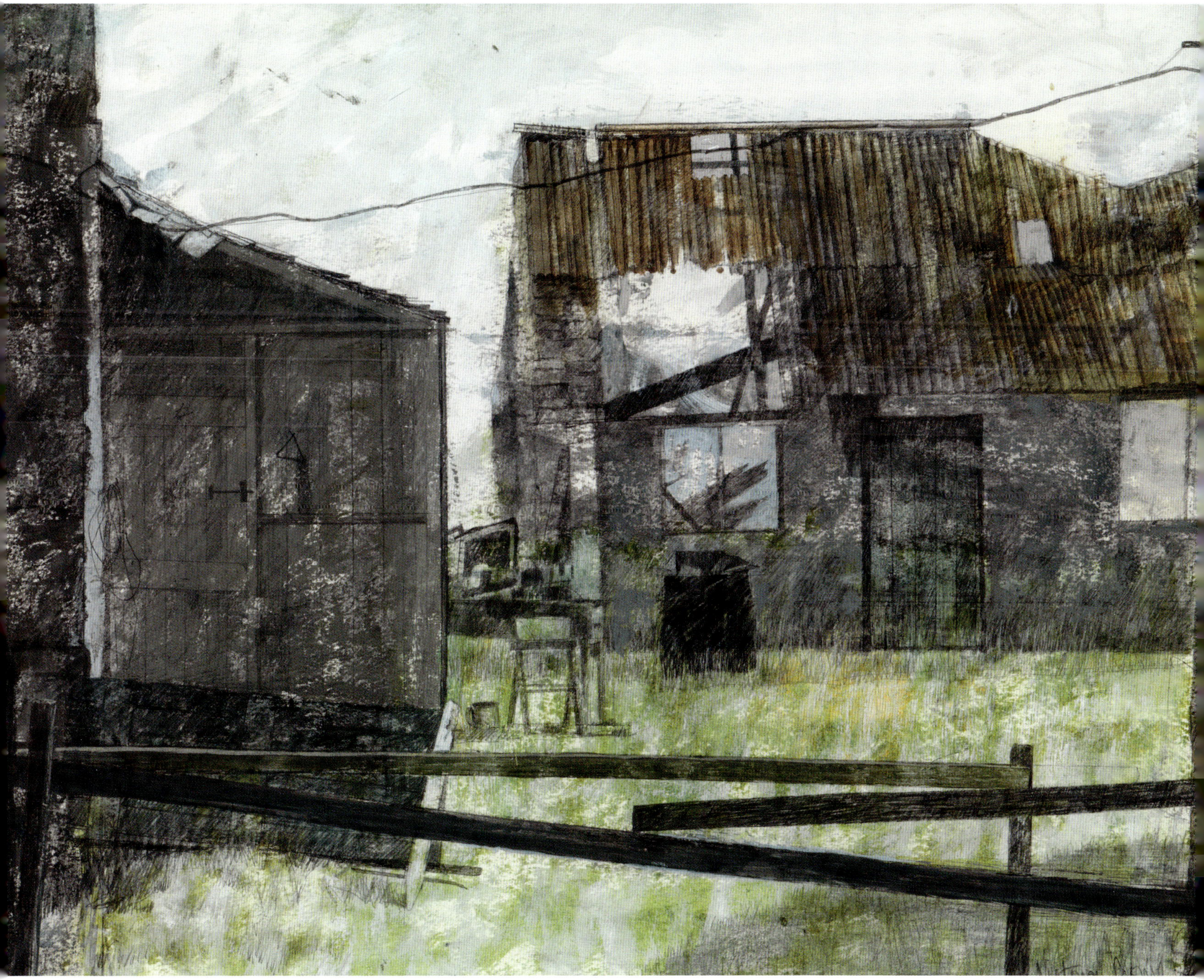

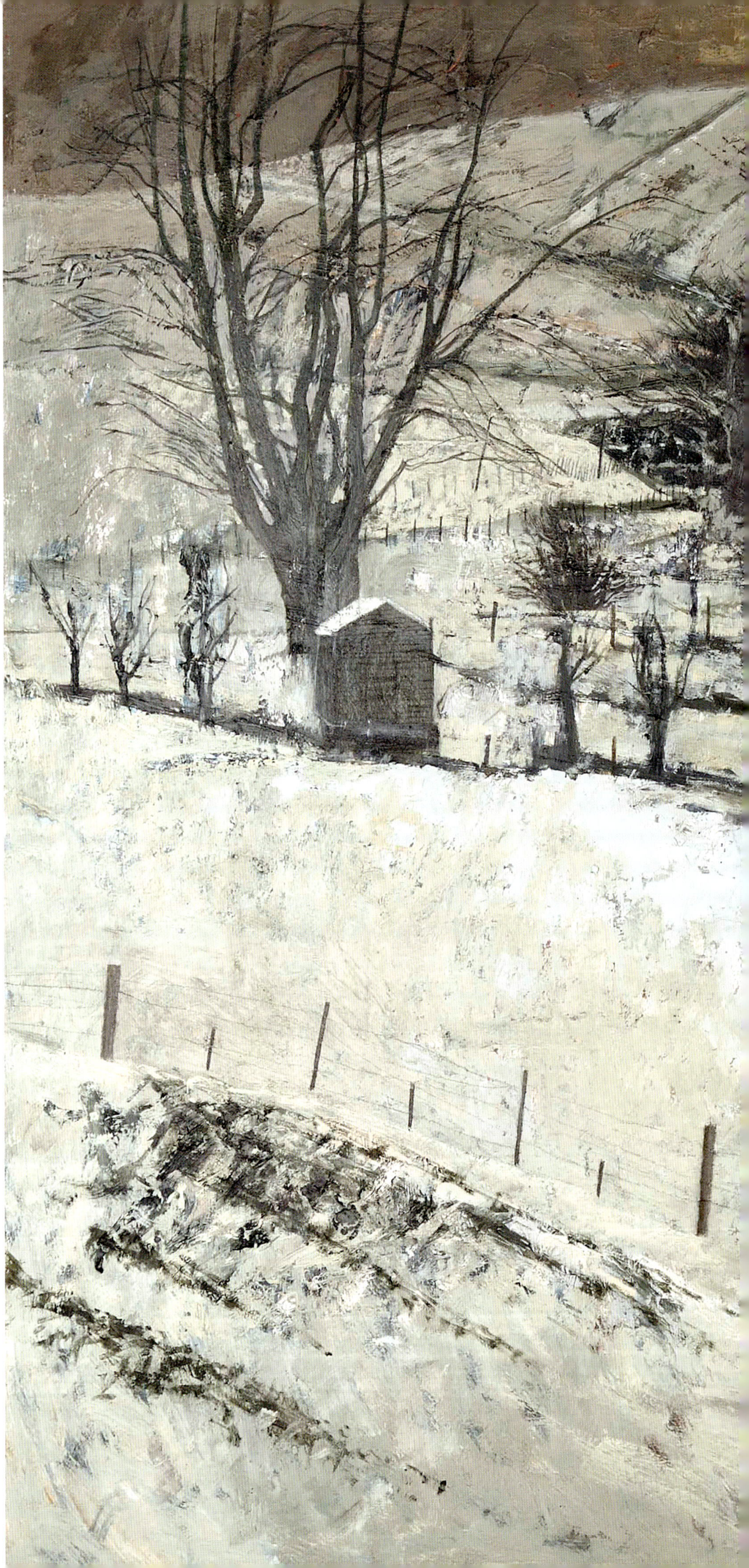

Kittleybrig, Winter

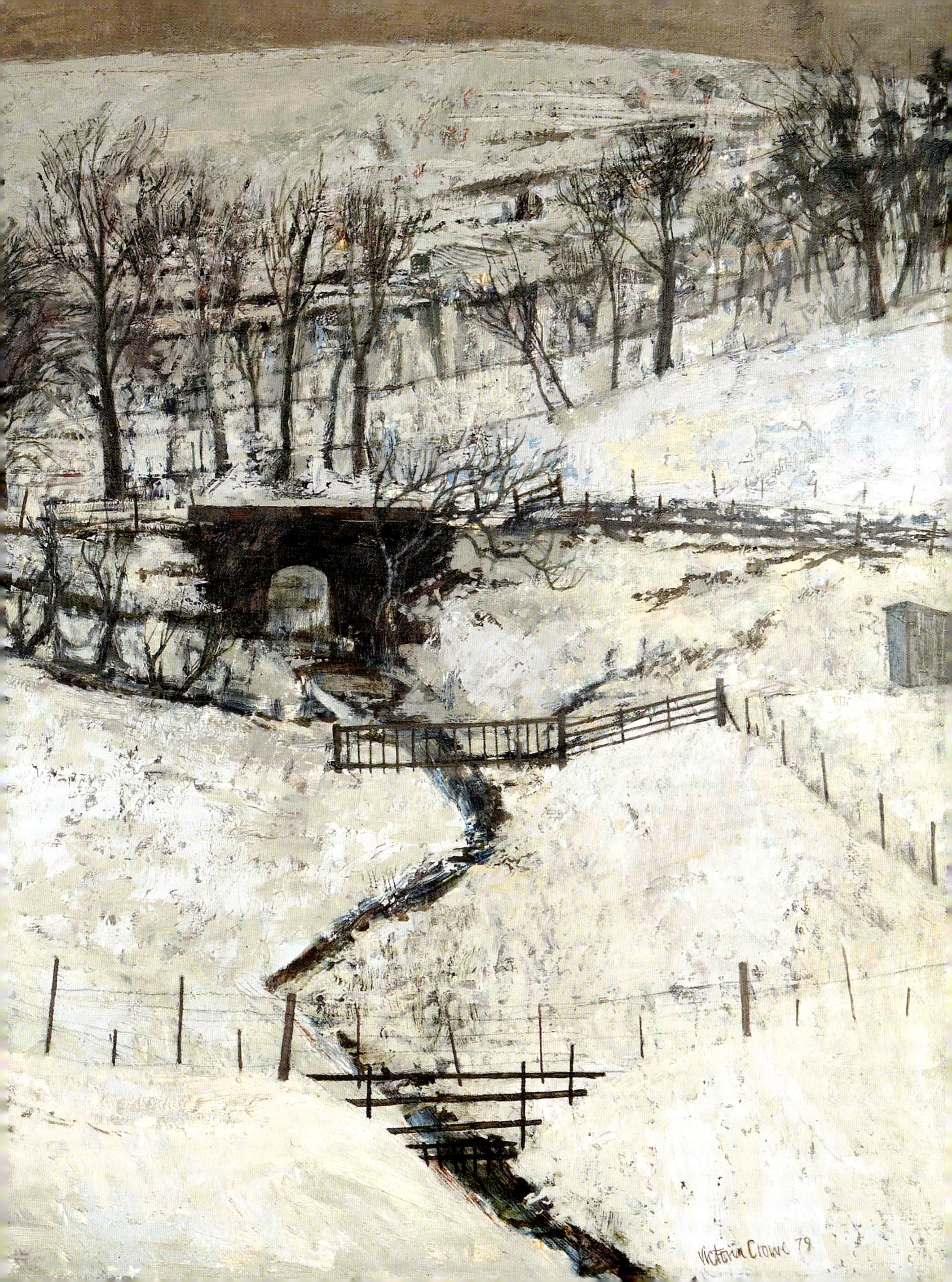
Victoria Crowe 79

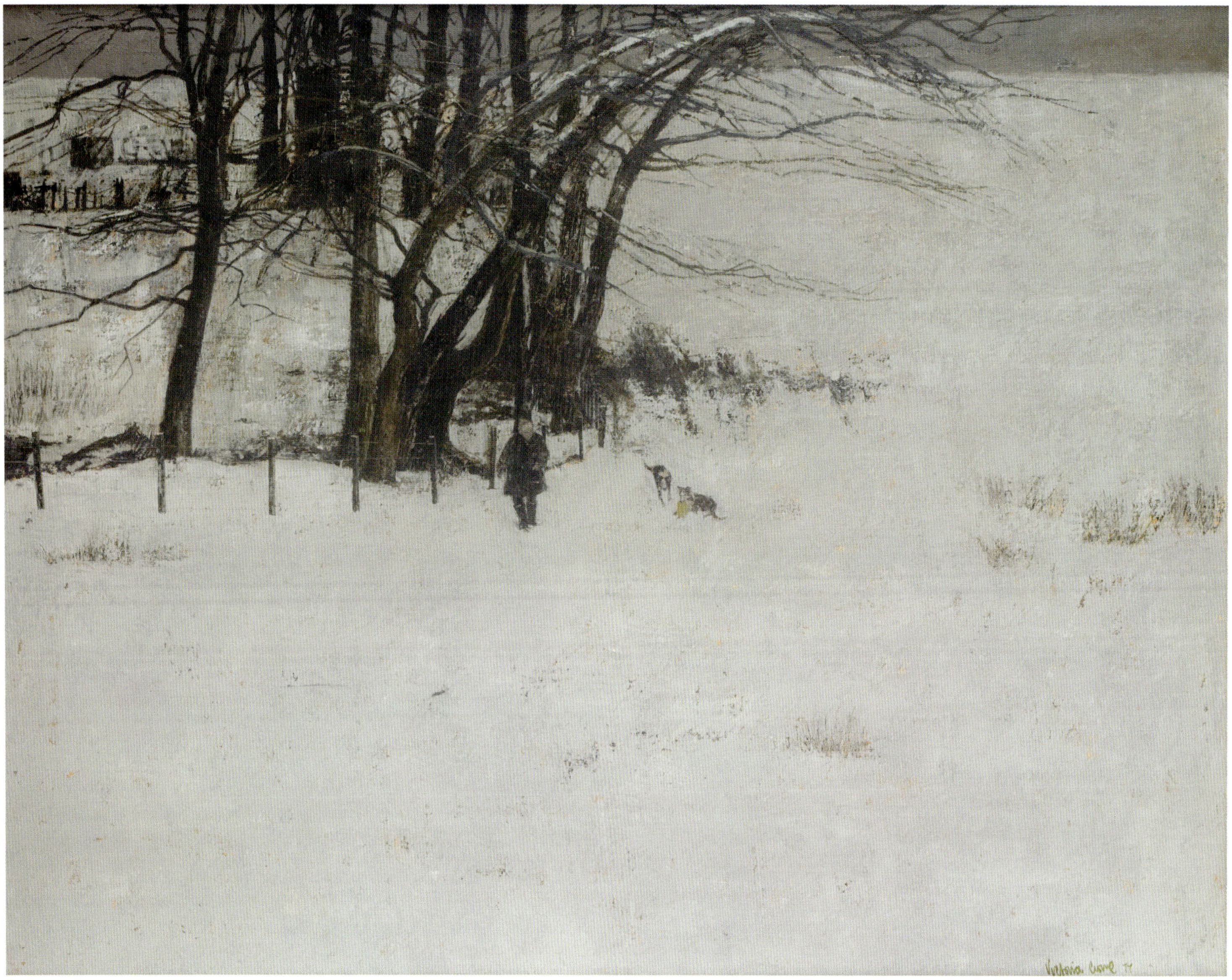

Winter Walk

In the picture, Jenny is a timeless figure. Her gesture with one arm raised against the landscape could be compared to images ranging from Raeburn's figure of Sir John Clerk stretching out his arm to embrace the landscape of Penicuik House, to Raeburn's model, Michelangelo and in turn Michelangelo's model the *Apollo Belvedere*. Without supposing it is beholden to any of these originals, it is nevertheless the echo of them in Jenny's gesture that makes it seem so timeless. Victoria also painted several oil sketches and small pictures of Jenny doing various things, including feeding her hens, the first dating from 1974. These early essays are beautiful pictures in themselves, but it was in them that she found this way of representing Jenny; she is an immediately recognisable figure and can be redeployed with variations in other paintings, but is not really a portrait. As the artist says herself, Jenny's figure was more like an icon, a formal image – not a simply representation alone – and one which, for that reason, does not lose significance if it is repeated.

Jenny, Sheep and Dogs

Landscape with Figures and Dogs

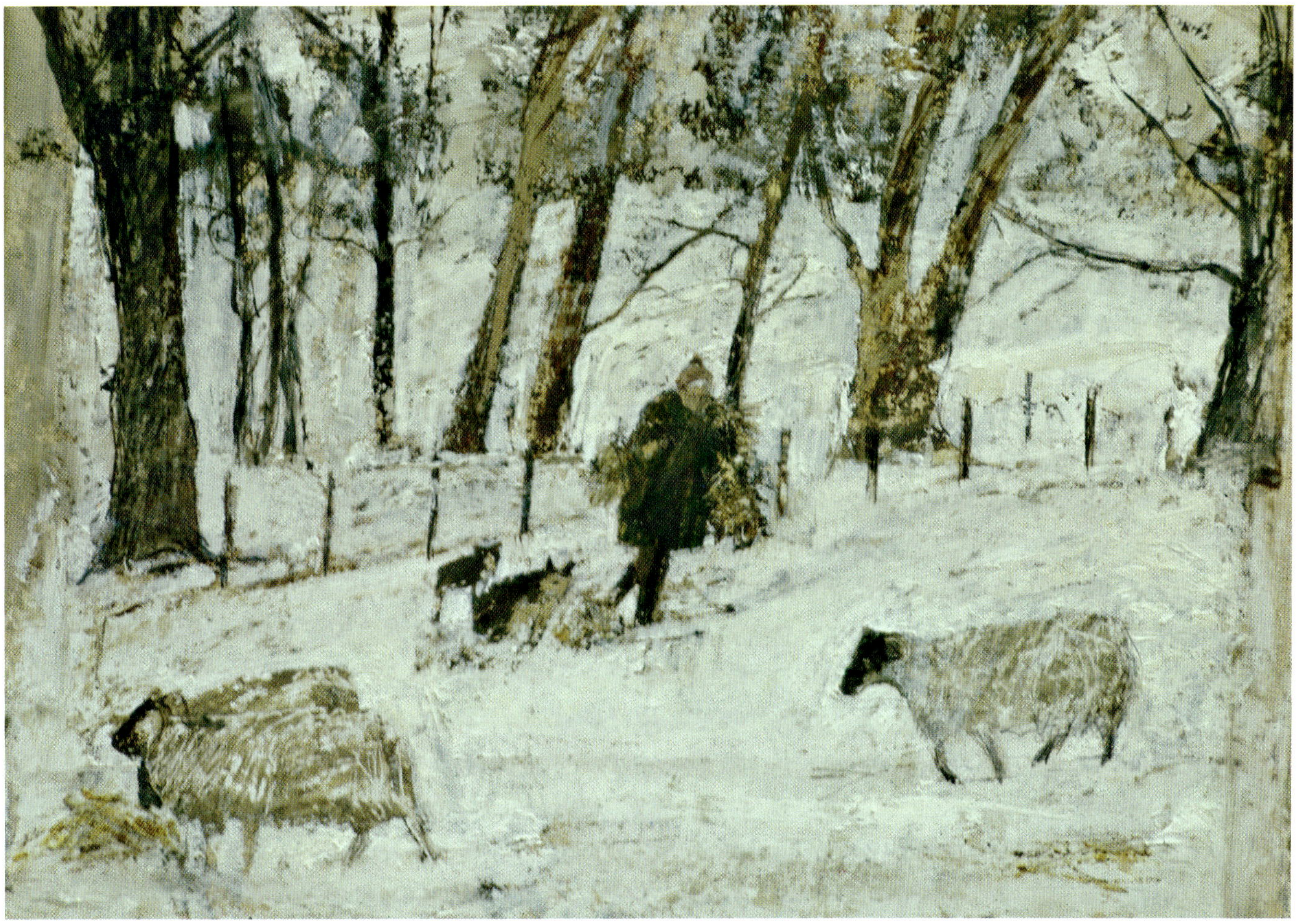

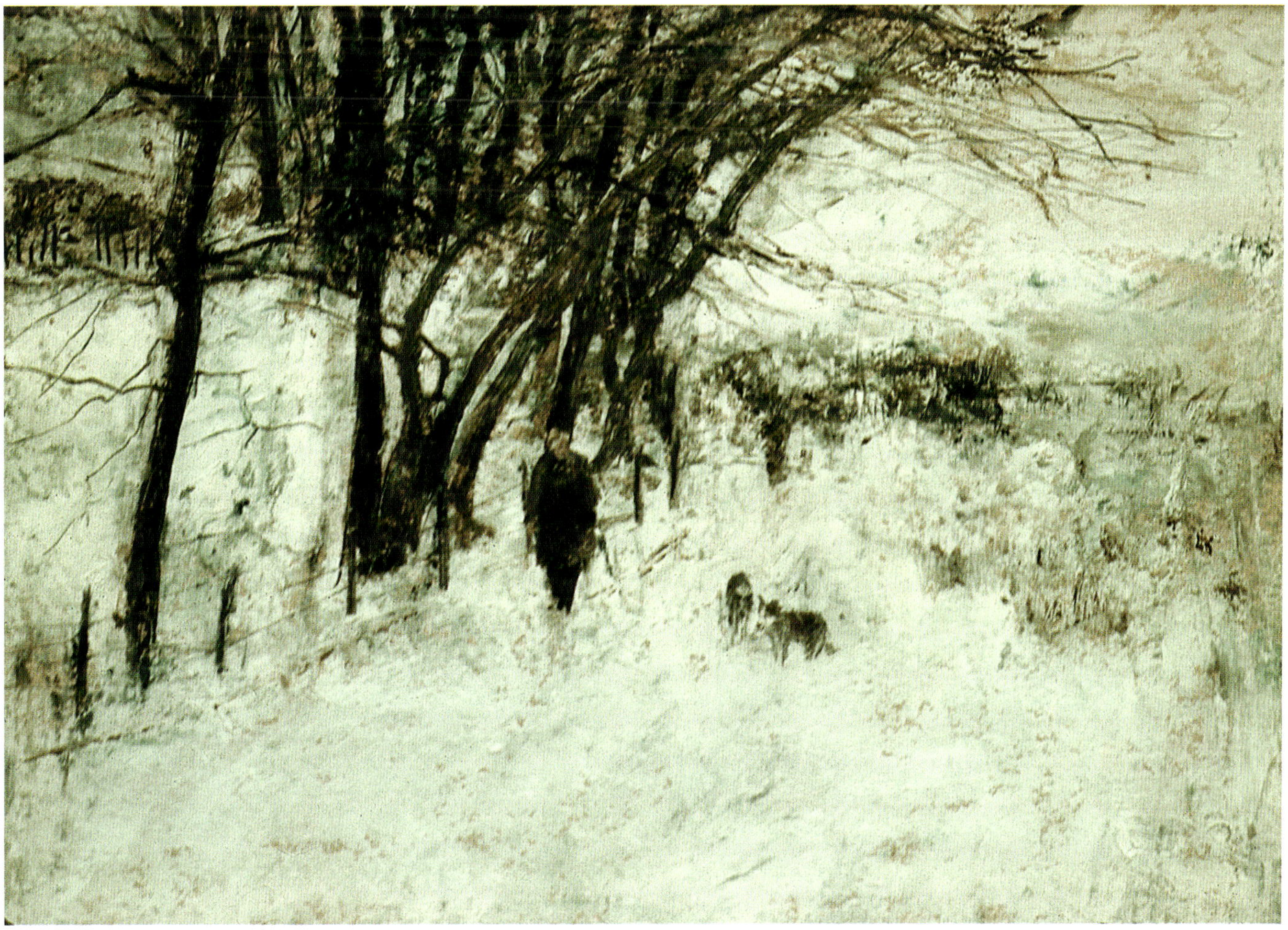

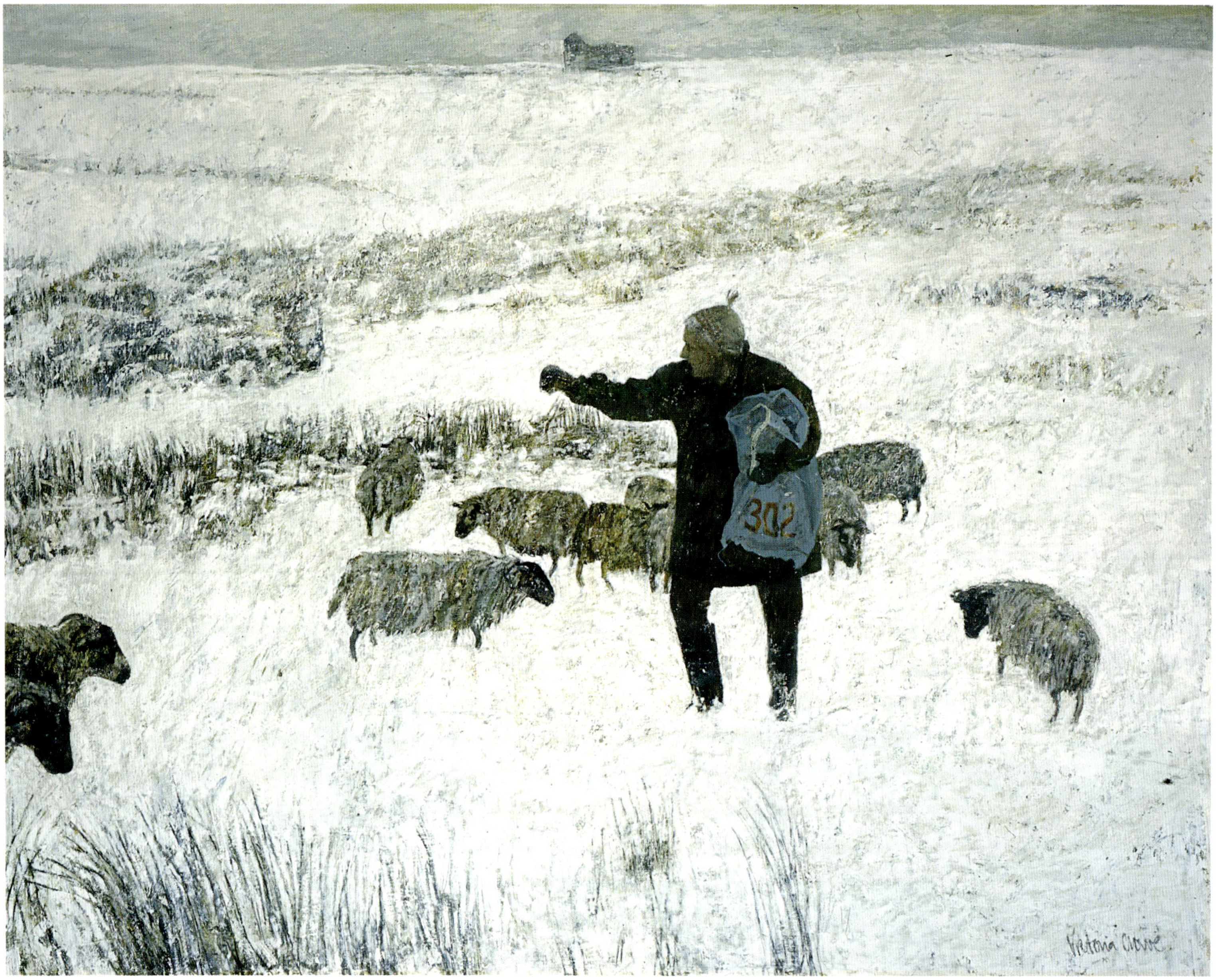

Sheep, Shepherdess and Harbour Craig

Small studies, drawings and watercolours are part of an elaborate process of preparation that underlies all these pictures. Drawings of a ramshackle fence that Jenny built, for instance, enumerate the number of planks and the precise position of the hinges of the gate. The final compositions are also always worked out in some detail, too, so the rich surface that these paintings have is not the result of expressive gestures, nor of successive changes of mind. It was already a feature of her earlier work, but now it is also descriptive, reflecting her concern with the texture of things, with their actuality. Nevertheless, this positive surface, the tangible presence of the picture as an object, is a reminder, even as her work became more objective and was based on such close study, that the end result is a made image. It is a product of thought, not of a conjurer's illusion.

Victoria herself became ever more closely involved with Kittleyknowe and its landscape. It came to be a constant in her life and Jenny Armstrong was its familiar spirit. *Snow Sky*, 1977, is a view of a fence and the gable of her house beneath a dark sky, heavy with snow. The picture is dramtic, but

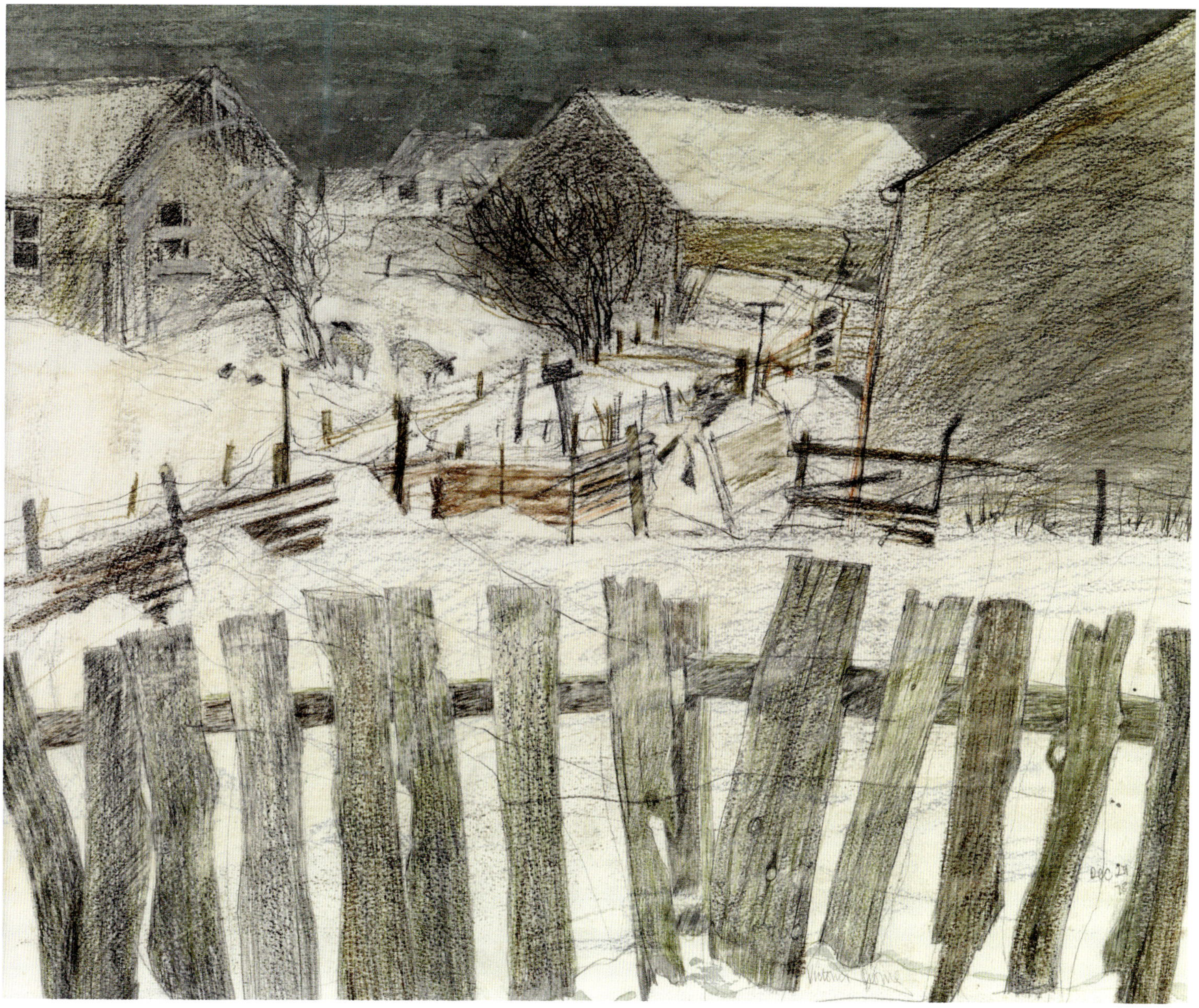

Jenny's Fence Looking Towards Kittleyknowe

it is not at all dramatised and indeed the great strength of all these pictures is that there is nothing sentimental about them. The closeness of observation on which they were based is an essential part of this. It is truly Ruskinian in its respect for truth. Indeed truth was the word she herself used when looking at her own detailed studies of the interior of Jenny's cottage that enumerate the objects on the mantlepiece. "It was", Victoria said, "important to record the truth." Because of the respect that this attitude entails, when she paints Jenny Armstrong, she does not, for a moment, patronise her, or distance her from us in a way that, so often in paintings of this kind in the past, subtly diminishes the subject's humanity. Jenny is entirely herself, secure in her dignity. This is perhaps one reason why these pictures are almost always set in winter. The purity and austerity of the snow and the starkness of the trees and other features of the landscape drawn against it exclude any risk of sentimentality. At the same time, *Snow Sky* is as much a picture of weather as of place, although in fact the weather at Kittleyknowe is almost definitive of the place. In winter there is little to stop the wind, and in the seventies too there was a series of hard, snowy winters.

Victoria's relationship with Jenny Armstrong and the landscape was central to her art up to and indeed for several years after Jenny's death at the age of eighty-two on 20 November 1985. She had been like a touchstone to test the truth of Victoria's own response to the landscape that they shared. As she herself bore two children, Gemma followed Ben in 1976, Victoria also recognised how the landscape could reflect much deeper concerns and the cycle of life itself. As she herself put it: "Watching Jenny at work and listening to her at home, had made me think of our relationship to the land, our impermanence vis à vis the enduring landscape and the rhythms of nature and season. I can see that I used my drawings and paintings to examine these questions of value and reality together with our function and purpose."[1]

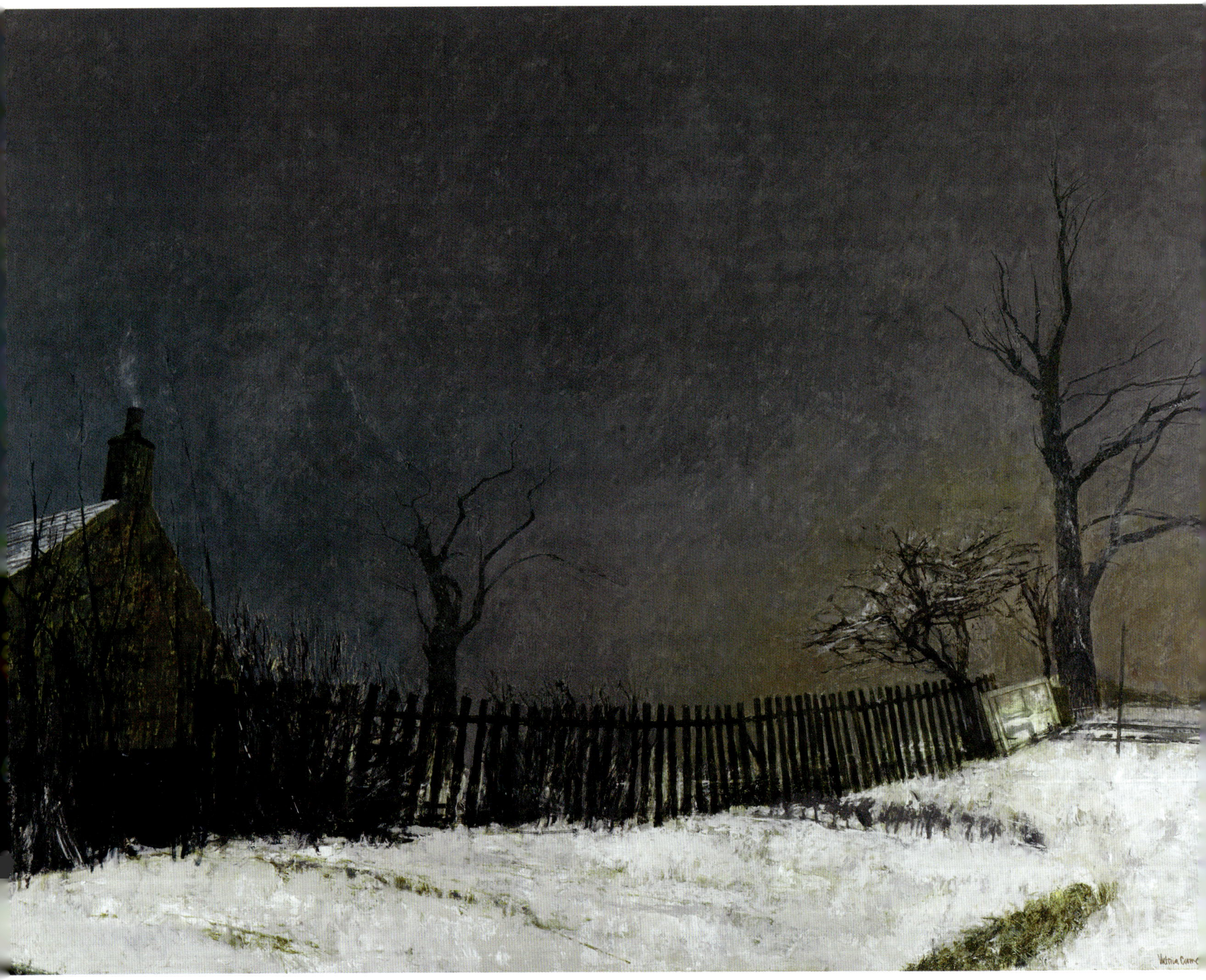

Snow Sky

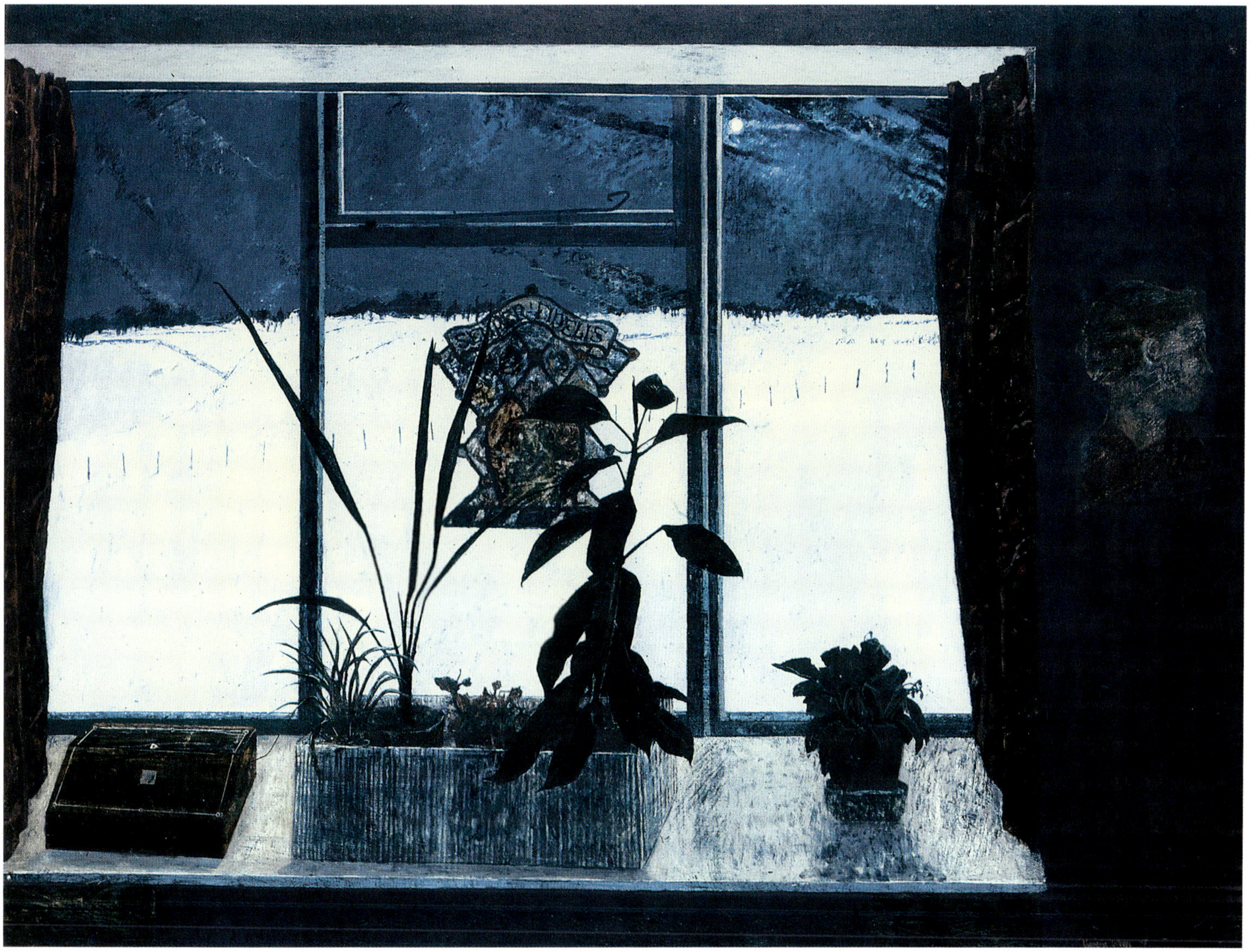

On the Inside Looking Out

Monksview and Monk's Cottage faced east, looking out onto moorland and across to Auchencorth Moss. To the north, the spectacular Pentland Hills stretched from the edges of Edinburgh well into the borders. While I was drawing Jenny working around her cottage and field and latterly the views from her windows, I painted 'On the Inside Looking Out'. This painting represents a parallel idea, looking out from our window, on to a moonlit, snow-filled landscape. As well as the plants and stained-glass panel, a small Italianate head, cast and glazed by Mike, can be seen to the right of the picture. A different window shape to Jenny's original small casements and a distinctly different interior, but both sharing the view of high moorland landscape and its powerful sense of quiet isolation.

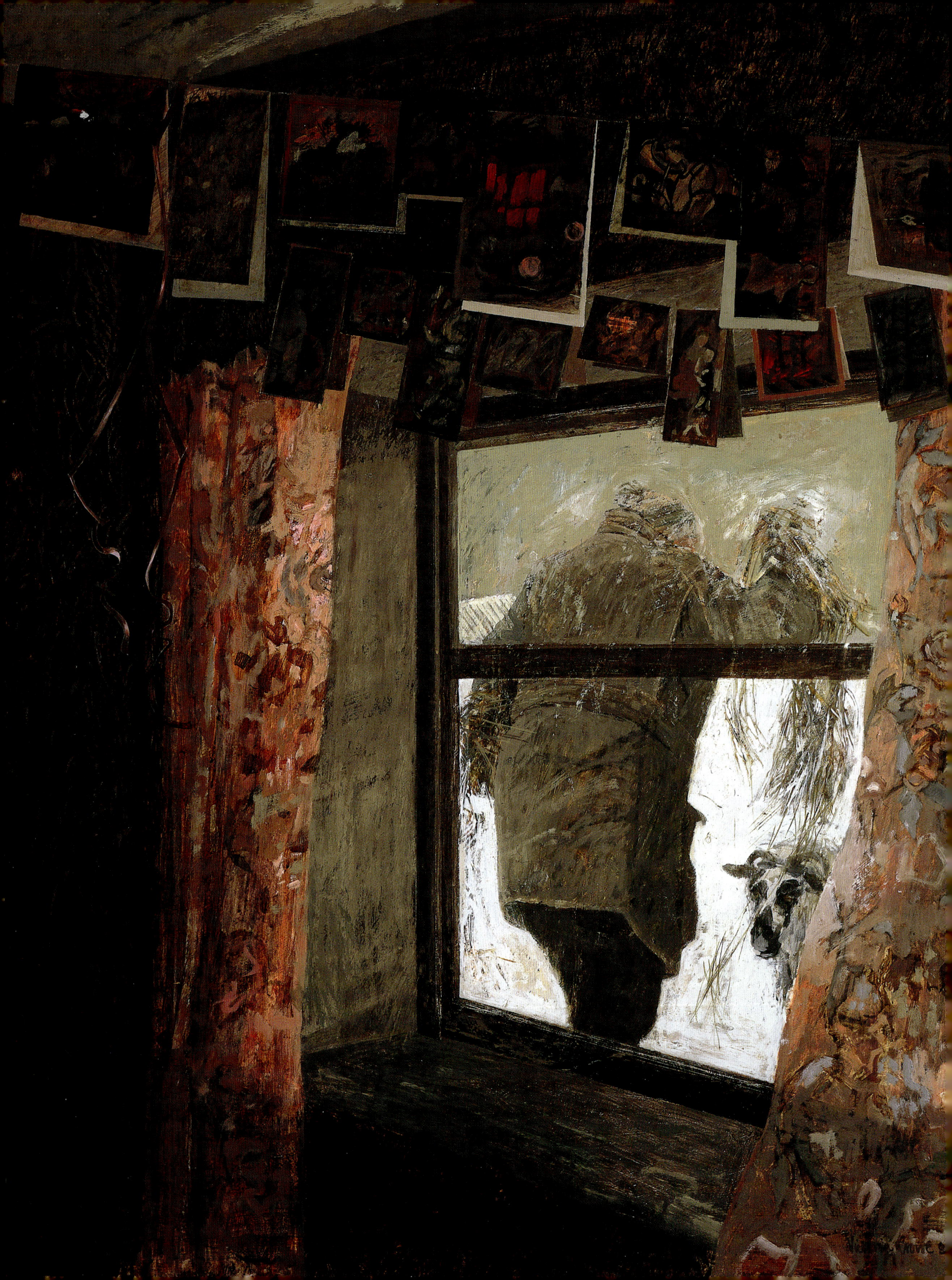

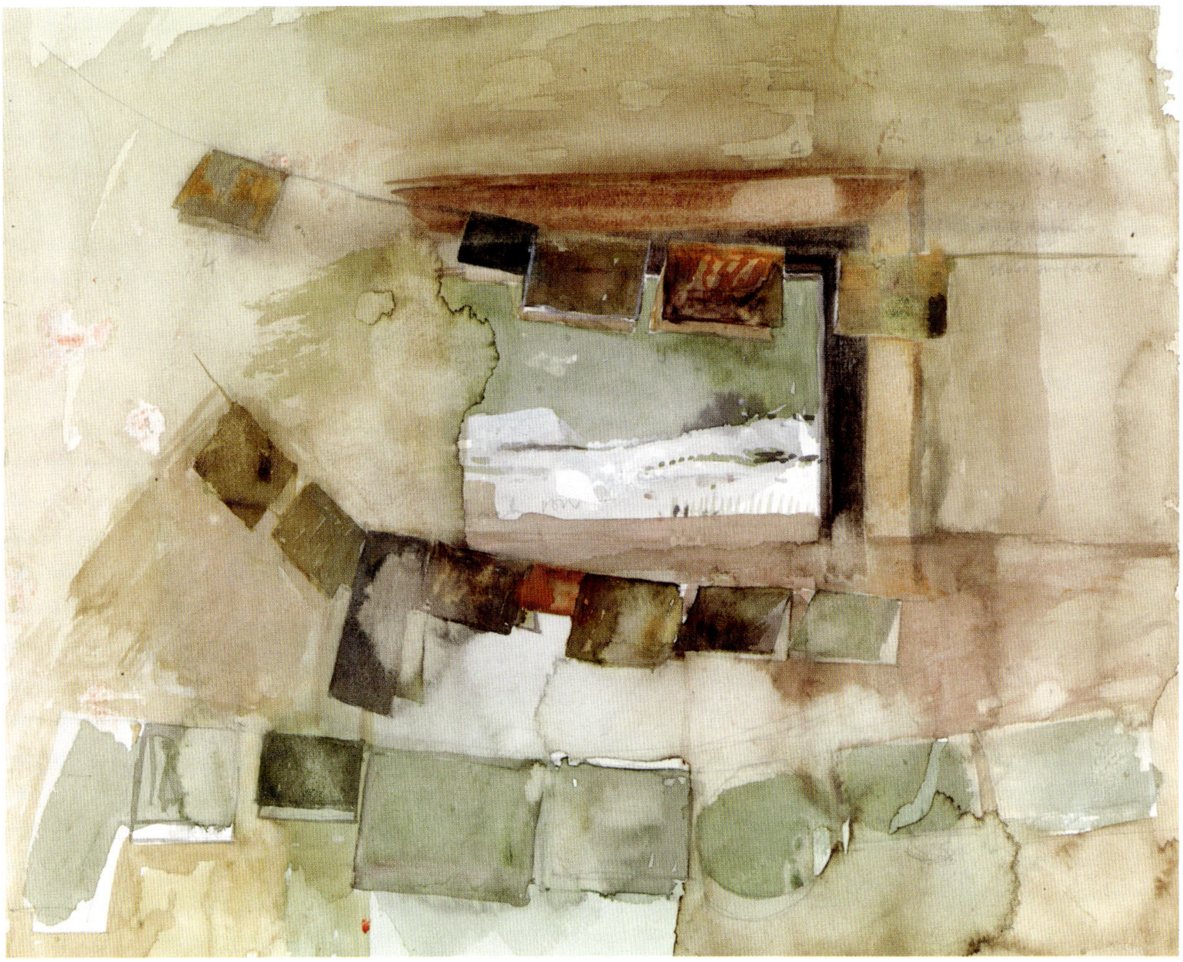

Study for December 25th

Interiors, Monk's Cottage

For the first few years of this relationship, Victoria saw and painted Jenny outside, but as she grew older and less able she began to spend more time indoors. Victoria would often join her there to keep her company and so the inside of her house became increasingly the subject and the context of her paintings. Sometimes and quite memorably, however, it was the outside seen from inside that the painter chose. There is a whole series of pictures of the windows, the views from them, and the interior seen in their light. In *Interior, Monk's Cottage,* the view beyond is the green of spring or summer, but one of the most memorable of these pictures is once again explicitly winter. The picture's title is its date, *December 25th* (1981). Jenny is seen framed by the window in characteristic pose, one arm raised to scatter hay for her sheep. The window is edged by curtains at either side, but above by rows of Christmas cards hung on strings. Christmas marks the winter solstice. It might be the still point in the turning year, but of course it is not. There is no pause, no stillness. The year spins on; the sheep must be fed. But whatever Christian iconography the cards carry – and although there is a beautiful watercolour study of them which

December 25th

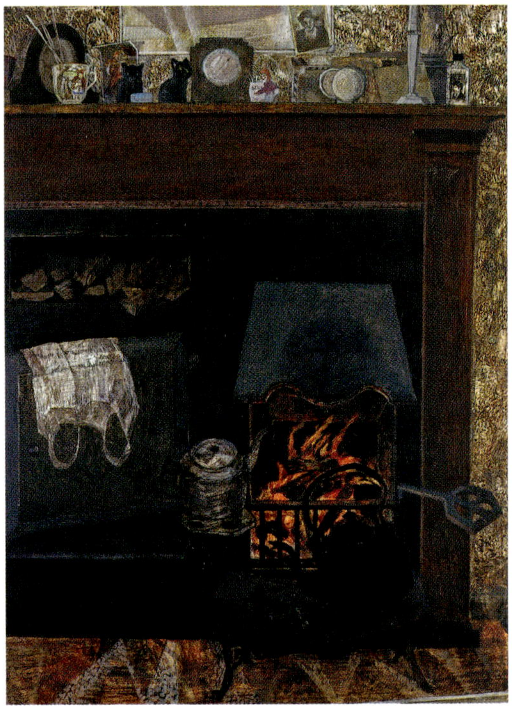

Range and Semmit

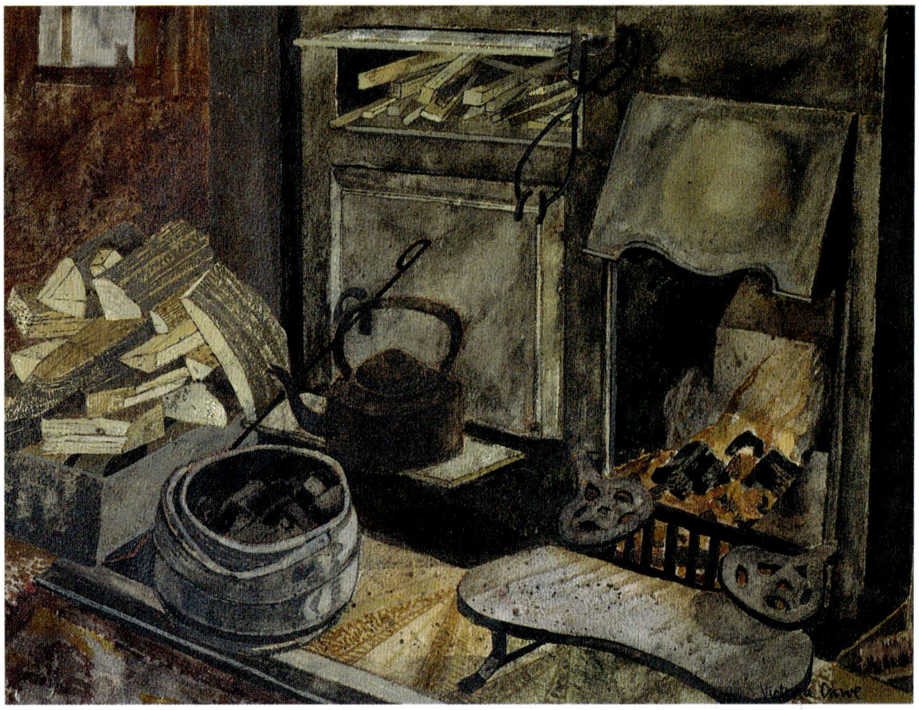

Winter Fuel

shows them blank – as the Good Shepherd, Jenny herself is the true Christian image. As Blake suggests in his *Book of Job*, Christianity is how a life is lived, not how the imagined rules it is lived by are respected.

There are also a good many paintings from these years of Jenny herself inside her cottage, often in the half dark, perhaps lit by the light of the logs burning in the range. Indeed one is reminded of George Paul Chalmers's painting *The Legend*, in which an old woman seated by the fire in her cottage is telling a tale to a group of children, their faces caught in the light, absorbed by the story. That in turn opens a whole history of images stretching back through Josef Israels to Rembrandt. Like their wider pastoral theme, these interiors are close to the heart of much that has happened in Western art. They are closely observed, too, and always based on study of the details of the scene, leading to a drawing on which the final composition is based. These drawings are also themselves often very beautiful. They record the detail of the fireplace, its tools and ornaments, even the patterns on the curtains, walls and floor. There is a watercolour of the range, for instance, with the coal bucket, logs, kettle and fire-irons all carefully described. Jenny herself is not always present in the finished paintings, so then these details themselves become the subject. *Range and Semmit*, for instance, is simply a painting of the fireplace. There are cards behind the clock on the mantlepiece. The logs in the fire are burning brightly. The tea pot is on the hob and the eponymous semmit is hung over the edge of the range to dry.

Jenny's hard life took its toll however. In 1982 she was hospitalised and suffered the amputation of both legs. It might have crushed the spirit of a lesser person to lose all her mobility after such

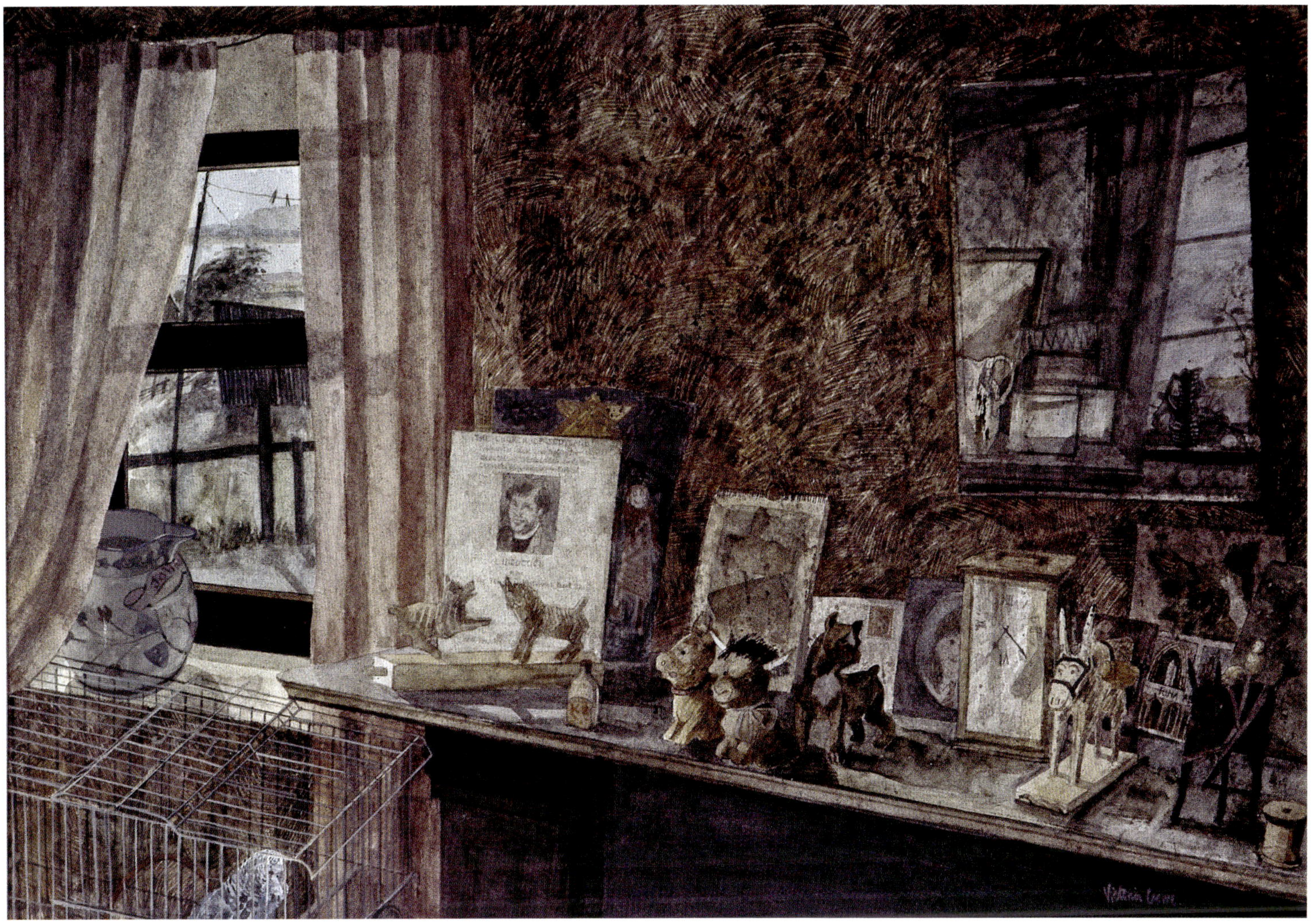

Induction Morning

an active life and then be limited to a wheelchair in one room. She was away from her home almost eighteen months, but when she returned her spirit was undimmed. There followed a series of paintings of Jenny in her wheelchair. She could no longer keep her collies, but had a budgie for company instead. The budgie and its cage also feature in the drawings and the paintings that they led up to. When Jenny was first taken to hospital, it was not clear that she would ever return. Marking her sense of imminent change, Victoria embarked on *Changing Landscapes,* an ambitious triptych of the changing seasons, autumn, winter and spring in Newhall woods. With its familiar spirit gone, she needed to look to a different landscape and this triptych seems almost classical beside the pictures she had been painting. The three panels are closely similar in composition, with tall trees reflected in water in the foreground, but with the colours changing appropriately to the season. The water creates beautiful reflections, but is not there in reality. The artist explained this saying, "I put water there – seeing landscape reflected in still lochs in the highlands made more of a complete 'world' of a landscape. That, in the triptych and changing seasons, was meant to encapsulate everything about the valley next to us. I think about it as the time my attention went to other aspects of the land." The neighbouring valley was also

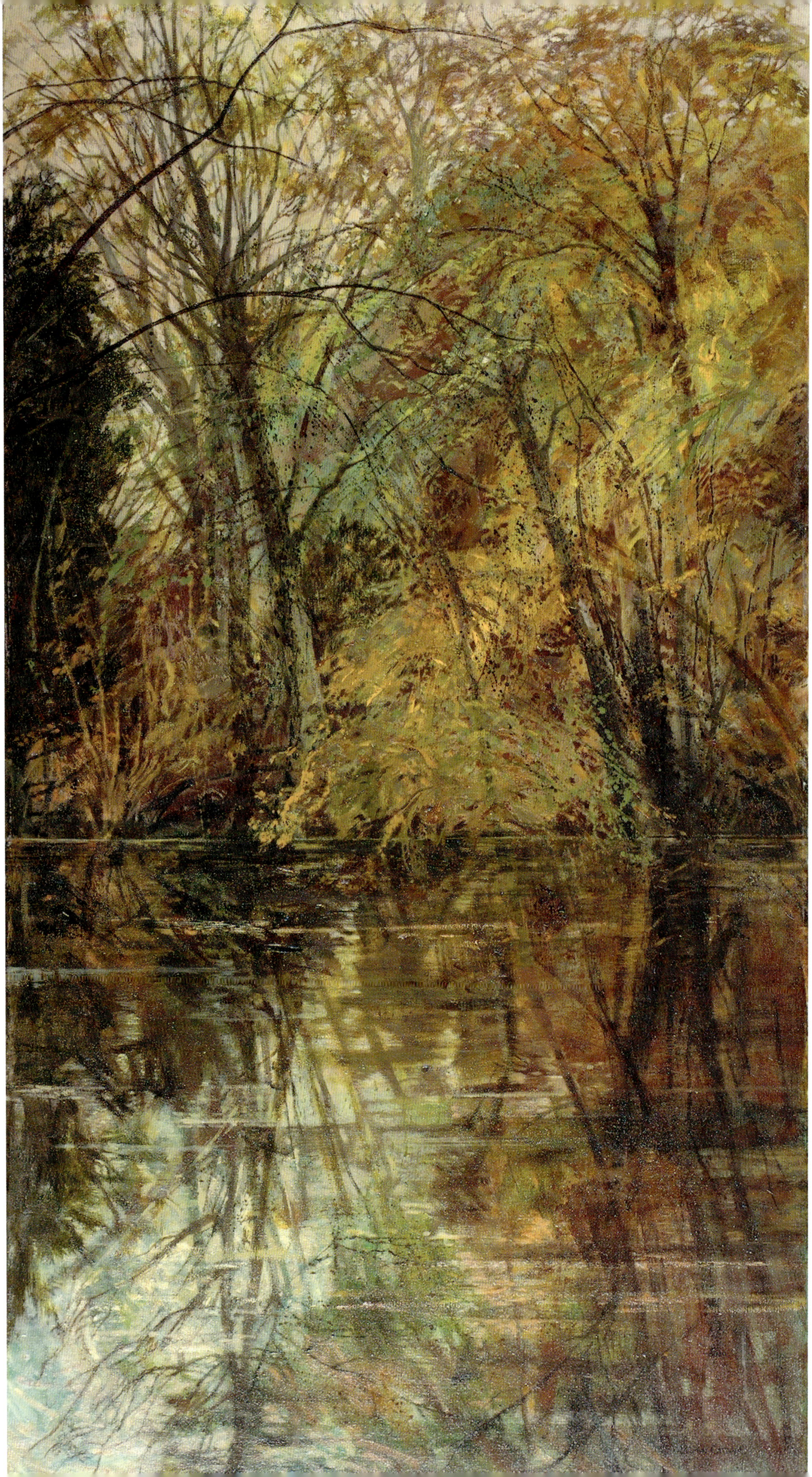

Changing Landscapes, Triptych

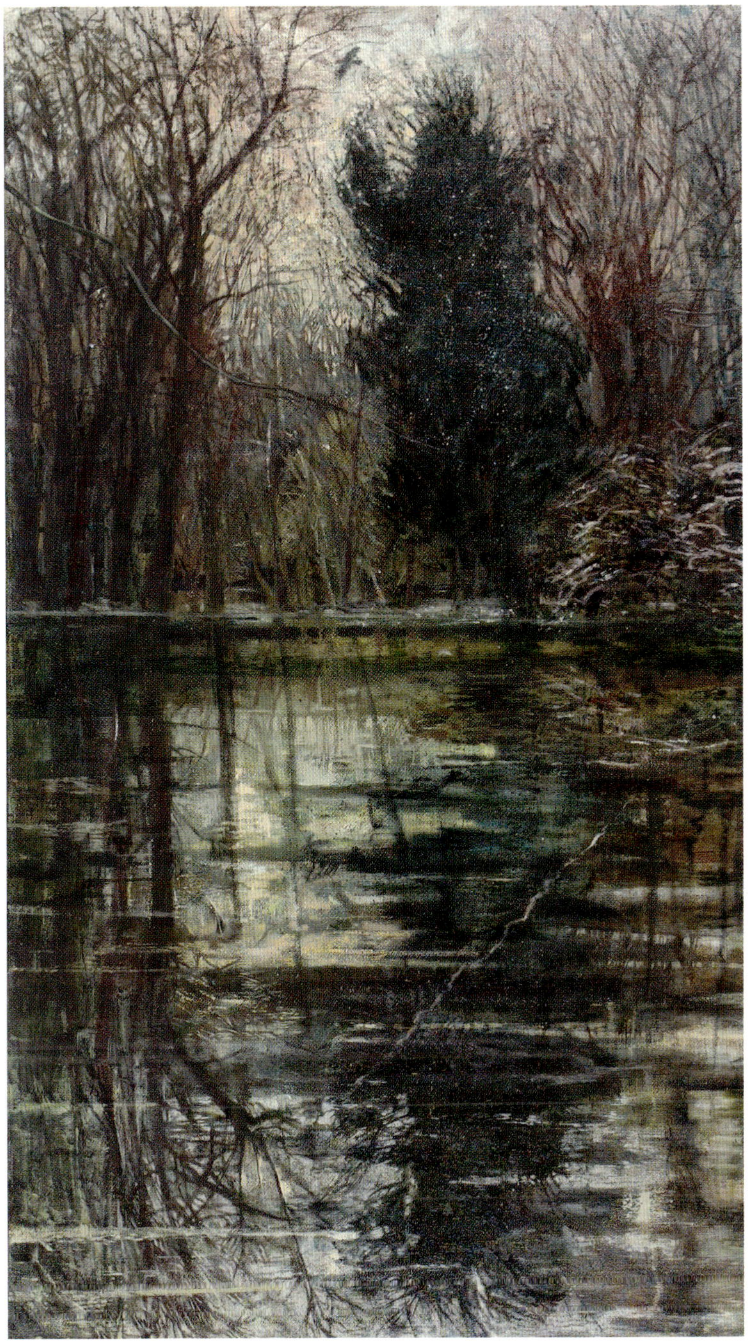

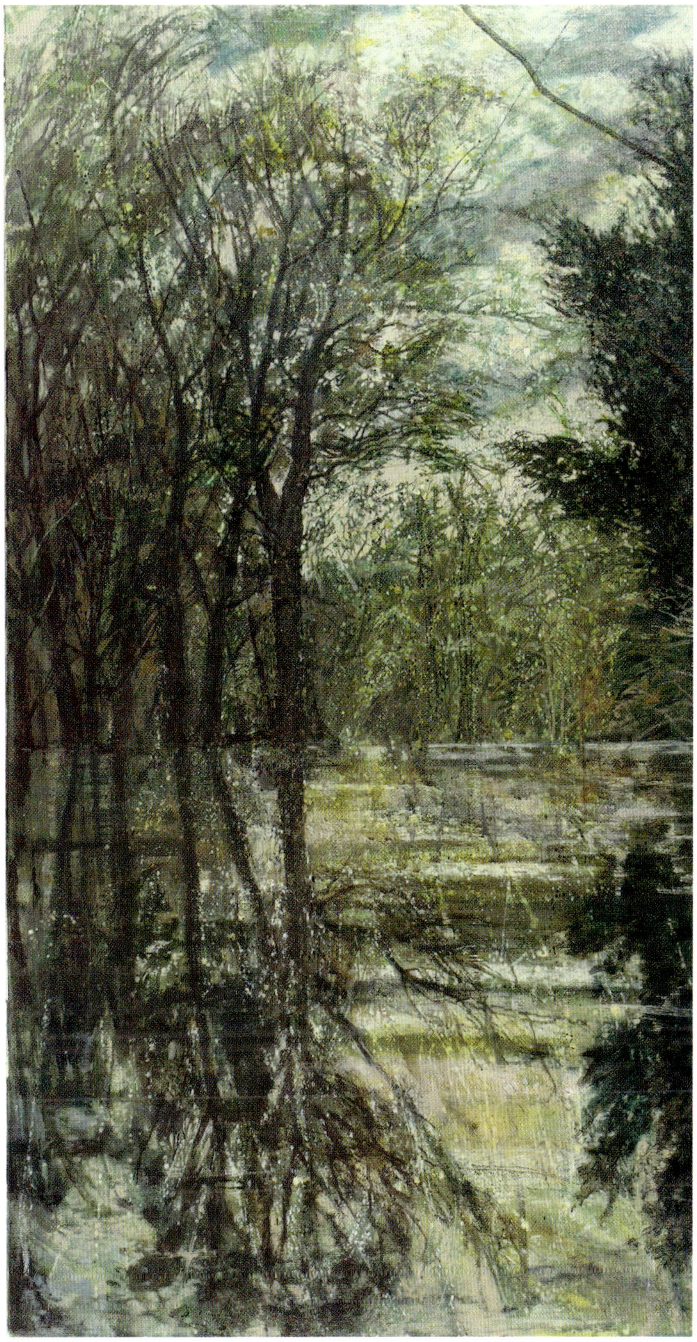

the glen in which the action of *The Gentle Shepherd* takes place, so you could see this beautiful image of the passing seasons as linking the artist's own pastoral to Allan Ramsay's famous play.

After Jenny's death, Victoria painted a series of pictures that were in effect memorials. These include a posthumous portrait, *Last Portrait of Jenny Armstrong*, 1986-7. She is sitting in her wheelchair, looking for something in her open handbag. Part of her bed is visible in the foreground. A cluttered table is beyond her. The curtains are drawn, but light is coming through them. One of the most striking features of the picture is the way this light focusses attention on Jenny even though it throws her face into shadow. The light is also a dominant feature in several pictures of the interior of her cottage seen without her. In place of Jenny the focus is on the objects that, by association, stand for the absent person. *Induction Morning,* for example, is a composition of the objects on the mantlepiece: the clock, photographs, figurines, the minister's

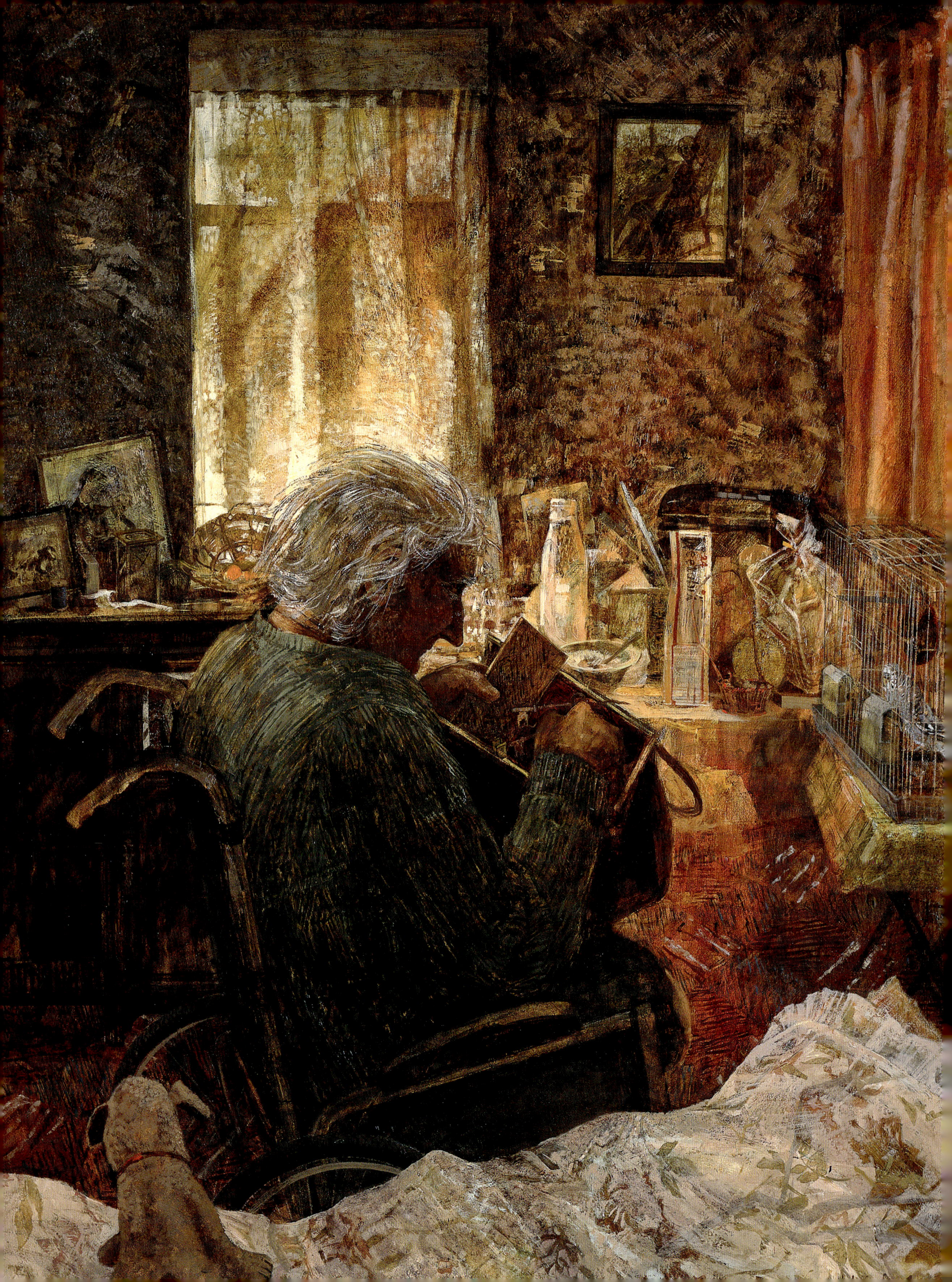

induction card and much else besides. To these are added, however, the view of a sunlit window reflected in a mirror that opens up the composition, brings in the world outside and widens the reference in the painting to include the shepherd's landscape. We see the same effect in *Private View with Plastic Tulips.* A ewer, a couple of ornaments and a vase of plastic tulips are seen against the light of the sun filtered through a lace curtain. These images of light carry their own meaning. Observed light in a painting indicating the transcendental goes back at least to Piero della Francesca's *Dream of Constantine* in Arezzo. Here, however, it does not stand for anything supernatural, unless perhaps it is Jenny's gentle ghost. Rather it is an emanation of memory. Strikingly, Victoria said that when she went into Jenny's cottage after her death, which she only did briefly, it was, in her words, "horrid, cold and grey". Jenny was the source of its warmth and light, and the house had died with her. Correspondingly, painting the warmth and light invokes her presence and distills and softens the mood of loss and memory that is the subject of the painting.

These paintings are visually objective, but in them Victoria achieves something that she had perhaps been seeking in her work since she first started painting from icons. There is a perfect elision between the image and its spiritual dimension. The image is neither through the surface, nor on it, but in a much bigger metaphysical space somewhere between. It is reminiscent of the mysterious light in her earlier paintings of icon screens. More than that, however, each of the objects so carefully studied on Jenny's mantlepiece holds a story that must now remain untold. Just like the votives hanging in front of the icons in Greece, they are forever mute, but are charged with meaning nevertheless.

A selection of the Jenny Armstrong paintings was put together in the exhibition 'A Shepherd's Life', at the Scottish National Portrait Gallery (SNPG) in 2000. The exhibition was at the suggestion of Mary Taubman. A friend, herself a painter and the author of a book on Gwen John, she also wrote an essay on the paintings for the catalogue. The exhibition made the point that together the pictures constitute a unique modern pastoral. If that is so, then the final pictures in the series, those of the empty room, are also a lament for the passing of a much loved shepherd, just like Milton's *Lycidas*, one of the finest pastoral poems in English.

Thee, Shepherd, thee the woods and desert caves,
With wild thyme and the gadding vine o'ergrown,
And all their echoes mourn.[1]

The paintings of the interior of Jenny Armstrong's cottage are pictures that work by association – the idea first formulated in the Scottish Enlightenment that beauty is not an absolute, but a function of the associations it has, of the connectedness we feel for certain things or scenes and the value they hold for us. As it was expounded by Archibald Alison in his *Essay in Taste*, the theory of association found its central expression in our relationship to the landscape. It also had an inescapable spiritual dimension, however. This theory was a primary inspiration for Constable and also for Ruskin. Quite independently, similar ideas were to become central in Victoria's later work. The idea also has a corollary, however. It means our judgements are subjective; our associations are our own.

Last Portrait of Jenny Armstrong

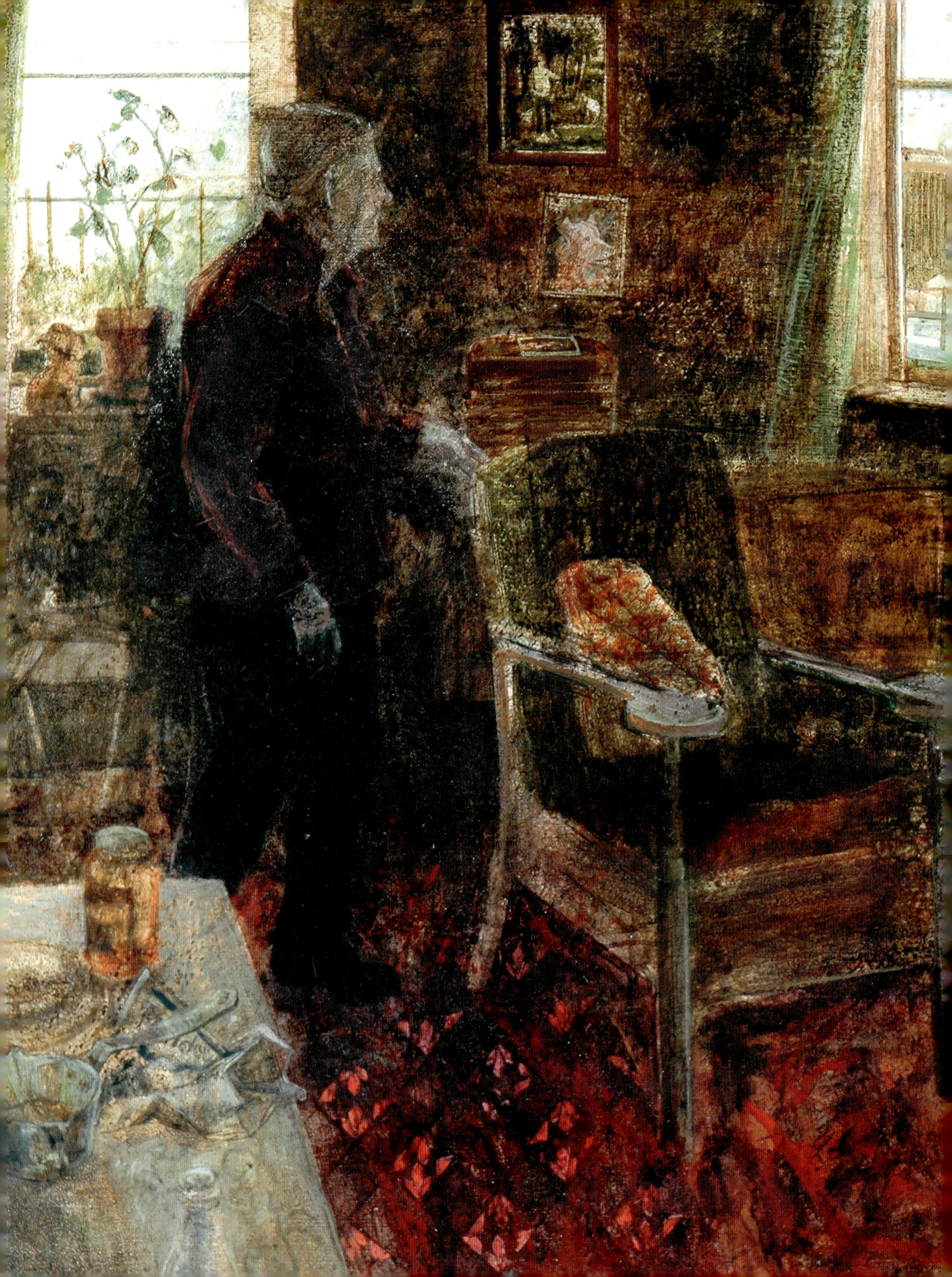

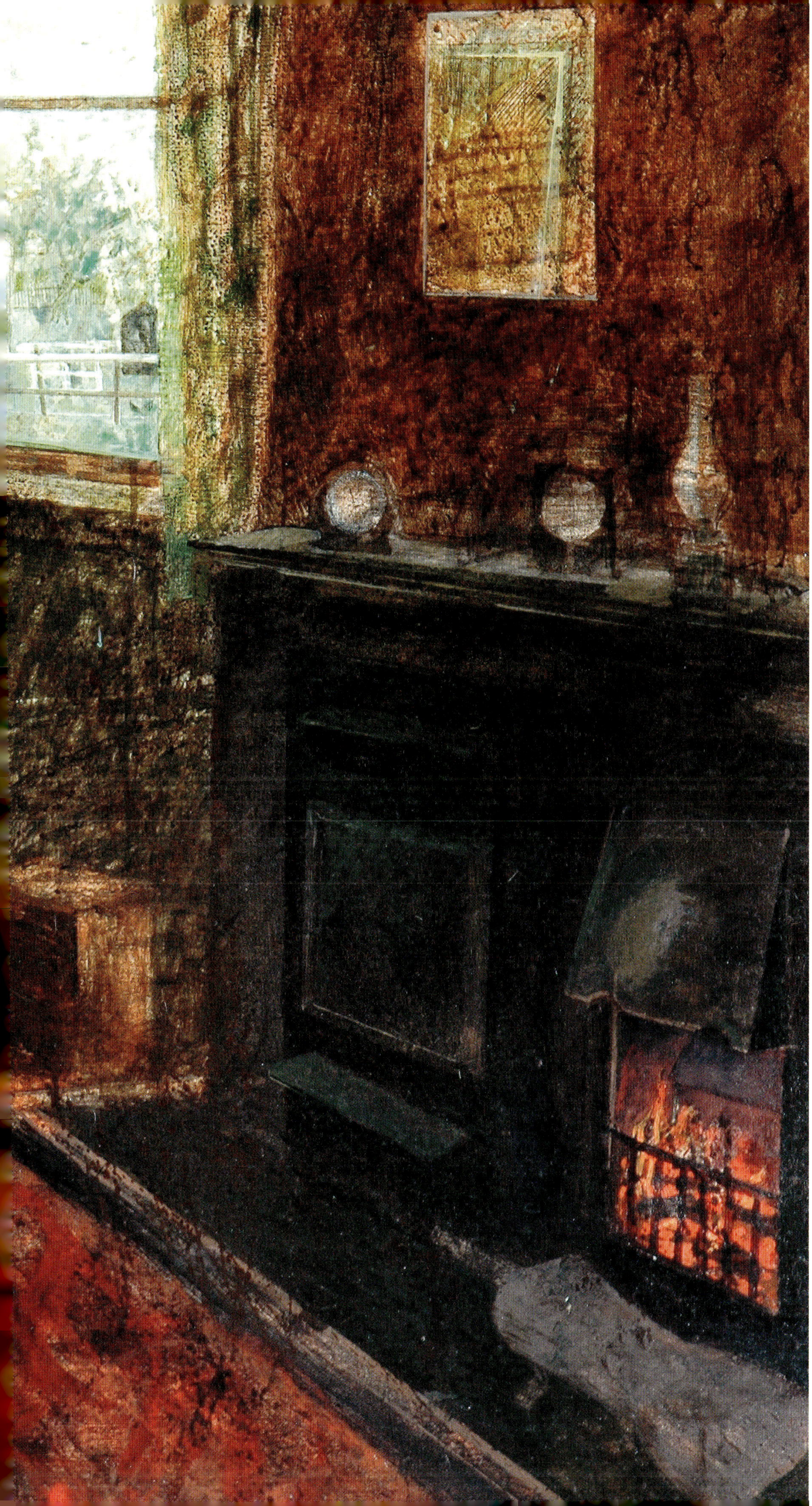

Interior,
Monk's Cottage

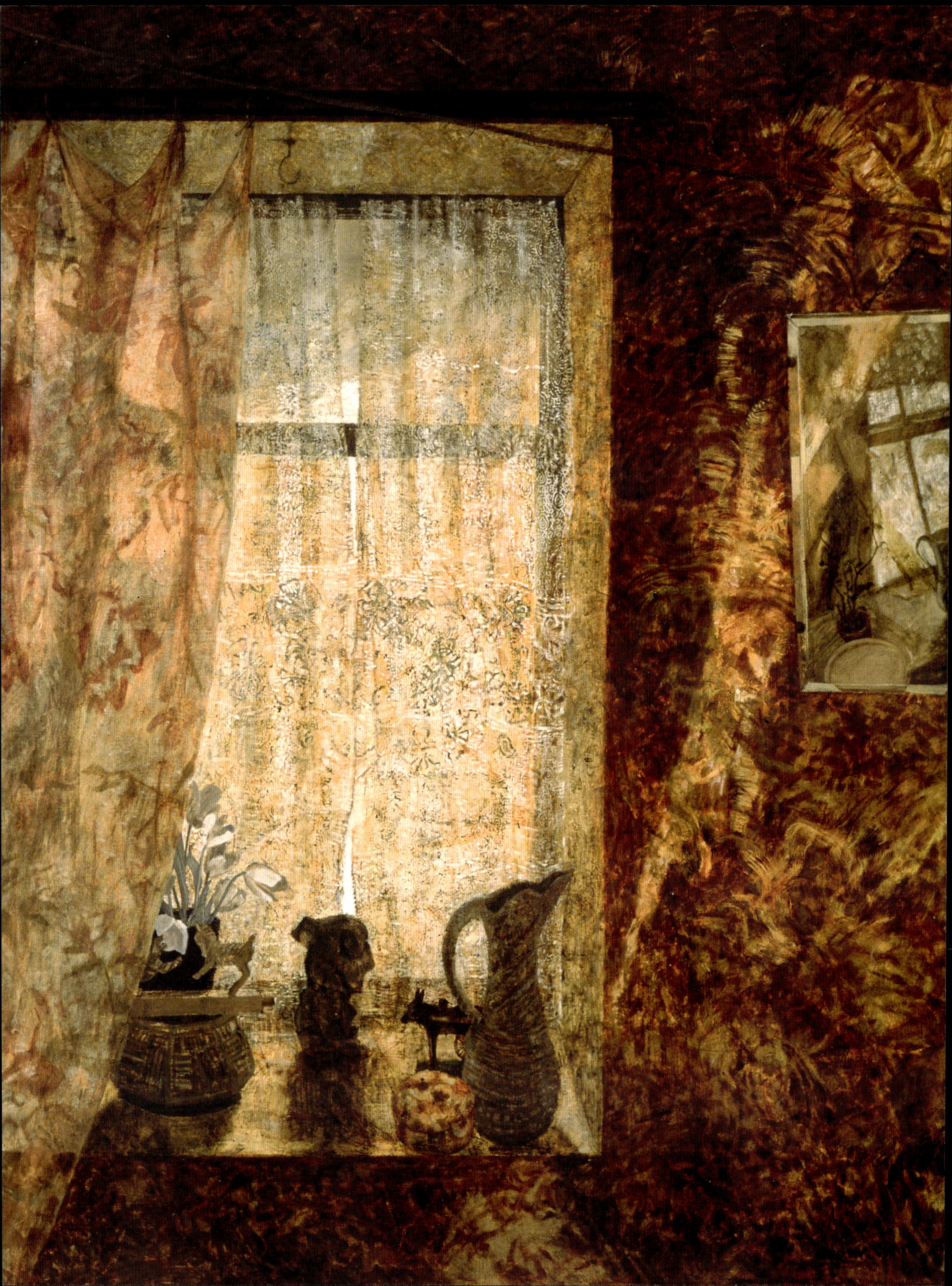

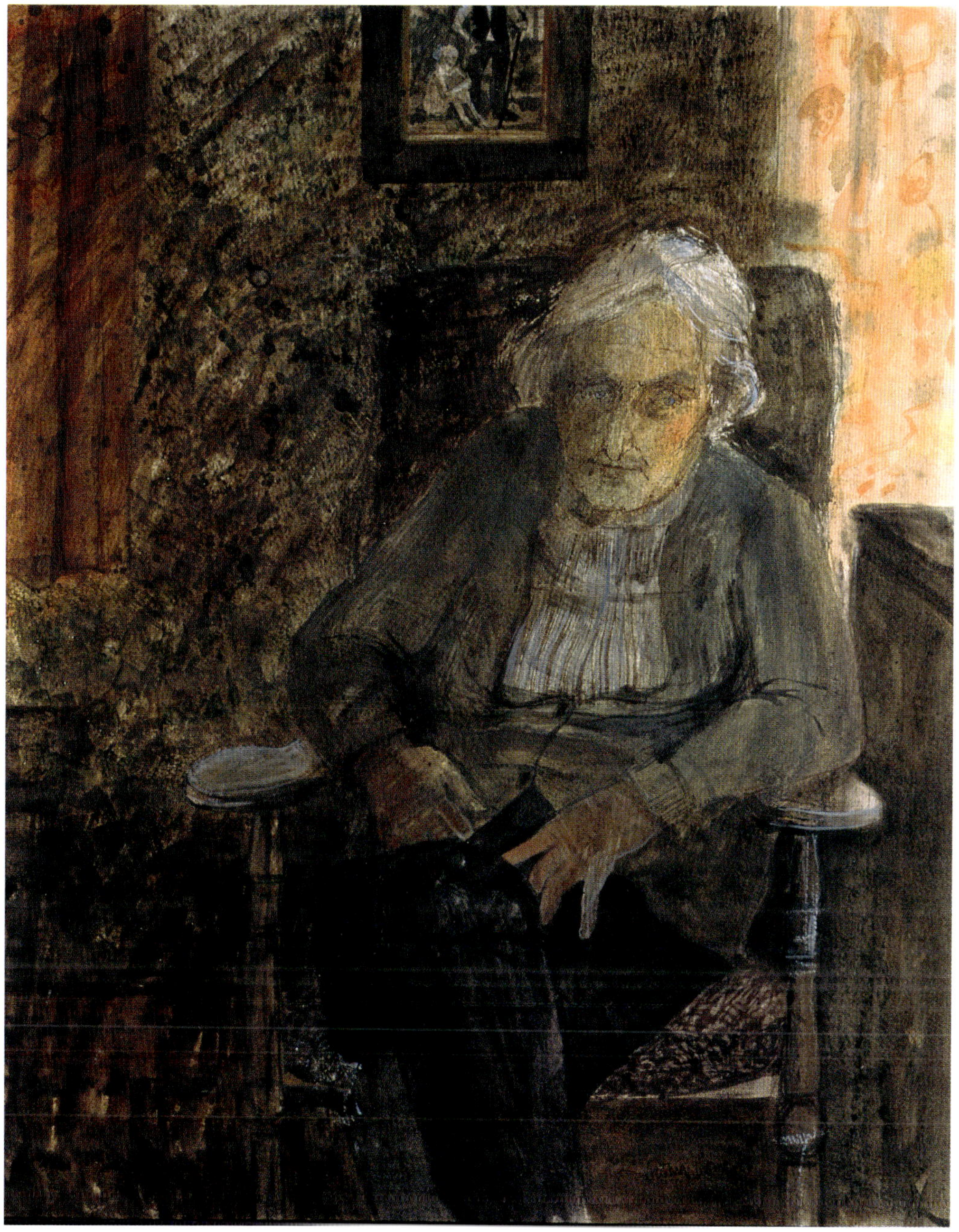

Jenny at Home

Victoria's pictures of the interior of Jenny Amstrong's cottage are also portraits without a sitter. Although she appears so often and is so easily recognisable, Victoria rekons she only once painted a true portrait of her shepherd friend. She did once set out to paint a double portrait of herself and Jenny, but it never got past the stage of preliminary drawings. The one portrait she did paint of Jenny is in watercolour. She is seated in her chair. Sunlight on a yellow curtain illuminates her face from the right. The window itself is unseen and the rest of the room is in shadow. Jenny is facing us, but with an inward expression, her blue eyes look past us and seem not to be focussed on anything in particular. Perhaps in this portrait it is we, the observers, who are absent. Jenny Armstrong is alone in her room, just as she lived. Without even her dogs for company, we feel her presence vividly. This is a very fine portrait, though hardly a formal one.

Private View with Plastic Tulips

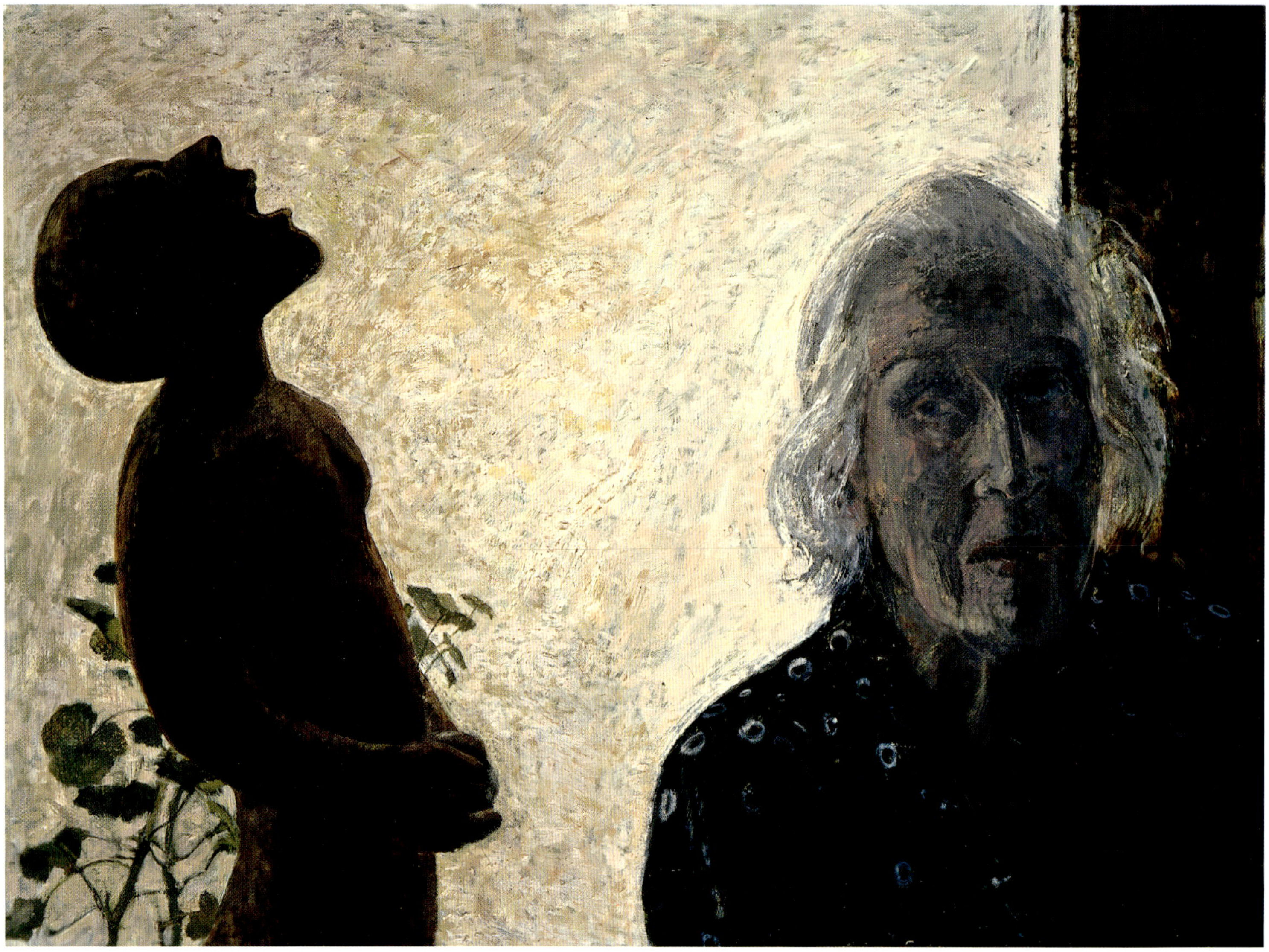

Dr Winifred Rushforth

First Portraits

It was perhaps a natural progression of ideas that Victoria should have begun to paint more formal portraits at this time and that she should bring to them something from her experience of trying to paint the wholeness of a life, as she had sought to do in the 'Shepherd's Life' pictures. The first formal portrait she undertook was of Winifred Rushforth. Painted in 1982 in two versions, it was a tribute to the sitter who was ninety-four when the artist first met her, but whom she came to admire very much. One version was bought for the SNPG. It is a striking portrait of a forceful and alert old lady. Beside her is a sculpture of a bushman, head raised and mouth open, apparently in a howl of protest at something unseen, or perhaps just at the human condition. In the second version of the portrait, beyond this image, dinosaurs roam in a primeval swamp. A doctor by training, Winifred Rushforth moved from medicine into psychology and became the first person to practise psychoanalysis in Scotland. However, by the time Victoria met her, she had moved on from conventional psychoanalysis, if there is such a thing, to a more spiritual approach. In her own words, "to be a freelance in this work it came to me ... that the psyche is the human spirit, and we can't exclude God and the creative purpose

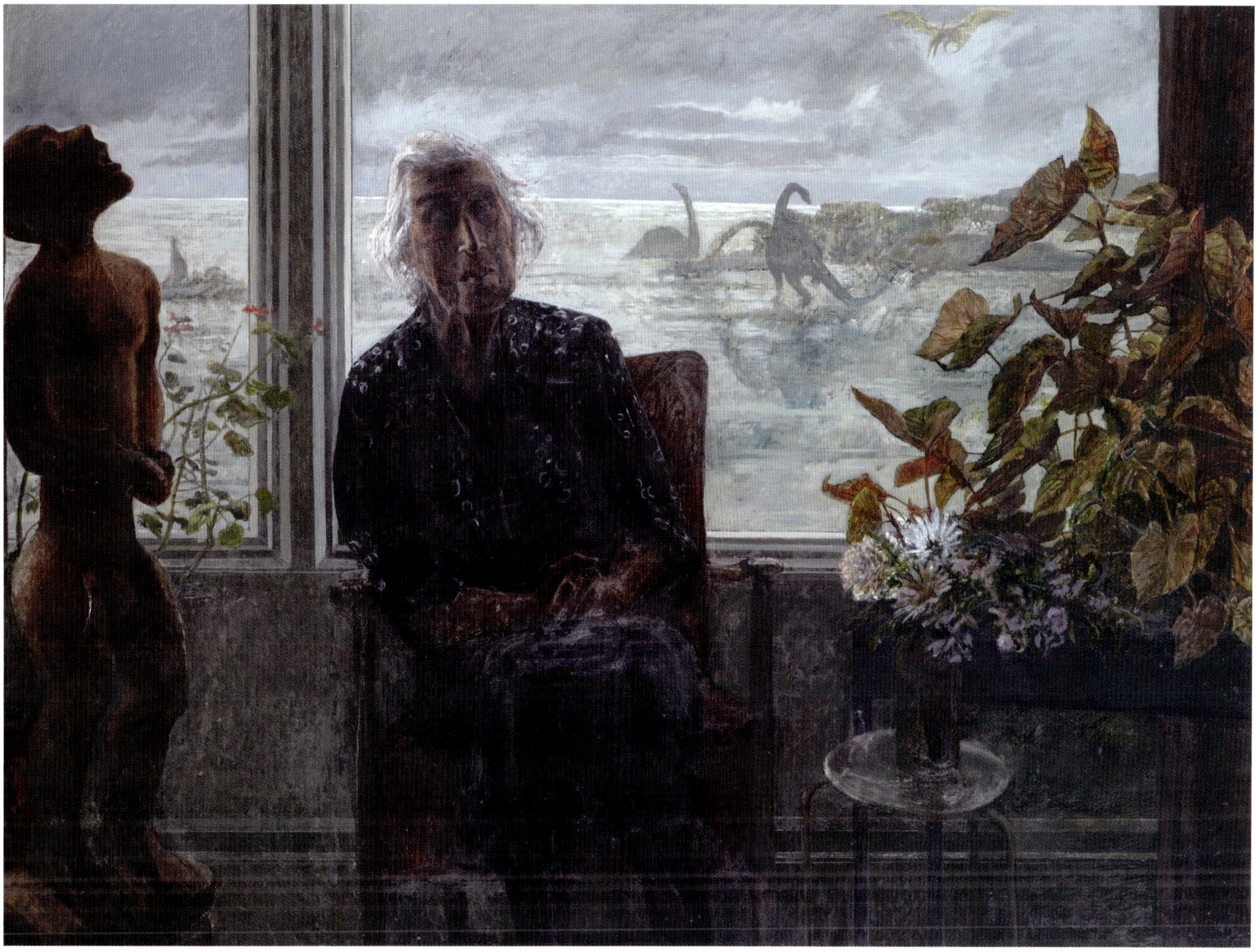

Dr Winifred Rushforth, Lauder Road

from our work."[1] She was at the time leading groups in dream therapy. Victoria met her at a party and subsequently joined in several of her dream groups. It is easy to see how such ideas about dreams and the nature of spirituality would chime with the painter's own spiritual quest, and that she would respond to her sitter as warmly as we can see that she did in the portrait. In fact, in the artist's own words, the meeting with Winifred Rushforth was for her "the beginning of an interest in dream and its imagery and the related symbolism of myth and archetype within a Jungian framework."[2]

The portrait of Winifred Rushforth was followed in 1984 by a commission from the SNPG to paint R.D. Laing. He was a psychiatrist of a highly individual kind and, like Winifred Rushforth, had pushed the boundaries of psychotherapy towards a more profound consideration of the whole of human nature, including our spiritual needs. His books *The Divided Self* and *Self and Others* had been current in the sixties. Victoria had known his work since her student days when she encountered schizophrenia in a friend and felt the need to try to understand it better. It was a process in which she found Laing's writing helpful. She has described the sometimes unsettling

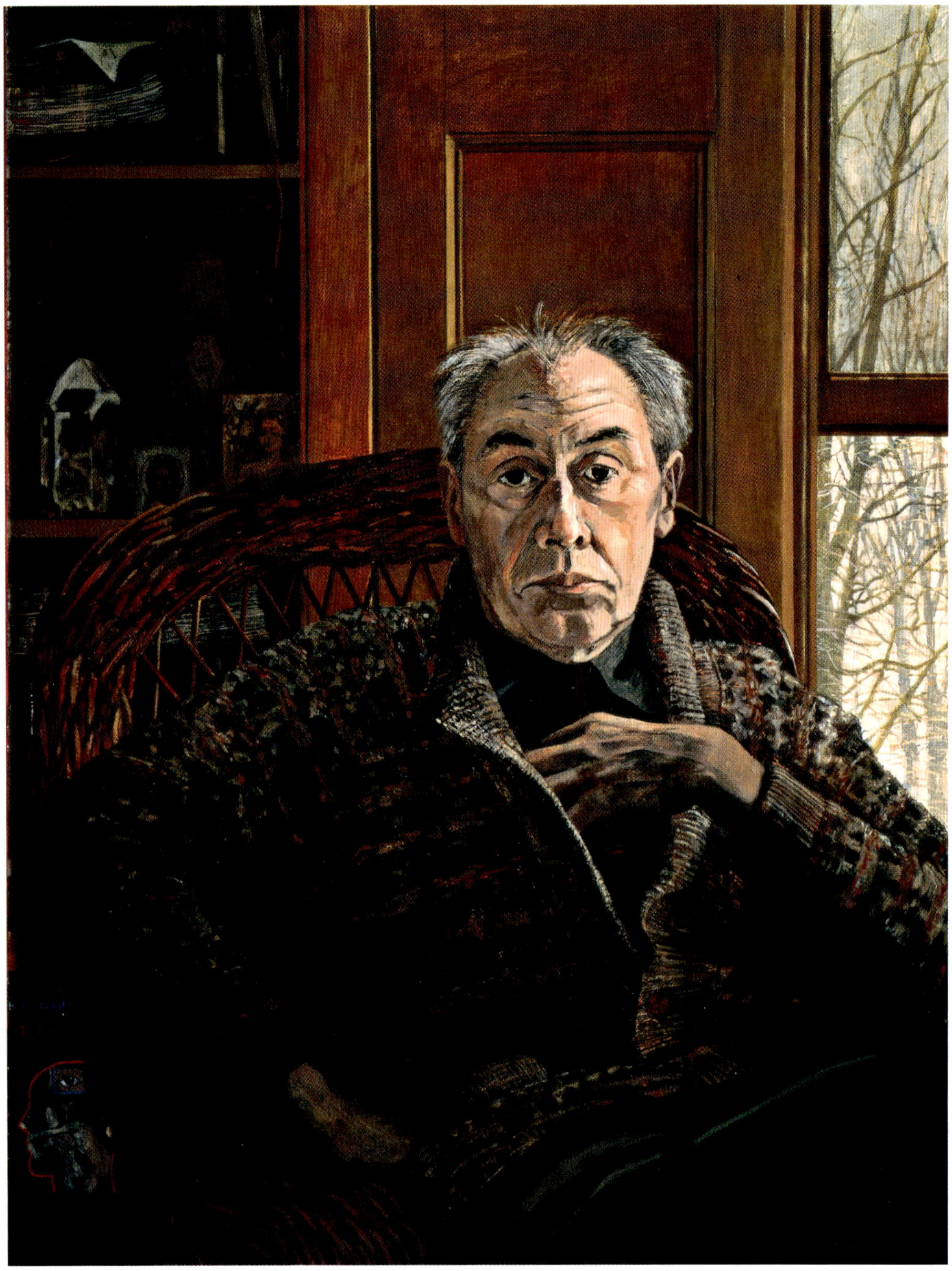

R.D. Laing
(photograph and study shown below)

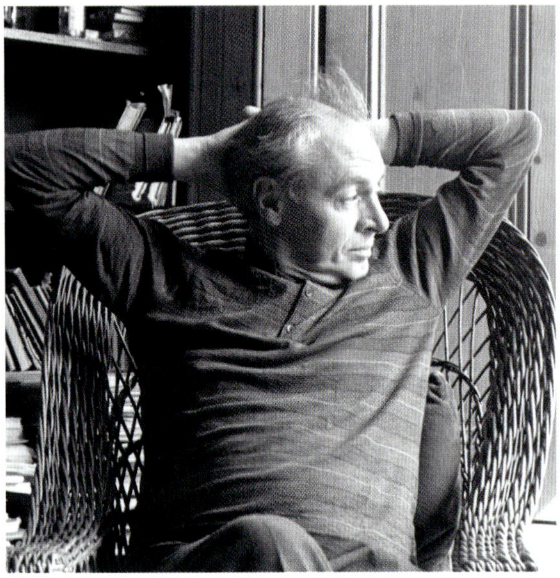

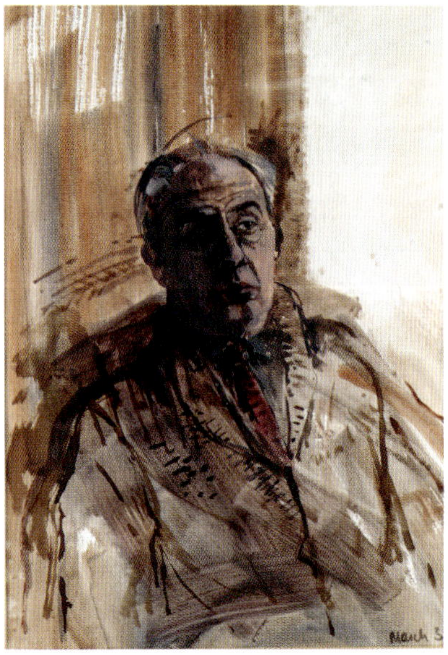

Kathleen Raine

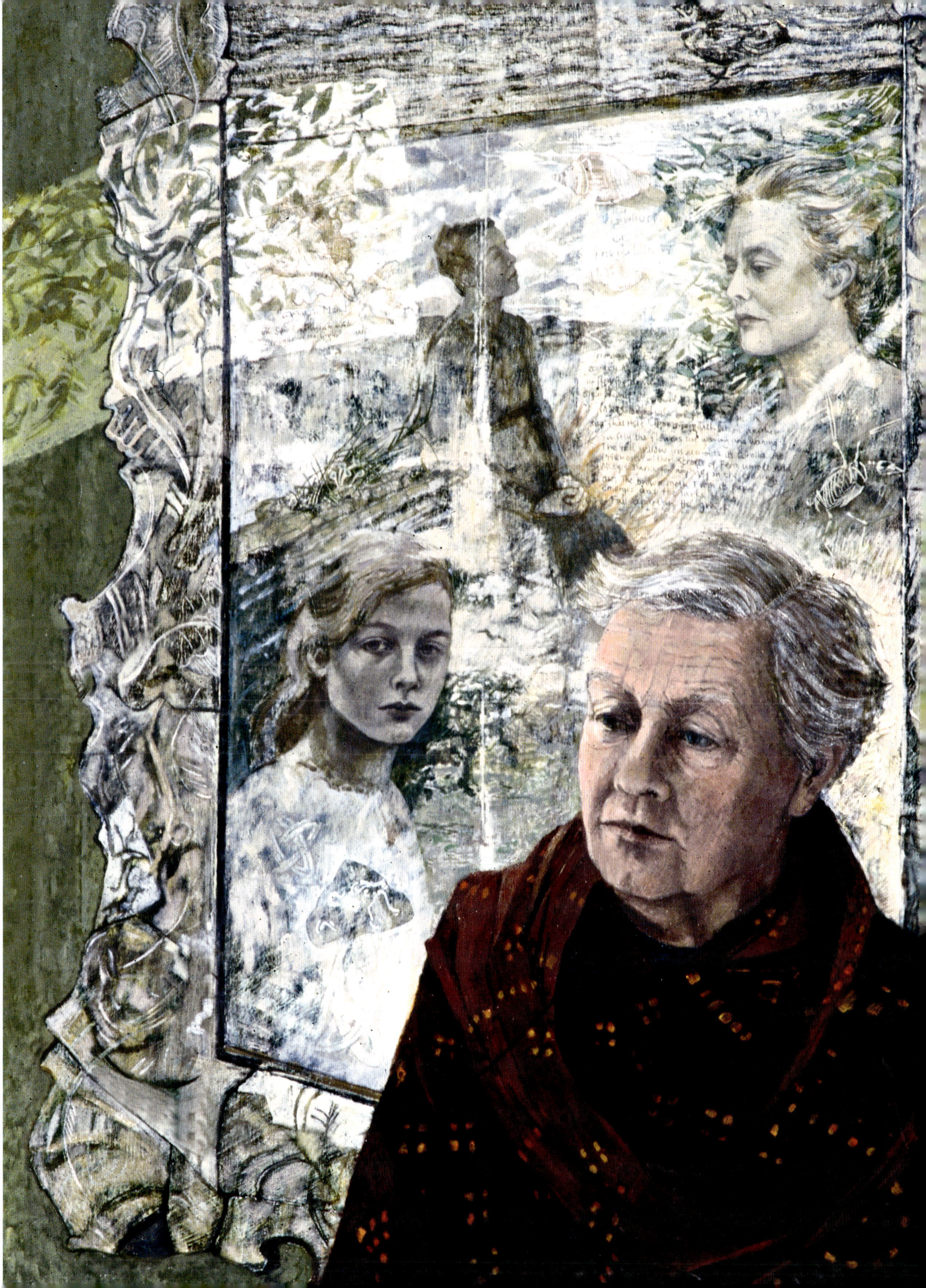

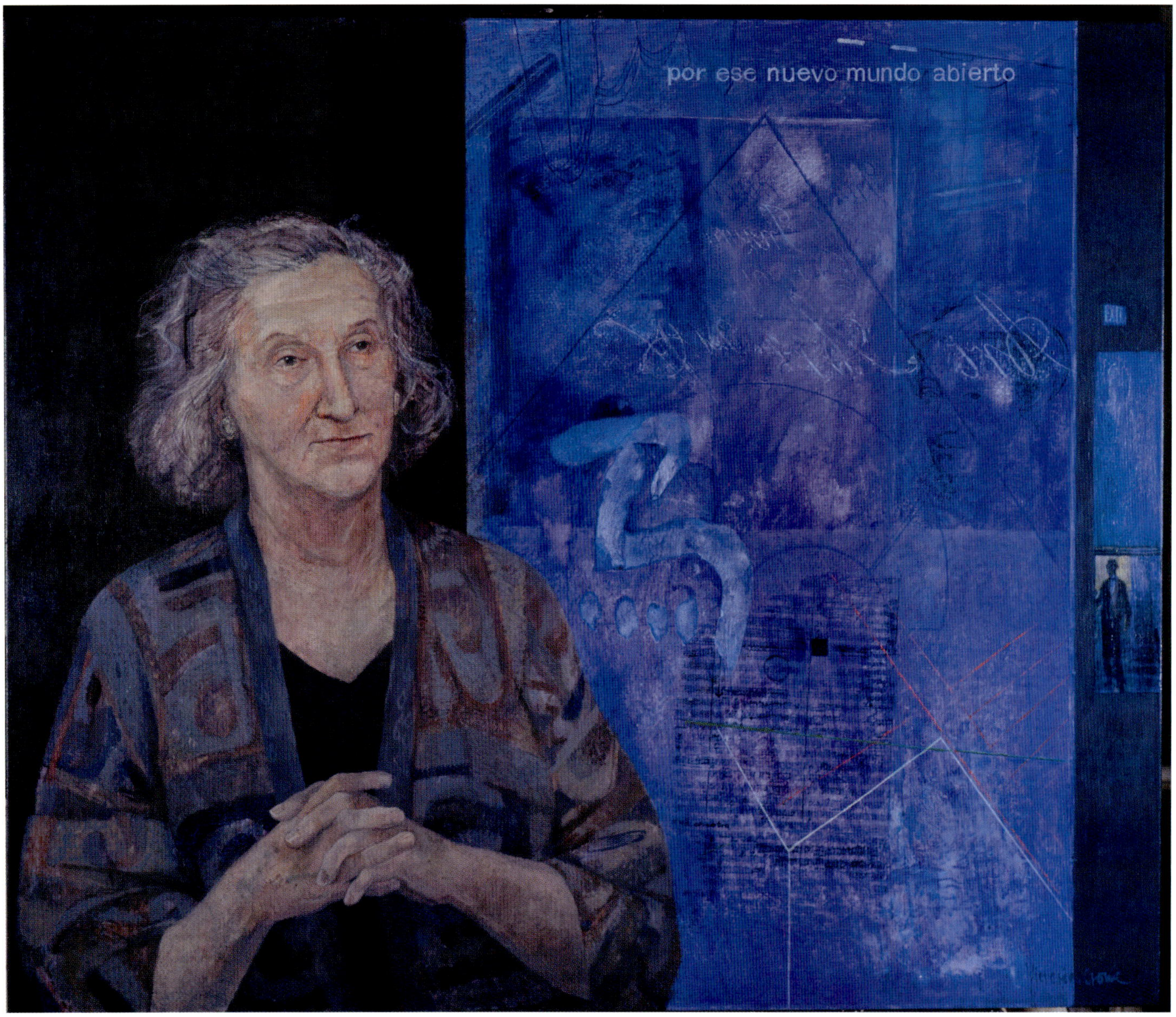

Thea Musgrave

experience of painting him in her contribution to a collection of tributes.[3] The eventual portrait is a vivid likeness. He is also painted with a carefully considered collection of objects behind him that form a kind of personal iconography. They include a metronome, referring to his love of music, a Byzantine head of Christ and a print of Blake's painting *Eve naming the Birds*. Eve was the artist's own feminine presence perhaps, but these objects also invoke both Laing's own spiritual search and the conversations during sittings that he and Victoria had on this common ground.

Other portraits with the painter's personal motivation behind them followed, notably of the musician Ronald Stevenson, who lived in West Linton, and of the poet and writer on William Blake, Kathleen Raine. Her portrait was a commission from the National Portrait Gallery (NPG) in London, but Kathleen Raine was once again someone whose work Victoria admired and whom she was delighted to have the opportunity to get to know. In *Painted Insights*,[4] she quotes at length from Kathleen Raine's poem *The Moment*, a soliloquy on time and the transience of all things. In

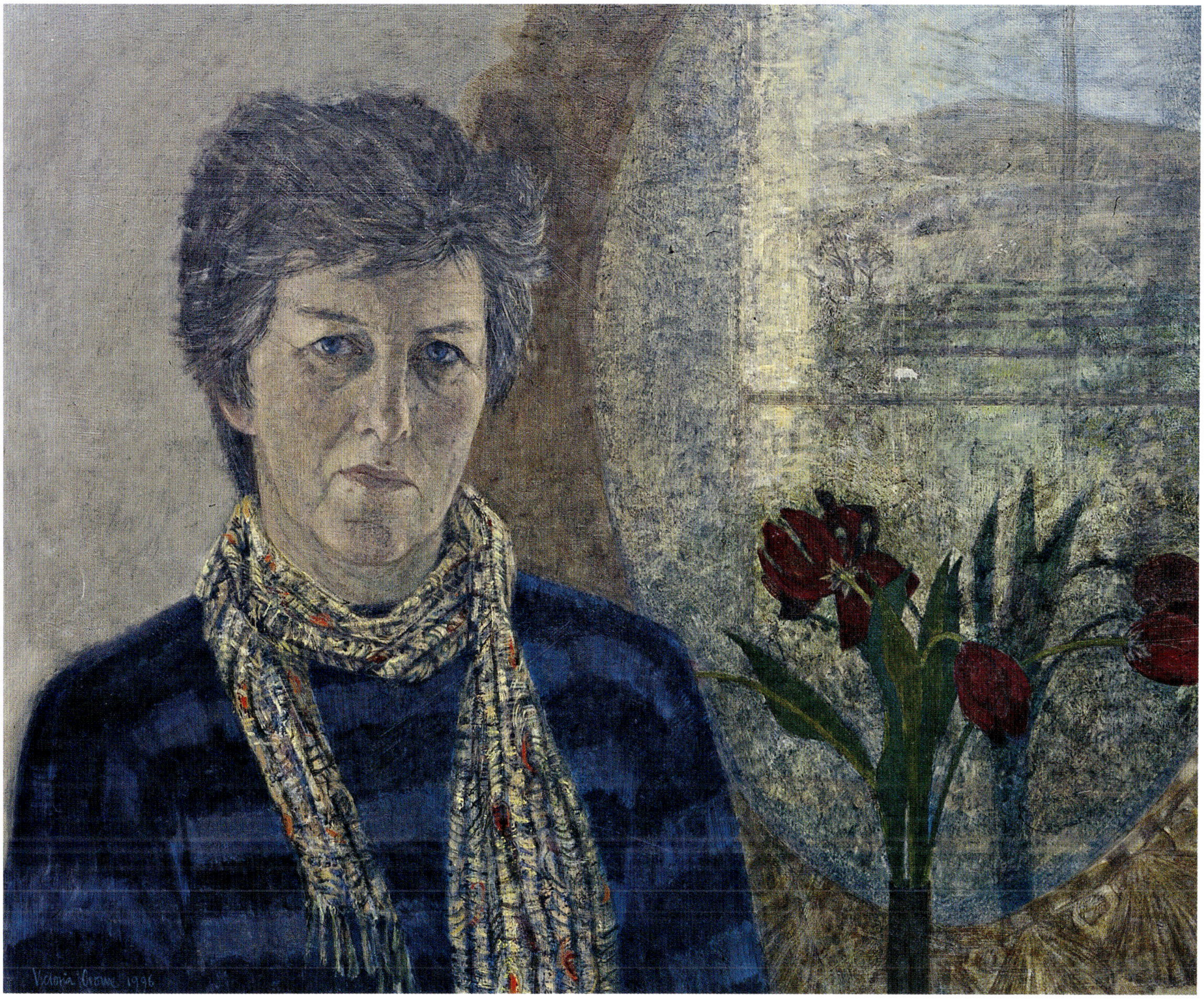

Emma Tennant

the portrait, the poet is shown looking down, her expression withdrawn and reflective. Behind her in an ornate mirror are three reflected images of her at different stages in her life. The only one of the four portraits in which her gaze meets ours, however, is that of the poet as the young and very beautiful girl she had been in her youth. Her beauty had, she felt, been a mixed blessing.

As a memorial, a portrait is anyway a kind of tangible memory, but by these multiple images, this one is more a picture *of* memory, of that dimension in consciousness that makes our past experience definitive of our present selves. The portrait, like the poem, is a soliloquy on transience, but also on the way portraiture can, like memory, lift us out of time. The poet's multiple images seen in the mirror are reflections in both senses of the word, of her and on the poem.

The success of these portraits led to further commissions and the list of Victoria's sitters now runs to some thirty names, many of them very distinguished.

West Linton

The late eighties brought change both to Kittleyknowe and to Victoria and her family. Jenny's death, which in a strange coincidence was followed within four days by the death of their other neighbour, Tom Wickham, marked the beginning of the end of the place as they had known and loved it. Both the houses made vacant by their owners' deaths were sold and converted into suburban-style dwellings rather out of keeping with the rural nature of the landscape. Opencast mining, begun illegally on the moor beyond the houses, was wrecking the landscape and brought machines and heavy lorries grinding past their cottage door. It was heartbreaking, but clearly it was time to move. This they did in 1990.

Their new home was Bank House in West Linton. Three or four miles further out from Edinburgh, West Linton is technically a village, but is more like a small country town with large houses, shops and the bank for whose manager their house had originally been built. Bank House was a Victorian villa with a sheltered south-facing garden. There was plenty of room both for the family and for studio space. Their new environment was hardly urban, but was very different from Monksview nevertheless. Victoria painted several pictures of Kittleyknowe in the first years after the move. Most poignantly, *Heroes and Villains* is a portrait of Ben in Monksview cottage. The title is from a Beach Boys song. He is standing with his back to the window, but lit by a second light source beyond him to the right. There are various still-life objects on a table behind him including a toy solider in a kilt and busby who seems to have wandered in from Jenny Armstrong's cottage. A drawing is pinned to the wall and a copy of a Quattrocento relief of a youth's head is propped beneath it. Framed in the window, an aeroplane is dropping parachutes on the moor. It is a startling sight, but it did actually happen and without warning. It was during the First Gulf War and was a military exercise. Victoria had painted the scene the year before in *Strange Occurrence at Auchencorth*. Nevertheless, like one of those unheralded events in Iris Murdoch's novels, or sudden cutting in a film, it is a dramatic intervention from right outside the narrative.

The move to West Linton was to prove a watershed in Victoria's art. The relationship with the landscape of Kittleyknowe which had nourished it for twenty years had ended. She had to find a new direction. Her choice was Italy, a place she had still never visited. This was not because she was indifferent to its appeal, rather that she felt its impact would be so momentous that she had to choose the moment when she would be able to deal with it. The opportunity came in 1992 with the conjunction of an award from the William Gillies Travel Bequest of the Royal Scottish Academy and a term's sabbatical leave from the College of Art. She went on her own to be able to concentrate on what she saw. What she looked at above all was fourteenth- and fifteenth-century painting. The result was a new departure, or perhaps the acceleration of changes that had already begun. Her first major work on her return was a self-portrait called *Being in Italy*. It is a confident picture. Split into three vertical parts, her own portrait is to the right of centre, just outside the picture space, but

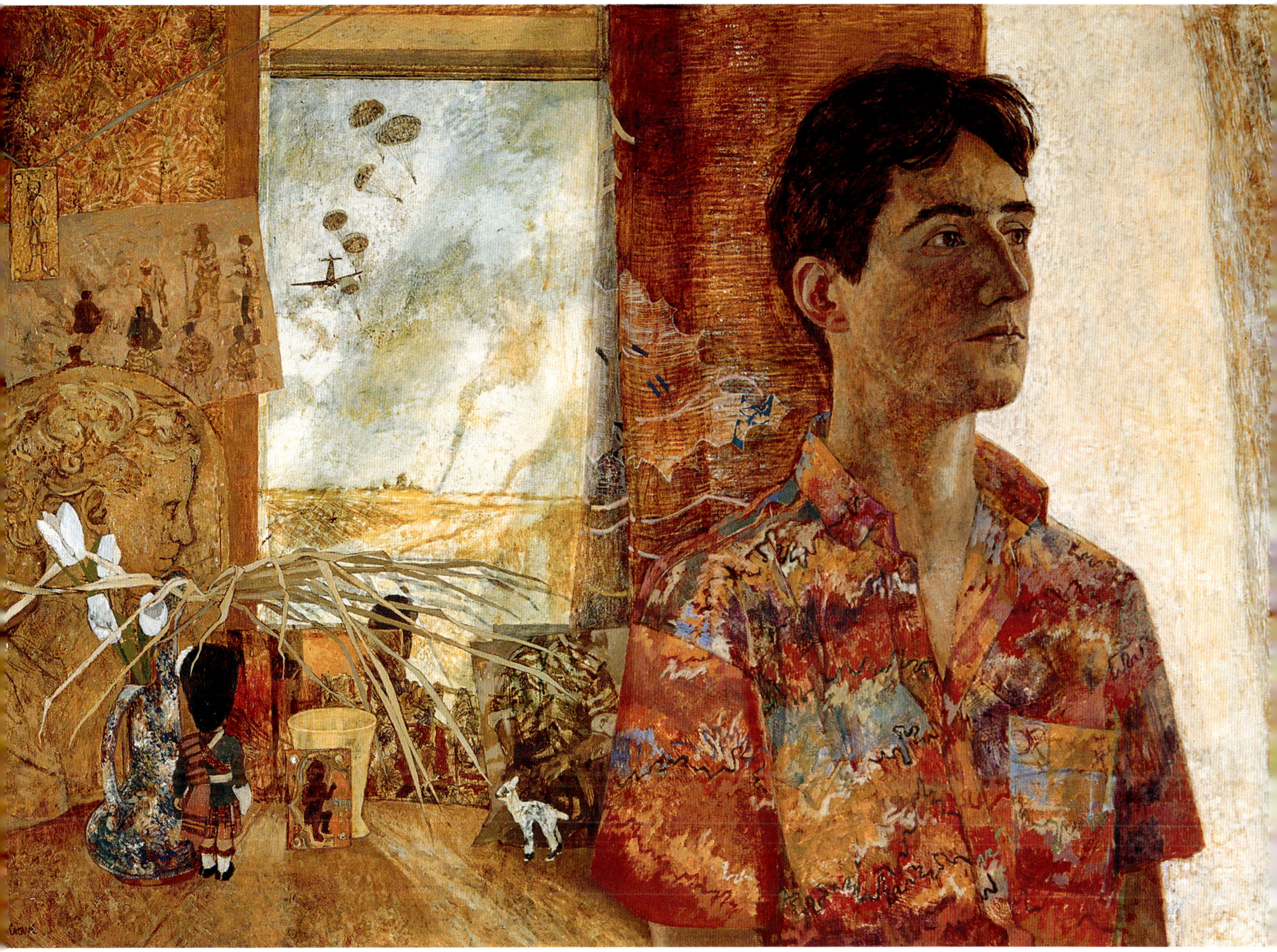

Heroes and Villains

standing in the light, looking in. On either side are darker passages with reflected or remembered images partly discernible in rubbed and scumbled red, black and gold. Most clearly recognisable is the angel from Leonardo's *Annunciation* in the Uffizi. Above it is a little passage of luminous landscape with cypress trees and olives against golden earth. It could be the background of a fifteenth-century painting and she remarked how you could still see Piero's landscapes in the Italian countryside. As we see it here, it could also be the reflection of one picture in the glass of another, or a memory of an actual landscape drifting into the scene and it was in fact based on a sketch.

The layering of the surface of *Being in Italy* is in some ways reminiscent of pictures Victoria had painted long before, as though she was going back to go forward. It recalls her portrait of Kathleen Raine, for instance, and also some of her pictures of Jenny seen against the light. Certainly this is a picture about a space somewhere in the imagination, or better, perhaps, about metaphysical space. Above all, it is about memory: about how memories seem to inhabit a place unlike any conventionally ordered space, but which nevertheless painting can perhaps emulate. That is what she seems to

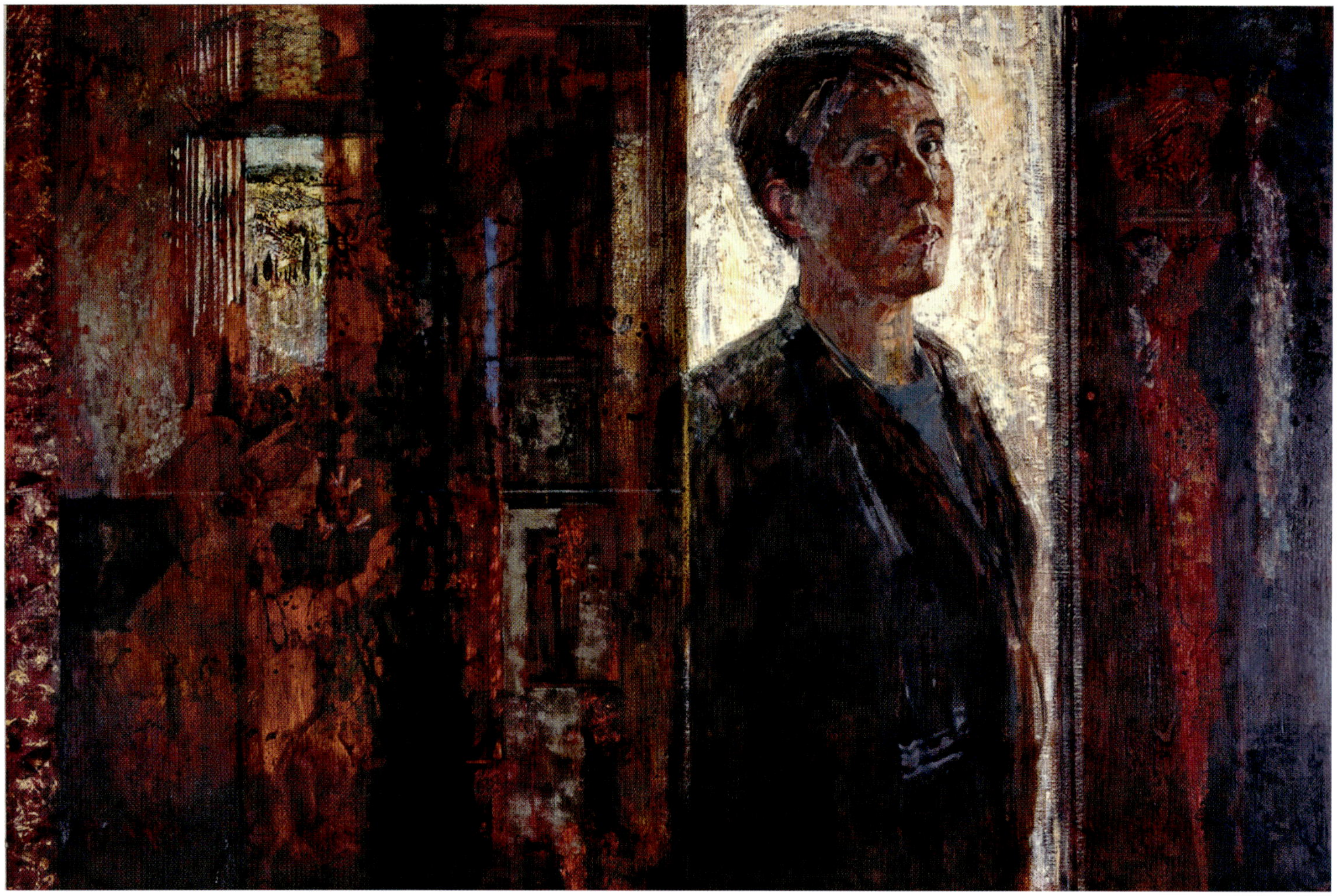

Being in Italy

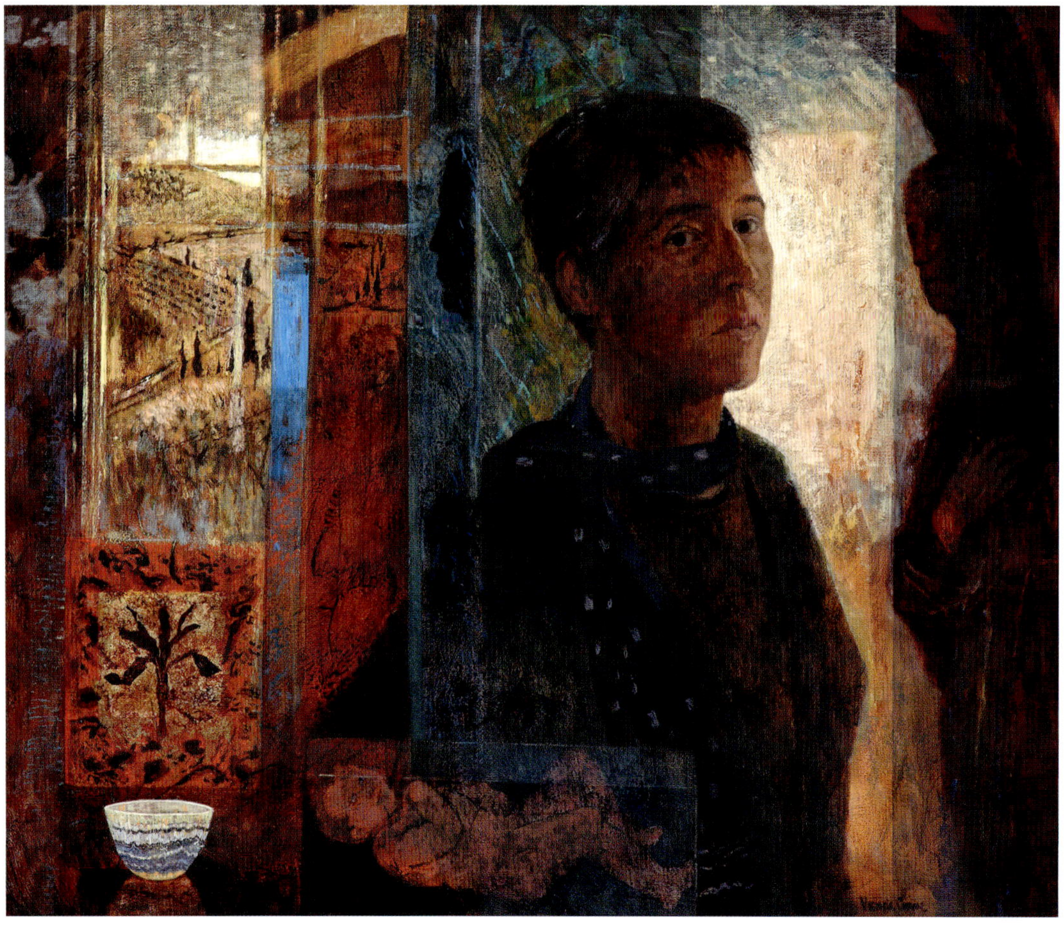

Italian Reflections

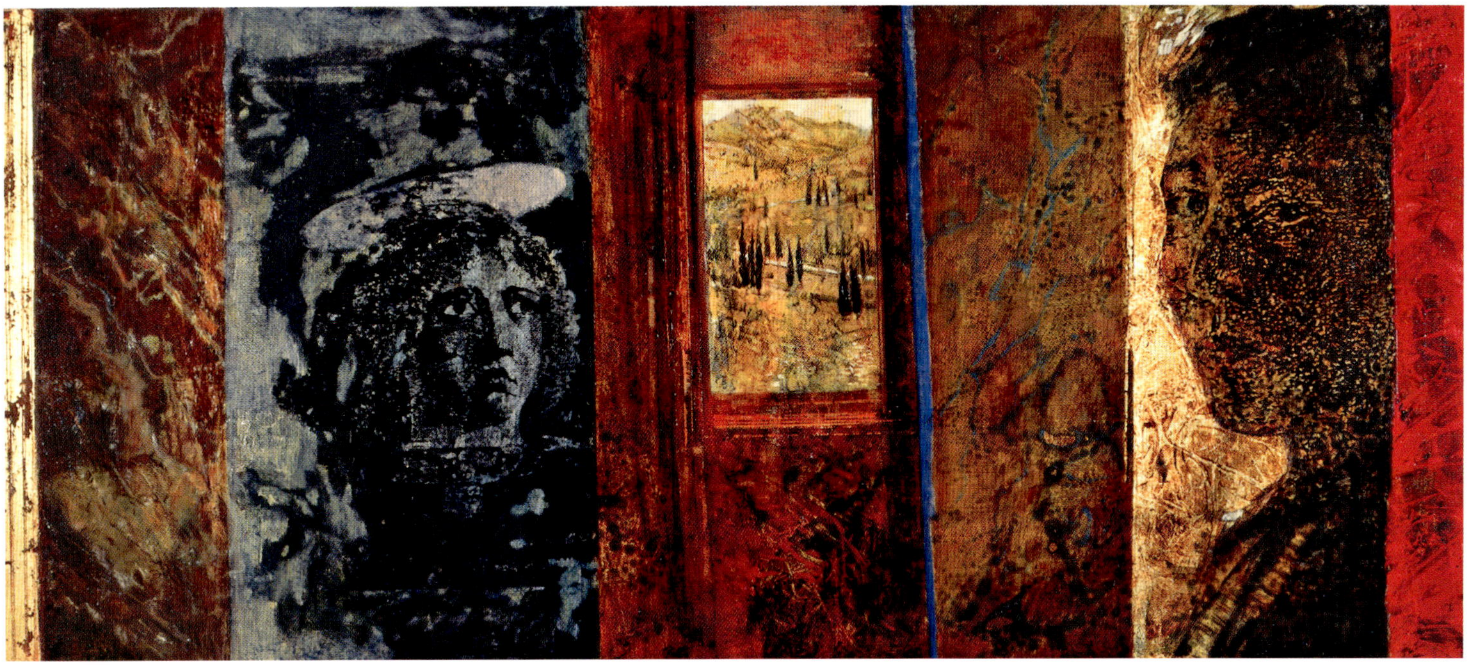

Dialogue in San Sepulcro

work towards. She had always been suspicious of the idea that pictorial space is a reflection of perceived space. Now she creates a pictorial space that is quite different. It is a metaphor for memory, for images that are somehow extended in time because they exist at once in both past and present. In *While in Italy (Variations)*, for instance, she creates a compound image out of remembered fragments of painting, architecture and decoration that is constructed like a collage, just as remembered images can overlay and intercut each other. Cinema is of course a construct of pictures extended in time and she often links her own use of collage with cutting in film.

This idea of painted memory was also enlarged after Victoria's encounters with Winifred Rushforth and R.D. Laing by the Jungian idea of collective memory. The wear and tear visible on the pictures and places she saw appealed to her in a way that perhaps reflected her own very personal feeling for this idea of collective memory. She often made notes of details of damage or deterioration in the pictures she saw and sought to make the surface of her own work as rich and suggestive of the passage of time. These effects seem to stand not just for time passing, however, but also for the vast shared experience that goes with it. It is as though as these ancient pictures have worked in so many people's imaginations over centuries, and so much giving has left its mark on them too.

Imitation of this kind of wear and tear is very marked in a second self-portrait, *Dialogue in San Sepulcro*. It has even less sense of physical space, indeed there is no constructed space at all in the way that there had been in Victoria's paintings of the past twenty years. Instead she uses layered, rich surfaces that allow the eye to explore, but do not lead it inwards. In a new departure, too, she uses gold, much as it was used in medieval altarpieces as both a precious adornment and a transcendental space. Her own head in this picture is scarcely defined in the round, but is painted against gold, rubbed like a passage in some altarpiece worn by time. The same landscape of cypress trees appears either through a window or in a painting. It is unclear which. To the left, a

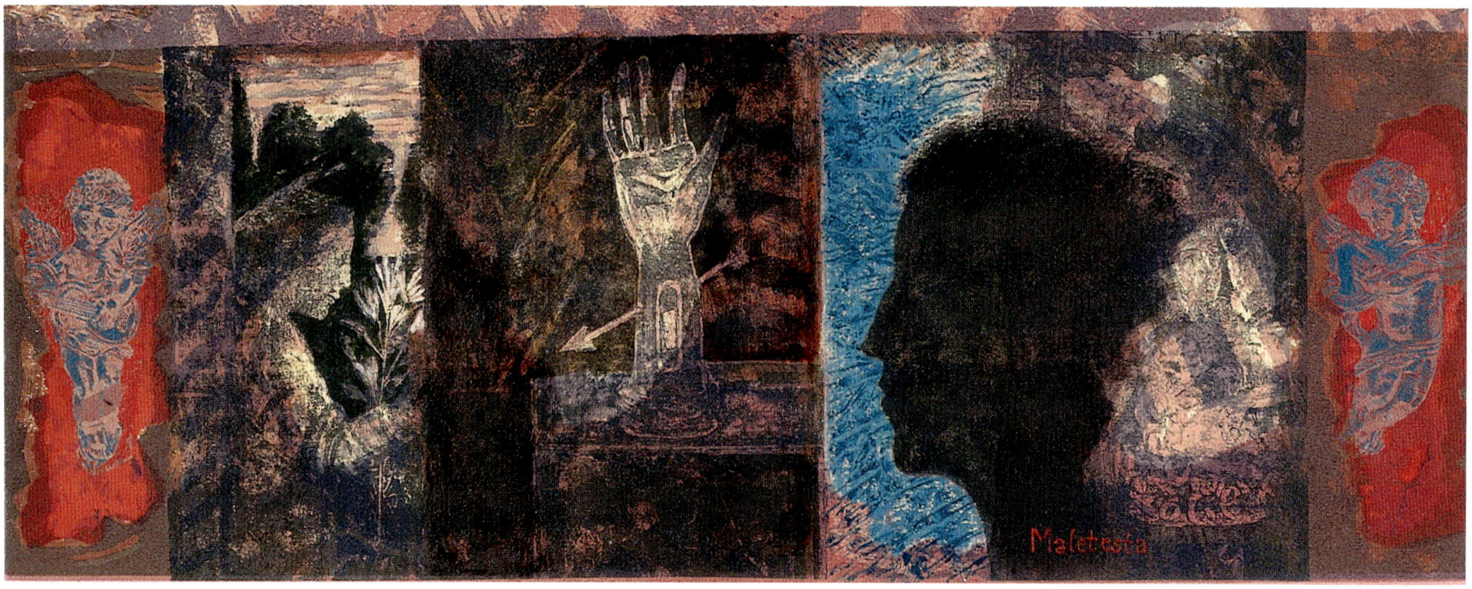

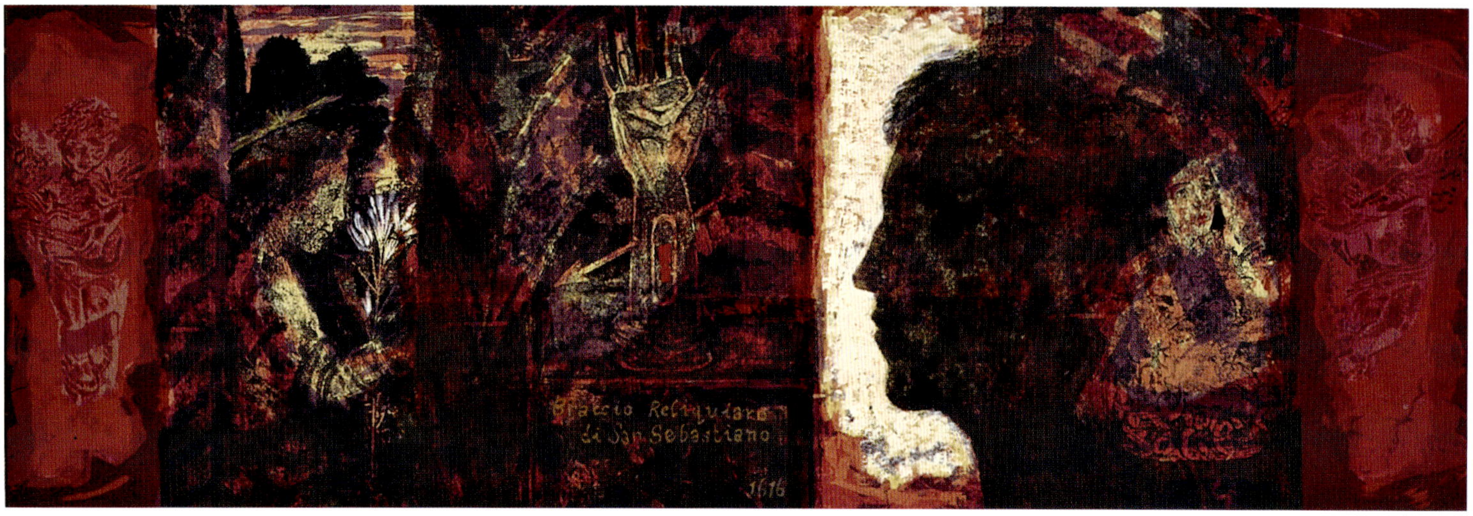

While in Italy; Variation

While in Italy; Variation Braccio Reliquario, San Sebastiano

broad band of transparent dark blue-black has turned the gold beneath to silver. Against this she has painted the head of *San Giuliano* by Piero from a fragmentary fresco in San Sepulcro, but she has reversed it so that the saint is facing her across the picture even as she herself looks away.

This self-portrait is a souvenir of Italy, but it also echoes a much earlier stage of her life. The saint is very like one of the angels in Piero's *Baptism* in London, the picture she had chosen to write about so unfashionably as student. Most strikingly too, the juxtaposition in the portrait of her own head with a head from a great religious image from the past clearly recalls the self-portrait she had painted more than twenty-five years before when she paired her own image with the head of Christ by Rublev behind her. The image by Piero is also, like the Rublev Christ, a fragment. Like an image lodged in memory, it is potent but incomplete. Its edges shade off into the broader and much vaguer field where memories are lodged, where time not space is the prevailing dimension. In her interview for *Artists' Lives* Victoria remarks how being alone in Italy and having time to reflect at her own pace did indeed take her back in some way to the girl she had been then.

There are other echoes, too, however. Long before, when Victoria first met Robin Philipson, she had admired the way he split up a surface architecturally and then layered things over it. As she put it herself, the artist felt this addressed the problem of the picture plane that she had been preoccupied with in her early work: trying to make it so that it is neither a window, nor simply a surface. Now she tackled it again, but with the self-confidence of experience. From the same date, *Within and Without*, for instance, seems to be a soliloquy on just that question: how to establish space in a picture as a place for the mind to roam, unhindered by conventions of spatial structure, a place for dreams in fact. An oculus with stained glass is partly visible in the central section of this picture which is divided into vertical panels. To the right a head is seen in shadowed profile. To the left is the edge of the architectural frame of an altarpiece and a beautifully rendered Annunciation lily.

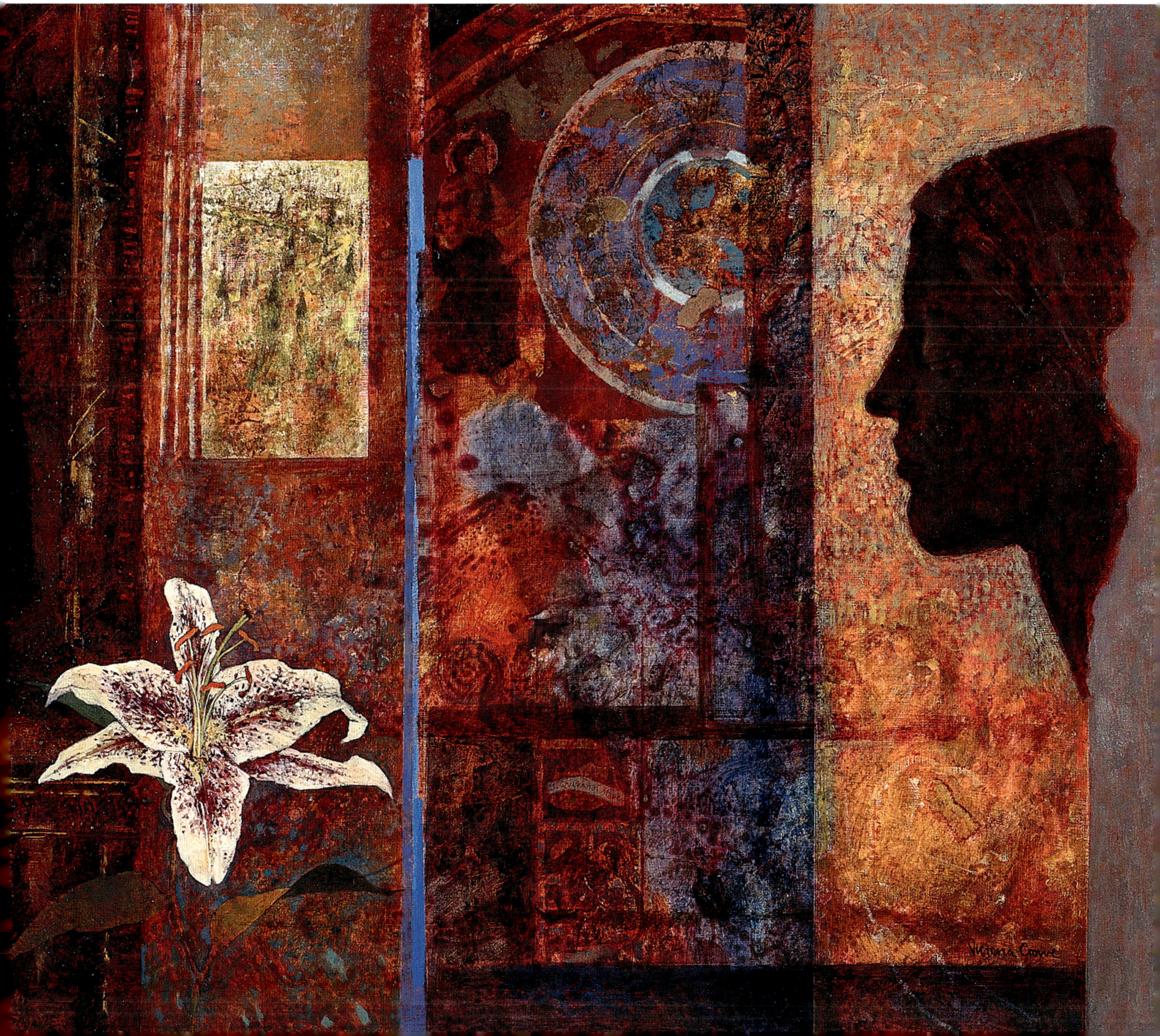

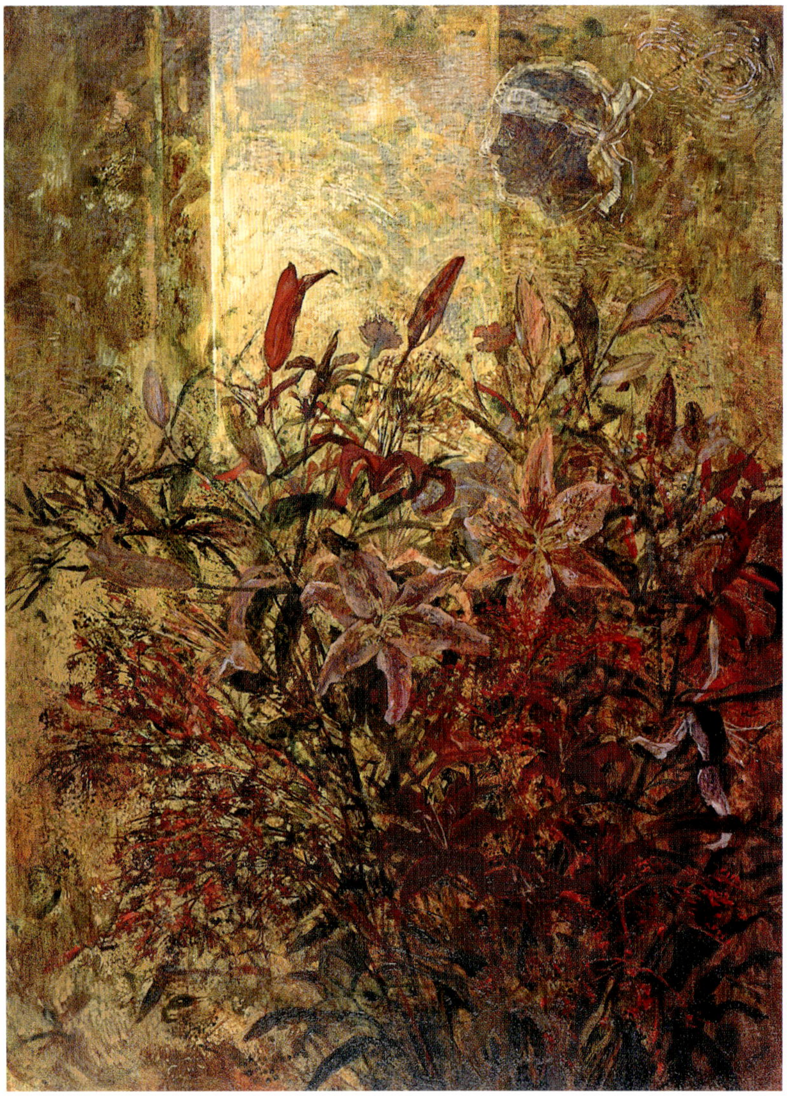

Bouquet for a Warrior

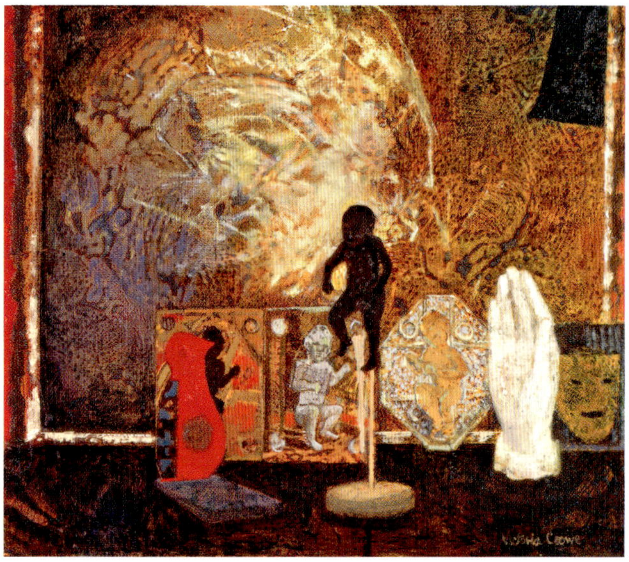

Myth and Message

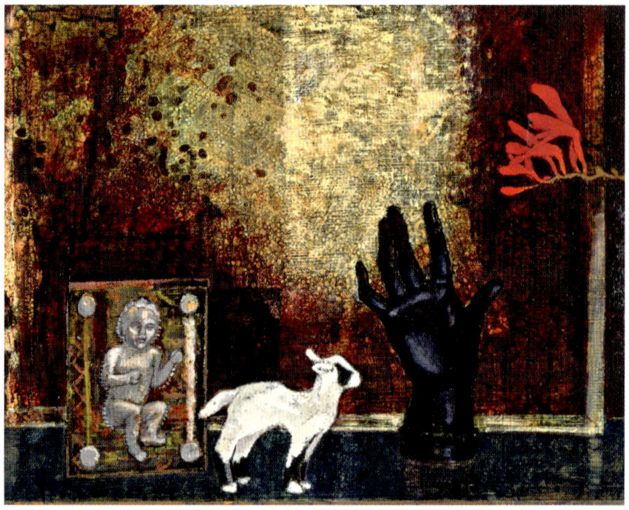

Lamb and Lucifer

Perhaps Victoria found some encouragement now in the model Philipson offered, but also in the work of James Cowie, whose work she had encountered back in the seventies. She had admired the way he weaves together symbols, observed objects and remembered images. Of all the Scottish artists whose work she came to know, he seemed closest temperamentally to herself. It is no more than a distant echo now, perhaps, but her watercolour, *Dialogue in Volterra*, brings together the heads of the Virgin and the angel from a sculptured *Annunciation* in the Pinacoteca against a landscape of Italian hills in a way that Cowie would have admired.

The lily that appears in *Within and Without* was to become a frequent image in her work, but the way it is rendered also points to the increasing importance of flowers and plants to her. In her sabbatical term in 1992, on her way to Italy, she went first to Poland with the Artists for Nature

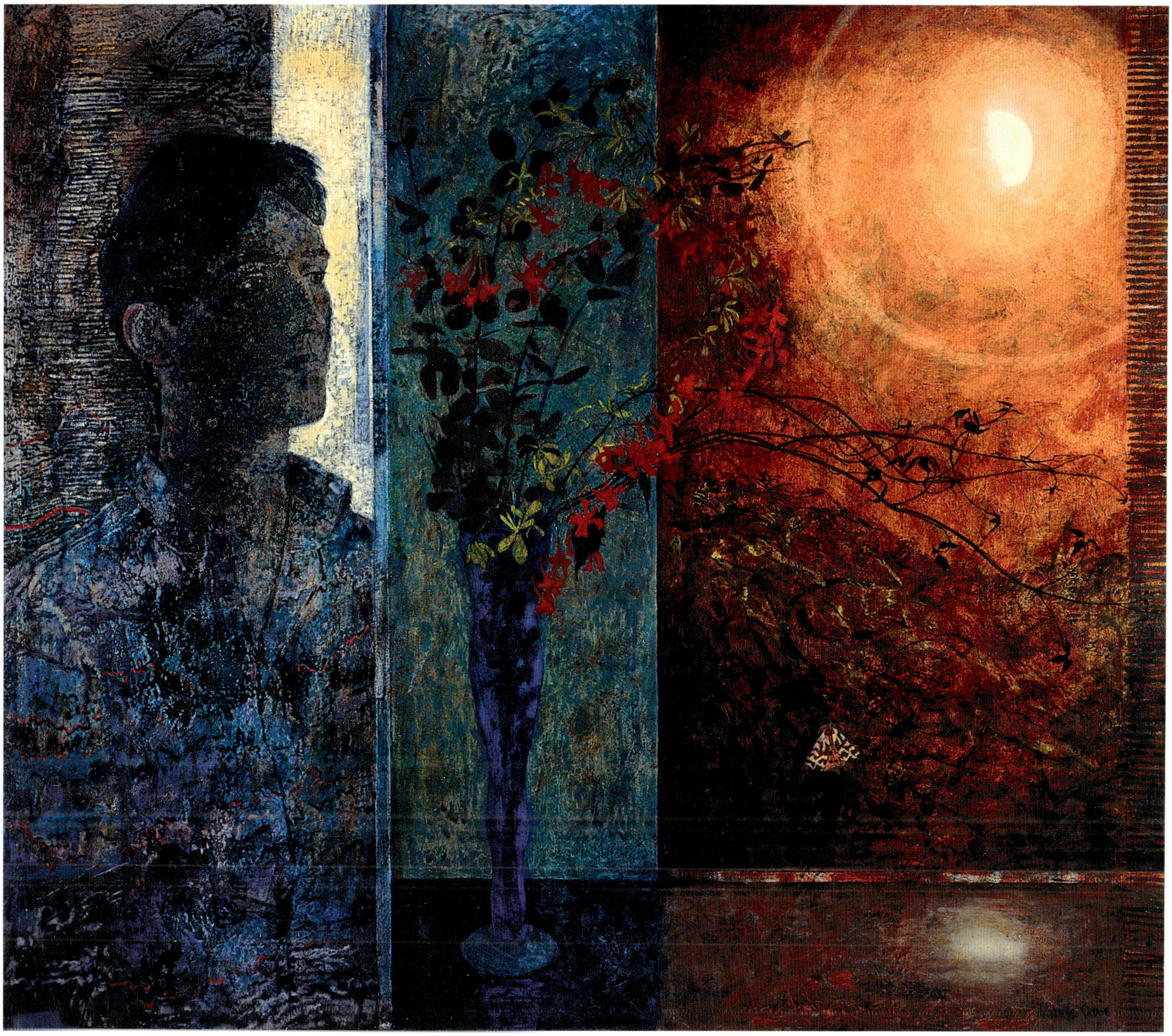

Travelling by Moonlight

Foundation, a conservation group with whom she was later to go to Spain and to India. In Poland she was working to record marshland plants threatened by agricultural drainage in wetlands near the Russian border. Through John Busby, a colleague at the College, she had earlier been invited to contribute to a series of four films on the seasons made for Grampian Television. Her season was spring and this involved making studies of the growth of flowers and grasses in the landscape. It was through this film that she had subsequently been invited to Poland. It was the beginning of an interest that was to become increasingly absorbing and indeed, on Elizabeth Blackadder's retirement, Victoria took over her botanical class at the College of Art. Flowers and plants begin to appear in a variety of contexts in her work including several dramatic still-lifes. *Vigil in Siena*, for example, exhibited in 1995, is a beautiful composition of flowers in a vase, though as they are seen against a dramatic sky, it is perhaps more than a simple still life.

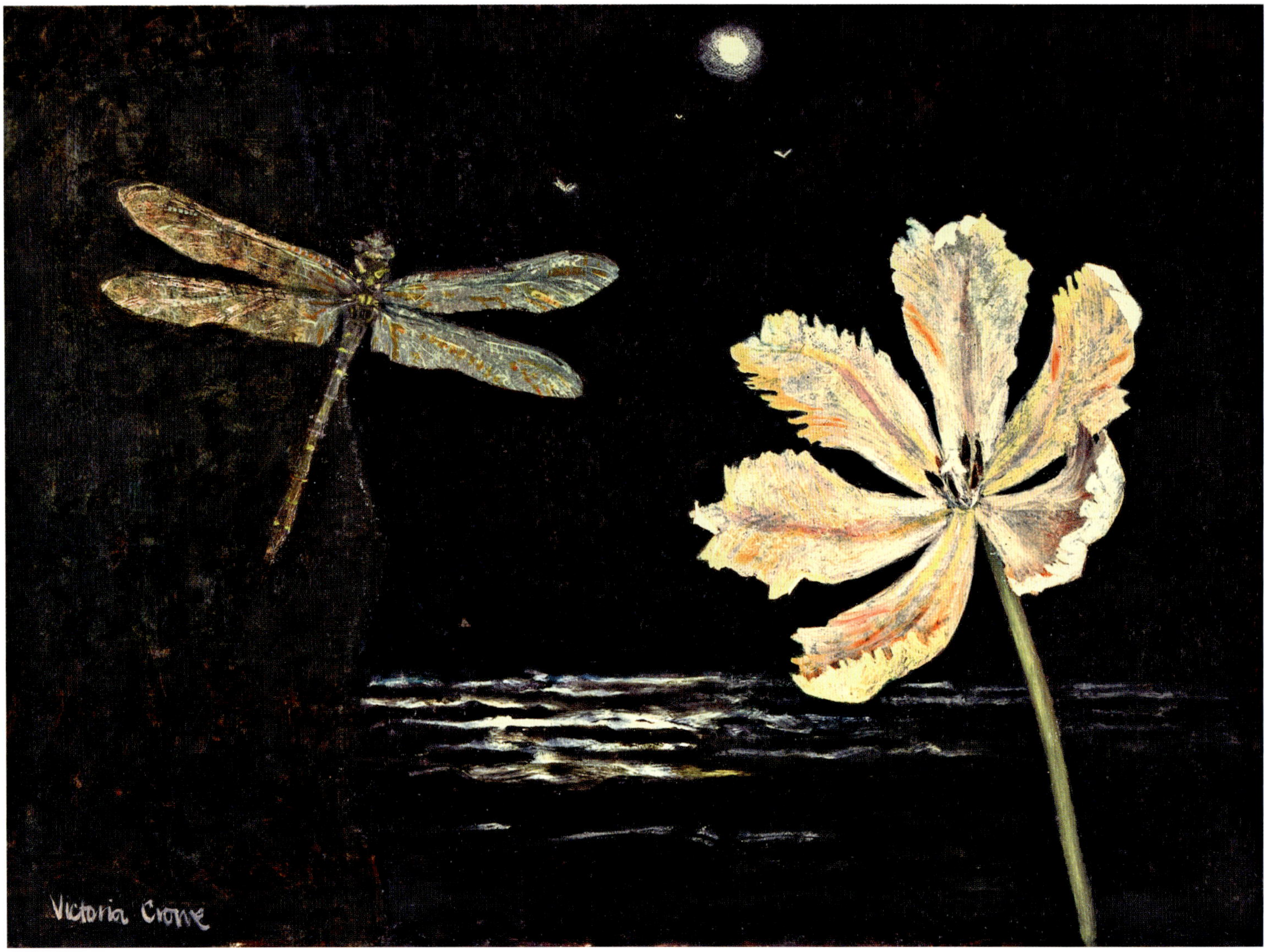

Night of the Dragonfly

Pages from Victoria's Polish sketchbooks were also turned into a series of prints using photo-etching. In the late seventies she had studied etching and produced some remarkable experimental results, but in 1993 she also started to make screen prints. The technique was to prove liberating. She had no interest in producing editions of identical prints. Rather she used print-making techniques as another way of layering the image, but also of working variations onto it. She tended to use the print as a matrix, but then work over it to create a series of separate individual works such as *While in Italy (Variations)* and *Dialogue in San Sepulcro*.

It was 1994. The children were growing up. In her art Victoria had embarked on a confident new phase and she seemed to be moving onto a plateau of achievement, but all this was as nothing when in December that year the family was devastated by a diagnosis which revealed that Ben had cancer. He was in his third year at Aberdeen University. The following June they were told it was terminal. He died in December 1995. He had been with the family a month before at the opening of Victoria's exhibition at the Scottish Gallery in November where she showed her portrait of him, *Travelling by Moonlight*. The fatal illness and death of a child is the worst thing that any parent could experience. The child is part of yourself, yet you cannot go with him, nor take his place as any parent would most willingly do. As that is impossible, the only thing left is the

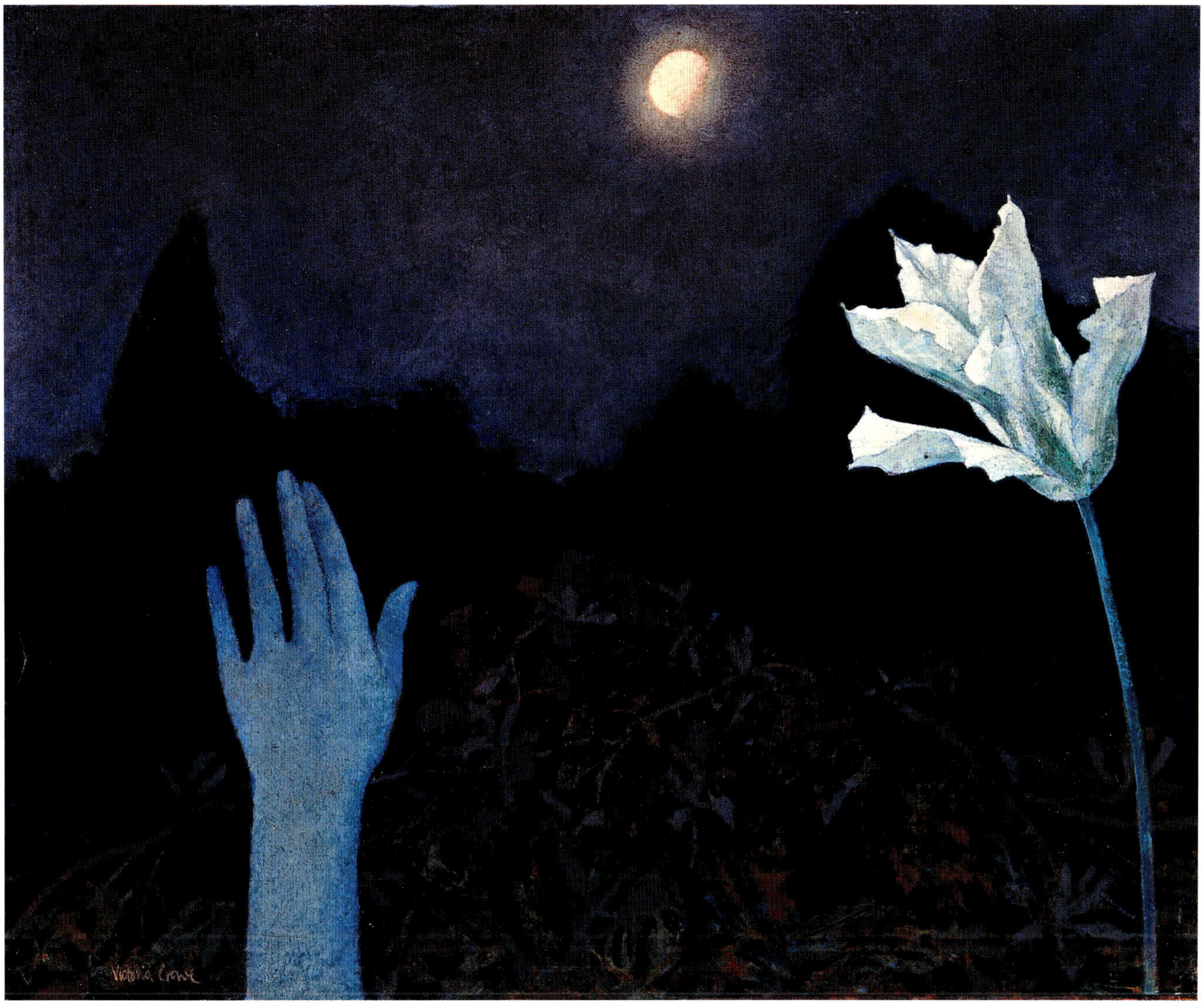

Midnight Garden

course that was chosen by Mike and Victoria, to live life more fully, first in support of him in his illness and then in memory of their lost son.

For Victoria this meant painting. It became a vehicle for the expression of her anxiety and her grief, first as a votive and then as a memorial. *Bouquet for a Warrior* was the former, a great bunch of lilies between darkness and a transcendental light. There are flowers again in *Travelling by Moonlight*. Ben's portrait is to the left silhouetted against gold. A delicate arrangement of clematis, berberis and scarlet tropaeolium stands in a tall blue vase at the centre. To the right, the composition opens towards a brilliant moon ringed in a golden haze. Traditionally, a ring around the moon heralds a storm, while beneath the moon a tiger moth, drawn to the light, is the image of the transience and fragility of life. This is one of a series of very beautiful paintings of the moon and moonlight painted during Ben's illness and in the years immediately after his death. They include *Night of the Dragonfly*, which has a particularly lovely passage of moonlight on water, *Midnight Stefanotis* and *Travellers in a Single Dream*. In *Midnight Garden* she raises her own hand against the night sky, her gesture matched by a tulip, ghostly white against the dark. These are sad and very beautiful pictures. They reflect the extraordinary courage with which the artist met her grief and found strength to express it, at once with such restraint and such power.

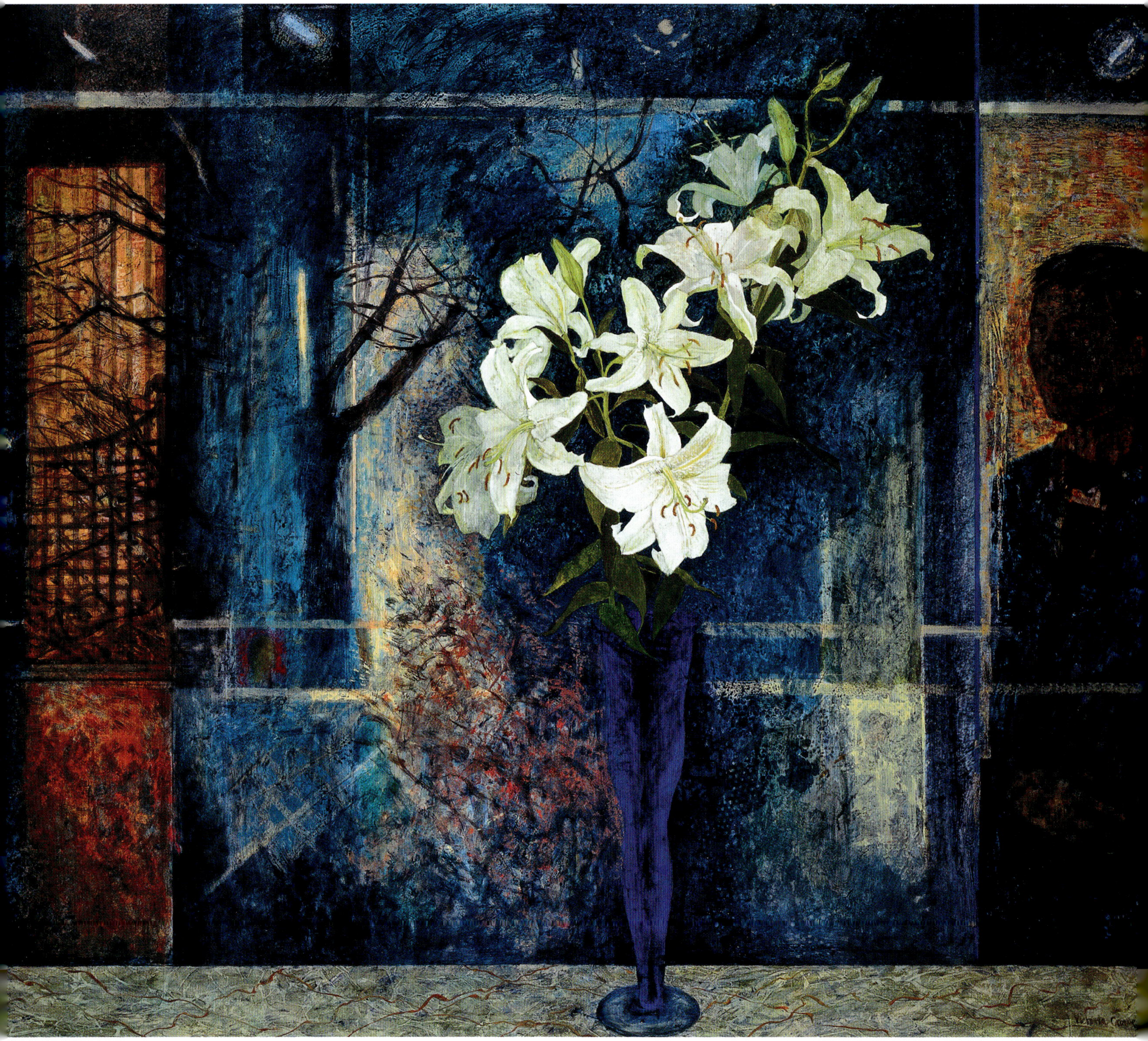

November Window Reflecting

Some of the pictures she produced at this time were small and so more focussed and more private. *Lamb and Lucifer* is a little still-life, just a foot square. The title seems to refer to objects, much as she had seen them in the Jenny Armstrong still-lifes, as votives, or talismans even. A little silver votive of a child appears in several similar compositions. Indeed a tiny little picture is called simply *Silver Votive*. It is paired with what seems to be a portrait of Ben set in a ground of silver foil. It appears again in *Votives for Male Children*, a little picture, typically now in mixed media, painted during Ben's illness. In a small watercolour, against a stormy ground, she pairs her own portrait, seen only in part

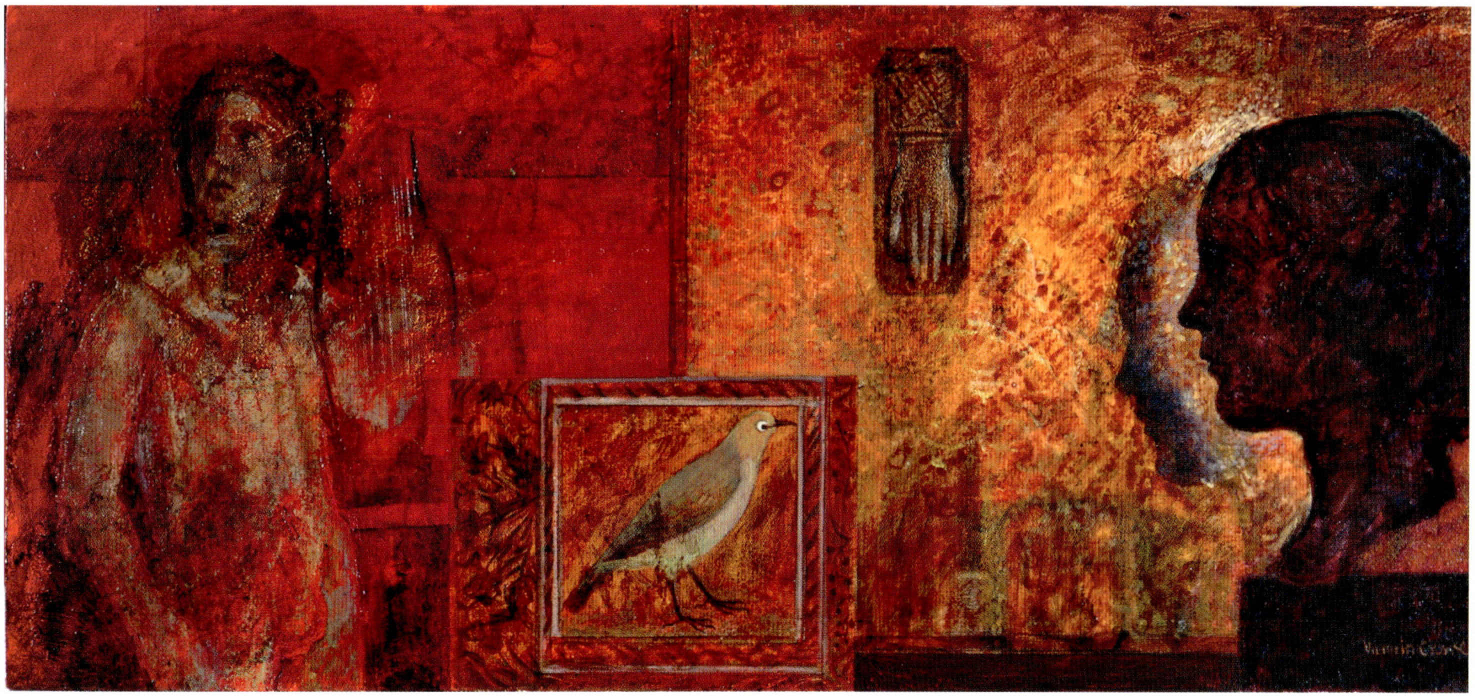

Contemplating the Mysteries

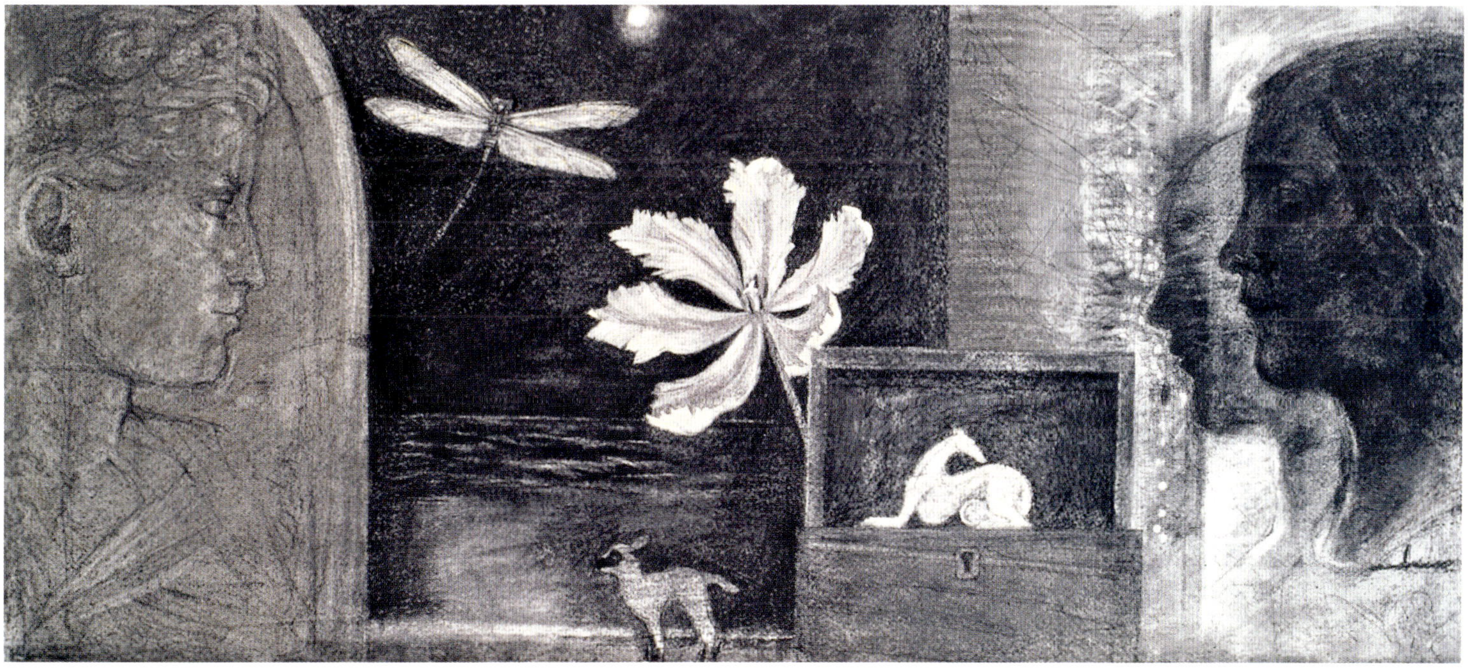

Night Travelling

in a hexagonal mirror, transfer-printed onto the panel, with a dark, strongly painted portrait of Ben. In the anguish of such tragic events, Victoria's reflections were deep and troubled, but they also found a vehicle in her art where the metaphorical exchange between actual reflection and reflective thought had long been a theme. It is there in the mirrors she painted in Jenny Armstrong's cottage. Now, contemplating loss and the questions of birth, life and death that it raised, inevitably her own reflections deepened and darkened. In several pictures a shadowy self-portrait is seen against gold leaf with votives and, in one instance, a parrot tulip, a flower remarkable for its brief splendour. In

November Window Reflecting, painted in 1997, both kinds of reflection interchange. We seem to be looking out of a window onto autumn leaves, bare trees and a trellis in a November garden, but that image is overlaid by reflections of the room in which we are standing. To the right is Victoria's own portrait, though in shadow against gold. The composition is dominated by a vase of tall Annunciation lilies, however, which, unlike everything else in the scene, are sharply defined so that their white petals stand out. Curiously, too, where so much is reflection, they seem not to have any reflection at all. It is as though they existed in a different reality.

This lily held a special meaning for Victoria. In *Artists' Lives*, speaking about her visit to Italy, she describes the anticipation she felt before her first encounter with Leonardo's *Annunciation* in the Uffizi. In the picture, the angel holds the lily always associated with that event in his left hand. She also looked at the treatment of the Annunciation by different artists. It became something of a theme of her visit. Perhaps as a mother it held special significance for Victoria but then, cruelly inverting the promise in the picture, her world was shattered by the very different annunciation of Ben's illness. With that knowledge, the lilies here, picked out as they are, assume a strange, otherworldly, almost sinister aspect. As she herself reflected, the subject of the Annunciation was to the Virgin 'not only the joyous announcement itself, but by implication also the shadow of future grief.'[1]

During Ben's illness, Victoria and her daughter Gemma travelled to Italy and visited Pompeii. A city cut-off suddenly in the middle of vigorous life understandably found resonances in Victoria's work. Deep Pompeiian red begins to feature in her painting. So does Pompeiian painting. A figure from the Villa of the Mysteries appears in *Contemplating the Mysteries*, for instance. There is a Roman mosaic of a bird in the centre and to the right a bust of Gemma with beyond its reflection, or its shadow. The picture is dominated by Pompeiian red, but the surface is broken as though it was an actual frescoed wall. There are other shadowy images in, or on it, too. In *Interior with Unheeding Dancer*, a naked bearded figure from a Roman fresco dances against a similar deep red ground. A branch with yellow leaves stretches in front of him and to the right, a Quattrocento angel seems to raise a banner against a background of battered frescoed wall. In the dancer's moment, frozen long ago, and the withered leaves of a present passing season, time and eternity intersect.

Do Not Disturb the Dreaming World, exhibited at the Scottish Gallery in 1995, is a major picture from this time. Although it was painted in a period of such anxiety, it is as though the artist's pictorial language was evolving to meet her needs. In the painting, a winged putto hangs against a mirror. It seems to be a reflection, yet the mirror is painted out in golden yellow, so it cannot be. The yellow in turn becomes a source of light, however. A vase of dry, curling grasses stands at the centre of the composition. The grasses are actually a three-dimensional, still-life object that Victoria had inherited from David Michie's studio when he retired as Head of Painting at the College, but here, against the dark background, they read as flat drawing. To the right, the artist's own portrait was transfer-printed onto the board and then worked over. Piero's *San Giuliano* looks on out of the shadows on the left. The picture is composed in rectangles, but they do not yield ground to each other as each claims to dominate the picture plane. There is no logical space, yet the mind is free to roam, to make associations, to follow allusions wherever they may lead.

After the tragic events of the mid-nineties, as gradually she and her family absorbed their loss, Victoria felt she had to continue to paint with more determination than ever. Because of these events her art had inevitably turned inwards, but as it did so, she also moved towards a freer,

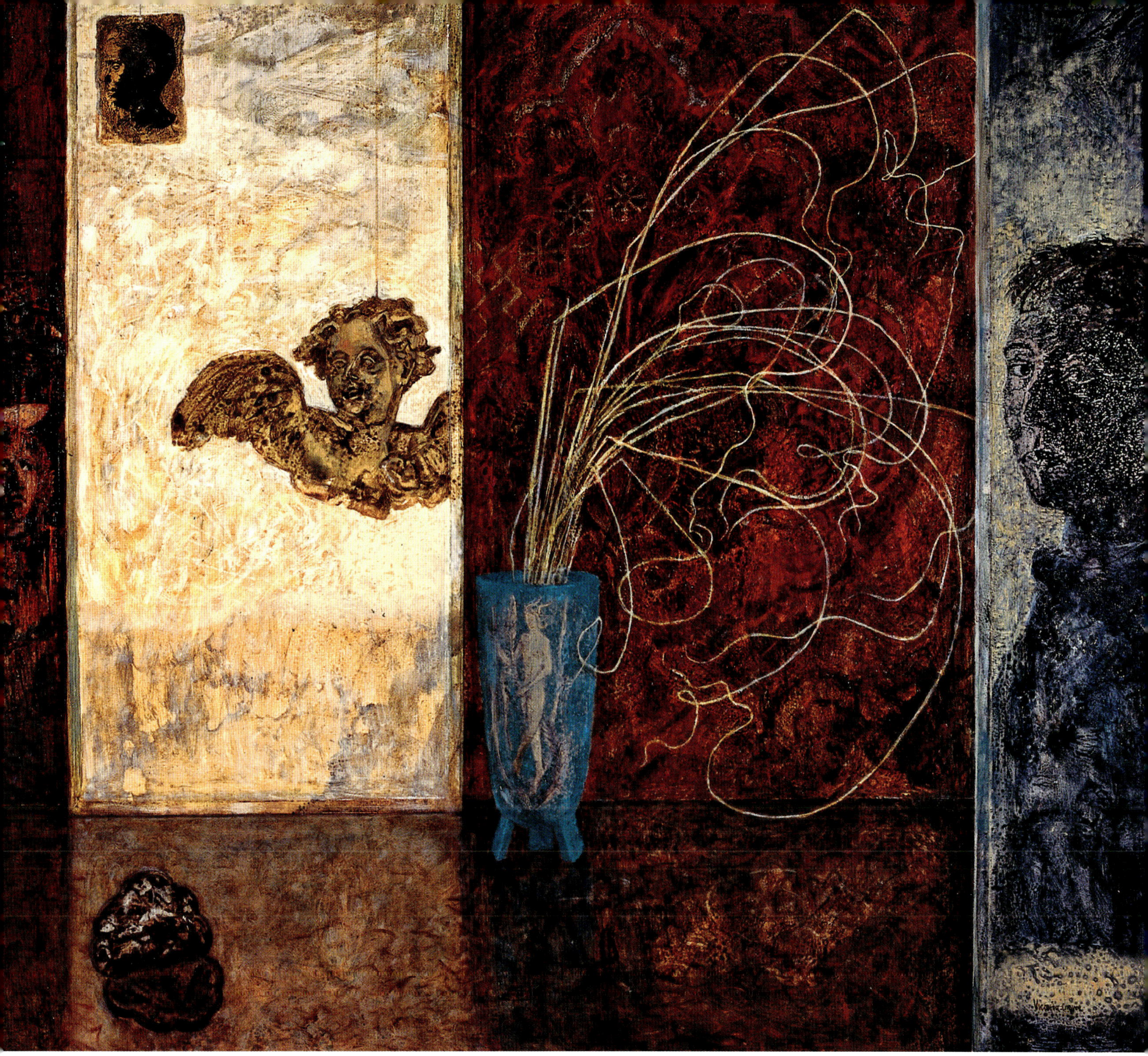

Do Not Disturb the Dreaming World

more open and more associative approach to composition. The surfaces she created were complex, often broken and so suggestive of the passage of time. Increasingly she used mixed media, combining collage and prints with painting and incorporating borrowed images that brought with them all sorts of associations. Among these it is above all the painters and sculptors of the Quattrocento – Uccello, Piero, Donatello, and others like them – whose work appears in her paintings, hovering in an indeterminate space. An exception from outside this Pre-Raphaelite period is a beautiful, but almost Baroque angel from *Annunciation* by Pontormo in the church of Santa Felicità in Florence which appears in a number of compositions.

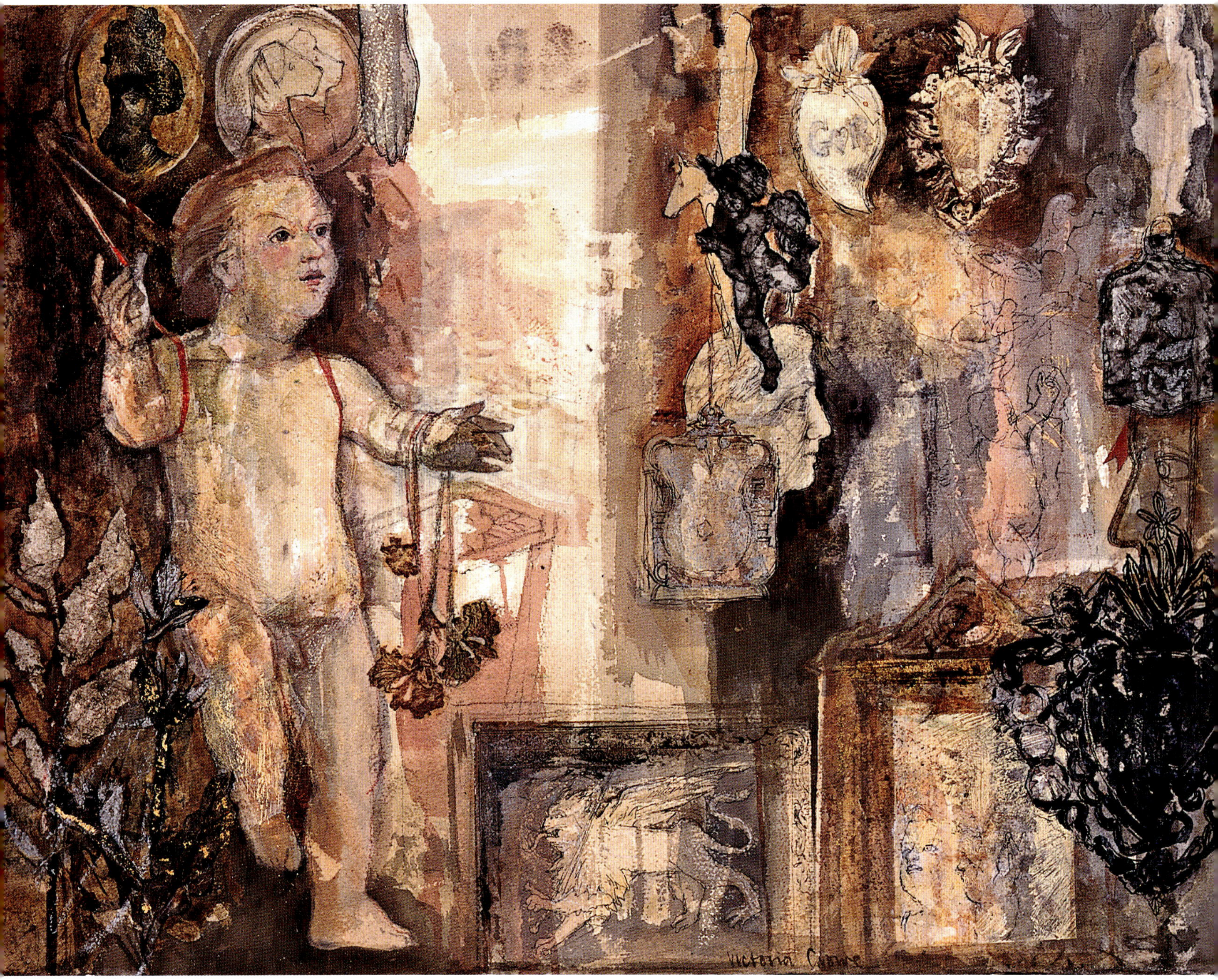

Dorsoduro Interior

Venice

Victoria's interest in the art of the Quattrocento probably began in the National Gallery when she was a teenager, for Italian art of that period is one of its great strengths. But what is it about the Quattrocento that she responded to so consistently over such a long time? The answer lies perhaps partly in the reason for its strong representation in the National Gallery in the first place: the Victorians, led by Ruskin, identified a special quality in this painting. Before Raphael, Italian art had a peculiar purity – artists seemed to see the world in its spiritual simplicity. After all, they were still known as the Italian Primitives. Later they lost that innocence and it was this idea that led the

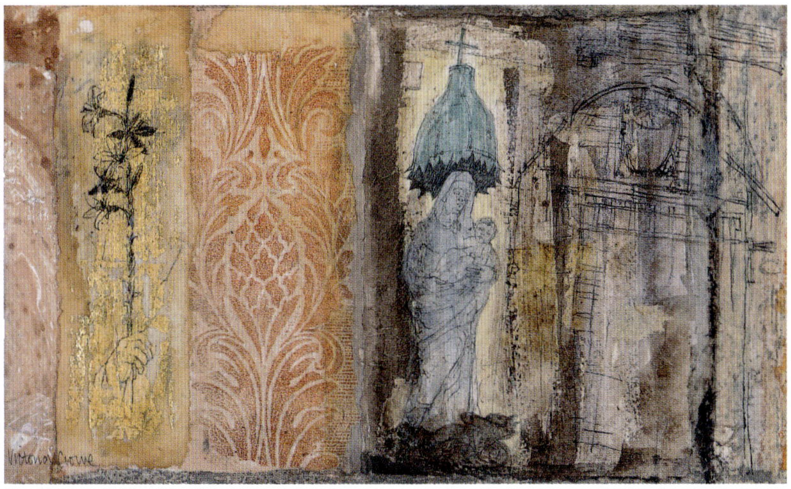

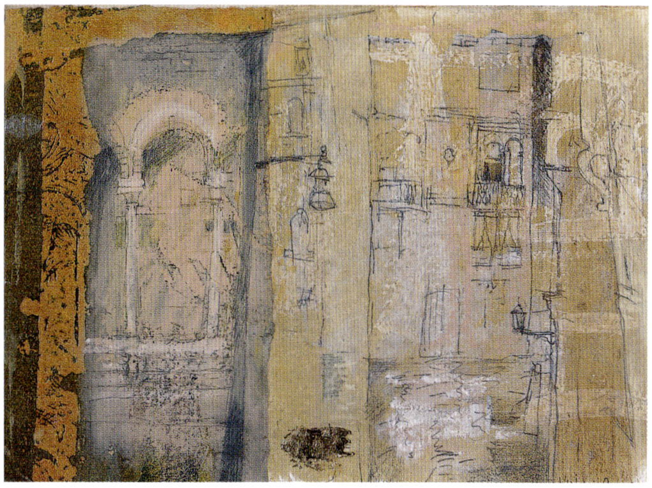

Across the City; La Madonnetta

Across the City; Cloister

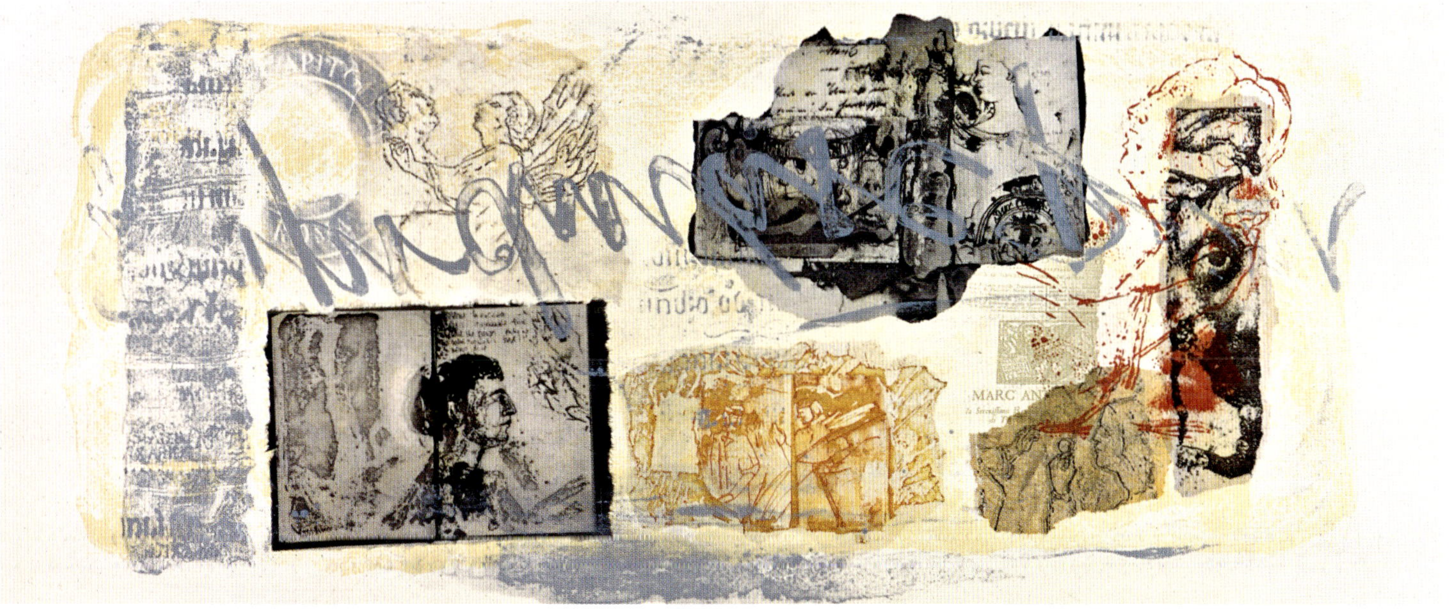

Drawn from Italy

English Pre-Raphaelites to choose their name. The pictures that the artists of early Renaissance Italy created are not reflections. They exist for us now, not in some reflected objectivity borrowed from the past; they have their own autonomy and that is why they can drift in our imaginations just as Victoria Crowe proposes they should do. For Ruskin, the key idea that he adapted from the Scottish philosophy of moral sense was that in art, truth, as we see it in these pictures, is first of all a quality of the imagination. It reflects purity of feeling. It is not merely a functional relationship to some objective reality. Truth of observation is a vehicle, a test of honesty and a source of wonder, but not the primary object of painting. Independently Victoria seems to have come to a similar position. For Ruskin, too, Bellini more than any other artist except Turner, personified his ideal of the balance of imaginative and objective truth. It was therefore perhaps intuitively following Ruskin, the city's greatest advocate, that Victoria found her spiritual home in Venice.

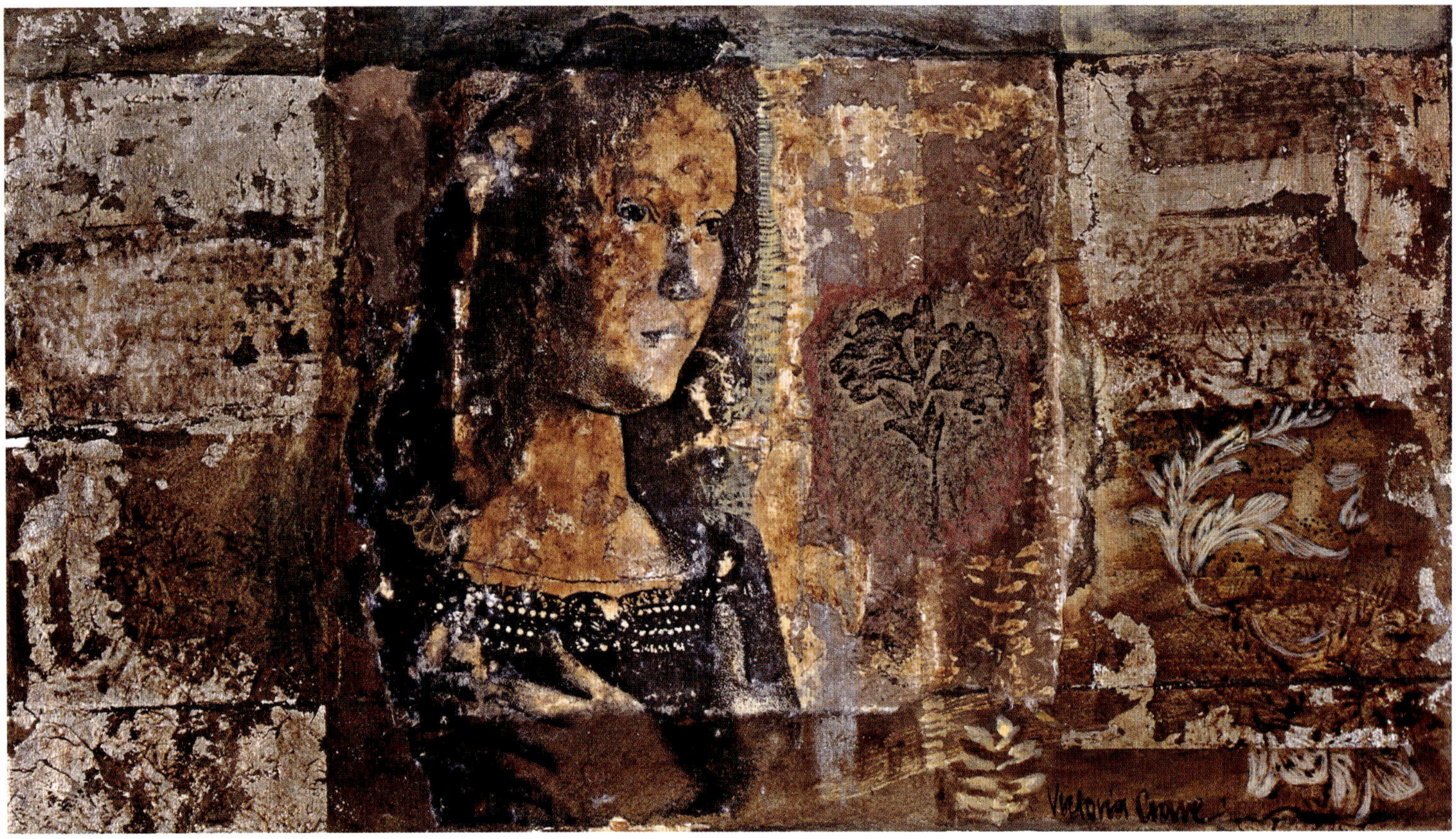

Fragile Traces, Venice

She first visited the city in 1998. Five years later she and Mike were to buy a studio on the Giudecca, and since then it has been a regular place of work and a source of inspiration for her. On this first visit, she travelled on her own and, as always, made notes and sketches of what she saw. To make it a bit more difficult for herself, she says, and to avoid the clichéd views of Venice, but perhaps also in response to the unique quality of the light, she drew on pages on which she had laid a ground of gold. The results are very beautiful and include many images which were to continue to echo in her work thereafter.

Some of the results of this first Venetian trip were shown at the Thackeray Gallery, the Bruton Gallery in Leeds and the Scottish Gallery, and reflections, memories and votives are words that appear frequently in the titles of the works she showed. Examples are *Interior with Many Reflections*, *Memories and Reflections*, *Assembled Votives* and *Dorsoduro Interior: Ex-votos*. The latter is a composition of votives hung in Italian churches with the Christ child from a Venetian crib, the lion of St Mark's and other objects all loosely associated in a space that glows with light, but has no obvious light source. In *Fragile Traces, Venice*, *Venice Fragile Secret*, *1st Day Venezia; Archangel with Wings of Fire* and the silk screen print *While in Venice,* the beautiful face of the Magdalen appears as she has done so frequently since. She is taken from a *Sacra Conversazione* by Bellini in the Accademia, a simple composition with two saints, half-length, standing on either side of the Madonna and child. The saints do not have haloes, nor any other attributes to identify them as saints. In consequence they seem like ordinary women and so are closer to us. The Magdalen stands to the right. Arms crossed on her breast, her focus is inward. Absorbed by the simple, inescapable facts of life and death that the mother and child

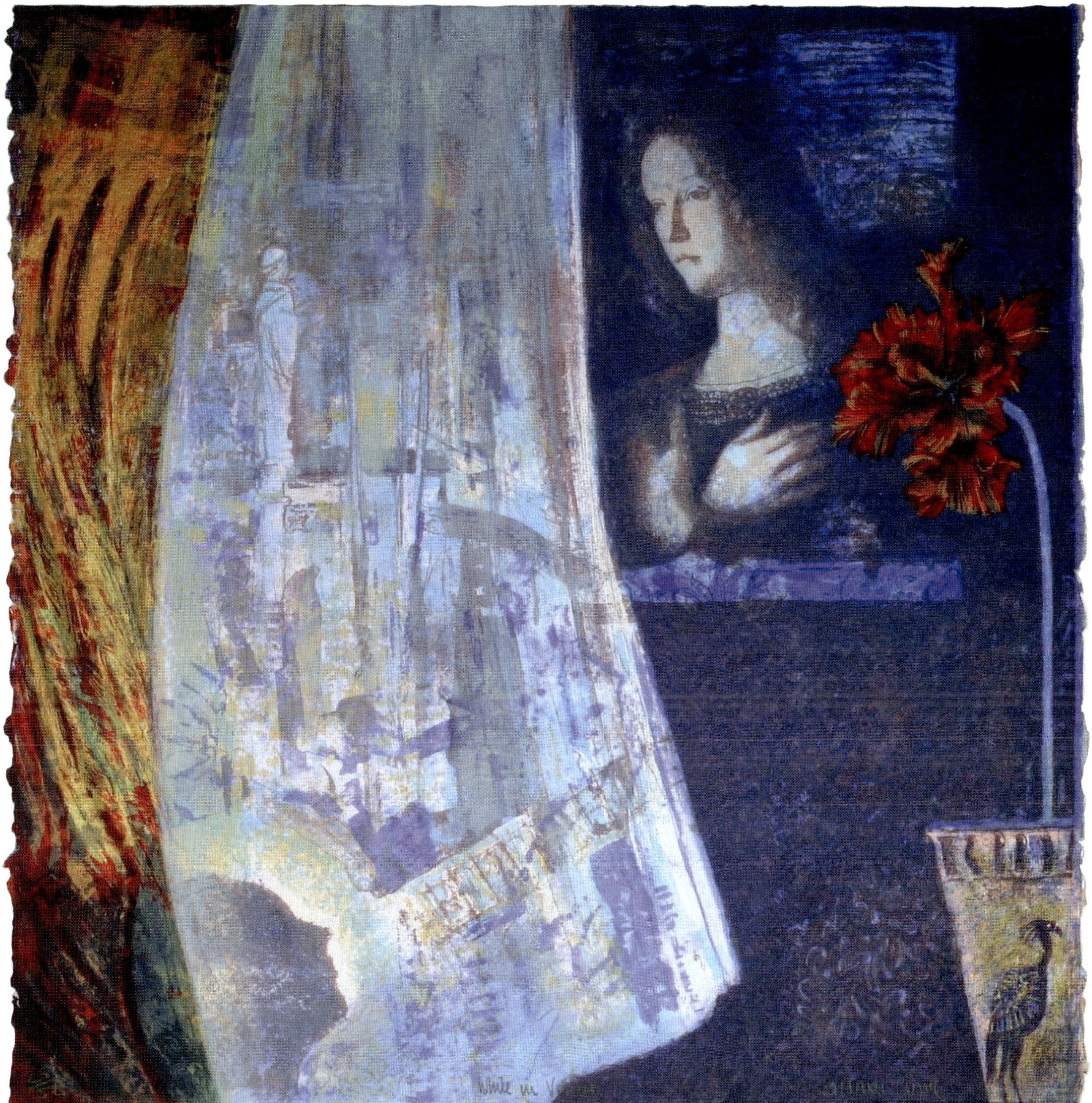

While in Venice

present to her, she personifies reflection as a mental state. The word itself with its double meaning of mirror and thought suggests a kind of inner optics, of images in inward mirrors, and that is what we see in her face. As if to endorse that double meaning, too, her image is sometimes reversed. We see her as though in a mirror.

It is easy to see why this figure has appealed so much to Victoria, and in *Fragile Traces, Venice* she is effectively the subject, but in a way that opens up our own reflections too. The surface of the picture, divided roughly into rectangles, suggests the crumbling stucco of a Venetian wall. At this time Victoria also began to add writing to the surface of the picture. The whole effect is like a palimpsest of graffiti, peeling posters and crumbling stucco. If she were not so arrestingly beautiful, the Magdalen's image could almost be a tattered poster for some forgotten event. Thus the wall becomes a metaphor for memory, a symbol of Venice itself. Later Victoria was to note of the graffiti on a Venetian door that she painted in *Across the City* that 'it contains a secret language of indecipherable messages – scrapings and scratchings as subtle to read as a snail's trail.'[1]

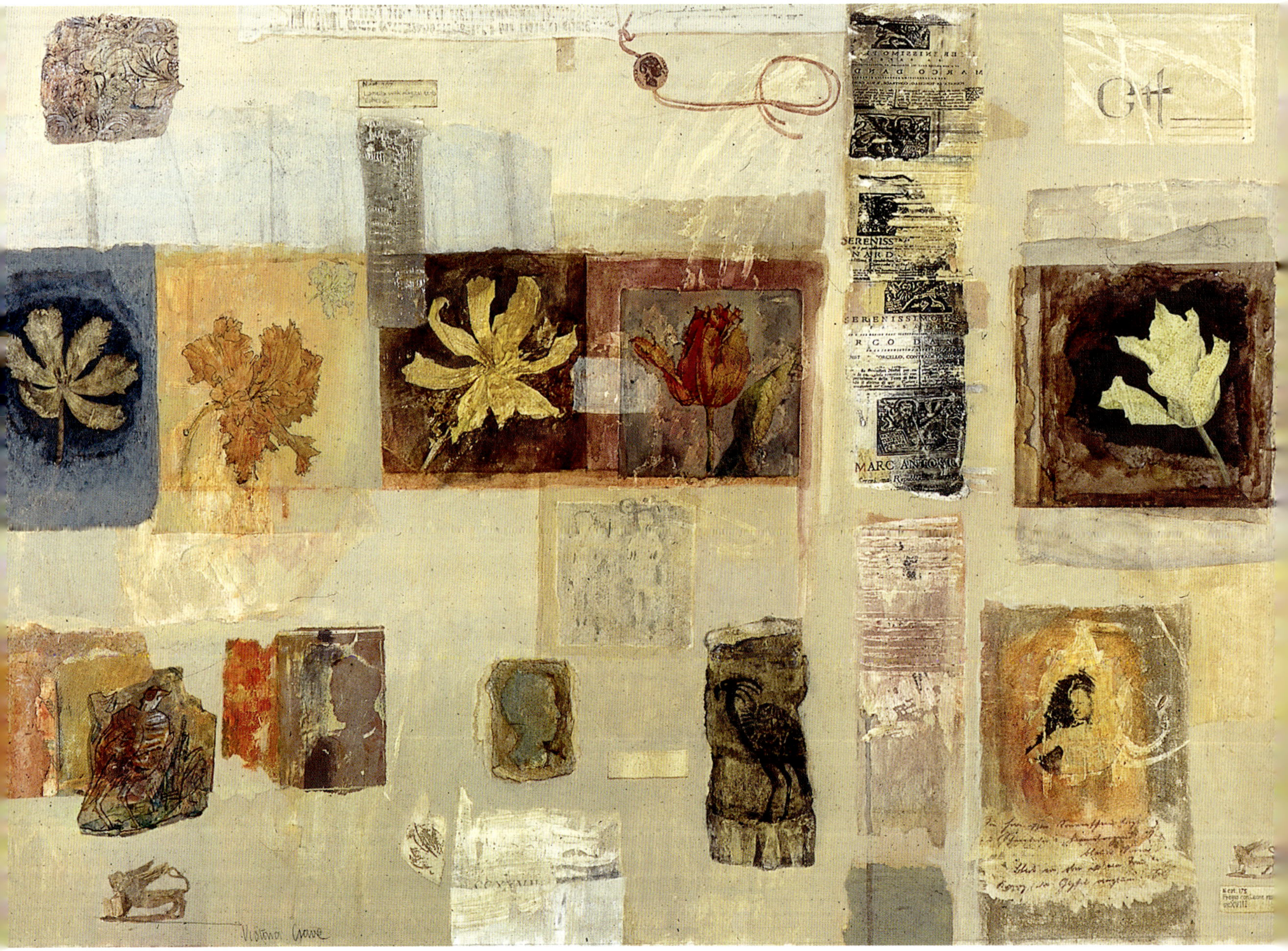

Artefacts and Magical Texts

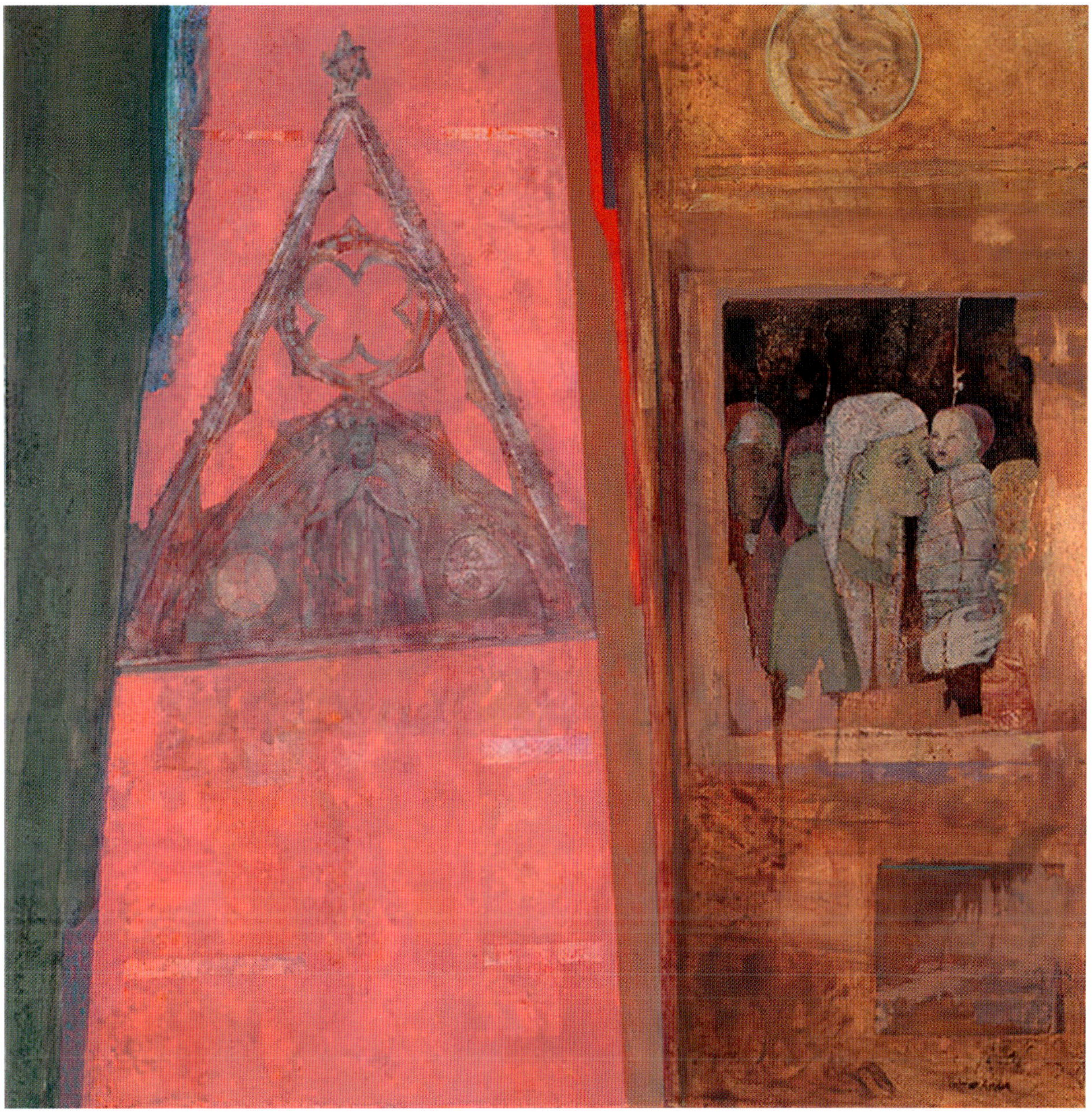

Pink Palazzo

In Victoria's show at the Scottish Gallery in 2001, writing graffiti and collaged or transfer-printed texts and the mixture of media that she uses to present them had become even more conspicuous in her work. *Drawn from Italy*, for instance, is typically a mixture of silkscreen and etching with *chine collé*, a method of printing that works in effect like collage. These methods of transfering the text often have the effect of reversing it so that it is once again a mirror image and not easily read, adding to the mystery even more. As it did for Braque and Picasso a century before, however, the use of printed and written texts also asserts the flatness of the picture plane. It denies illusion, something Victoria had always been concerned with, but as she uses it, it also greatly enlarges the scope for allusion. For the Cubists, too, collage reflected something similar that was central to the profound shift their painting made in the preoccupations of artists. The introduction of bits of newspaper and other time-specific ephemera made explicit the intention to incorporate time and memory into painting, not just as so much narrative, but as an actual dimension in the image, intuitively apprehended. Henri Bergson who, after Cézanne, was a key inspiration to the Cubists, wrote of memory that 'by allowing us to grasp in a single

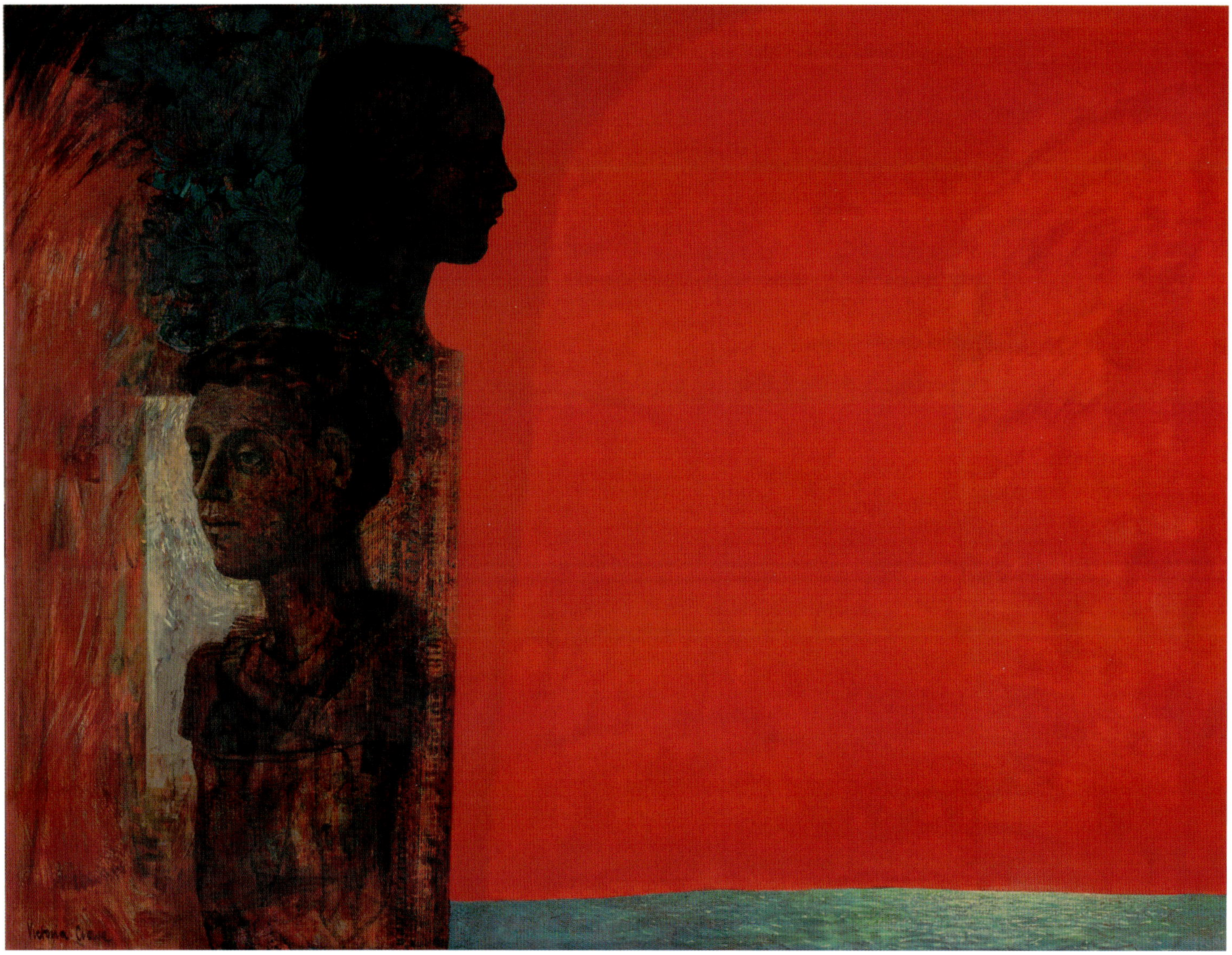

Near Rialto

intuition multiple moments of duration, it frees us from the movement of the flow of things, that is to say, from the rhythm of necessity'.[2]

Perhaps you could say that for the painter this means he or she is freed from the need to construct an apparently rational space, from trying to describe a fixed objective world, but rather to reflect the actual flux of experience. Indeed flux was a key word for Bergson and he also saw the analogy with film, which can of course work that way. Considering this aspect of her work, Victoria herself frequently cites her love of film. She was responding in her own way to this central concern of modernism, making explicit what had been implicit: through memory to make the field in her pictures extended in time, not space. Like the votives she has used so often, even though these pieces of text evidently carry stories, they keep their secrets. Like Proust's madeleine again, they may be small but they support 'the vast structure of recollection', and Proust was of course the great modernist master of time and memory.

In *Artifacts and Magical Texts* Victoria uses silkscreen, transfer prints and collage to introduce fragments of newspaper and other printed texts alongside separate images of flowers, a fragment of a picture of a statue in a niche and other things noted in her sketchbooks. The effect is like the

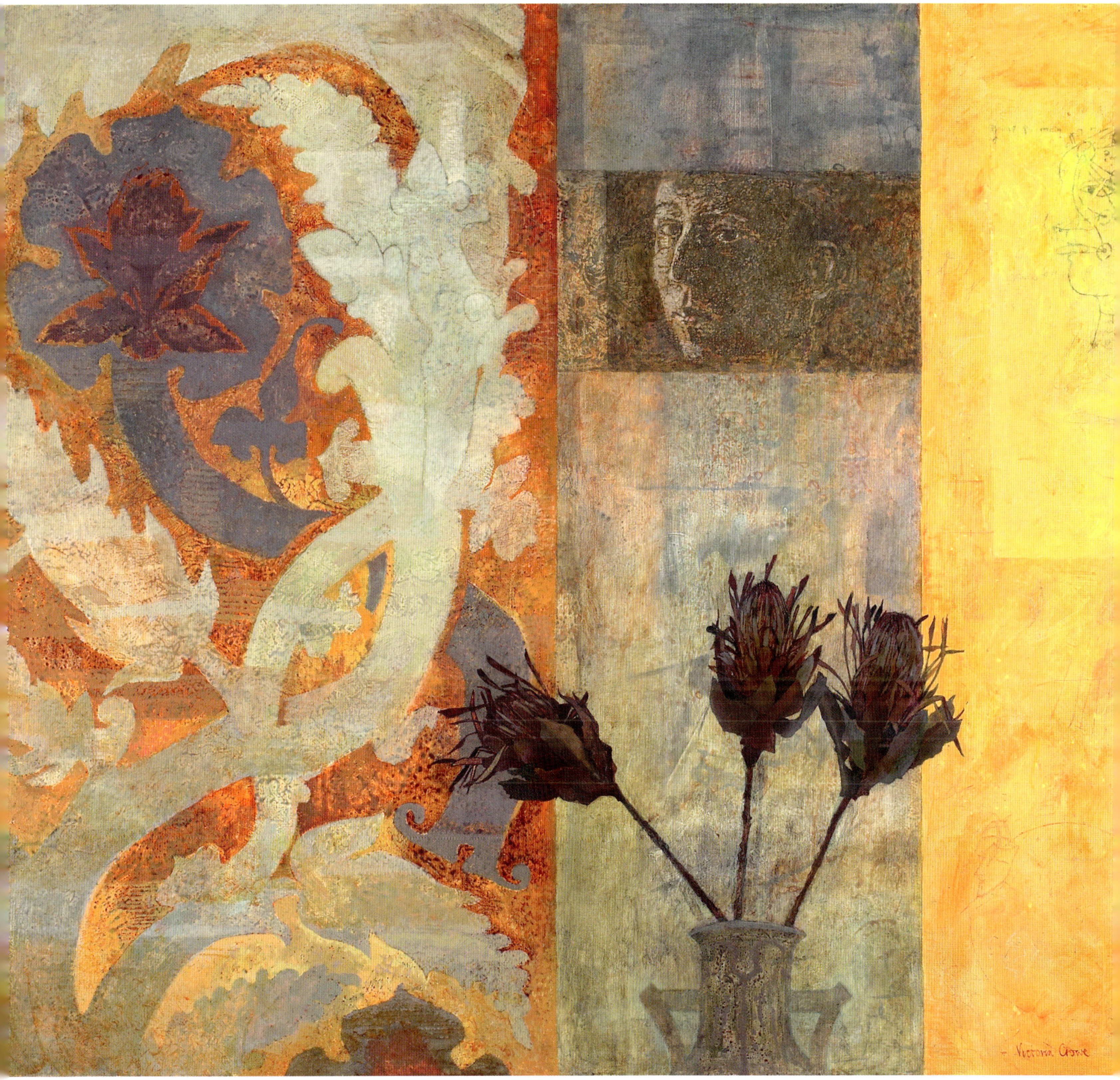

Sensual Processes

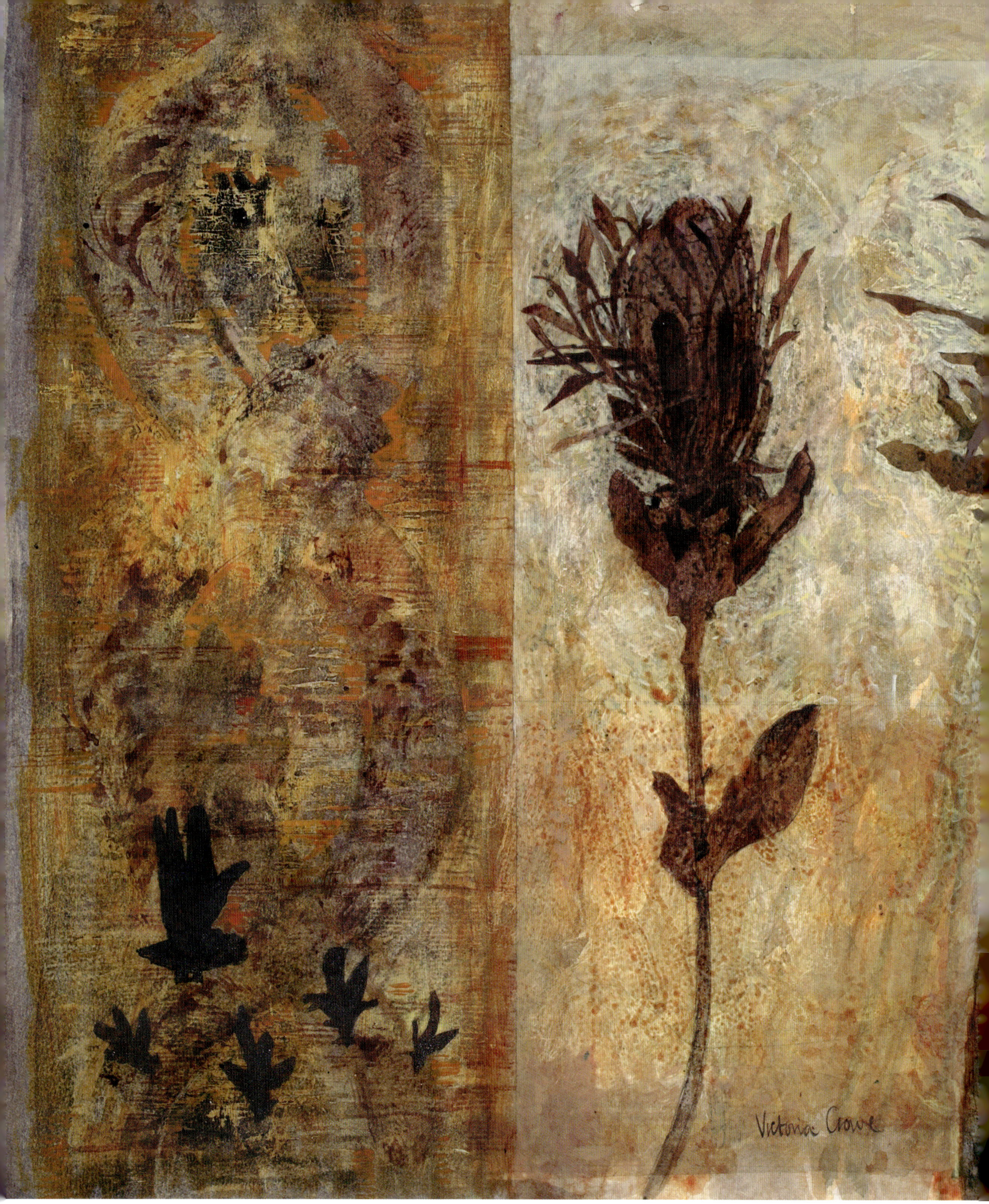
Victoria Crowe

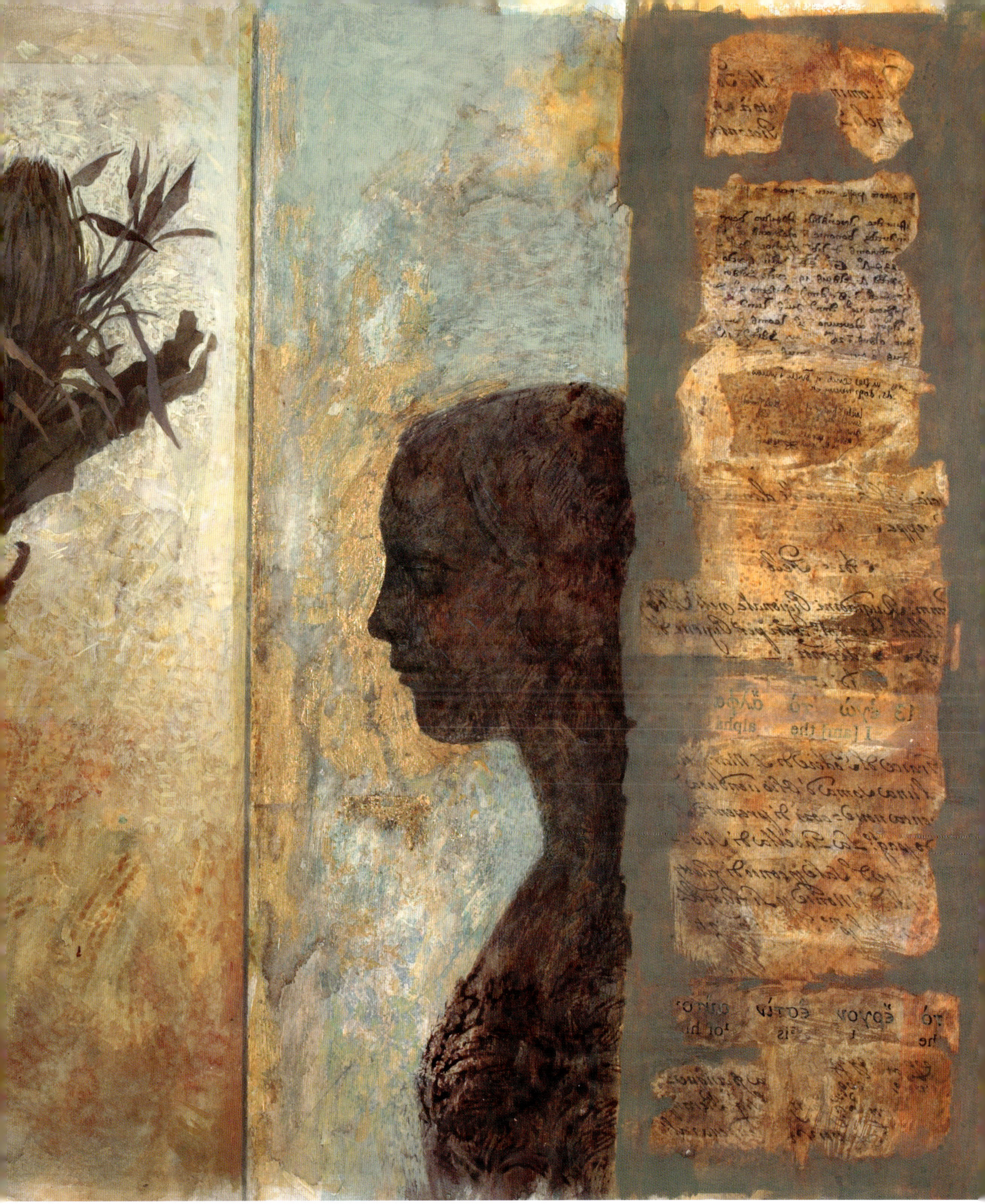

The Moment

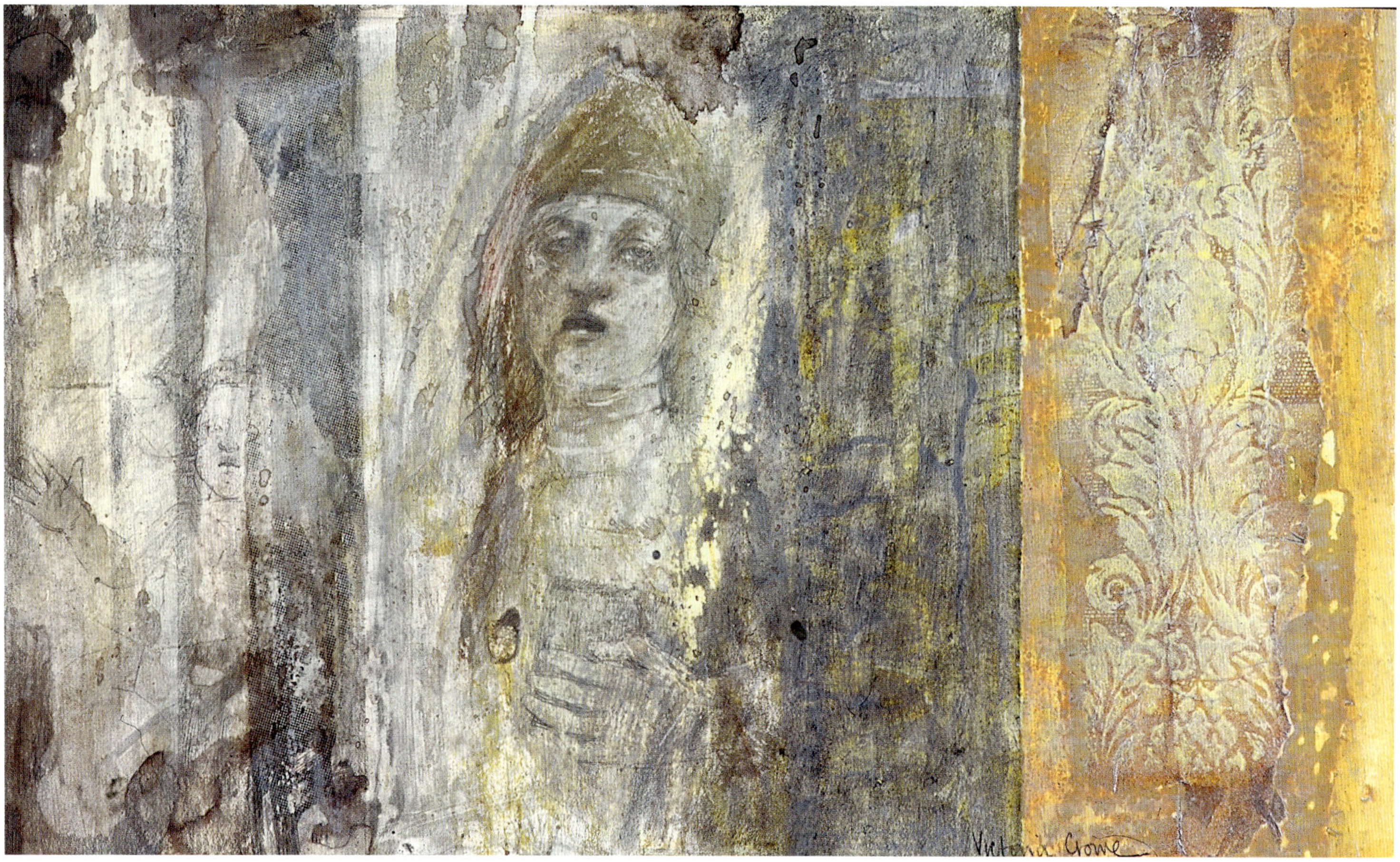

Reflected Time

pin-board that, as many artists do, she keeps in her studio with post-cards, feathers, butterflies, dried flowers, leaves and other things pinned to it in no particular order. It is in its own way a memory wall. Indeed like a pin-board, memories jostle together and seem to surface at random into our consciousness. Even so, they do inhabit a place where in some way we think of them spatially and it is that which these pictures invoke. They are a metaphor for this kind of mental space and we recognise them as such, but the use of texts that we cannot really read also raises the question of what is represented. There is much that we can share, but also there is much that remains enigmatic. Even if the artist volunteers to identify what is represented, we do not know the chain of connections that put it there. That remains inward and unseen. Like a poem, the image distills thought, but by that very process leaves much more unsaid. Our exchanges with each other, no matter how intimate, are always incomplete. Though intuition and sympathy can help fill the gaps, as they do in these pictures, there is always the enigma of otherness. When there is mystery in Victoria's art, as there often is, it is not because there is a key, but because it is missing. It simply reflects the way things are.

In the years since Victoria's first visit to Italy, the south and its imagery had entered her art and changed it decisively in many ways. She did not abandon the north however. Both north and south are brought together in *Mirror of the South*, but the south is in the major key, the north in the minor; the picture is split between the cold, blue snow-covered garden of the north to the left and the

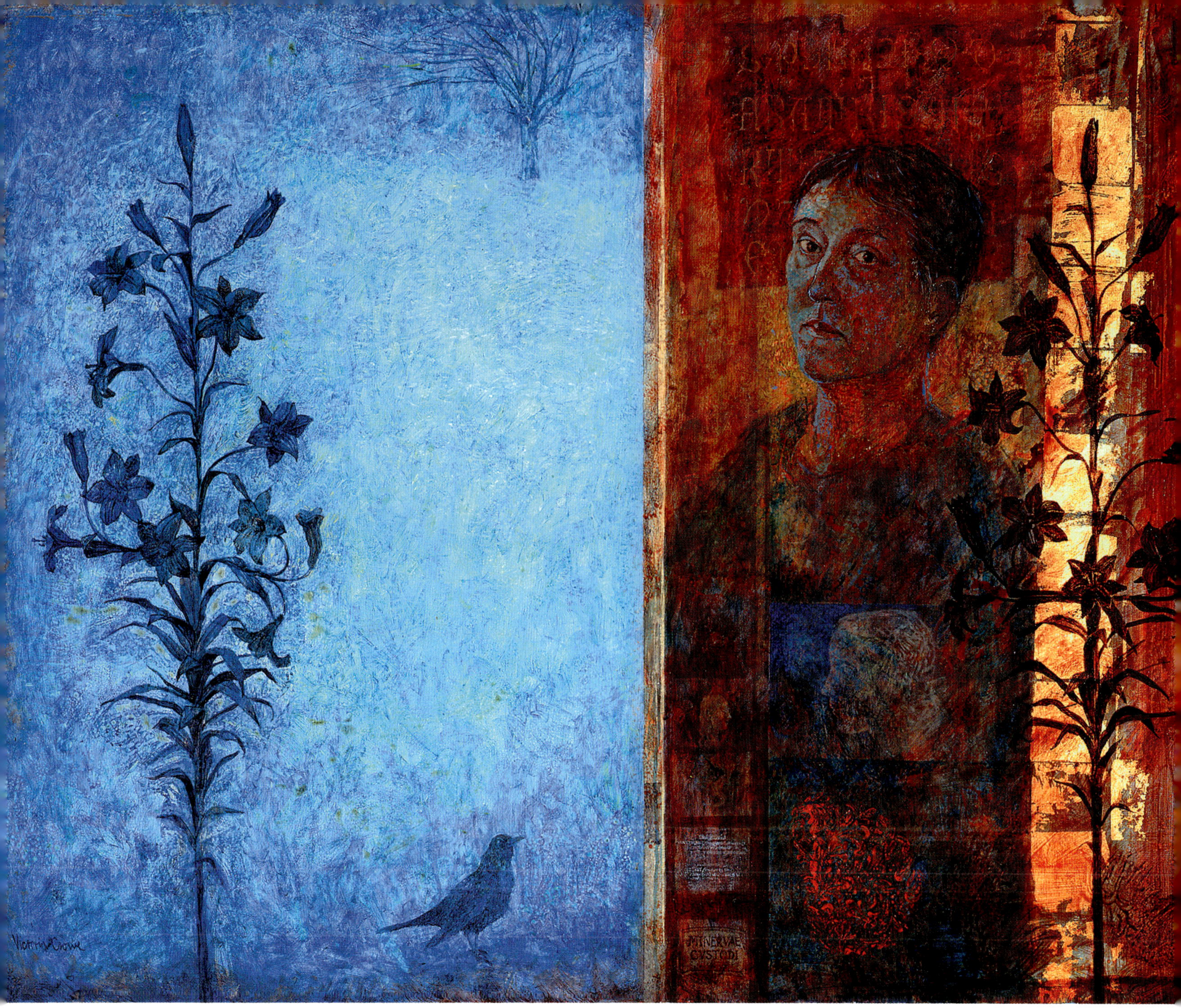

Mirror of the South

warm red and gold of the south to the right. Her self-portrait looks out from the right-hand side, too, but a tall Annunciation lily, repeated, stands in front of both parts as her experience links them. *Feeding the Birds* and *Millennium Dusk* are both pictures whose point of departure is the garden at Bank House under snow; distinctly northern scenes, in pale blue, pink and gold, they are once again in the minor key. In *Interior with Many Reflections* from 1999, however, the two are again combined. The picture represents a window at Bank House. A cat is walking across pale, moonlit snow in the garden. Beneath the moon, the spire of West Linton church is visible beyond the trees. A curtain closes the composition on the left, but as though reflected in the window, with her own self portrait to the right, the scene is framed by elements of Victoria's Italian experience.

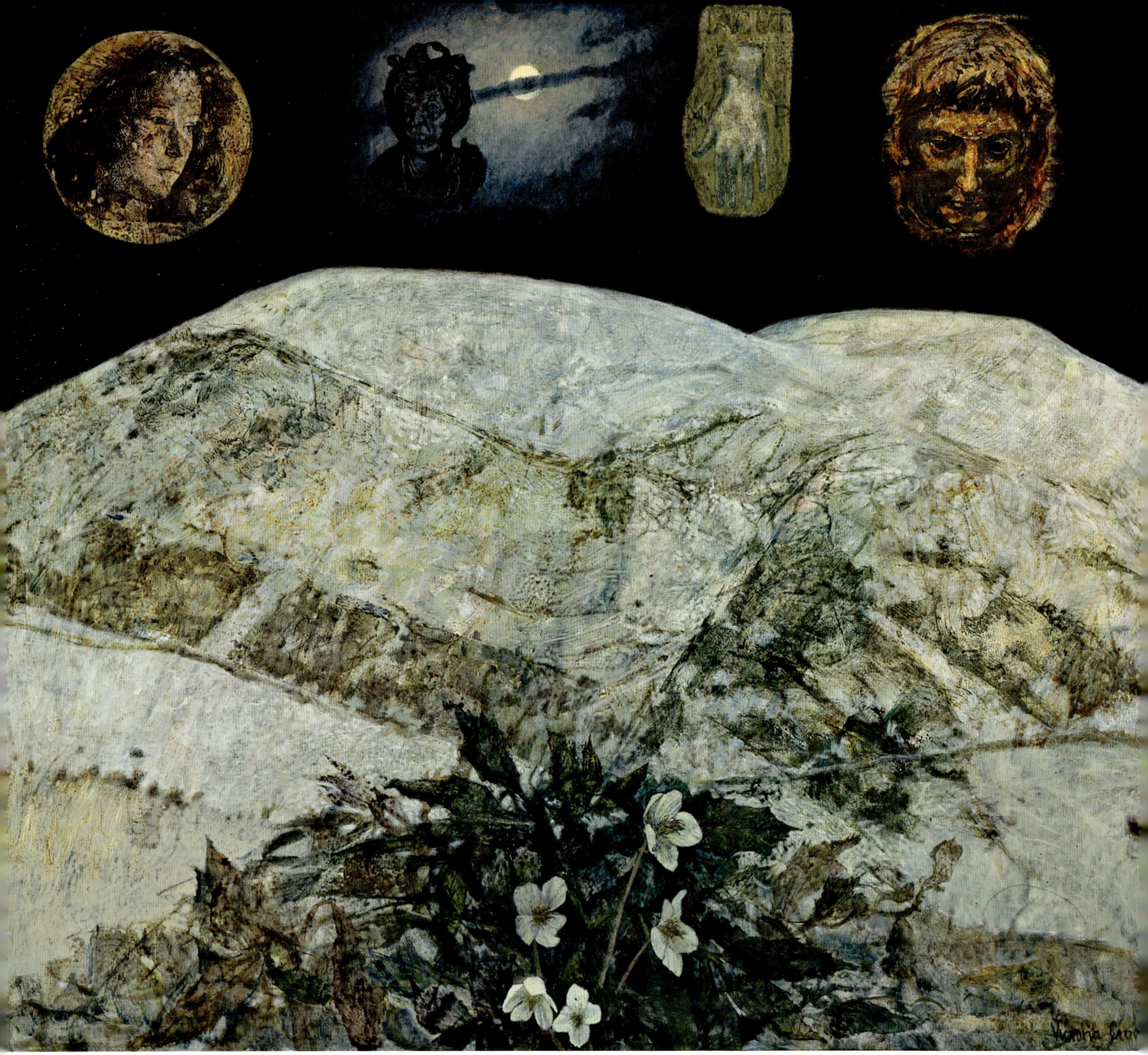

Into an Older Land

Affirming the continued importance of the northern landscape, Victoria also returned to the wild country of the Pentlands, but it was a long time since she had painted the hills themselves as directly as she did in *Into an Older Land*. Snow-covered hills glimmer in moonlight. In the foreground a Christmas rose, touched with frost, echoes their white and silvery green. The moon hangs in a dark sky above, crossed by a single line of cloud. Beside it, to the left, looking on like the spirit of Italy, Bellini's Magdalene is framed in a circle like the full moon. To the right is Ian Hamilton Finlay's golden head of an angry Apollo, the sun god, from Little Sparta, his brilliance a little dimmed, but another southern reference transported to these northern hills. Between the two hang votives, a silver hand and a woman's head.

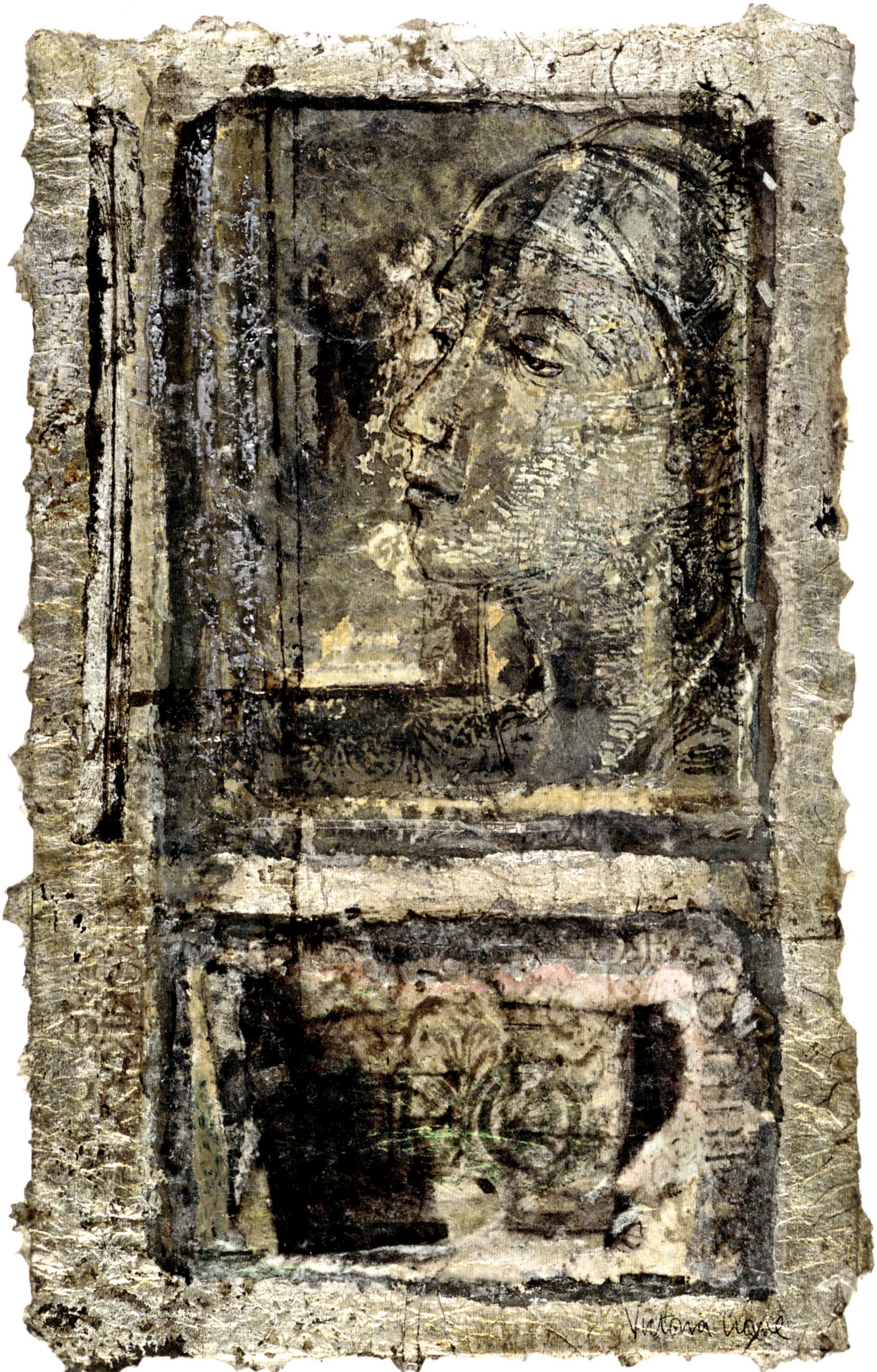

Recovered Reflection

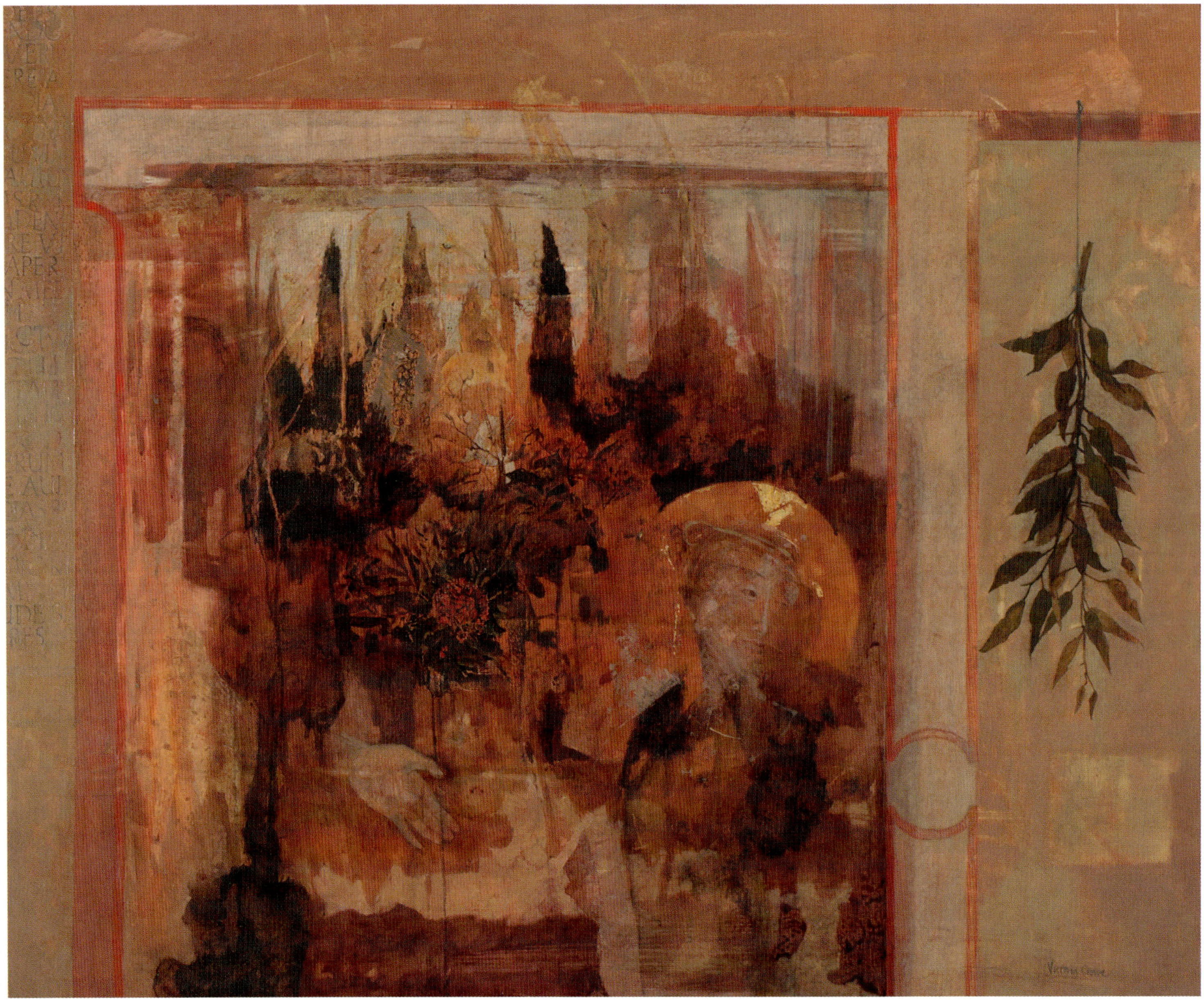

All that Remains, Padova

Victoria had made regular visits to Italy since that first occasion in 1992, but the purchase of the studio in Venice brought a deeper engagement. Living in a place is quite different from being there as a visitor. As Ruskin saw, Venice is an aesthetic statement in itself, in his view it was a moral one, too. Certainly its beauty and the extent to which the whole great city is unchanged since the moment of its glory in the Renaissance, yet is visibly so fragile, make it more than anywhere else a city of memory, a landscape of time where permanence and transience meet. The past surrounds you. The future is uncertain. It was not the views of Venice that attracted Victoria, however, or at least she did not feel able to at this stage to deal with them. It was the layered texture of the city, the physical witness of time. The peeling stucco, the graffiti, the details, still vividly present, but witnesses from another time. A statue of the *Madonna Misericordia* in a Gothic frame in the Calle del Paradiso appears in *Pink Palazzo*, for example. The artist has noted on the quick sketch that she made of it that 'it is flat right up to the picture plane'. It is indeed an extraordinary object, hardly sculpture, more like a vision hanging in the sky. Beside it in the picture is a Bellini Madonna and child which she did actually see as a peeling poster on a wall somewhere. The glorious *Madonna* in the apse of Torcello Cathedral

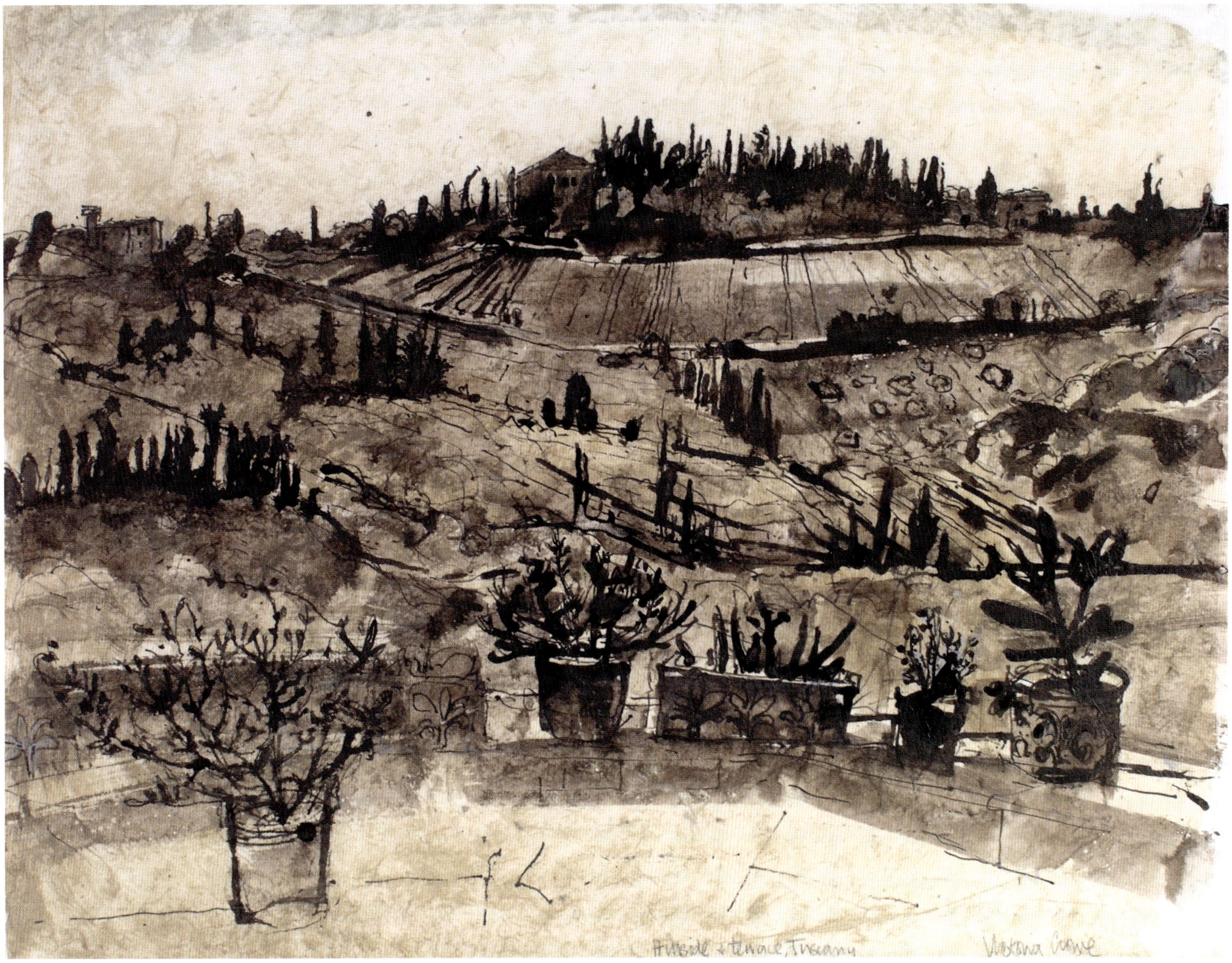

Hillside and Terrace, Tuscany

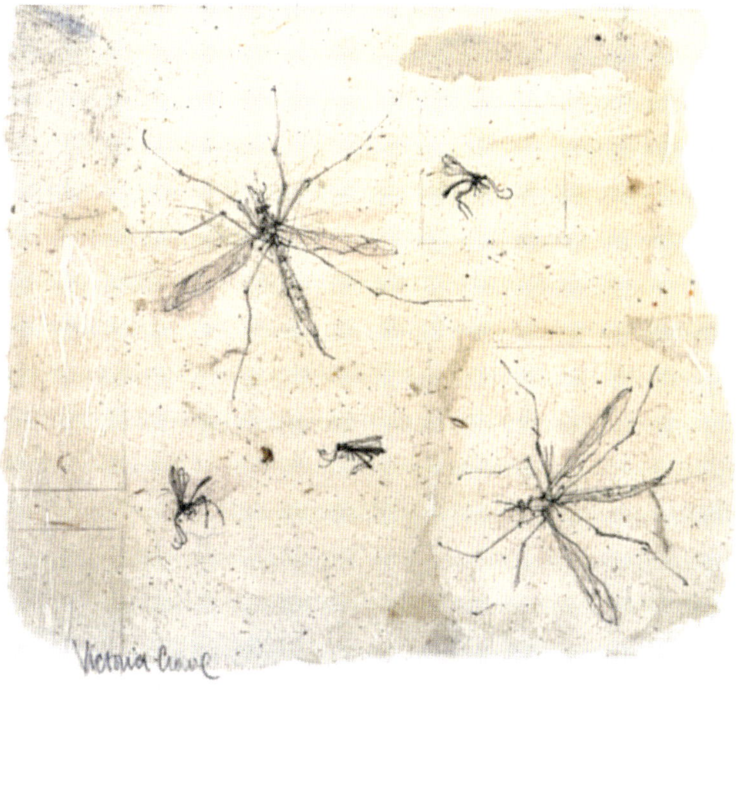

Fragile Creatures

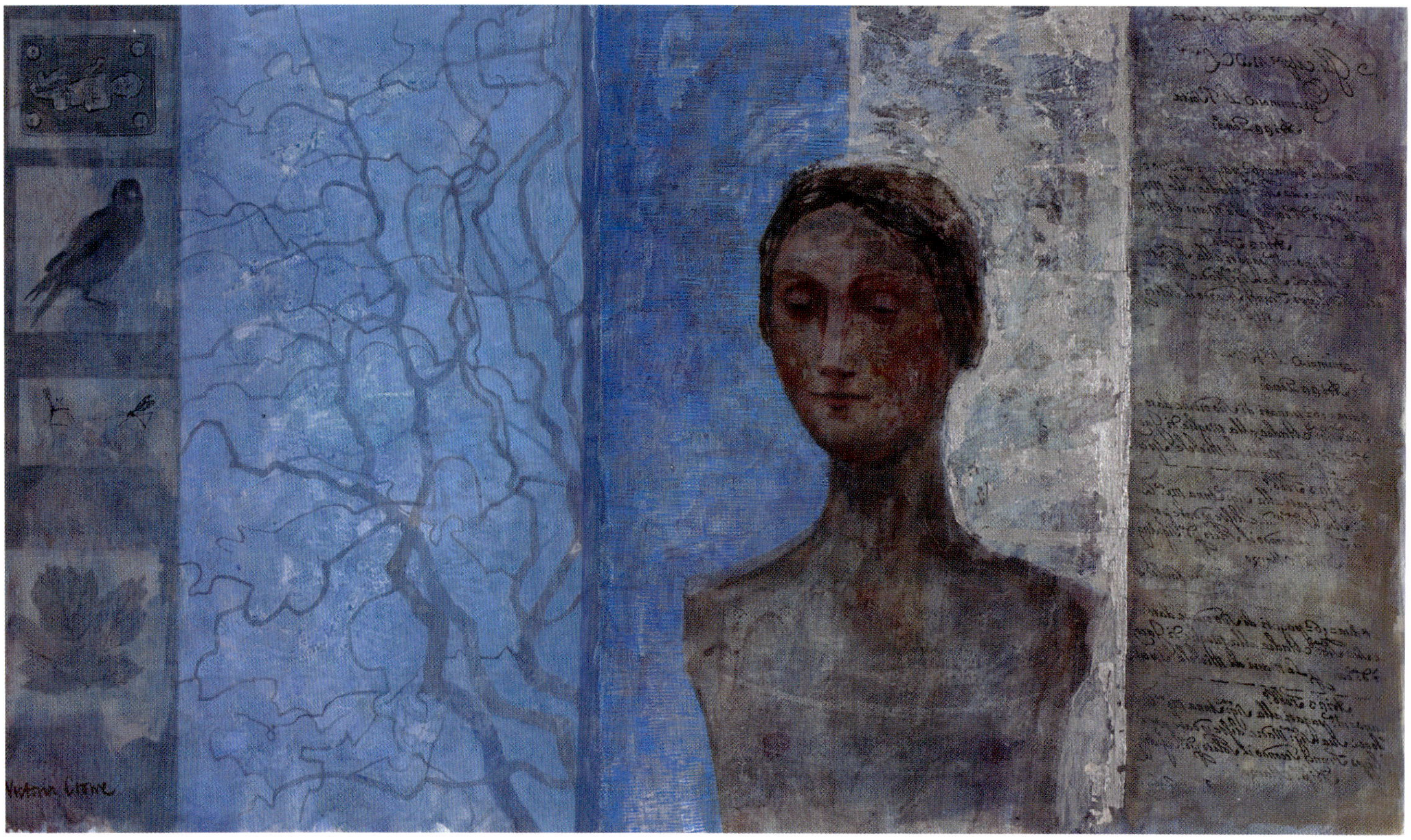

Florentine Winter

appears in *Immutable Image, Torcello*. Salome from a mosaic in the narthex of St Mark's is the dancer in *Dancer and Graffiti*. A piece of fabric from the Fortuny Museum provides a background in *Sensual Processes*. *Near Rialto* is dominated by a field of bright red with a narrow strip of green beneath. It is the fish market by the Rialto. The bright red is the colour of the tarpaulins that the merchants use, the green the water of the Grand Canal. Schematic busts of Ben and Gemma hover to the left, witnesses to the artist's thoughts and so to her presence. But if this is a picture of an actual place, as a view of Venice it is distinctly oblique and in fact actual views of the city appear hardly at all in her work at this time. In spite of its title, *Lagoon View*, for instance, is equally oblique. The map of the Lagoon is all that we see of Venice in the picture.

Antique mirrors in rococo frames are a striking feature of historic Venetian interiors. Their silver, dim with age, adds a new dimension to reflection in both its senses and they inspired some of Victoria's most beautiful responses to Venice. She wrote about them in a note on *Reflected Moment* and *Reflected Time*, two pictures which mimic their surfaces and misty depths: 'The flaking silver backing and pitted surface of mirrors capture past and present within their structure telling of another memory, suggesting another reality.'[3] In the same catalogue, she comments on how she has achieved a mirror-like surface in *Recovered Reflection*. 'This fragment of mirror-surface has been built up on hand-made paper with layers of silver leaf, wax, collage and paint. Rather than a transitory illusive reflection, it has become much more physical – an enduring object in its own right.'

Reflected Winter

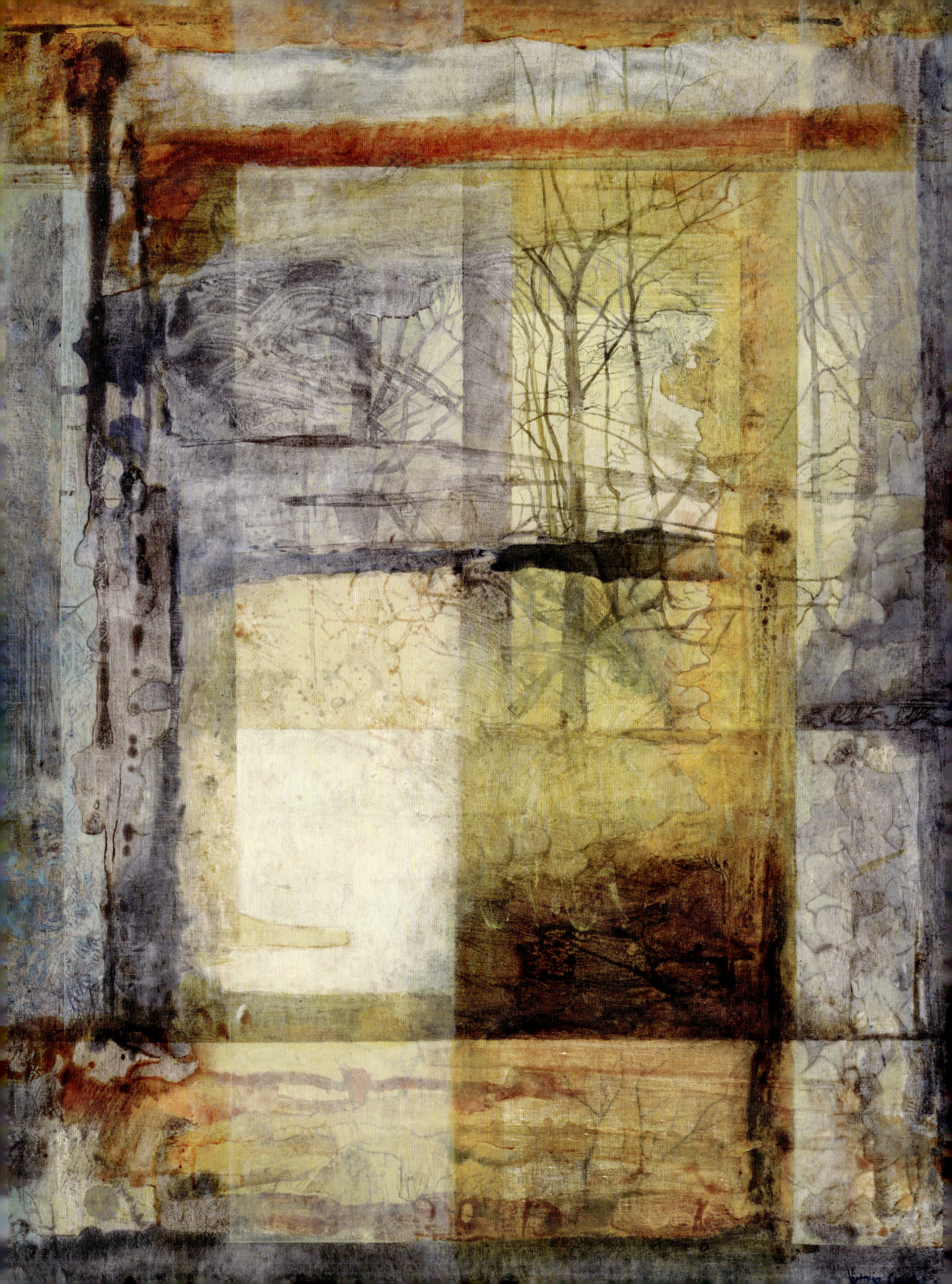

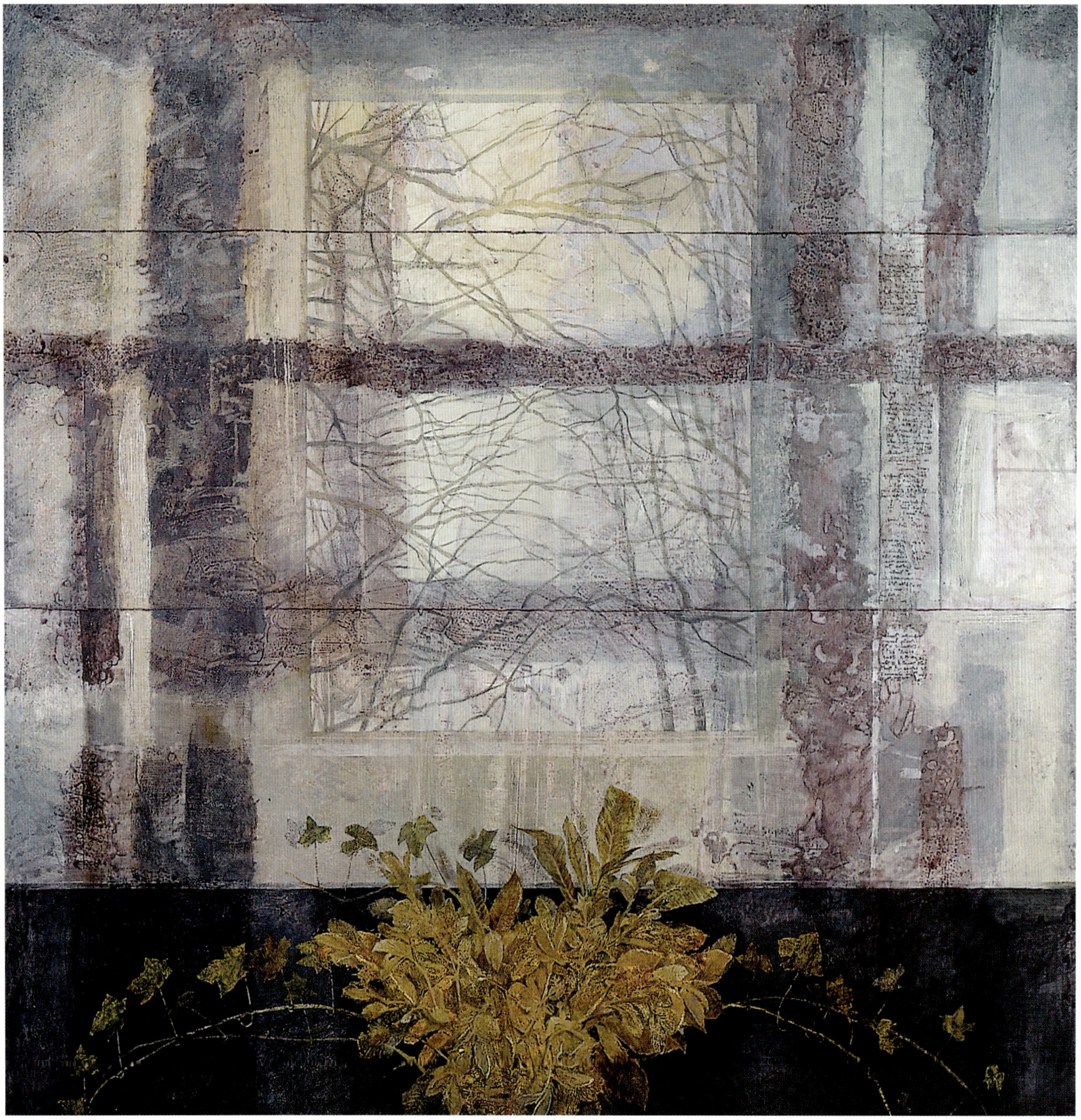

On Reflection

Venice was not exclusive, however, even when the city's mirrors were her inspiration. In both *On Reflection* and *Winter Studio*, northern trees are reflected in the faded mirror. In *Reflected, Winter* and *Landscape on the Mirror's Surface*, it is the familiar landscape of Kittleyknowe whose wind-blown beech trees appear in a mirror's foxed and ancient silver. The different panels of the mirror give different angles and so it becomes a composite image: Kittleyknowe remembered in the warmth and light of Venice where the past is a constant presence. *Florentine Reflections, Winter*, is another beautiful variation on this north-south theme. A Florentine polychrome bust of a woman is seen against a ground of silver and blue. At the right-hand edge, in mirror image, are fragments of an old account book. To the left a Kittleyknowe tree is seen in silhouette,

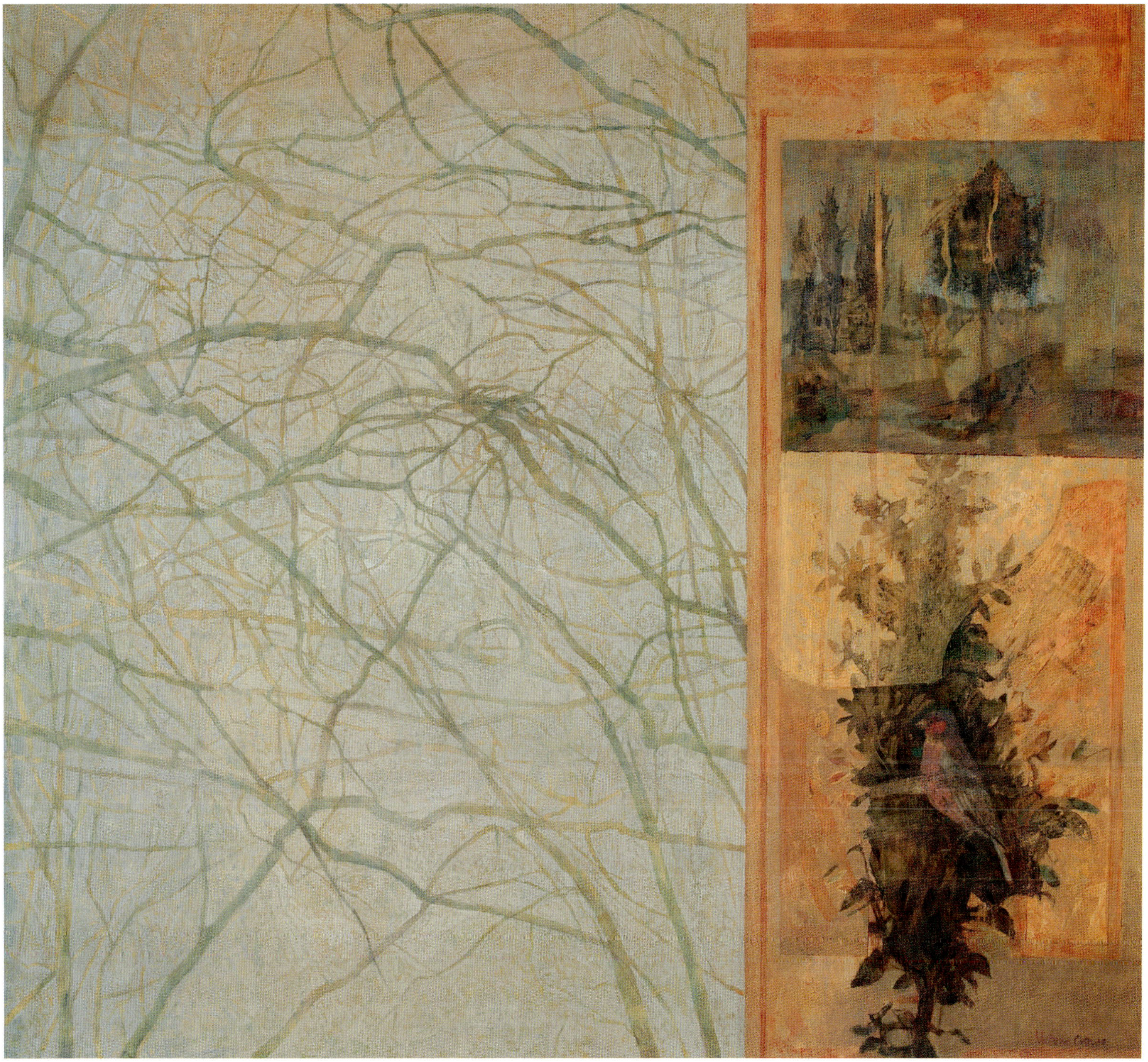

Echoed Landscape

northern blue on blue, and the composition is closed by a silver votive, a leaf, a crane fly, or perhaps a mayfly, an insect that is proverbially short-lived – in French it is an *éphémère* – and a goldfinch, the Renaissance symbol of the passion. In *Echoed Landscape*, the bare branches of a northern beech in pale, cool green are contrasted with southern cypresses, softly rendered as though in an old photograph, and a little bush with a goldfinch perched in it. *The Moment* is a similar composition with a profile of Gemma looking like a Renaissance bust, some writing and two dried protea flower heads, all against southern gold. The title is a homage to Kathleen Raine and the youthful bust of Gemma makes the picture, like the poem and indeed the poet's portrait, a soliloquy on youth and time.

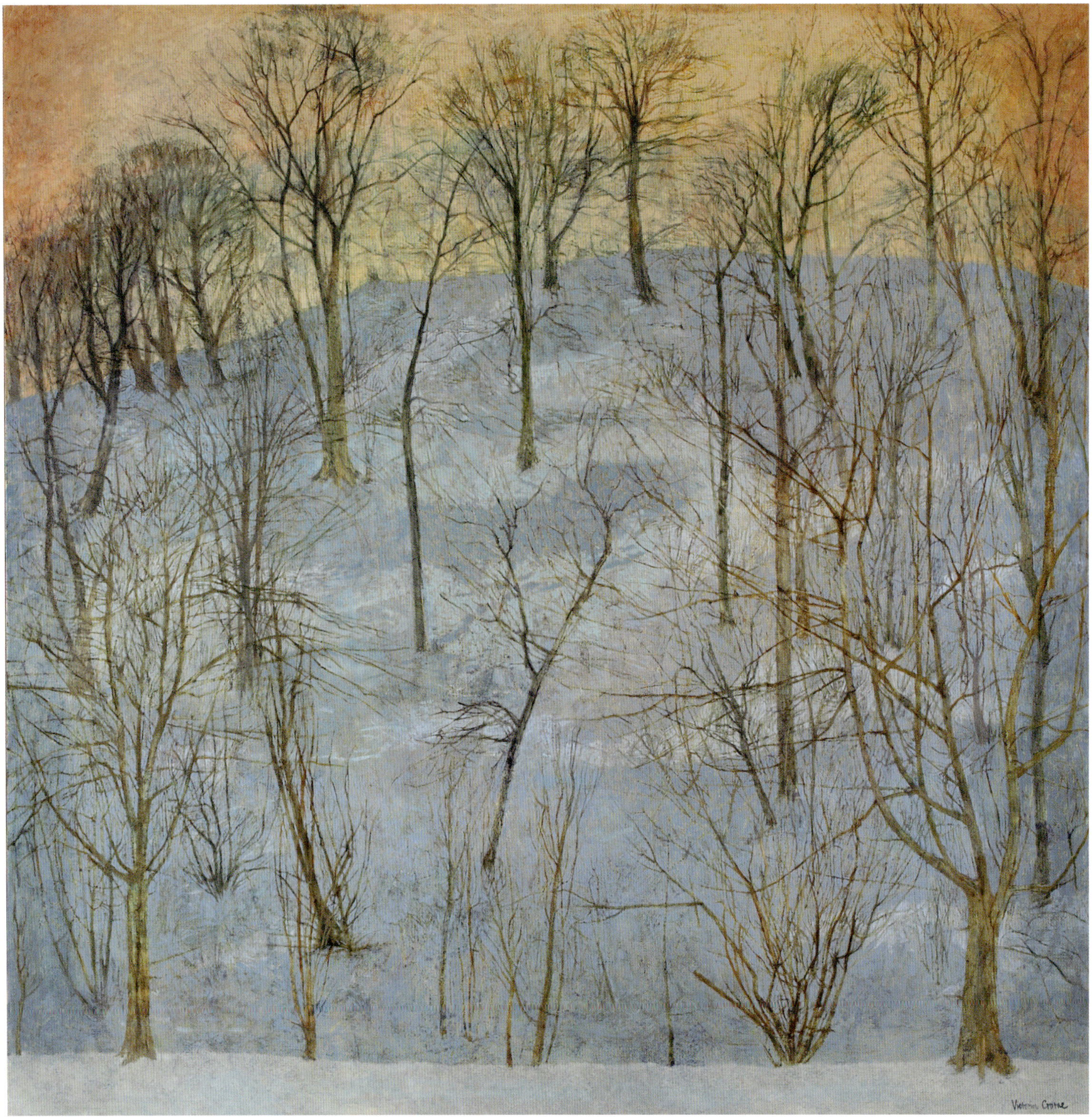

Landscape Against the Light

Landscape on the Mirror's Surface

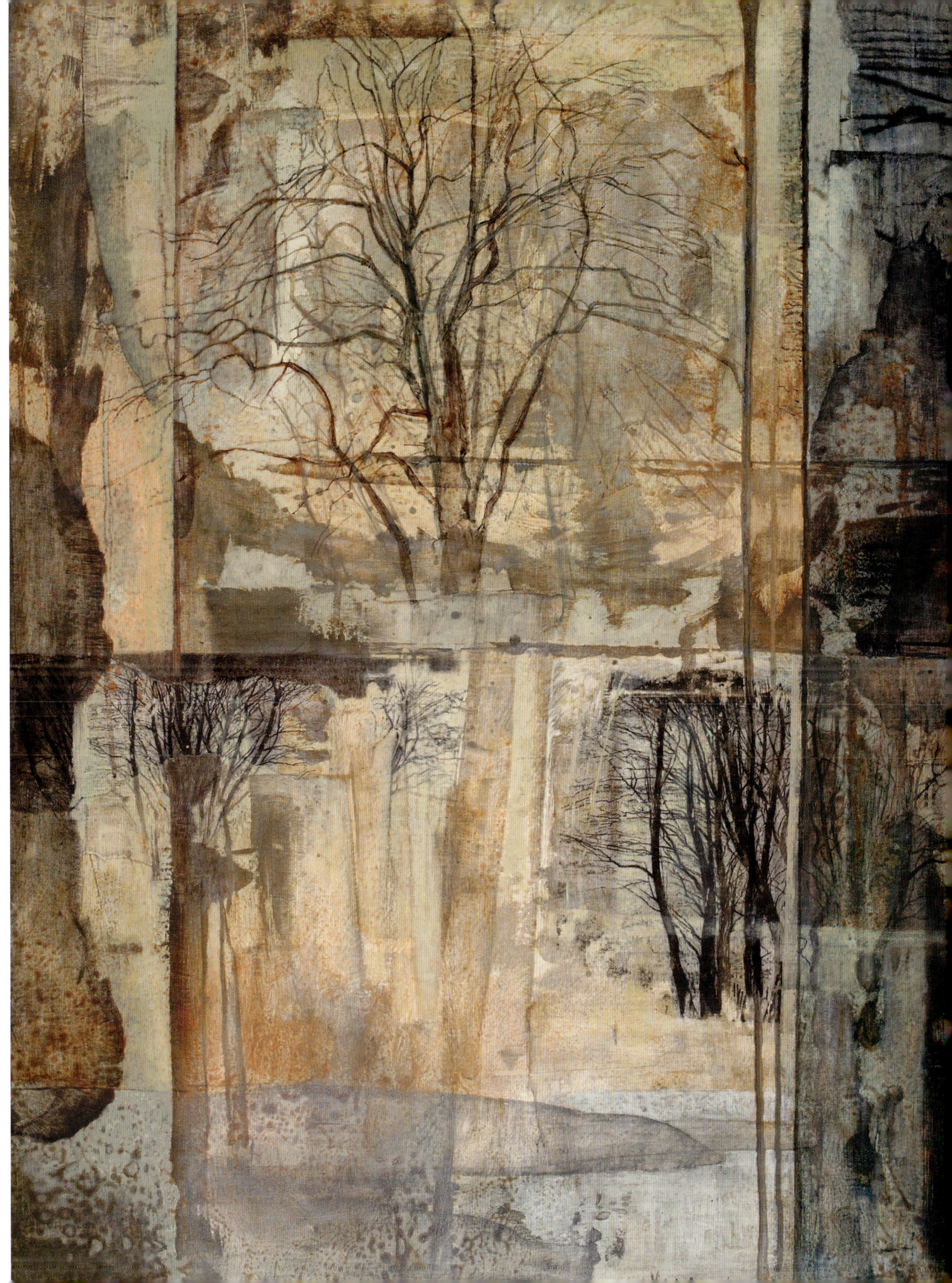

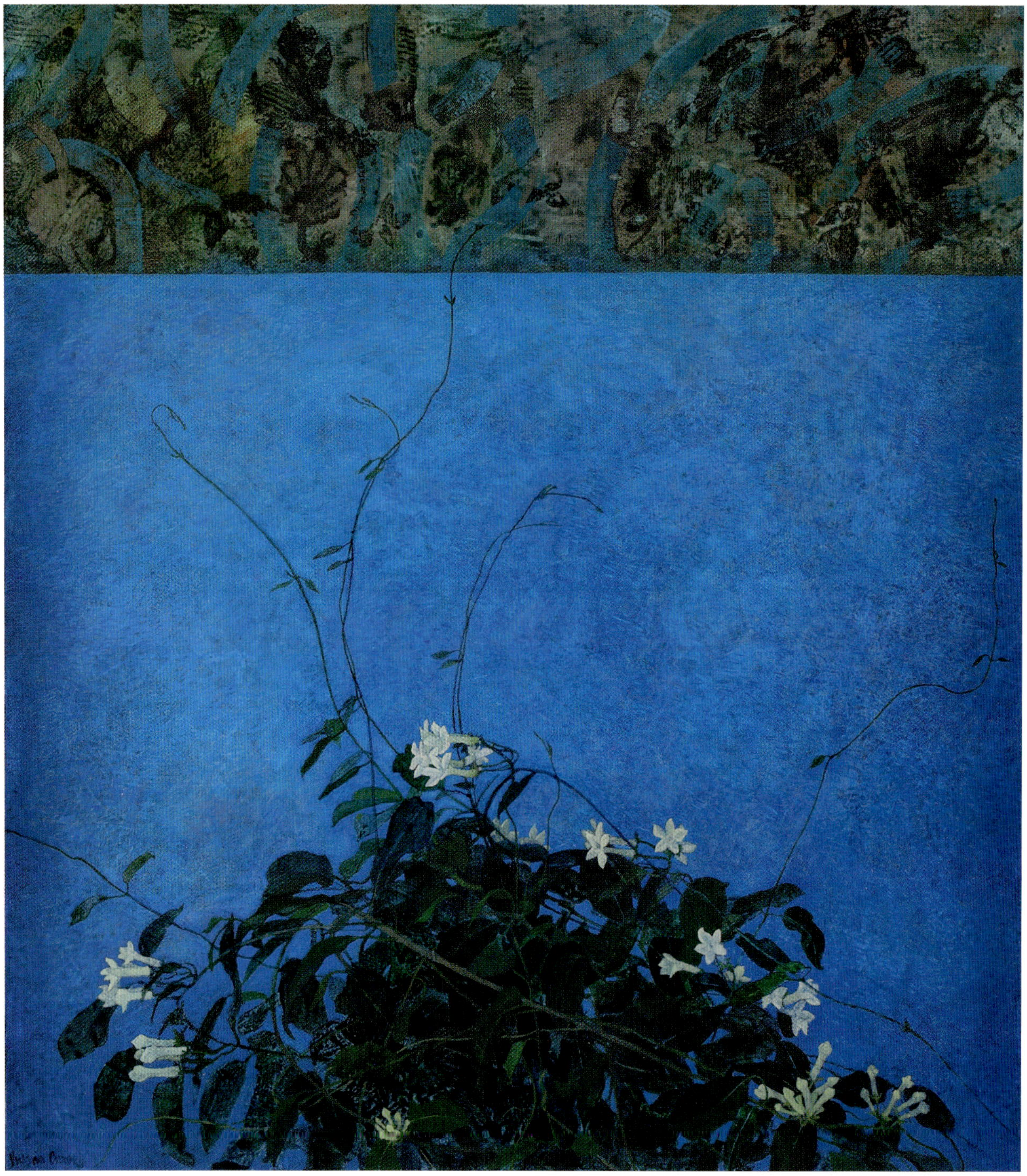

Stephanotis Ascending

Plant Memories

Flowers and plants also become increasingly prominent in Victoria's work. A lavender bush appears with the same Florentine bust in *Marriage Piece* and a moth orchid with Ben's portrait beneath the moon in *Walking the Way of Time*. She found the orchid on a skip and nursed it back to life. White stefanotis stands against deep blue in *Stephanotis Ascending*. In the magical painting, *Piazetta with Lily and Moon*, the lily is exquisitely painted against a black sky with a pale blue curtain and the moon above. Plants had certainly been part of the artist's pictorial vocabulary for some time. They are, after

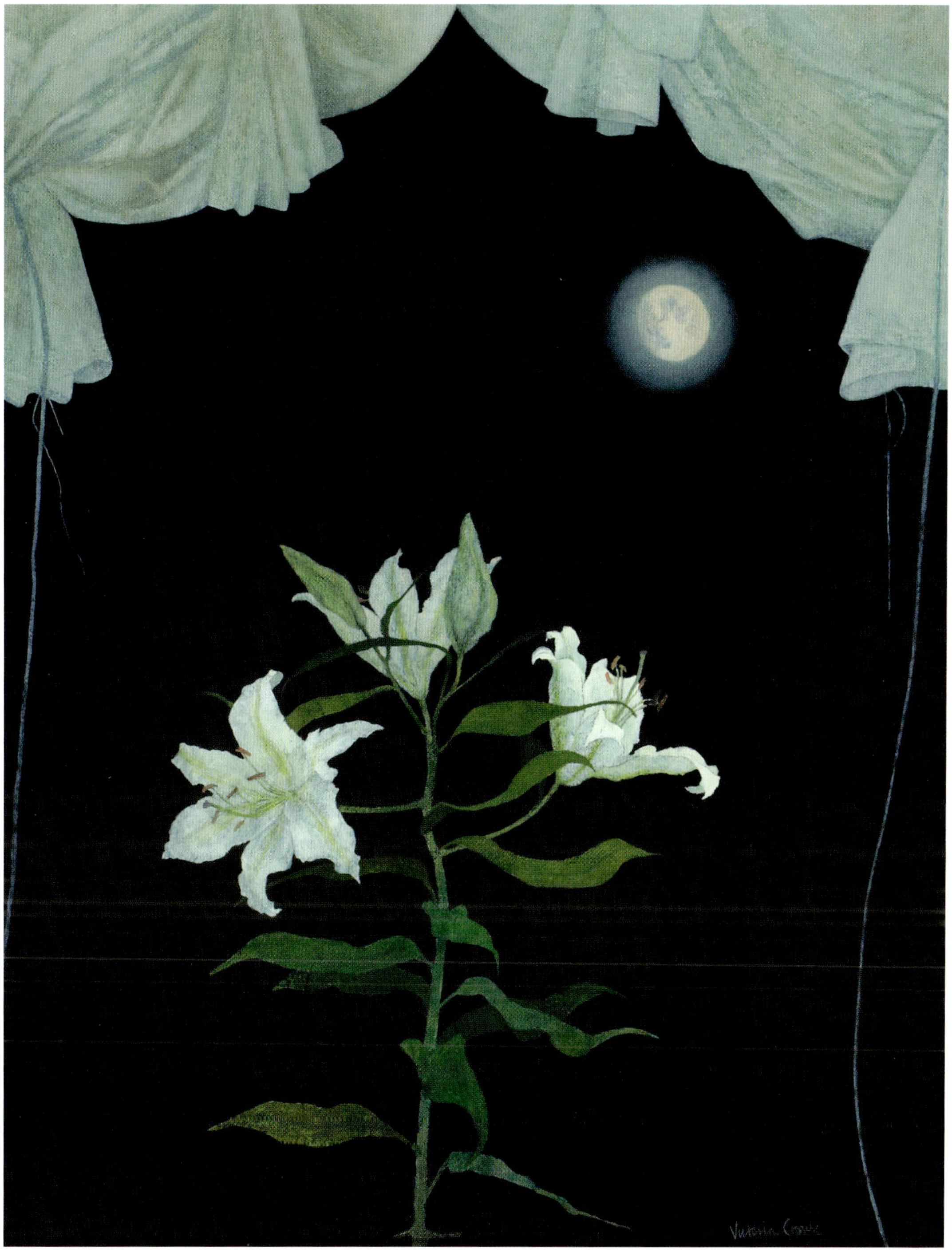

Piazetta with Lily and Moon

all, an integral part of the early Renaissance painting that she admired so much. Victoria's interest deepened, however, after meeting the distinguished botanist David Ingram. She was commissioned to paint his portrait in 2003 for St Catharine's College, Cambridge, where he was Master. He had also been Regius Keeper of the Botanical Gardens in Edinburgh from 1990 to 1998.

The sittings for the portrait became a meeting of art and science, and led to recognition by both artist and sitter that they were engaged in a common pursuit. The shared ground of art and science is perhaps most easily seen with botany where their partnership is both ancient and enduring, but in the beginning of modern empirical science, artists and scientists were indistinguishable. Both set

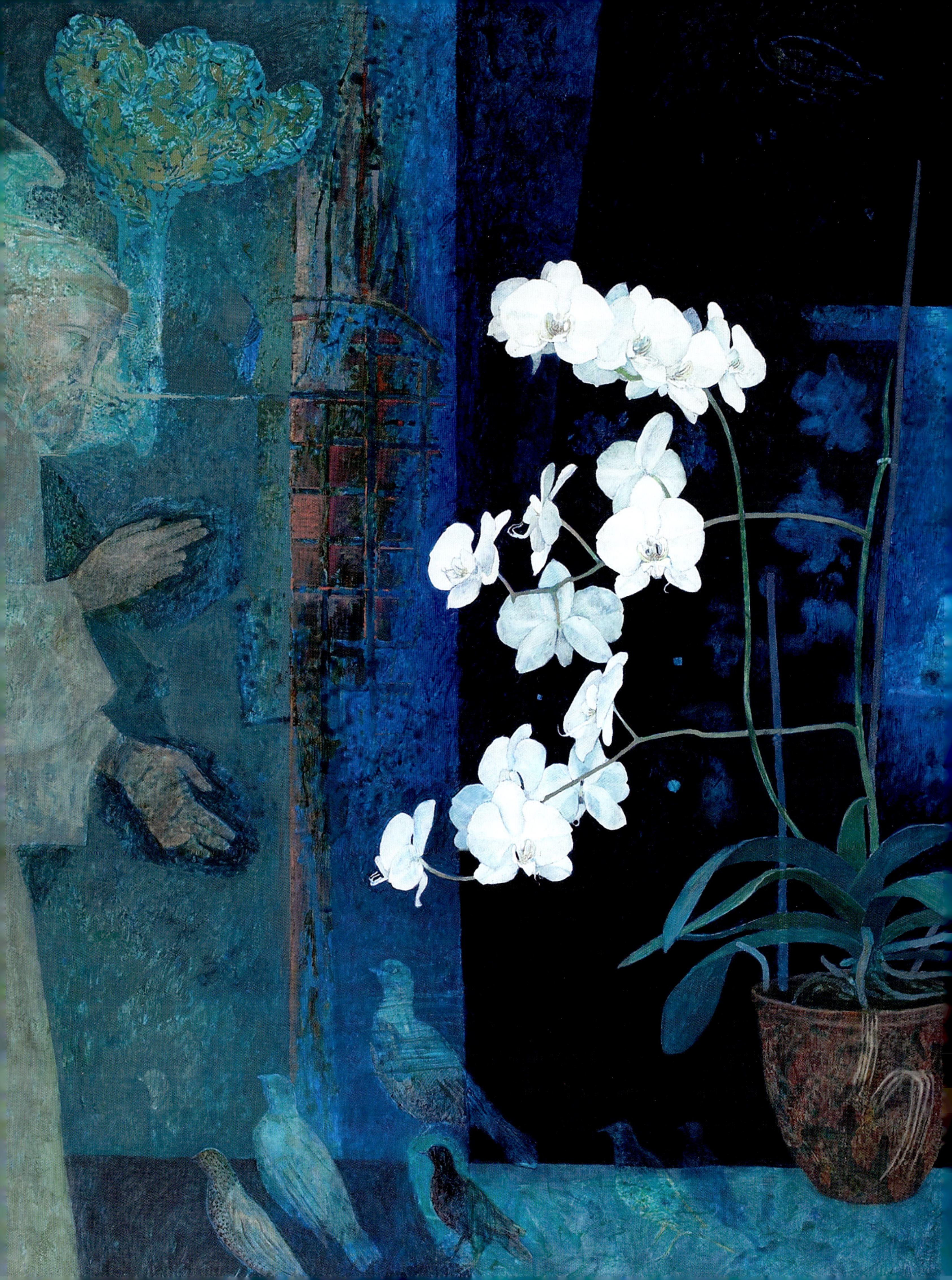

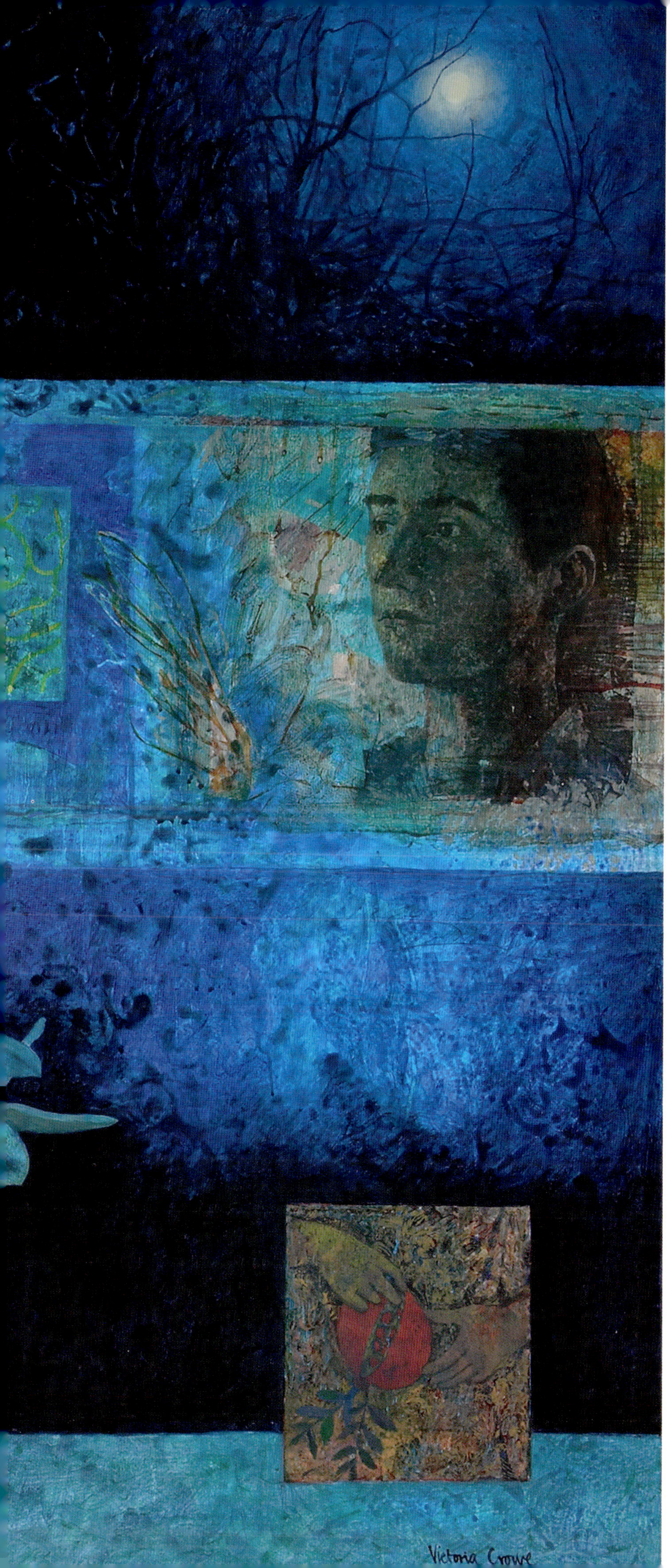

Walking the Way of Time

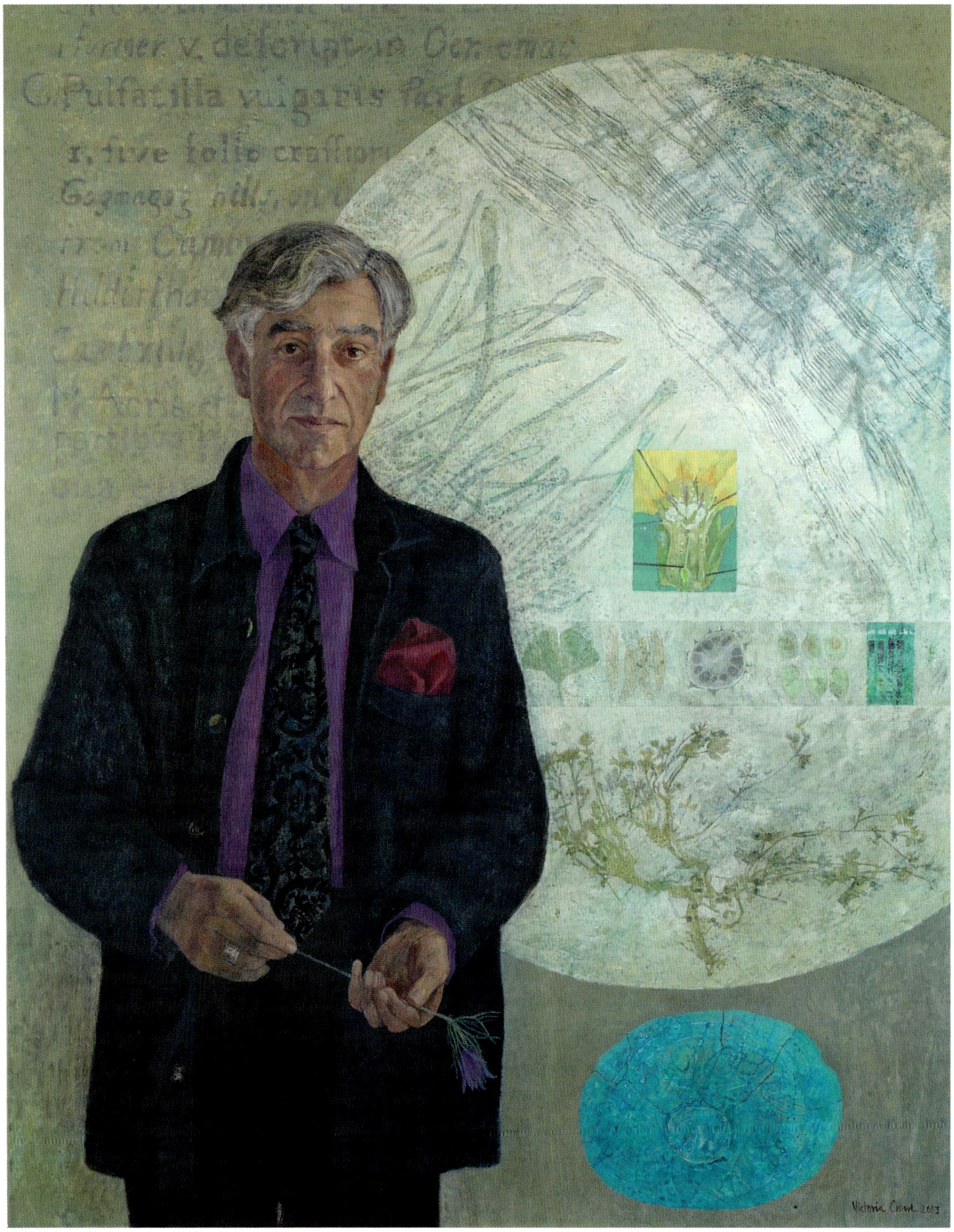

Portrait of David Ingram

out to try to understand the world by describing it. They subsequently parted company because early on artists understood that the claim to objectivity so necessary to science was ultimately untenable. Rembrandt, for instance, clearly saw that reality was not the objective 'out there'. It is the subjective 'in here'; it is the ever-moving point of individual consciousness with its dazzling halo of feelings and its comet's tail of memories, individual, collective and indeed genetic. It is this that artists had to try to describe, not some imagined, static reality. It was Hume who, after Rembrandt, first articulated this central problem of empiricism: 'how can I describe what I am part of?' or as Proust put it, 'when he, the searcher, is also the dark region through which he must search'.[1]

Recognition of this conundrum was the motor of modern art. Intuitively Victoria had engaged with it from the beginning, but as her work had moved increasingly towards a metaphor for memory, for experience extended in time, she had poetically restated it in a way that is all the more crucial when modern art has lost sight of its own origins. As a modern artist, therefore, she came to her conversations with the botanist as heir to generations of artists who had tried to deal with the question that scientists had perforce ignored. This was how she put it herself: 'We look for meaning and clarity through a glass darkly but we see only fragments and possibilities – hints of the real world which lie beyond the physical here and now.'[2]

In his portrait, Ingram is standing full face with the light behind him. His purple shirt matches the Pasque flower he is holding. The flower is described by John Ray, a previous botanist at the College, in his pioneering *Plants of England in 1670* and his description is written behind the sitter's head. Ingram himself had planted a Pasque flower in honour of his predecessor and it had flowered out of season as though to coincide with his portrait. Behind Ingram is a visual essay on botany, or rather a botanical autobiography of the sitter, including microscopic images of plant pathogens, an electron microscope image of chloroplast, the vehicle of photosynthesis and some sections of DNA, extracted in a school experiment.

Following the completion of the portrait, a visiting scholarship to St Catharine's College gave Victoria access to the Cambridge Herbarium. The result was the remarkable exhibition 'Plant Memory' held at the RSA in 2007 for which David Ingram wrote the catalogue. Outside the usual gallery shows, this exhibition was thematic and conceived as a unit. It included paintings, drawings and prints, mostly in mixed media, inspired by the history of botany from early printed books, but also in the remarkable physical form in which it is preserved in the Cambridge and other herbaria that the artist visited. These are collections of plant specimens, fragile, extraordinarily beautiful and often several hundred years old. Like Sleeping Beauty, too, because of modern DNA techniques these specimens can still contain the germ of life, memory incarnate. (Indeed in *Milan Gateway*, a picture painted a couple of years earlier, an unobtrusive length of DNA appears.) Other plants sadly are now extinct, their delicate traces in the Herbarium little more than a ghost.

In the commentary he wrote on his portrait, David Ingram attaches special importance to the inclusion of *Sibbaldia procumbens*, a plant that flourishes high in the Scottish mountains and which was named after Robert Sibbald, pioneer of Scottish science and one of the founders of the Edinburgh Botanical Gardens. The image in the painting is of a dried and pressed specimen in the Cambridge Herbarium. Ingram comments on this, and by extension all Victoria's herbarium studies, that 'the significance of this herbarium specimen ... was I believe, that she found embodied in it that same tension between timelessness and fragility which is the hallmark of her work ... and the reason for her fascination with the timeless fragile beauty of Venice.'[3] In the exhibition, the fragility and beauty of the Herbarium specimens is a constant theme, but it is layered and combined with other things in a way that extends its relevance beyond botany to life itself and the role of memory in our understanding. Memory is seen not only as a faculty of the individual, but through art and books, the herbaria themselves, and all the other ways in which we accumulate knowledge and hand it on from generation to generation, as a marvellous form of collective memory. To convey this the artist used mixed media images in which screen print, etching and transfer printing are combined with drawings, watercolour and impressions from actual plants, text and illustrations from early botanical books, folk names of plants and much else.

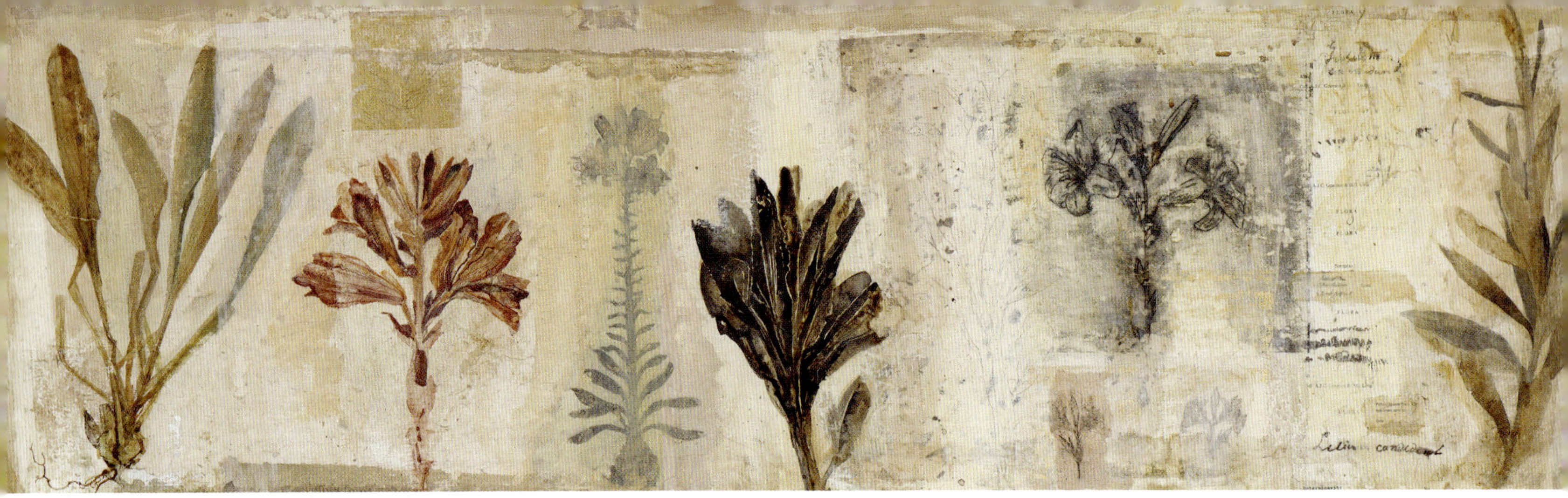

Lilium Candidum I

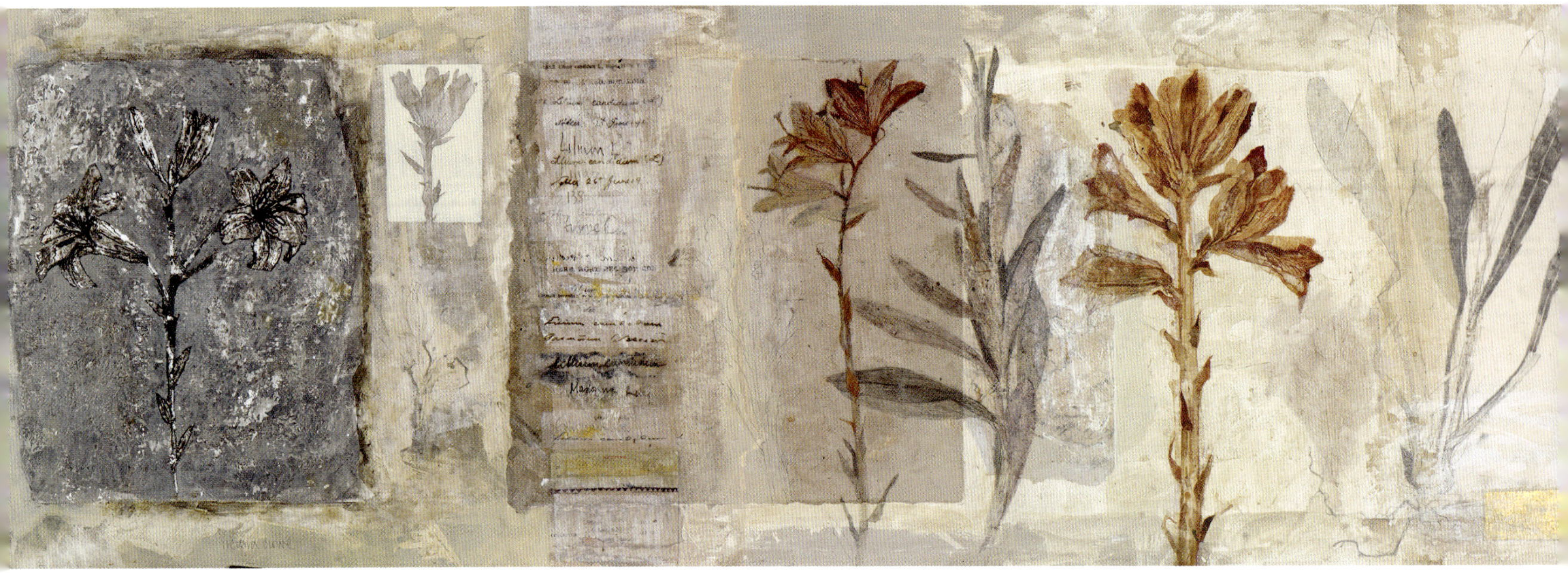

Lilium Candidum II

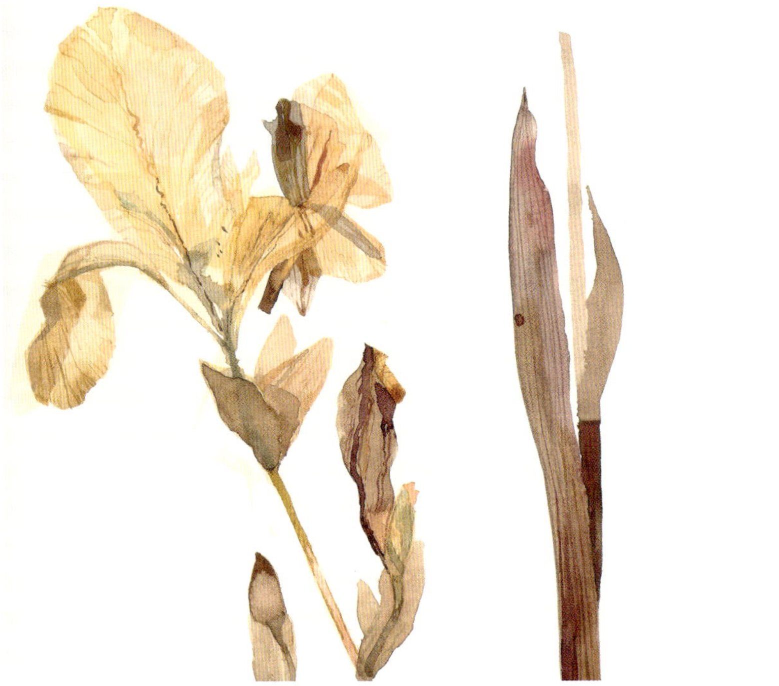

Iris Albicans (detail)

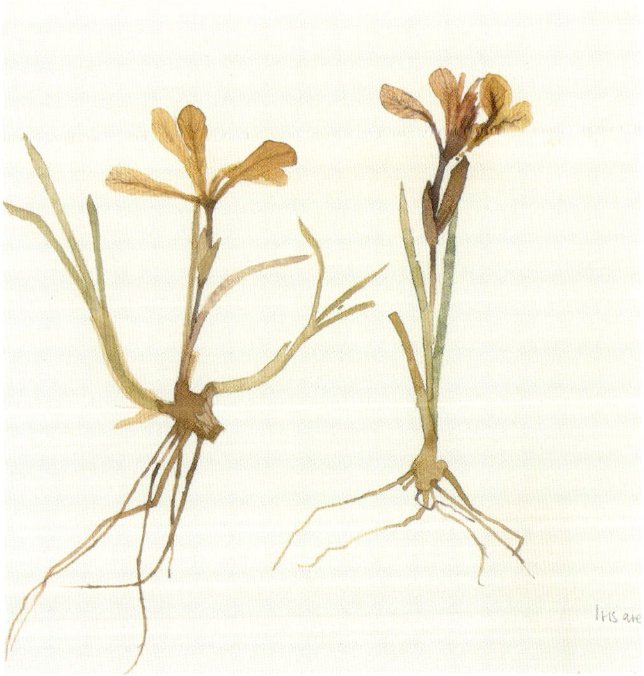

Iris Arenaria (detail)

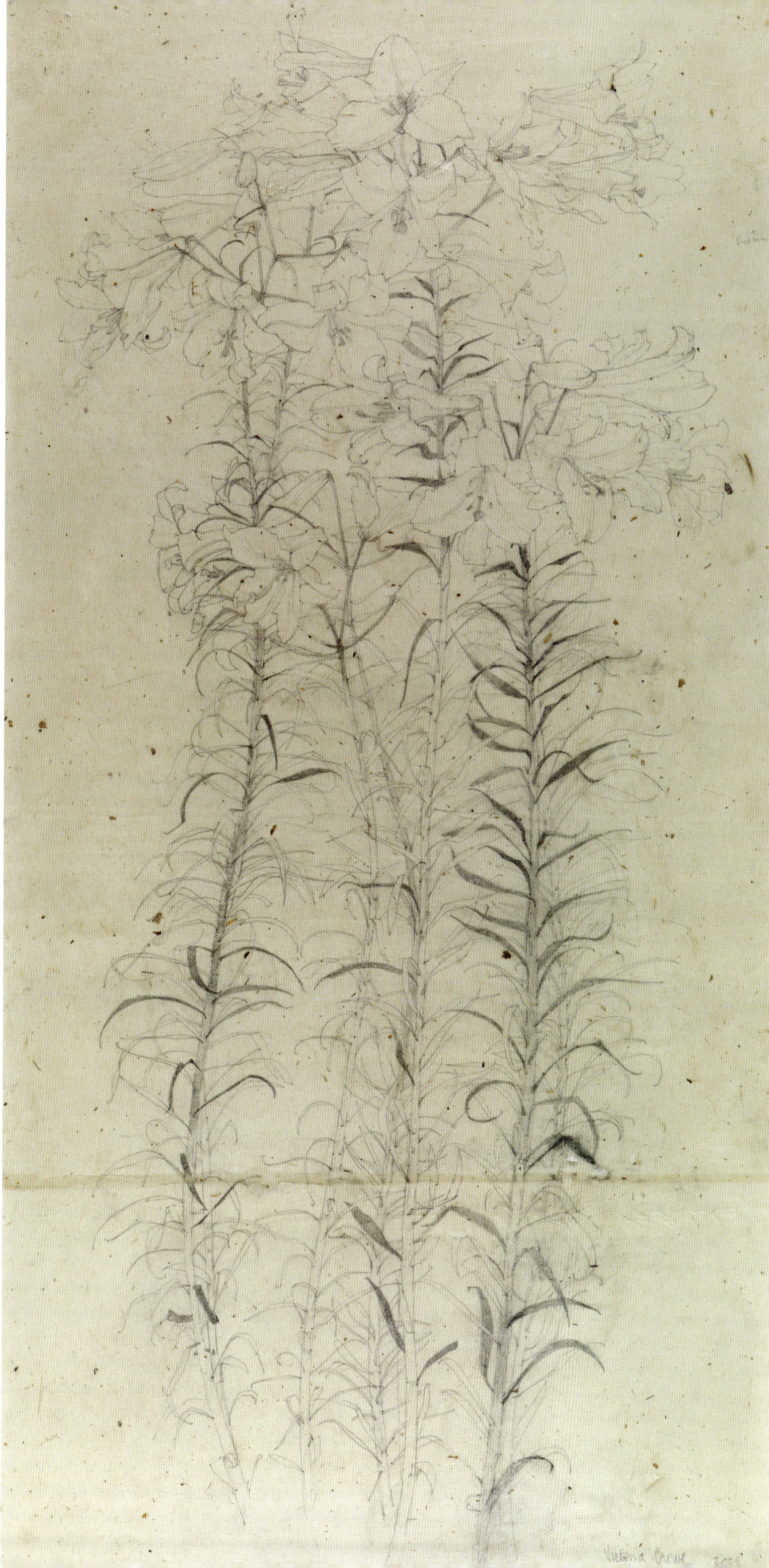

Madonna Lily

Sign and Symbol, Herbarium Pages from the exhibition is a composition that looks as though it was a collage of notes and drawings on scraps of paper. It is worth quoting her own account of the processes that she used to indicate their complexity, but thereby also the complexity of her ambition:

> "In the painting *Sign and Symbol – Herbarium Pages* I've used a collage of paper, applied linen and thickened the primer with pumice powder to split up and distress the surface, making some areas very absorbent, others very crisp. I used the iris watercolours as a basis, treating each individual image very differently – sometimes drawn, or as a thin stain on an absorbent part, scratched with gold leaf like Byzantine paintings, made into a linear pattern or silkscreen printed. Scraps of labels, descriptions, a book's frontispiece, botanical cross section are all there. They have became a kind of poetic subtext and the plants, far from 'reality' now, become ciphers or hieroglyphs."[4]

The exhibition was a whole anthology of plant history and plant lore and a selection was brought together in a beautiful artist's book. In it, Bear's Breeches, for instance, is a folk name for acanthus, so an image taken from a woodcut of a bear is joined with early descriptive text, drawings of acanthus leaves and of Corinthian capitals. Another page is simply a list in the artist's hand-writing of wonderful plant names like Jack by the Hedge and Old Man's Beard. A detail from one of the earliest maps of Venice shows how the Giudecca, where Victoria and Mike's studio now is, was once all gardens.

One starting point for 'Plant Memory' was the flowers and plants in early paintings that had appeared in the artist's work so often before, and on this occasion the *Portinari Altarpiece* by Hugo van der Goes was a particular inspiration. Orange lilies, blue and white irises, carnations and columbines stand in two vases in the foreground. Violets are scattered on the ground around them. In the altarpiece each flower has a different significance. The iris is most prominent as a symbol both of Florence, thus a compliment to the Portinari family, and of the sword of grief that was to pierce Mary's heart. The lily is her flower. Carnations are for the blood of Christ, columbines are also associated with Christ. These flowers were the starting point for many of the images in the exhibition and for a kind of botanical enquiry that evolved from them in which lilies and irises in various forms figured prominently. In the altarpiece the flowers are so beautifully described that they would qualify as scientific observation. Predating the beginning of empirical science by more than a century, they point to the common origin of art and science. Returning to Ruskin, however, their beauty which Victoria develops so eloquently is also a function of the reverence and awe, the feeling in fact, that the artist has brought to the description and not merely of the description itself. It was fitting that two of Victoria's studies of irises should have been included in 'Ruskin's Flora', an exhibition of Ruskin's own plant studies at the Ruskin Library organised by David Ingram in 2011.

As its title declares, 'Plant Memory' was a rich and complex essay in memory and so calls Proust to mind once again, or indeed Proust's cousin, Henri Bergson, who wrote in *Matter and Memory*: 'The truth is that memory does not consist in a regression from the present to the past, but, on the contrary, in a progress from the past to the present',[5] which is indeed what the exhibition presented. That said, it is also striking that Proust held Ruskin in deep reverence, indeed he translated *Praeterita*, Ruskin's own essay in memory. Proust, Bergson and Ruskin, or indeed Hume and Archibald Alison, may seem at first to have little bearing upon art in the twenty-first century, but citing them here points to the link between them and Victoria's art, not with something nostalgic and backward-looking as it might seem, but with the vital alternative tradition in modern art.

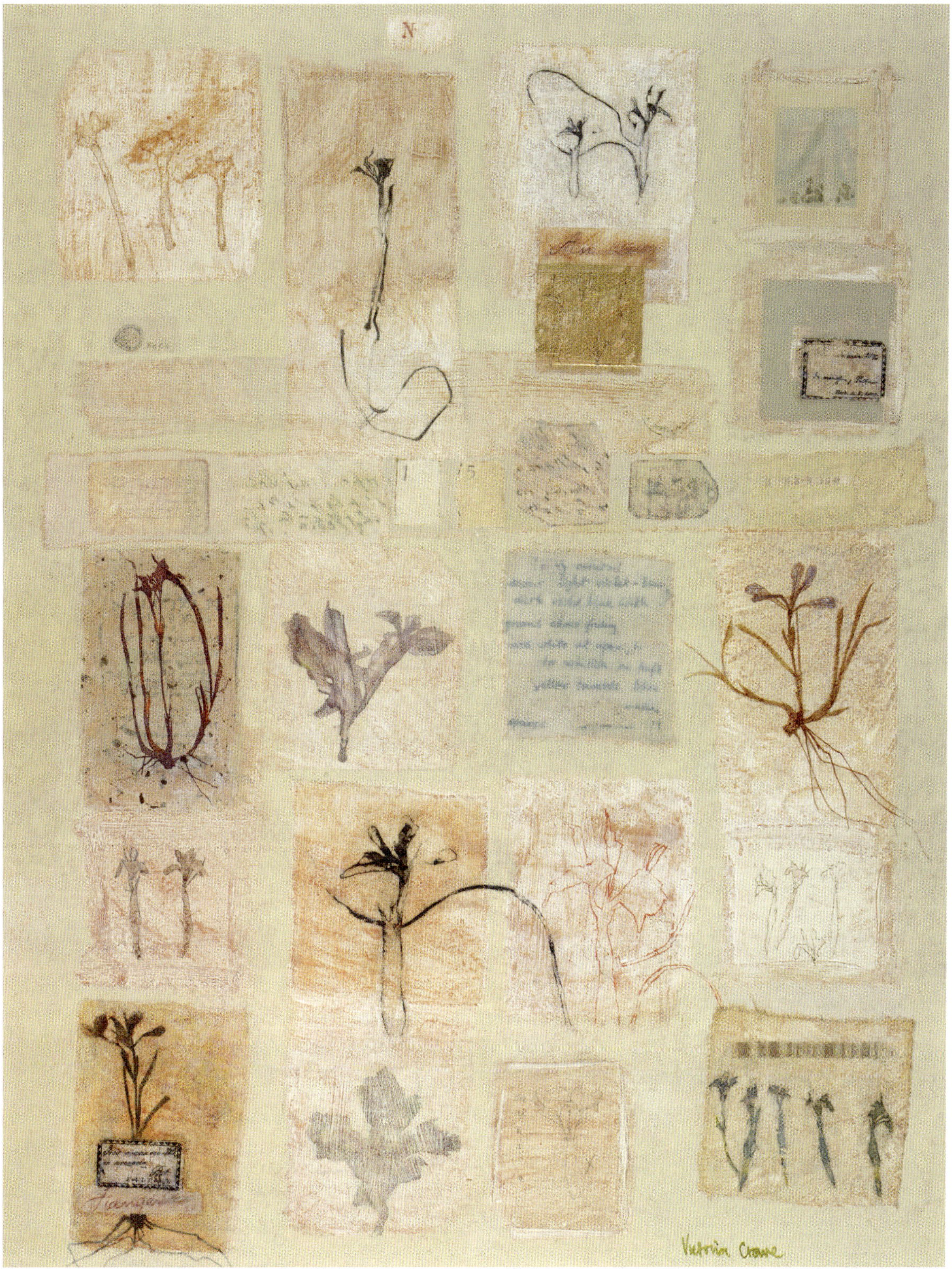

Sign and Symbol – Herbarium Pages

The dominant contemporary tradition follows Nietszche: art is the supreme expression of the individual will. That is why, for most contemporary artists, Duchamp is a hero: he reduced art to a simple act of will. The alternative and much longer tradition reflects the very different idea that the function of art is to lead us in the search for understanding of the nature of experience, however difficult that search may prove to be, or into whatever dark regions it may lead. André Breton's *First Surrealist Manifesto* formulated this for his time. So, too, did much of the teaching of the

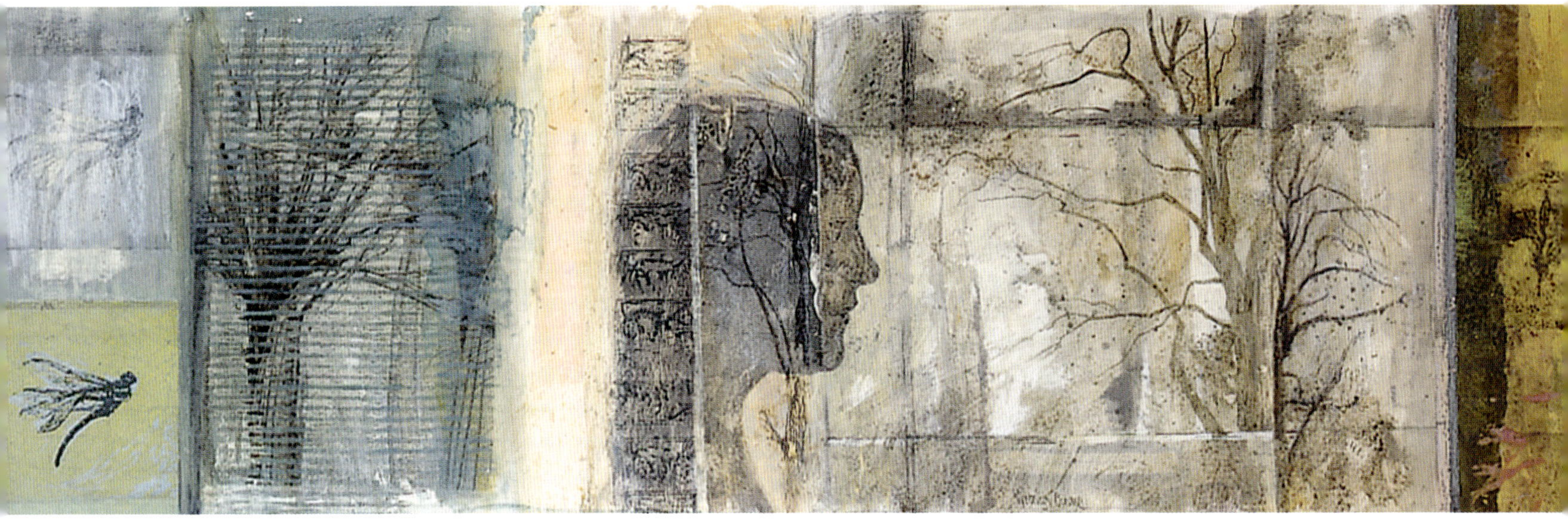

Reflected Sequence

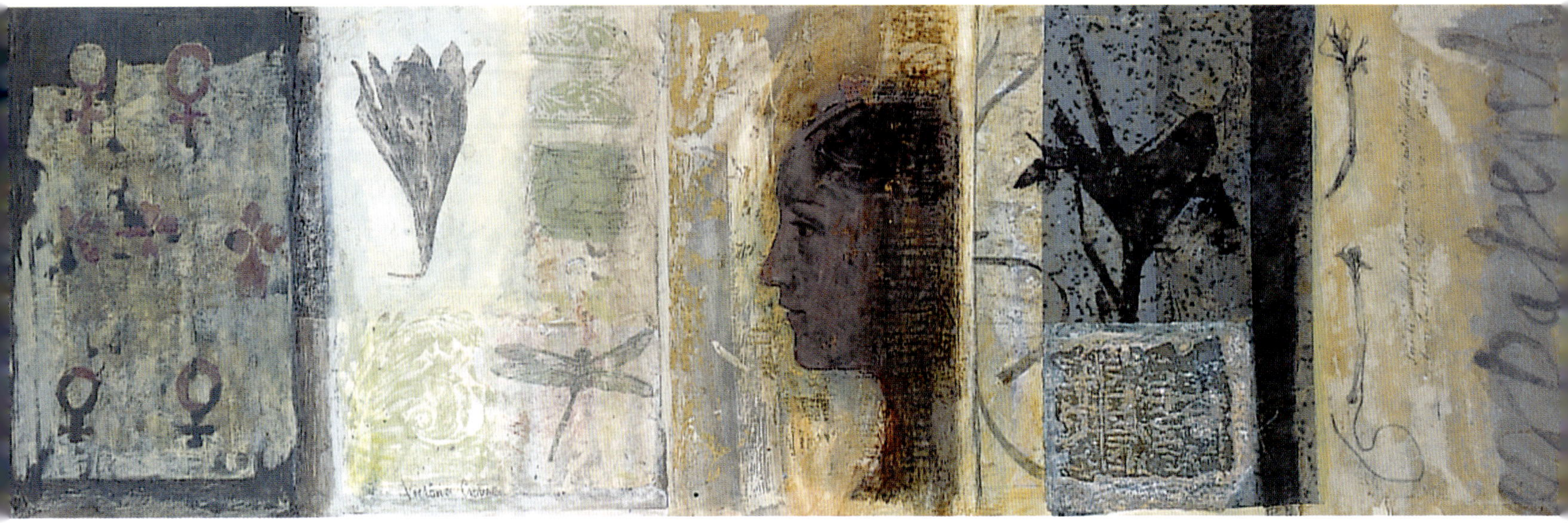

Observed Sequence

Bauhaus, heir in so many ways to the Arts and Crafts Movement, shaped in turn by Ruskin. Paul Klee and Wassily Kandinsky were the greatest artists associated with the Bauhaus. Among the Surrealists it was perhaps Miró who most closely reflected these ideas. The work of Eduardo Paolozzi, Alan Davie and Ian Hamilton Finlay, for all their differences, also belongs here. Victoria's work certainly resembles none of these. Nevertheless they were all artists, as she is, for whom the imagination, whether its manifestations are to be sought in the conscious or the subconscious mind, is the only field for art. It follows that the concern of art is not to assert the distinctiveness of the individual ego; on the contrary, it is the things we share and that bind us together. This tradition looks back through Ruskin to Hume and the philosophy of moral sense, and so to the role of the imagination in our struggle to understand the world, not only objectively, but in the moral and spiritual dimensions to which any objective inquiry must inevitably lead.

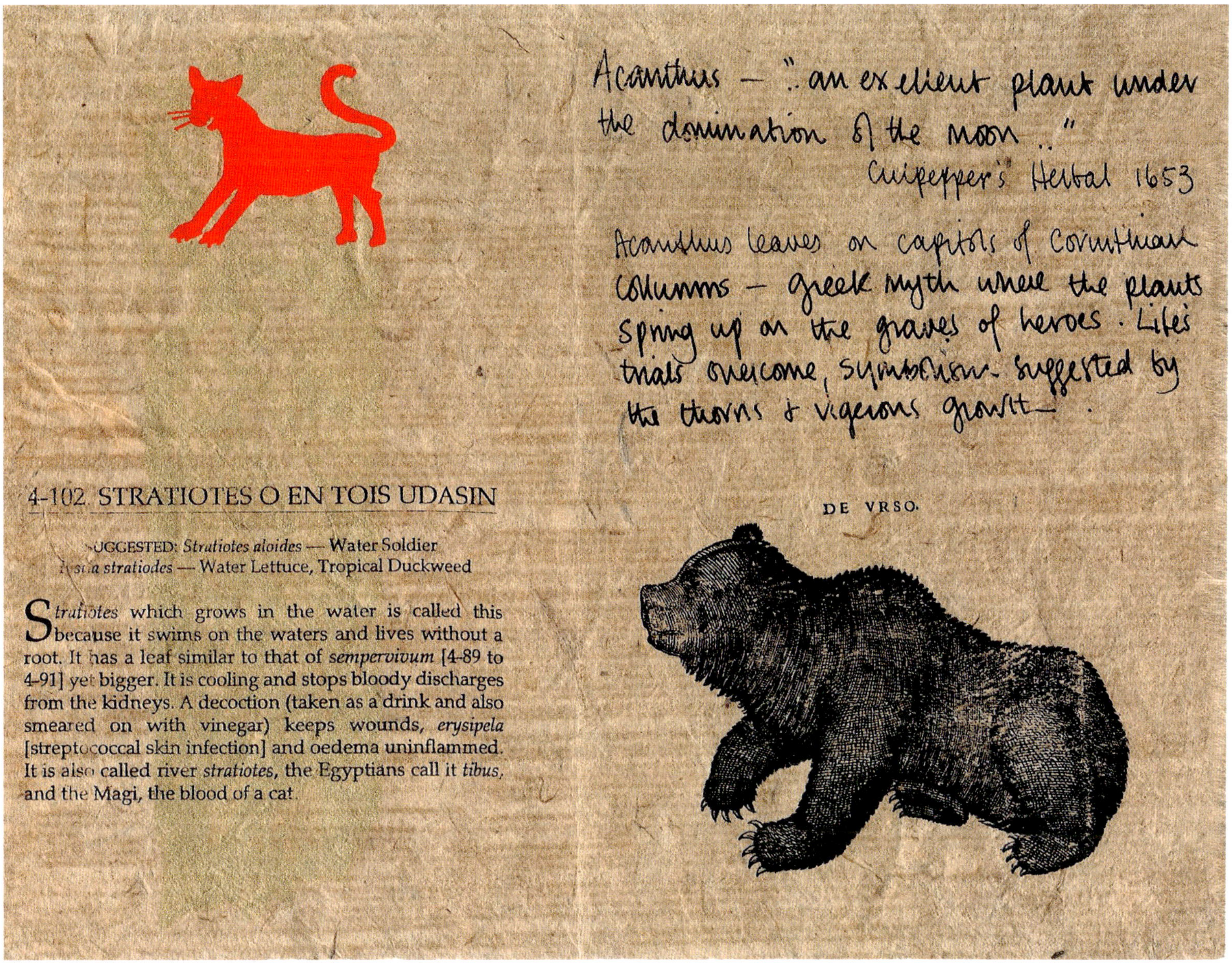

A spread from 'Inflorescence'

Inspired by the herbals and early plant manuscripts, I worked on a series of 'open-book' images, each one a unique mixed media piece, over-printed with a sketch-book matrix (see pp. 114-115). In collaboration with Robert Adam and Carol Robertson of Graal Press, I also produced an Artist's Book – 'Inflorescence'. A limited ediion of 10 books, Inflorescence exists as an object somewhere between a diary and a missal, a sketchbook & a book of hours. There's no didactic logic to it – it evolves & is held together by visual & symbolic links. It's a tactile experience made with about 20 hand-made papers ranging from fine tissue to heavy embossed paper. It was hand-bound in Venice; it is meant to be precious – to be a contemplative experience and an antidote to the form of knowledge presented through a plastic screen and a cold text. Its images are either hand-drawn, silk screen printed, collaged or etched, each book subtly different.

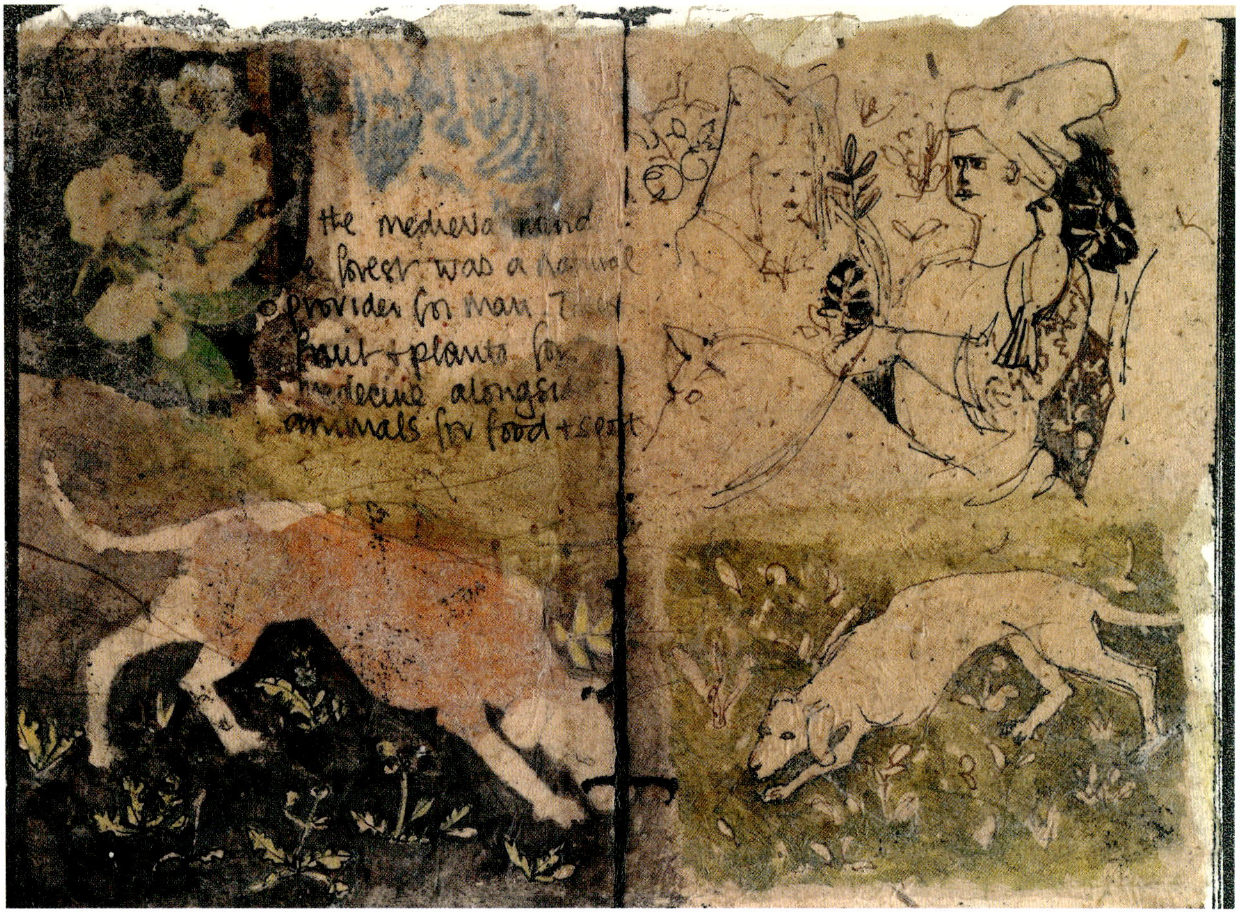

Medieval Mind

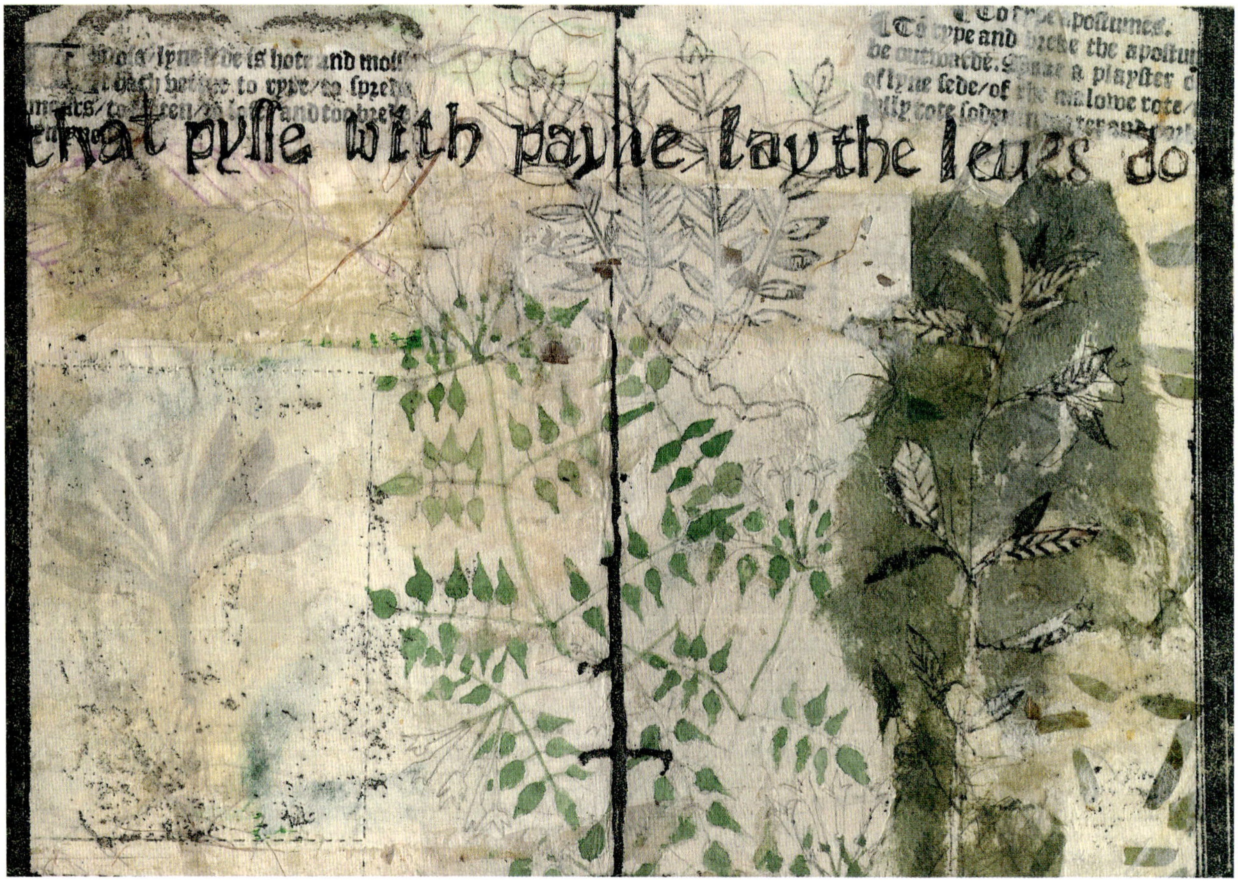

Herbal Remedies

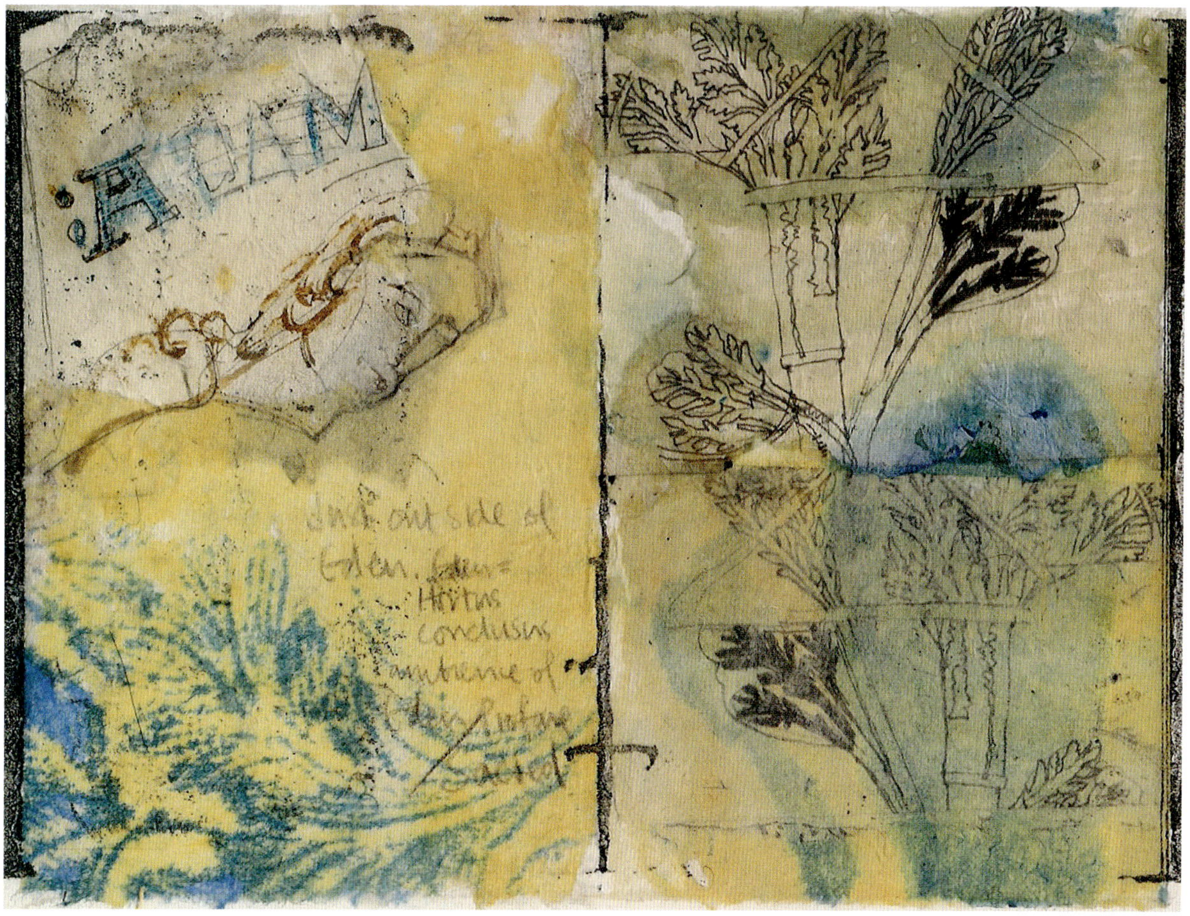

Outside Eden

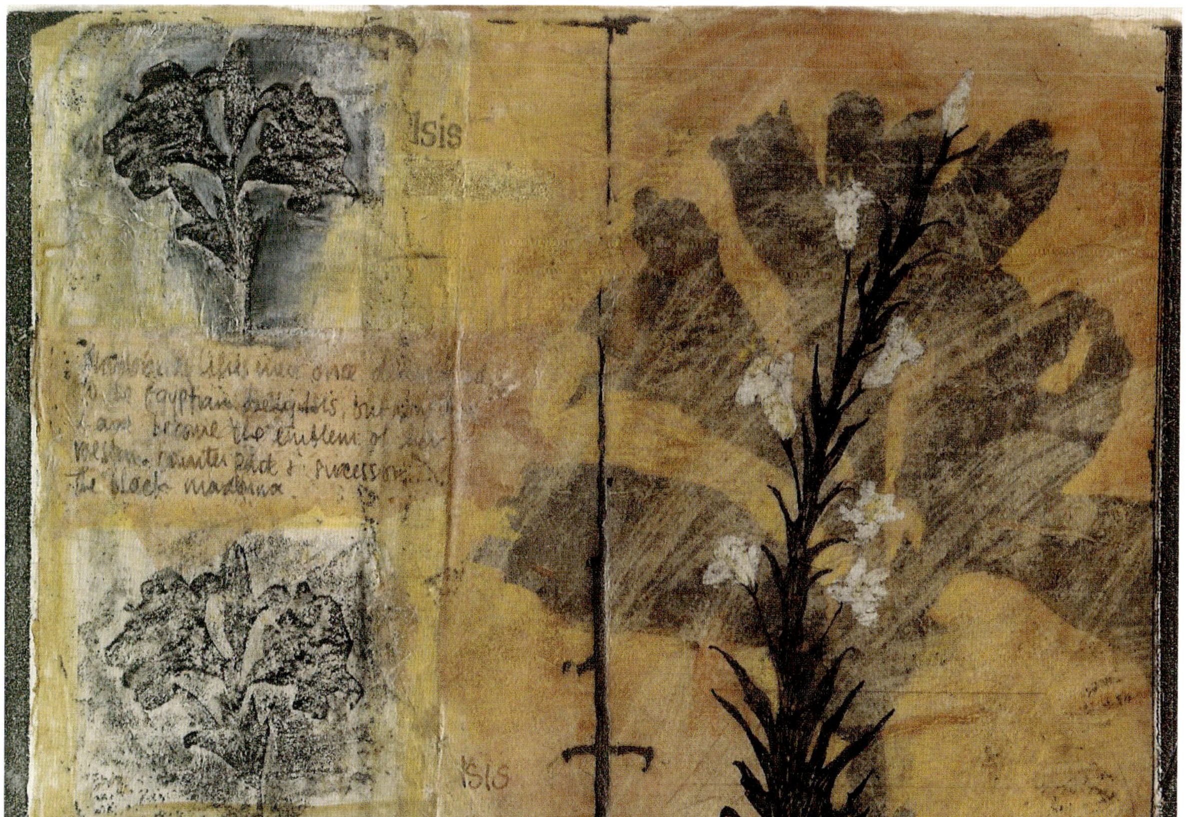

Isis Madonna

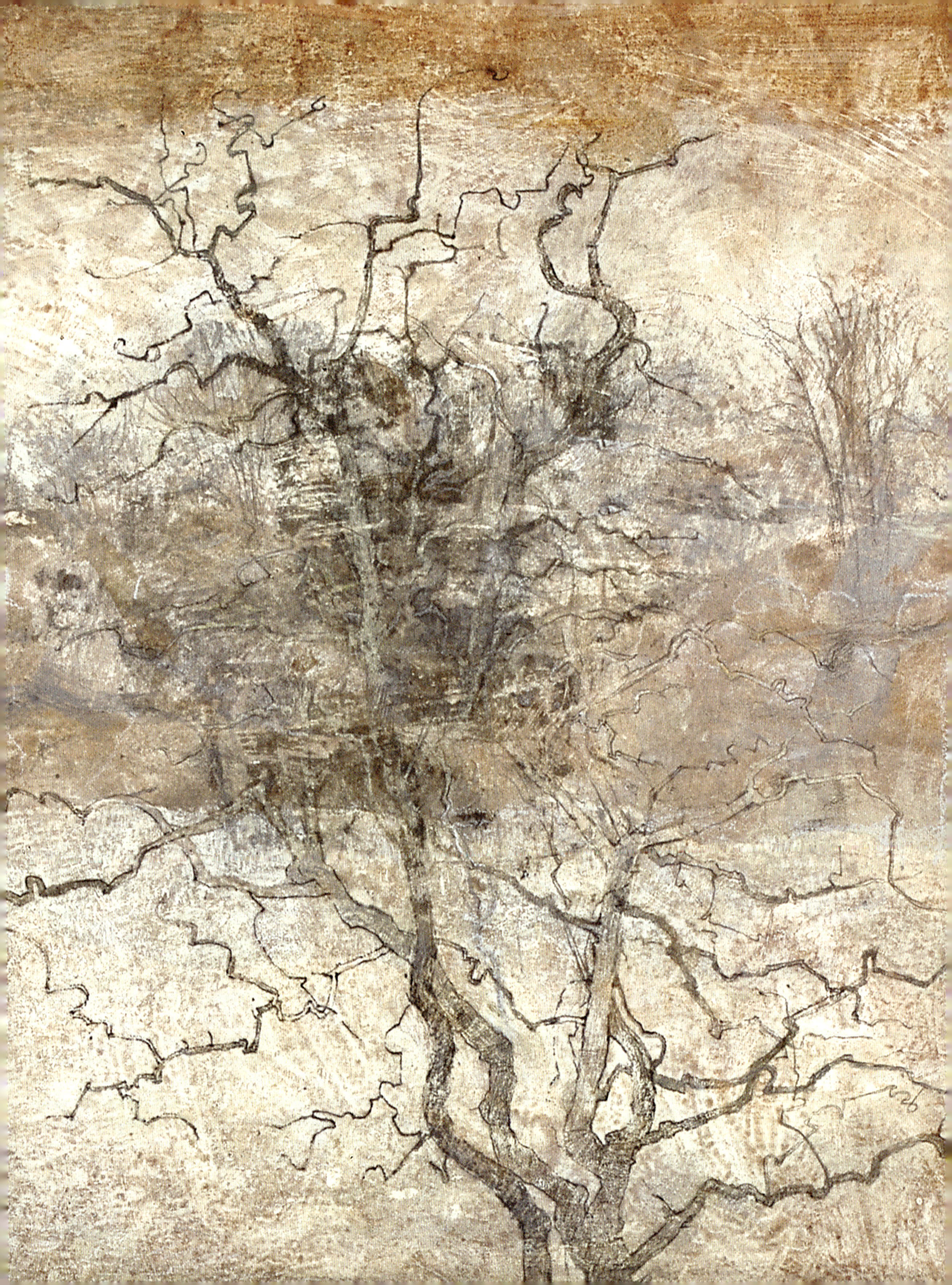

New Departures

'Plant Memory' brought together strands in Victoria's thinking that had hitherto crossed, but which were now much more intertwined. With the strength that brought, her art since then has become more spacious, lighter in tone and more elegiac. In 2008 at the Scottish Gallery she showed a series of works where the gold and silver of Venetian mirrors mingled with the whites and golds of the winter landscape of the Pentlands, softened now since her austere paintings of twenty years before. She also tends to introduce light, no longer only as general luminosity, as the glimmer of gold, but from a directional source. In *Mellow Winter*, for instance, a twisted hazel tree that grows in the West Linton garden is seen against snow, its branches touched by the pink light of the setting sun. The whole scene is painted in misty bands of muted colour, almost reminiscent of the trees she painted in Richmond Park forty years before. *Luminous Winter*, a loosely composed series of images of trees and landscape, says it all in its title. In *Dominance of the Moon* we are looking at a lit window with a bare tree silhouetted against it. In both these pictures, there are little elements of other things arranged along the bottom – a leaf, a piece of fabric, a Japanese lacquer bowl, some writing, simple reminders of the other thoughts that we always carry with us.

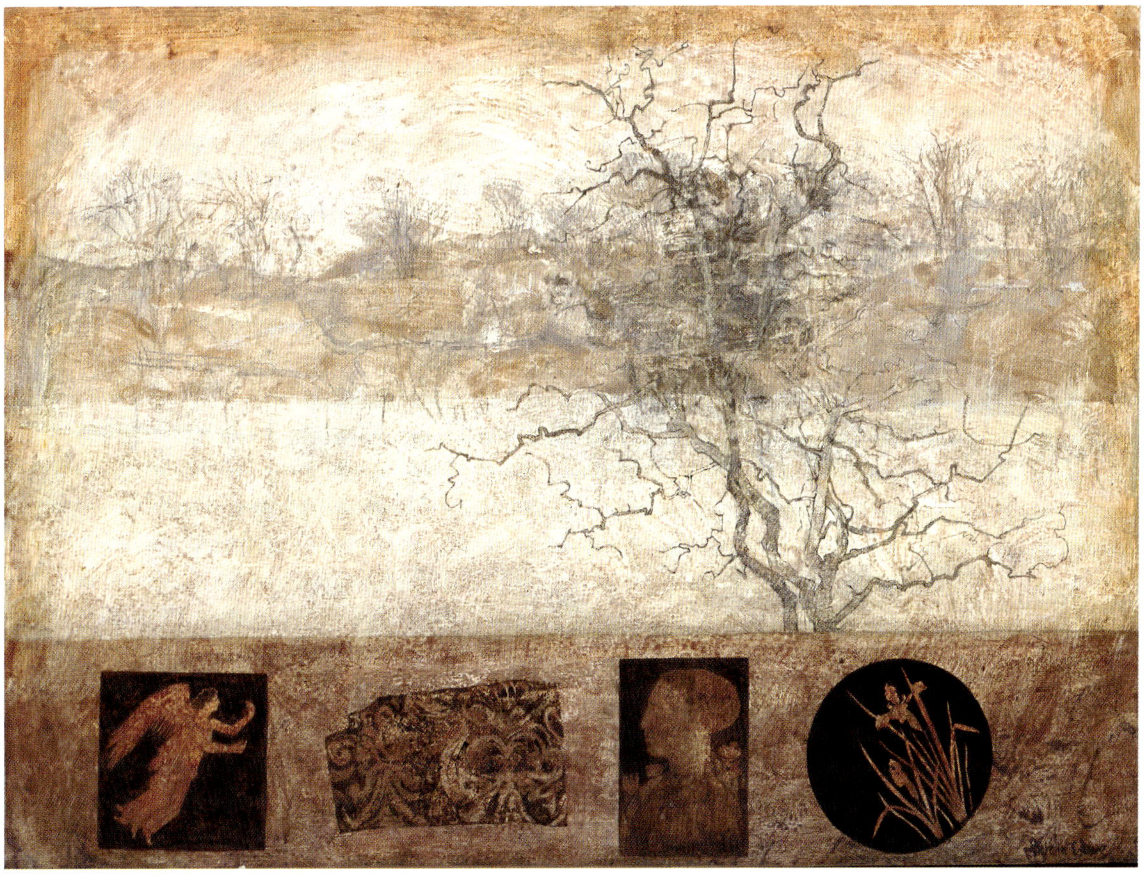

Litany

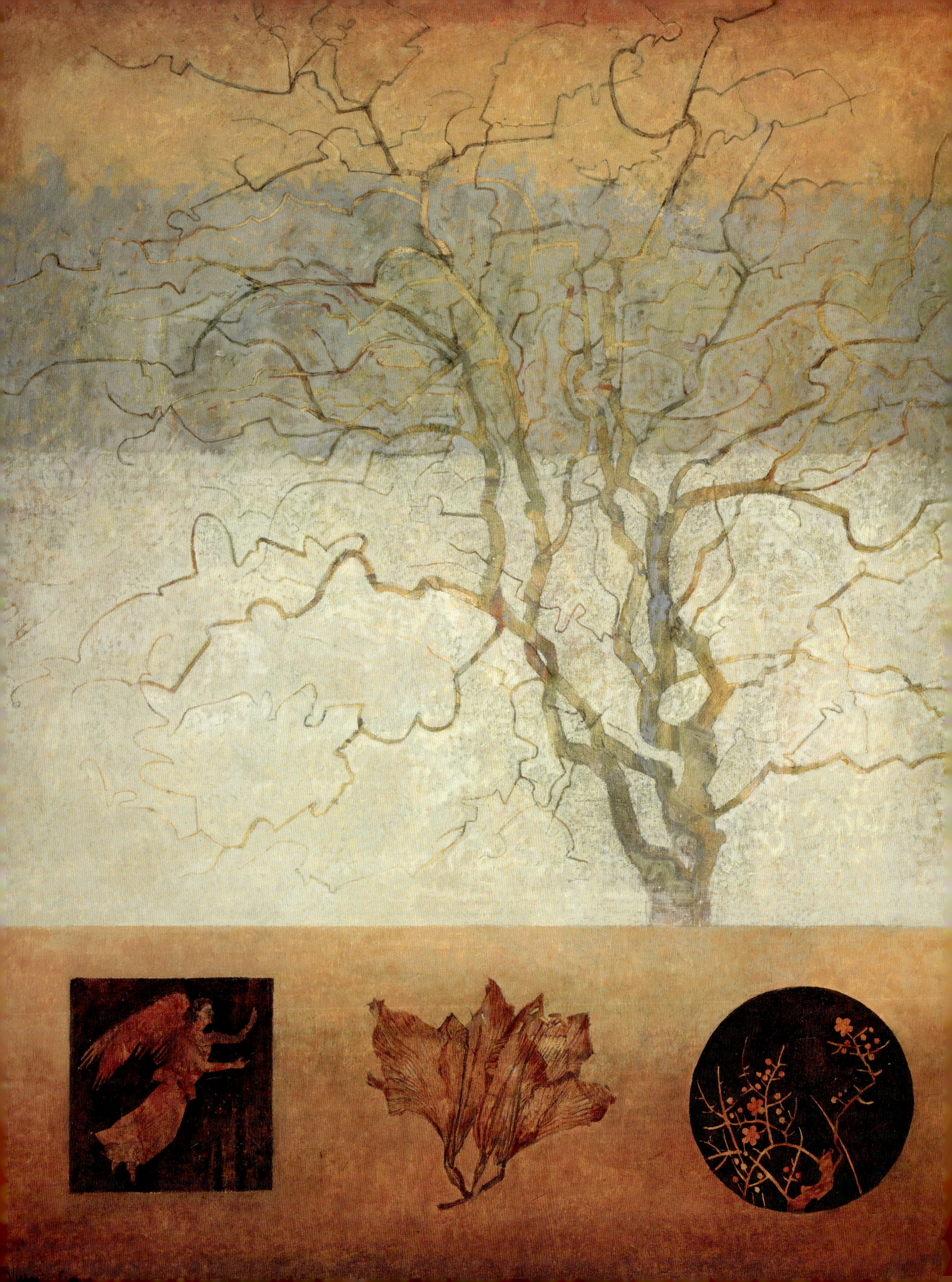

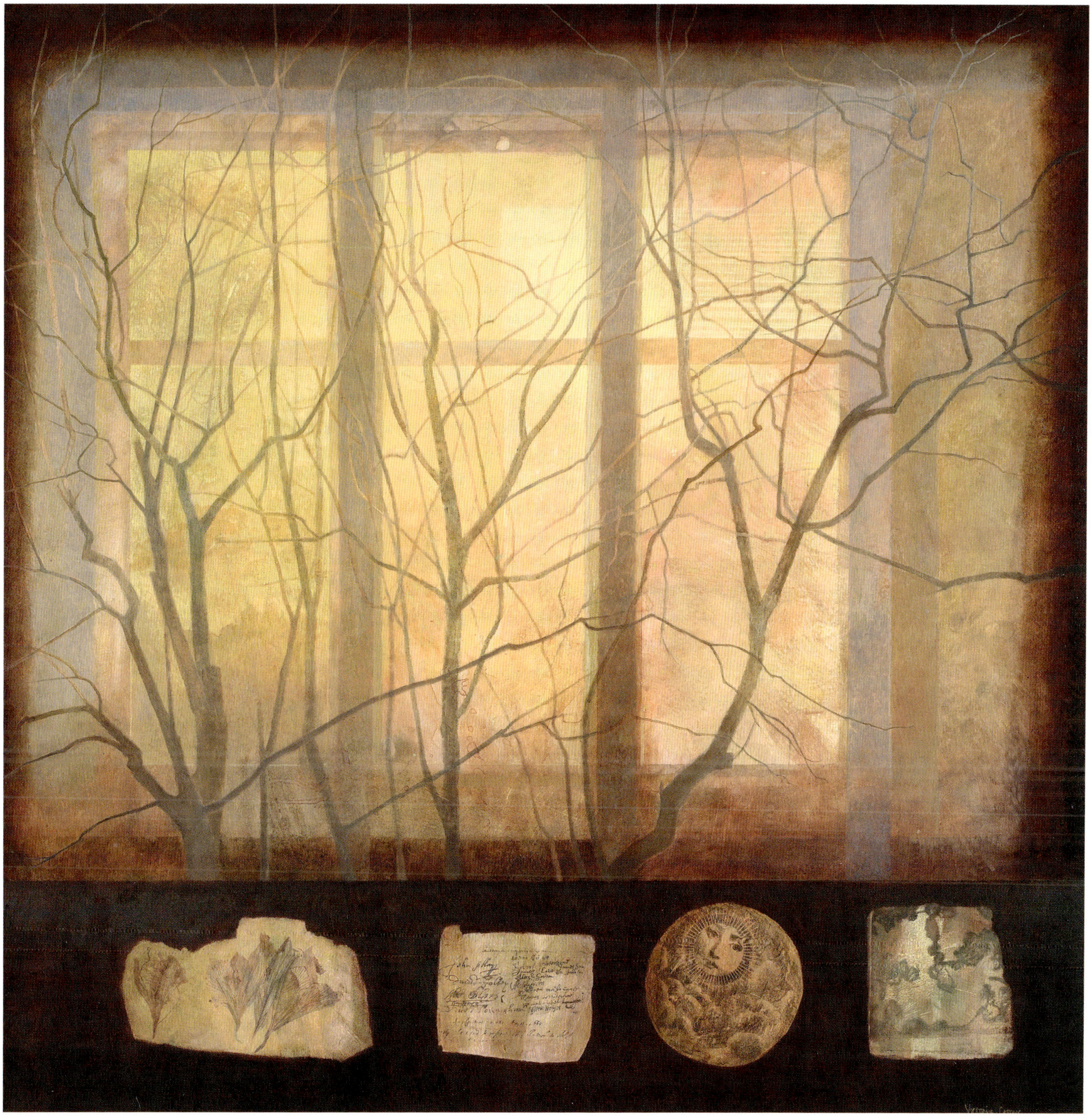

Dominance of the Moon

Mellow Winter

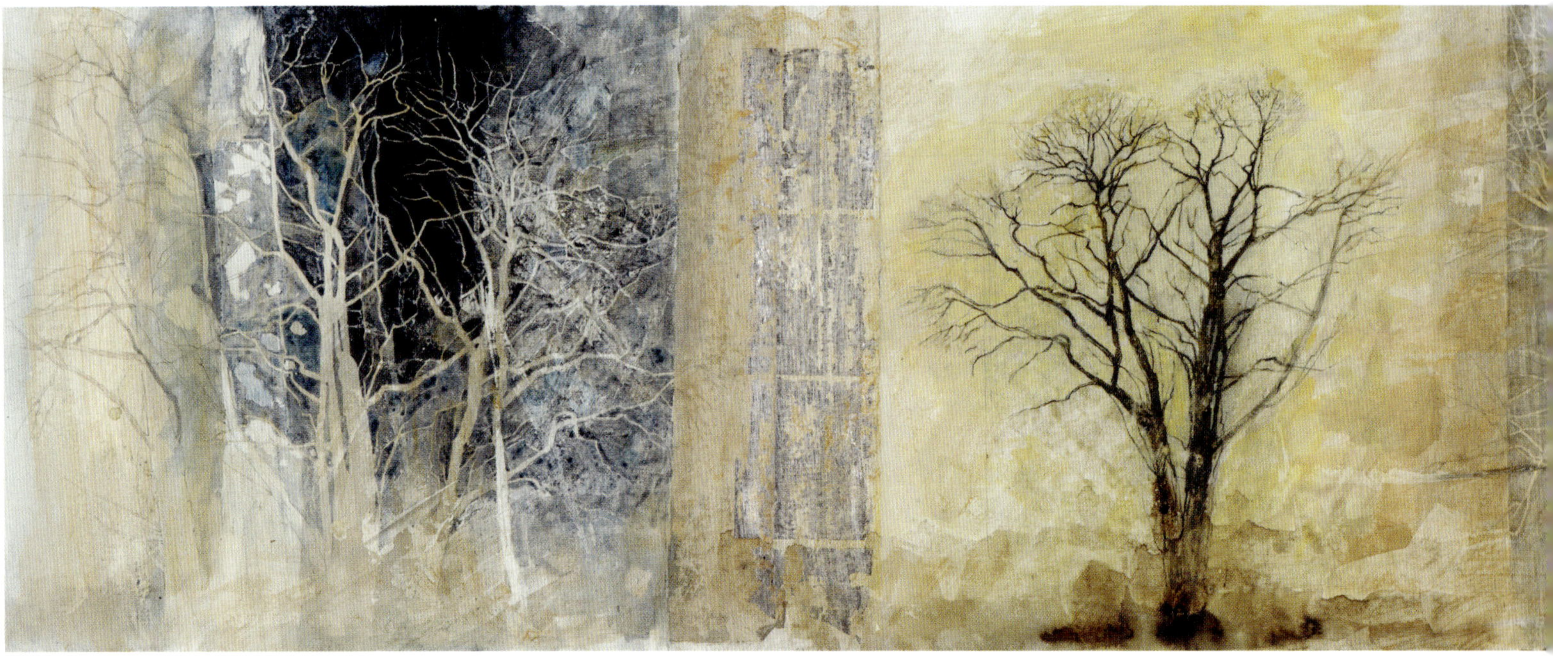

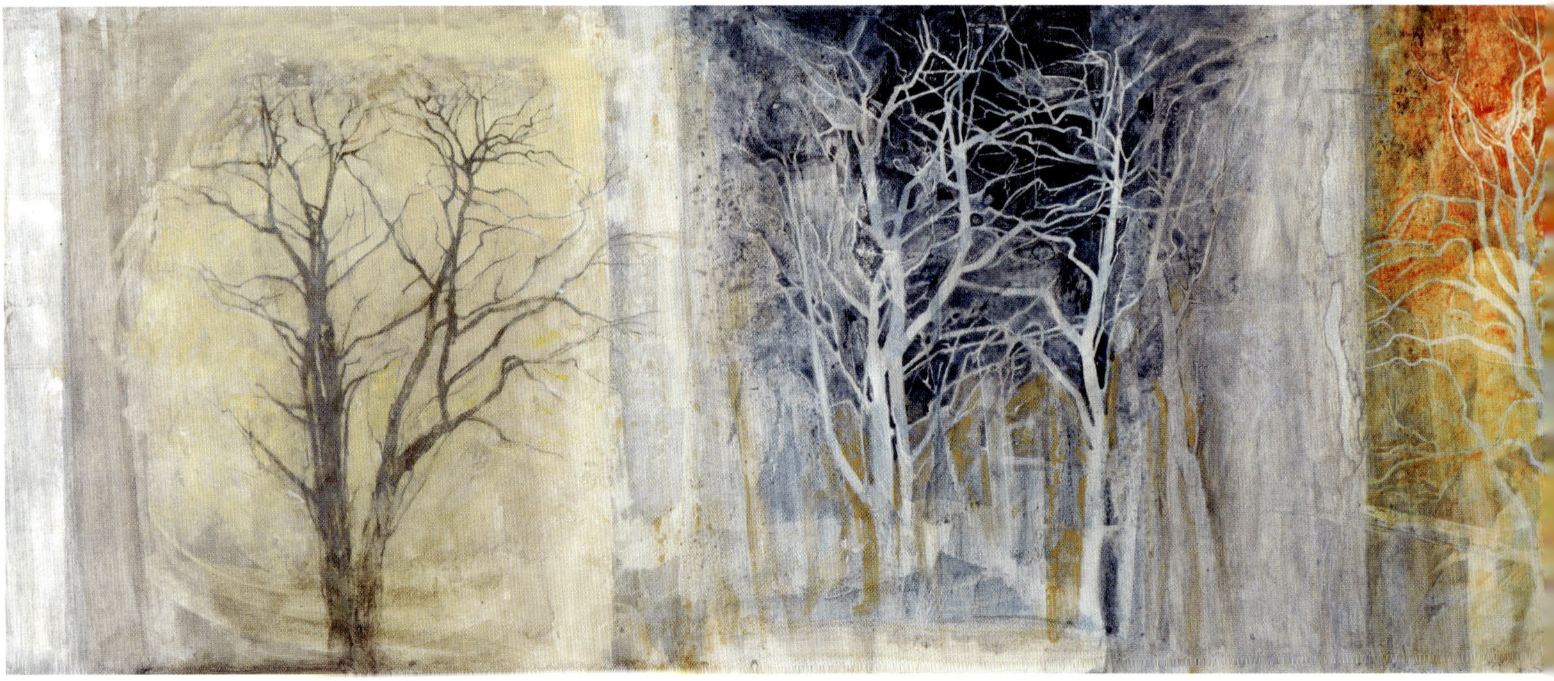

Frost Sequence

Winter Sequence

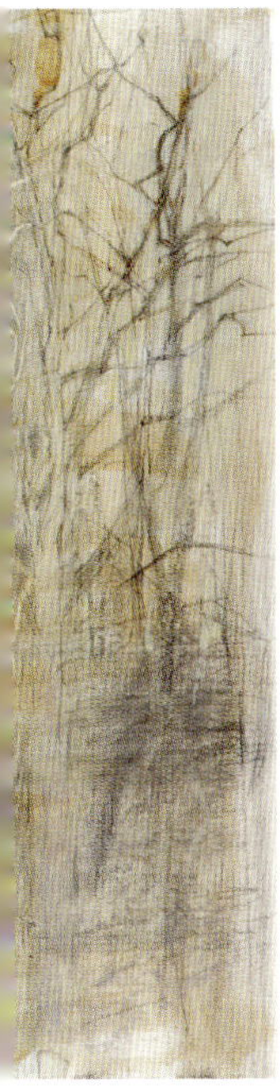

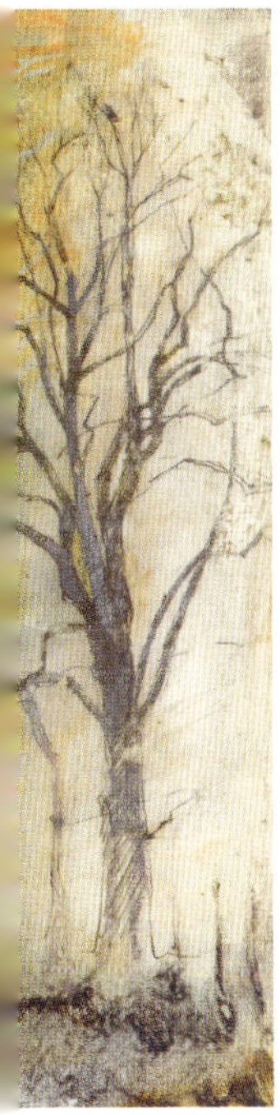

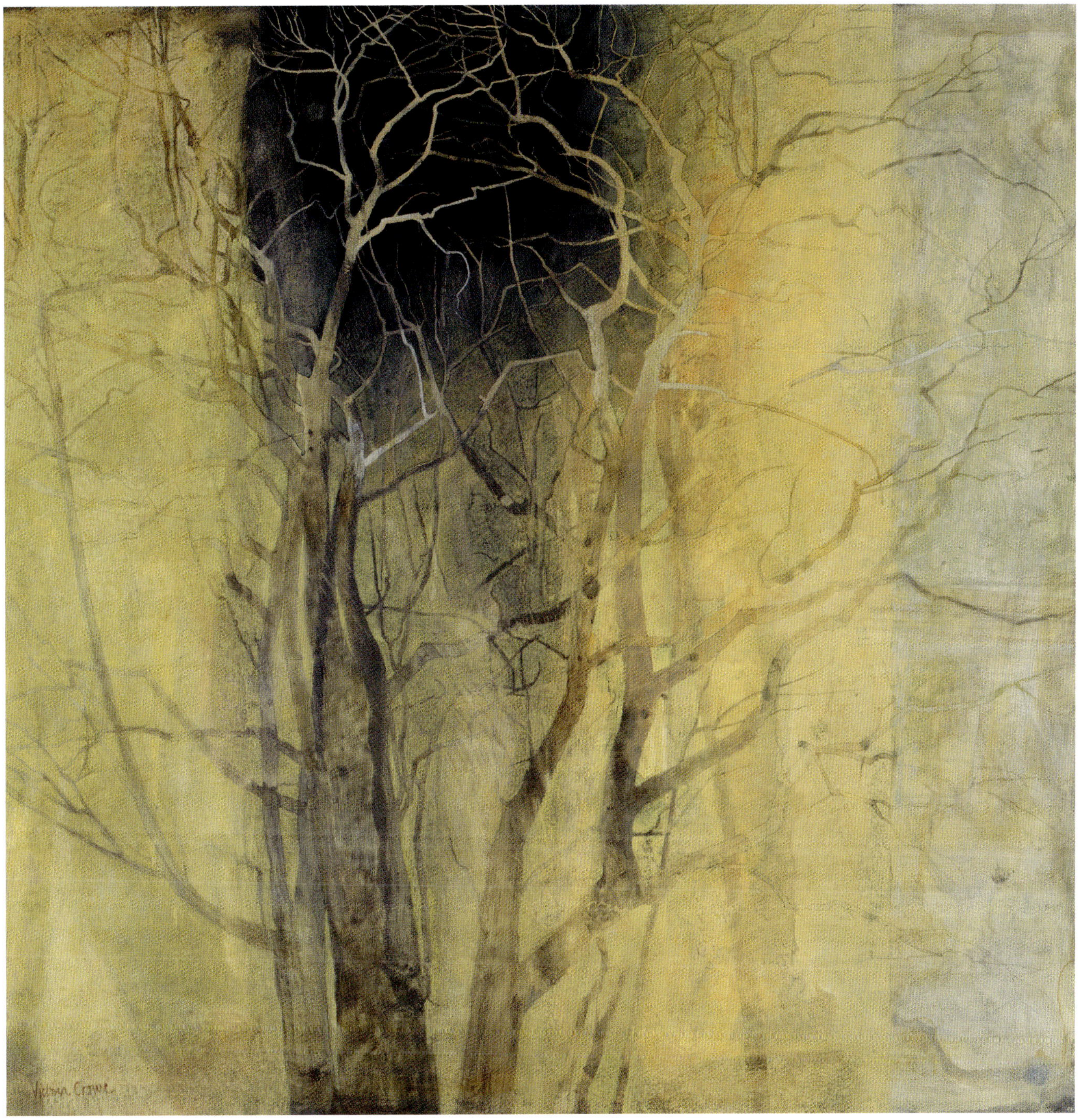

Frost Pocket

Overleaf: *Snowlines*

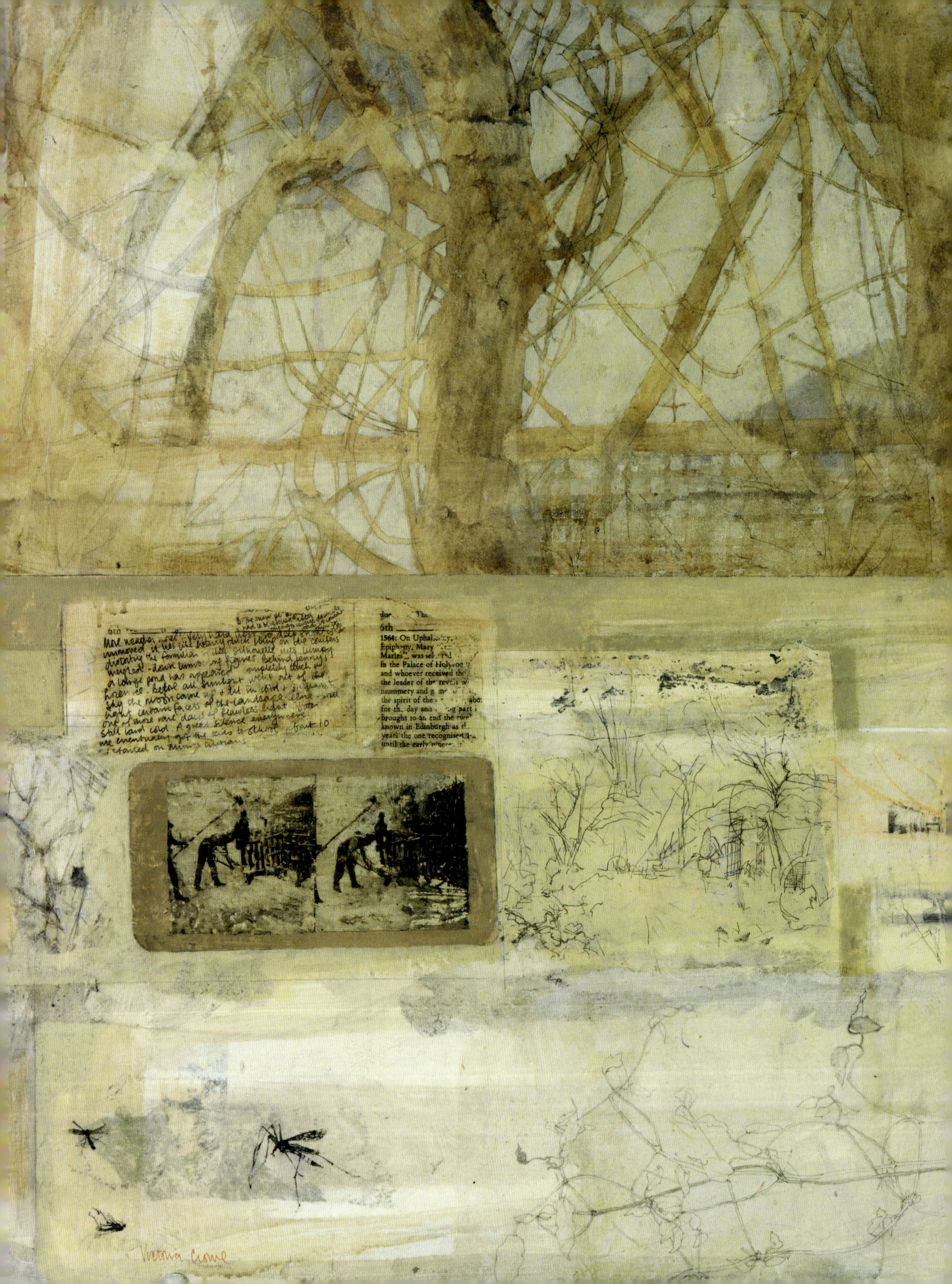
6th
1564: On
Mary
was
in the Palace of
and whoever received
the leader of
mummery and
the spirit of the
for
day
brought to
end the
known in Edinburgh as
the one
until the early
Victoria Crowe

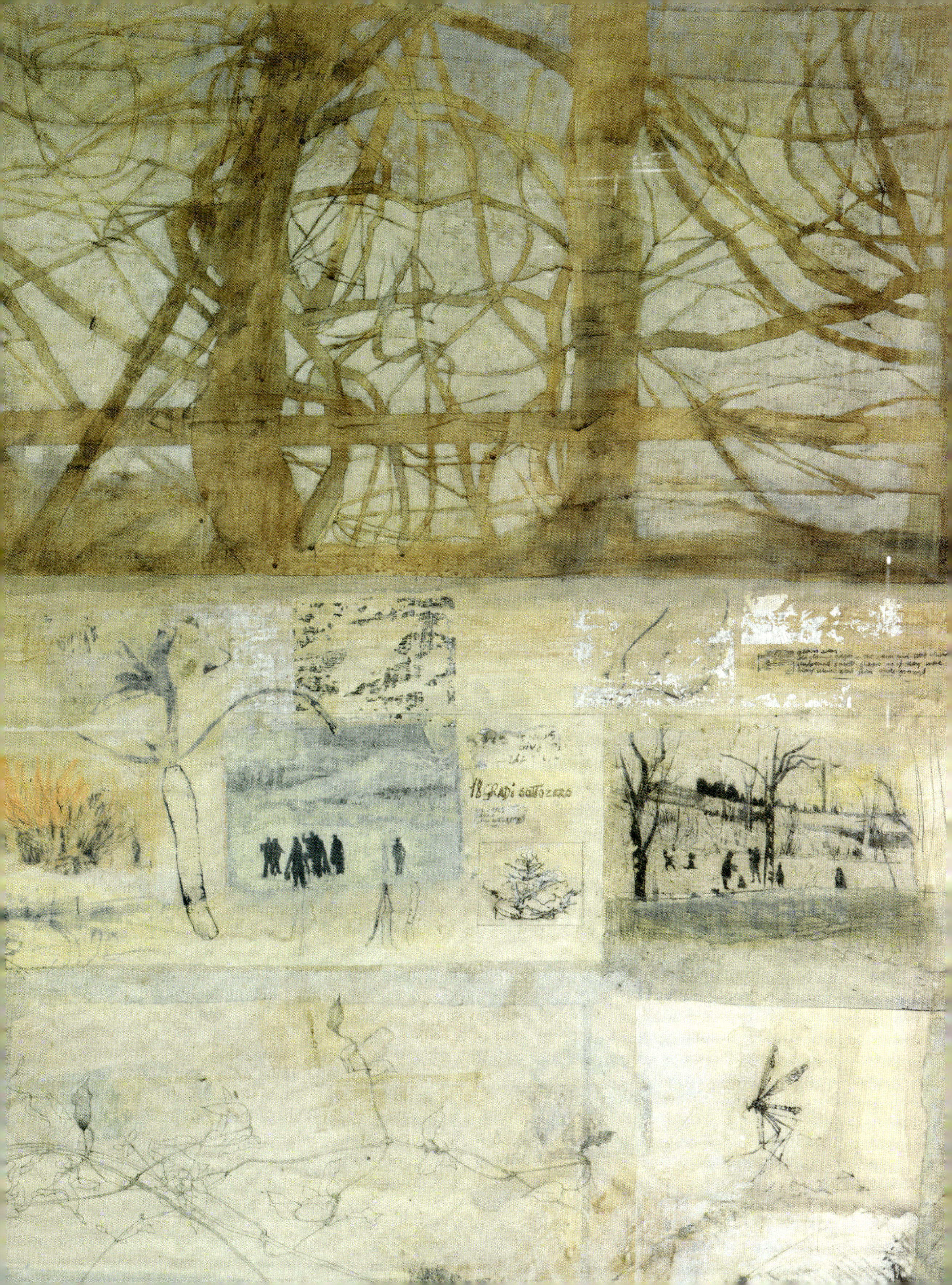
18 GRADI sottozero

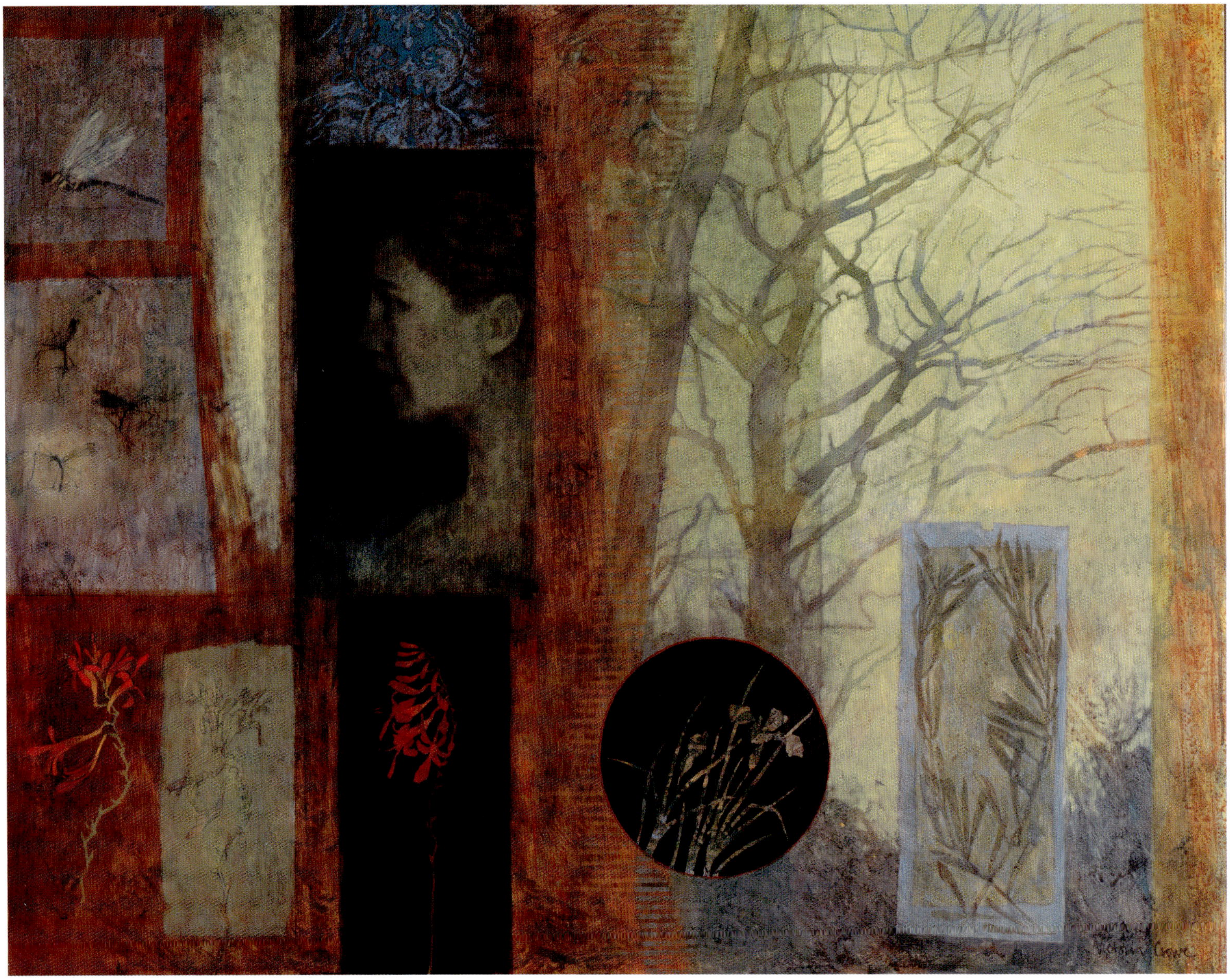

Continuum

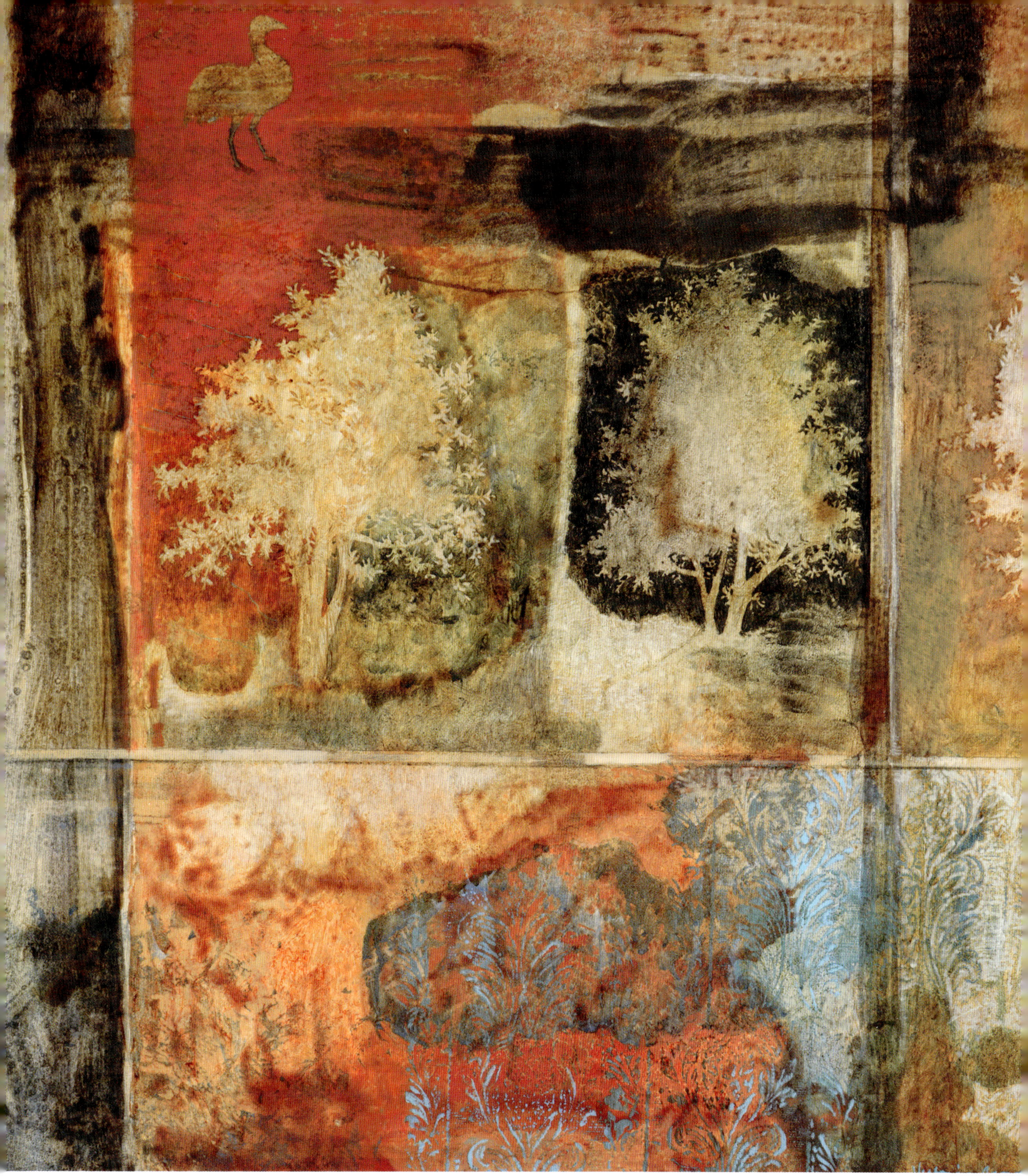

Interior with Reflected Landscape

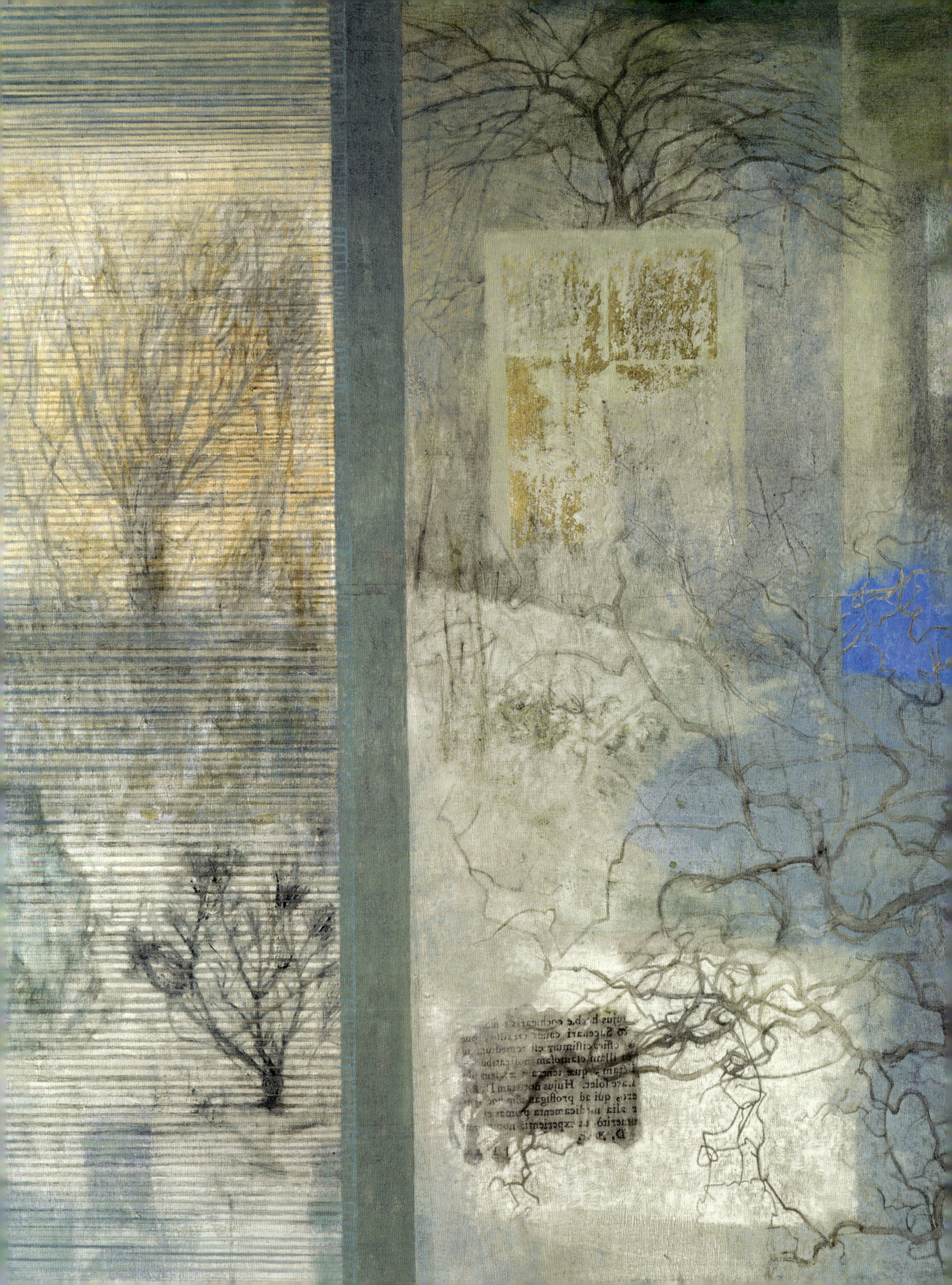

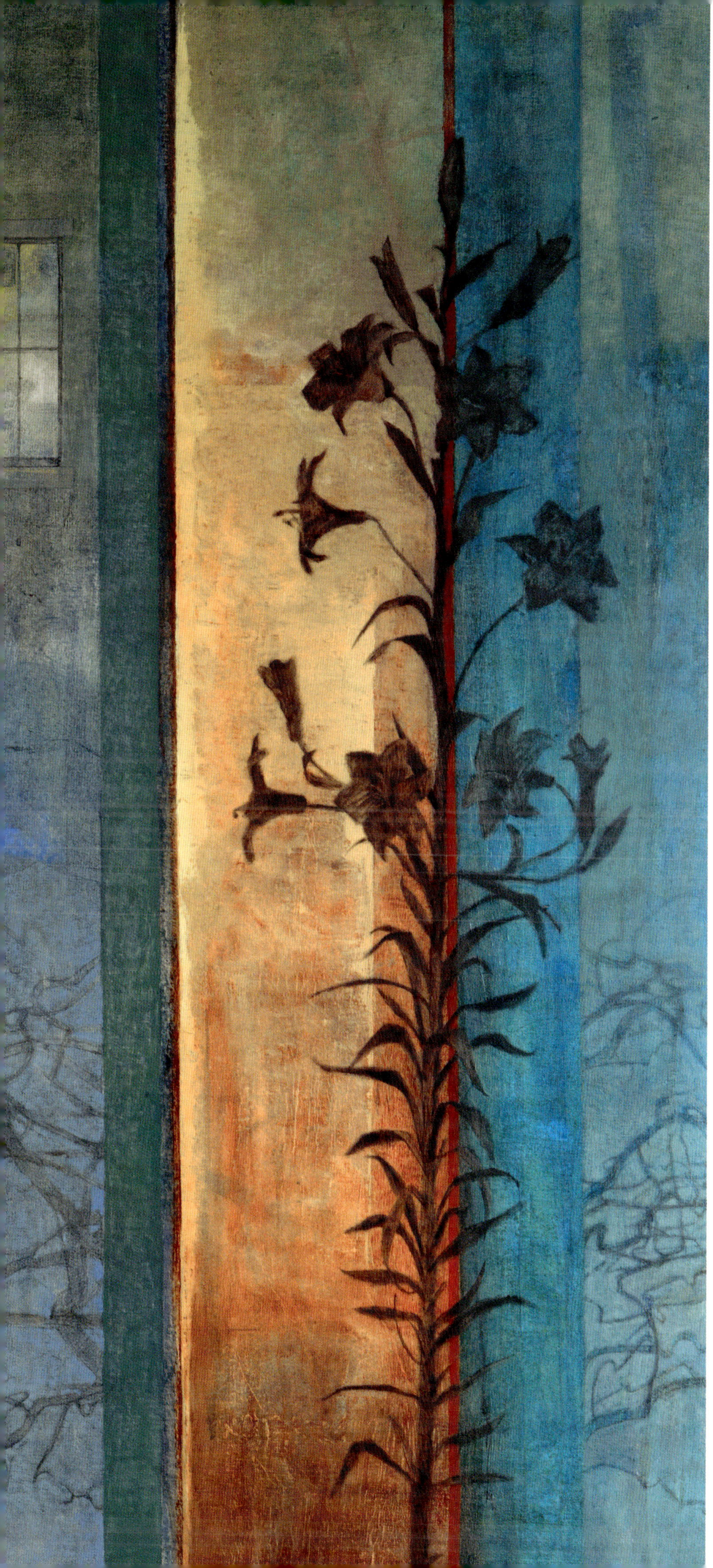

Garden Room – A View from the Interior

Always industrious, Victoria had another major show just two years later in the Edinburgh Festival exhibition at the Scottish Gallery in 2010. She continued to paint shifting, allusive pictures of Venice and some touch on the history of the city itself. In *Reflection on a Lost Empire*, for instance, a picture that is a reflection in both uses of the word, the lost empire is Venice. In *Trade Routes and Messages*, swatches of material from the Fortuny Museum are annotated in an antique hand, invoking the trade in luxury goods that created the city's wealth. Raphael's self-portrait peers out of the shadows of a faded sliver mirror, but begins to look increasingly like her own self-portrait. She does include herself in *Circumspice*, a picture of the view from her studio in Venice and incorporating an oblique self-portrait. She sees herself in profile by using double mirrors, double reflections again. She is reflected in the mirror just as she reflects on what she sees and what she paints.

The portrait in *Italian Portrait with Artichoke*, from 2008, is Raphael's self portrait again. It was painted in Florence before he went to Rome – where in the nineteenth century his art was held to have declined disastrously – and so when he was still himself in a sense Pre-Raphaelite. Framed on either side by northern trees in golden light, he looks out at us, not so much as though he was in a painting, but as though we were seeing him in a bathroom mirror. We have

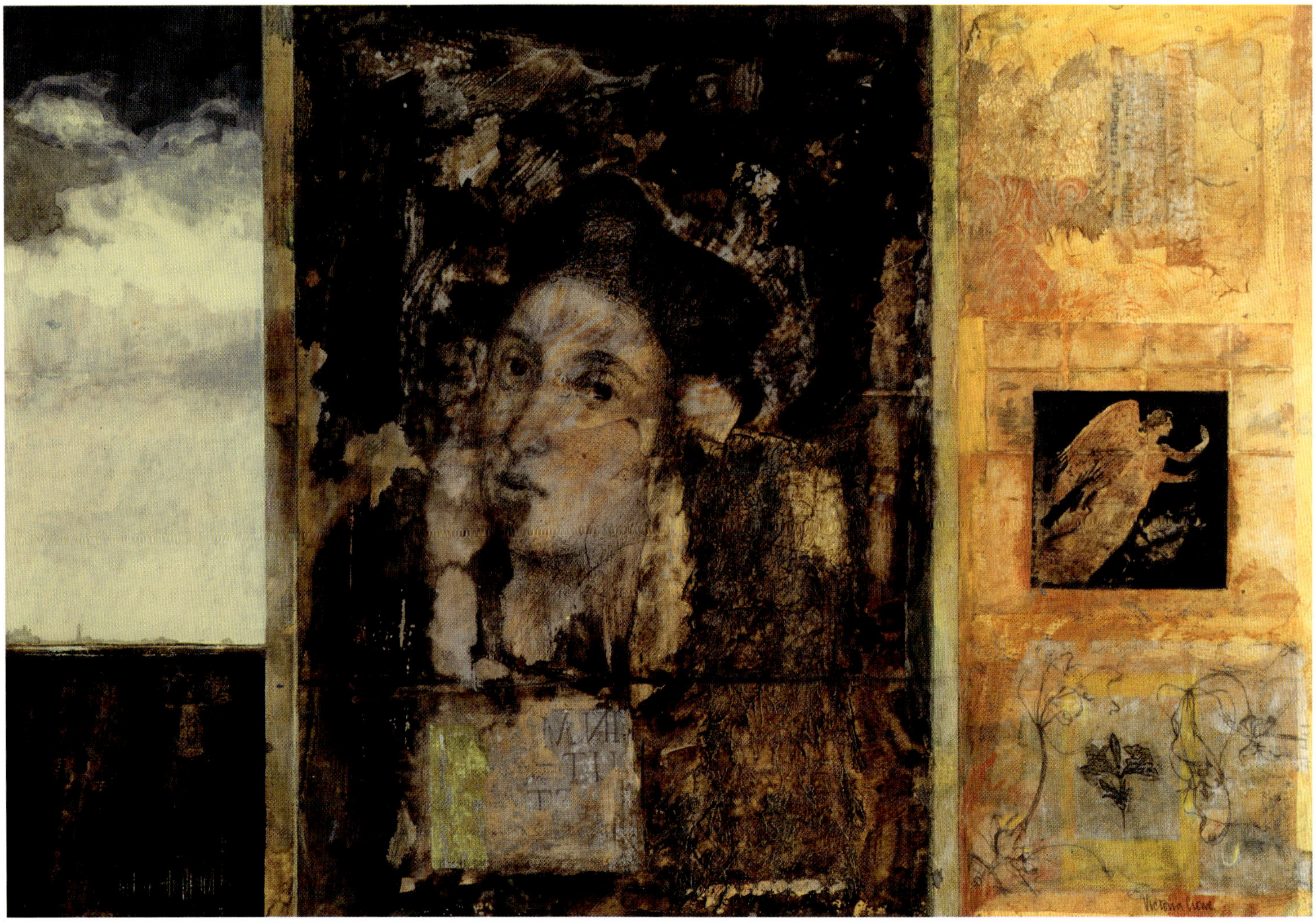

Venice Reflected

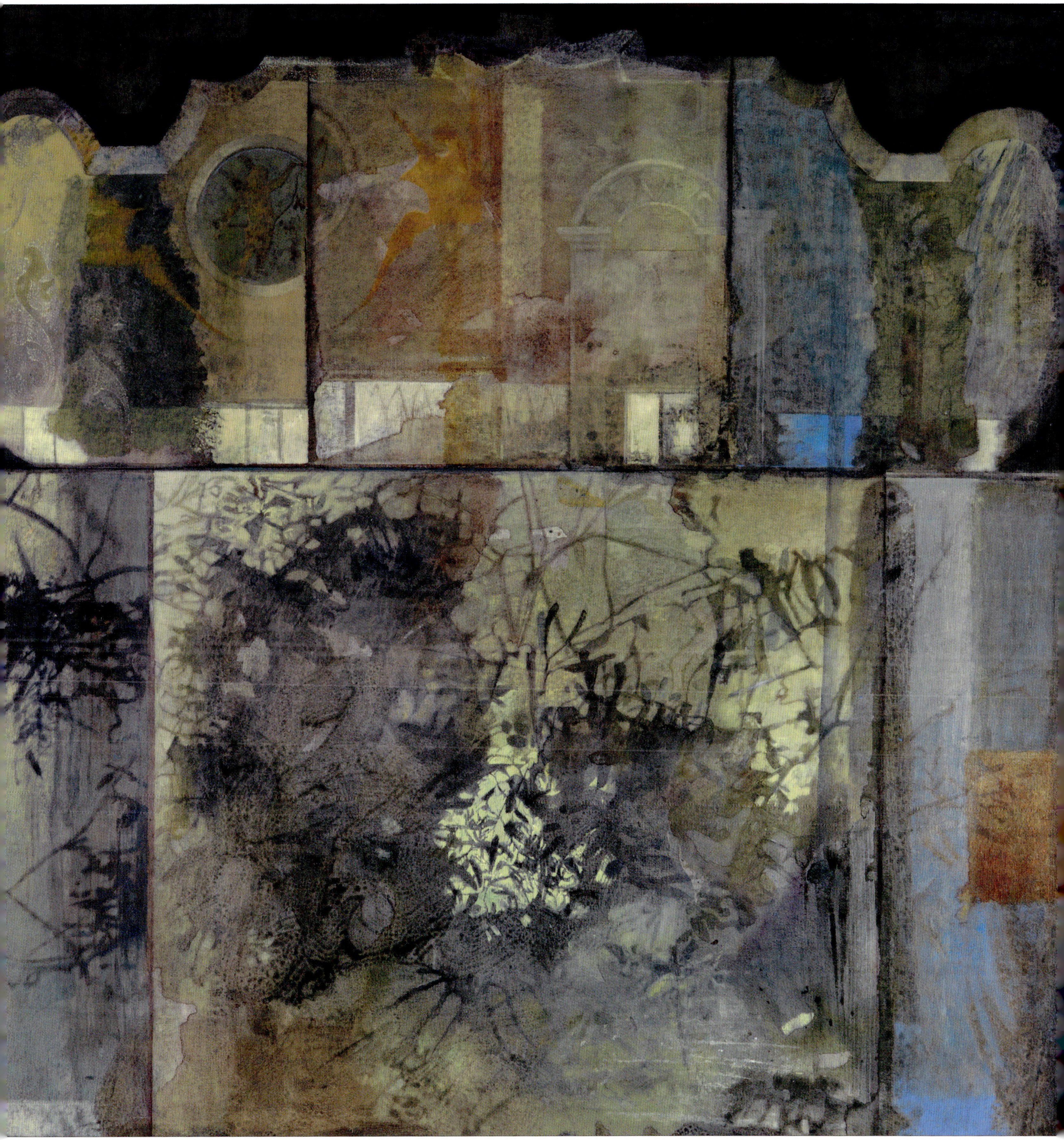

Reflection on a Lost Empire

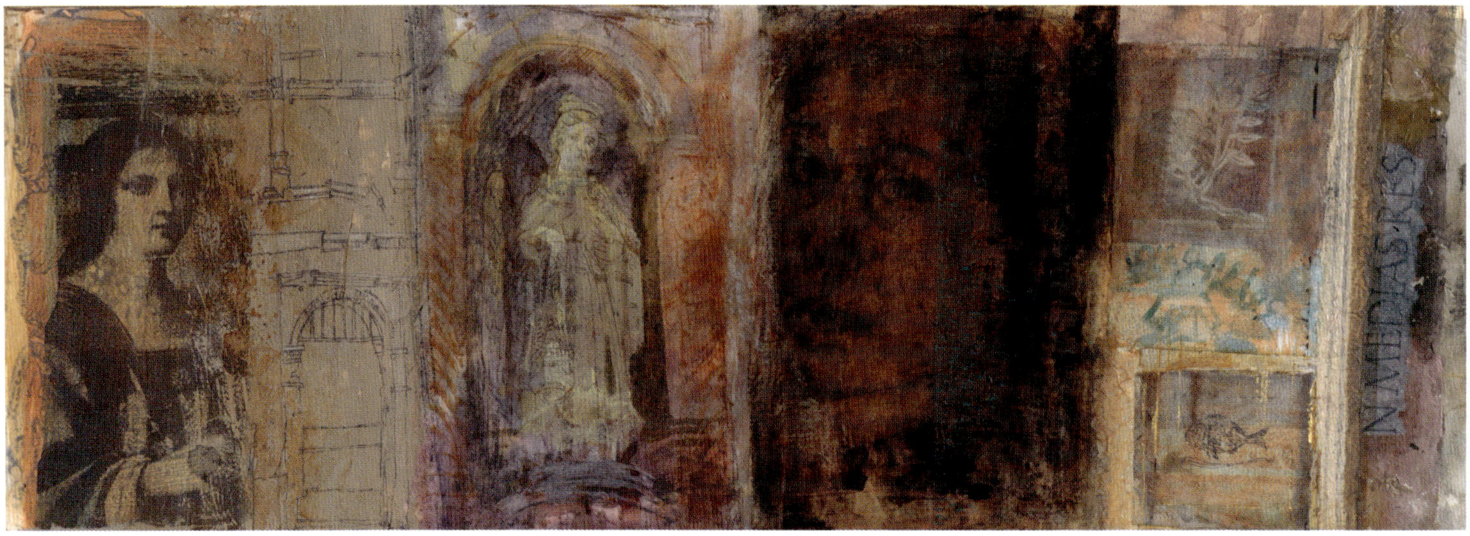

Walking and Thinking in Venice

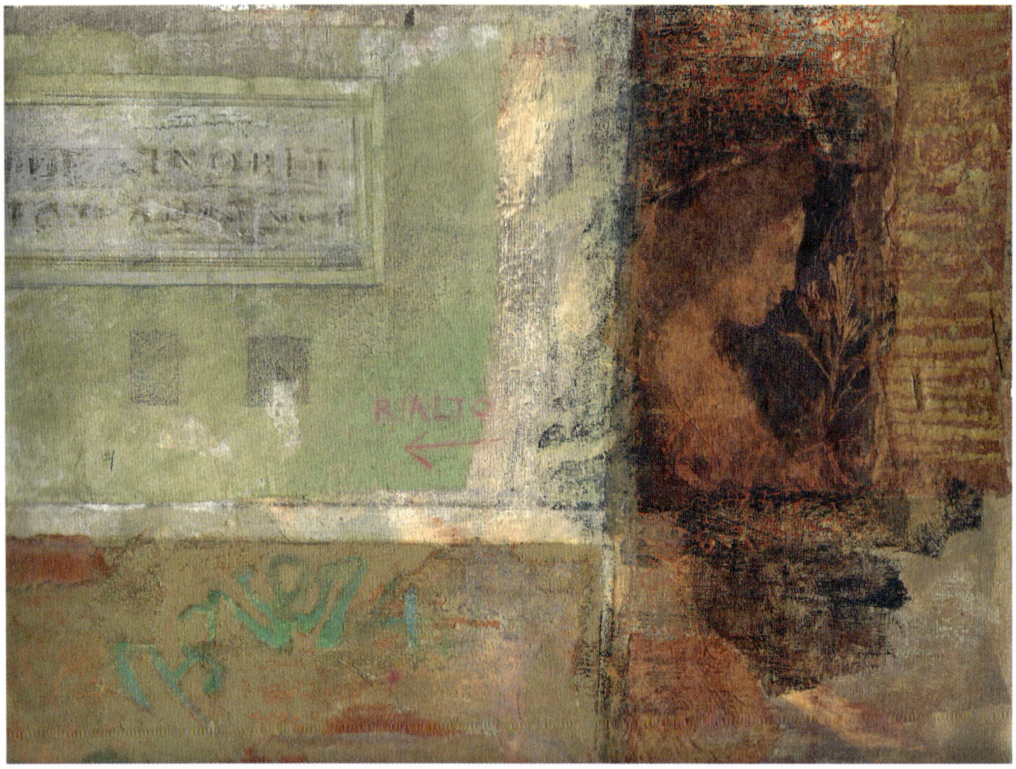

Rialto?

displaced him, or at least the artist has. The artichoke in front of him, the most Italian of vegetables, brings us back to earth. It is Victoria's own shadowy self-portrait that gazes out of *Walking and Thinking in Venice*, however, where it is seen in the patchy silver of an antique mirror together with a figure of a saint in a niche, some fragmentary drawing of a Venetian watergate and a face from a painting by Sebastiano del Piombo. The inclusion of her self-portrait and the title of the picture together suggest, too, how she passes her time in Venice. Her sketchbooks document this as she notes all kinds of things that she has seen – details of pictures, damage to a Madonna in the Accademia, or to a fresco in Padua that inspired the picture *All that Remains, Padova*. She notes bits of graffiti that then turn up in a little picture like *Rialto?* which takes its title from the word written on the wall with a pointing arrow by some exasperated Venetian, tired of giving directions to dumb tourists.

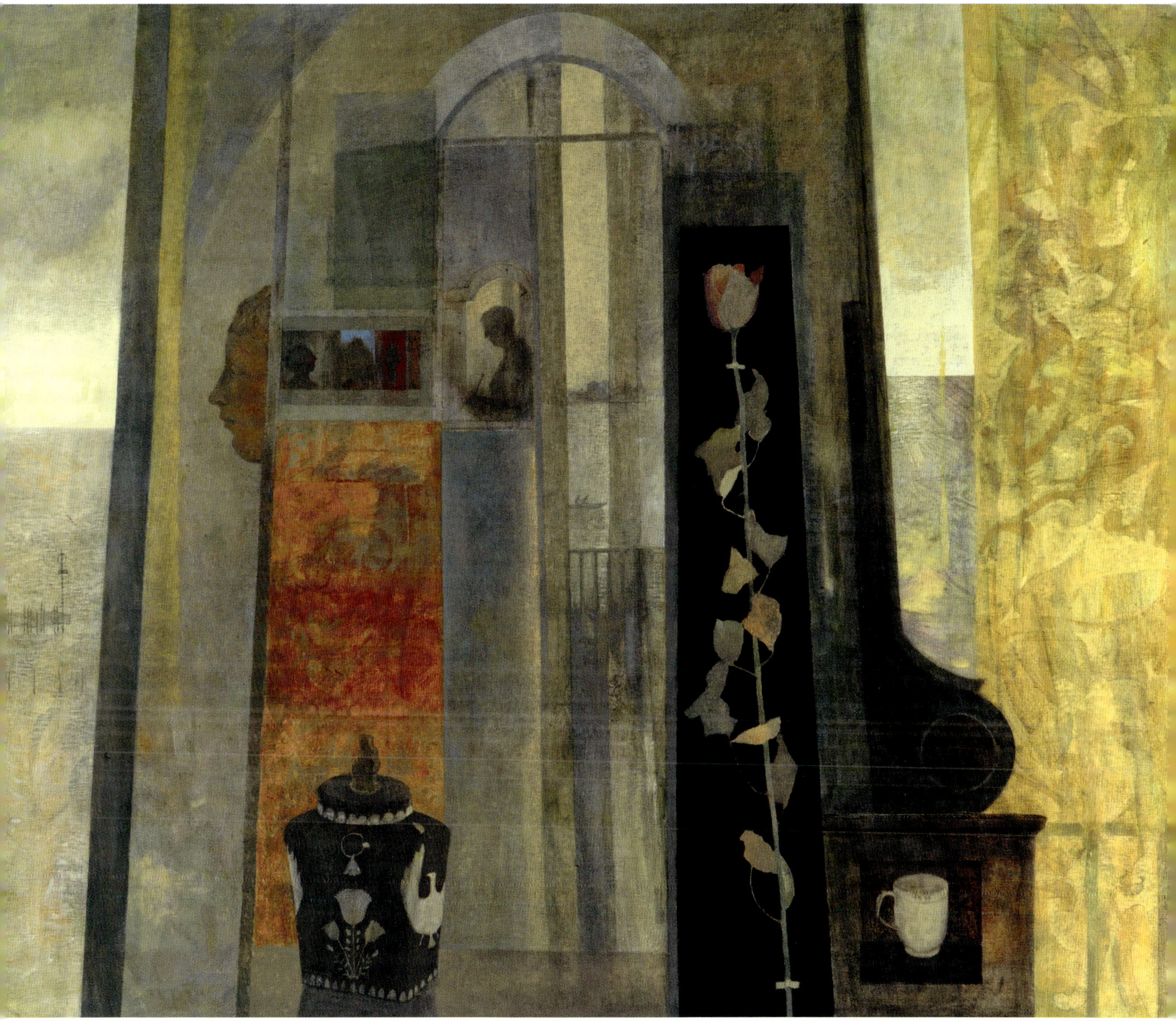

Circumspice — The Studio Venice

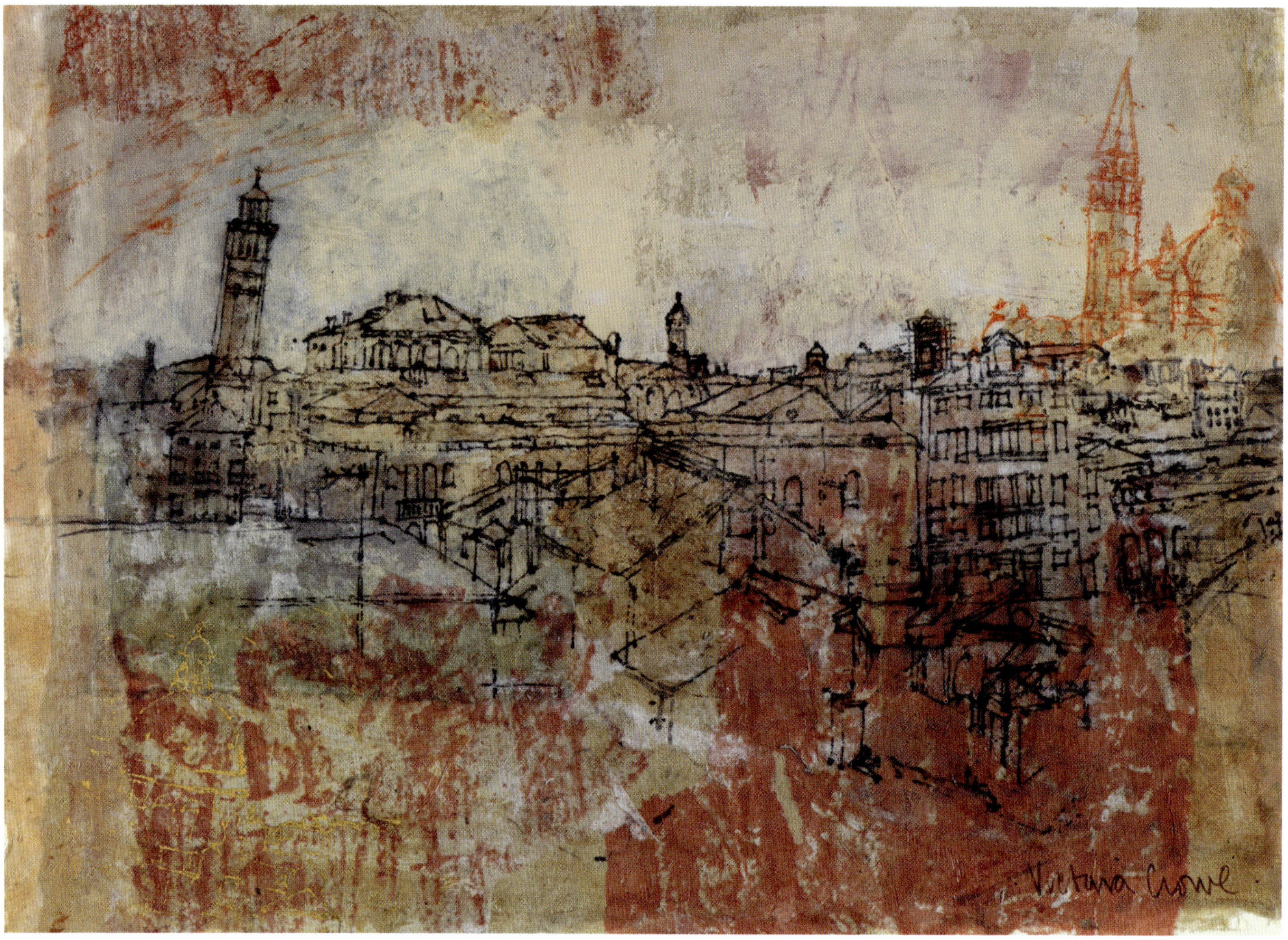

Skyline, Venice

It has only been in recent years that Victoria has been able to tackle the extraordinary townscape of Venice directly. She found it daunting, not just because of its beauty, but also because it has been tackled by so many artists so often before, not least by Turner and Whistler. Her first approach was deliberately low-key. She drew the panorama from her studio looking across to the Zattere, to the dome of the Salute and the Campanile of St Mark's beyond it and nearer at hand to the neighbouring roofs of the Giudecca. She chose to do this with a simple pen line, precise, but free enough to preserve spontaneity in what is in fact a remarkably sustained piece of drawing that faithfully follows the complicated roof line and all the details of the buildings.

Once she had done that, Victoria felt able to start to incorporate elements of the view into more characteristic paintings where the discipline is relaxed a little, or at least the detailed drawing is floating in a more associative space and, as in all her art, we start to see mental processes of reflection and memory shape the composition. In *Reflections on the City*, for instance, part of the drawing is echoed in gold, shifting it from the observed to the imagined or remembered. This is developed in a number of watercolours like *Thoughts on the City* and *Skyline, Venice* as well as in major recent paintings like *Studio Venice*, *Mirrored View* and *Morning, Reflections Across the Water*. In the latter picture the view is layered with Fortuny fabric, a window and dazzling light on water. One of the most beautiful works in this series, *Tramonto* catches the moment at dusk when, as the shadows develop within the enveloping warmth of the setting sun, the lights start to come on along the Zattere opposite the studio.

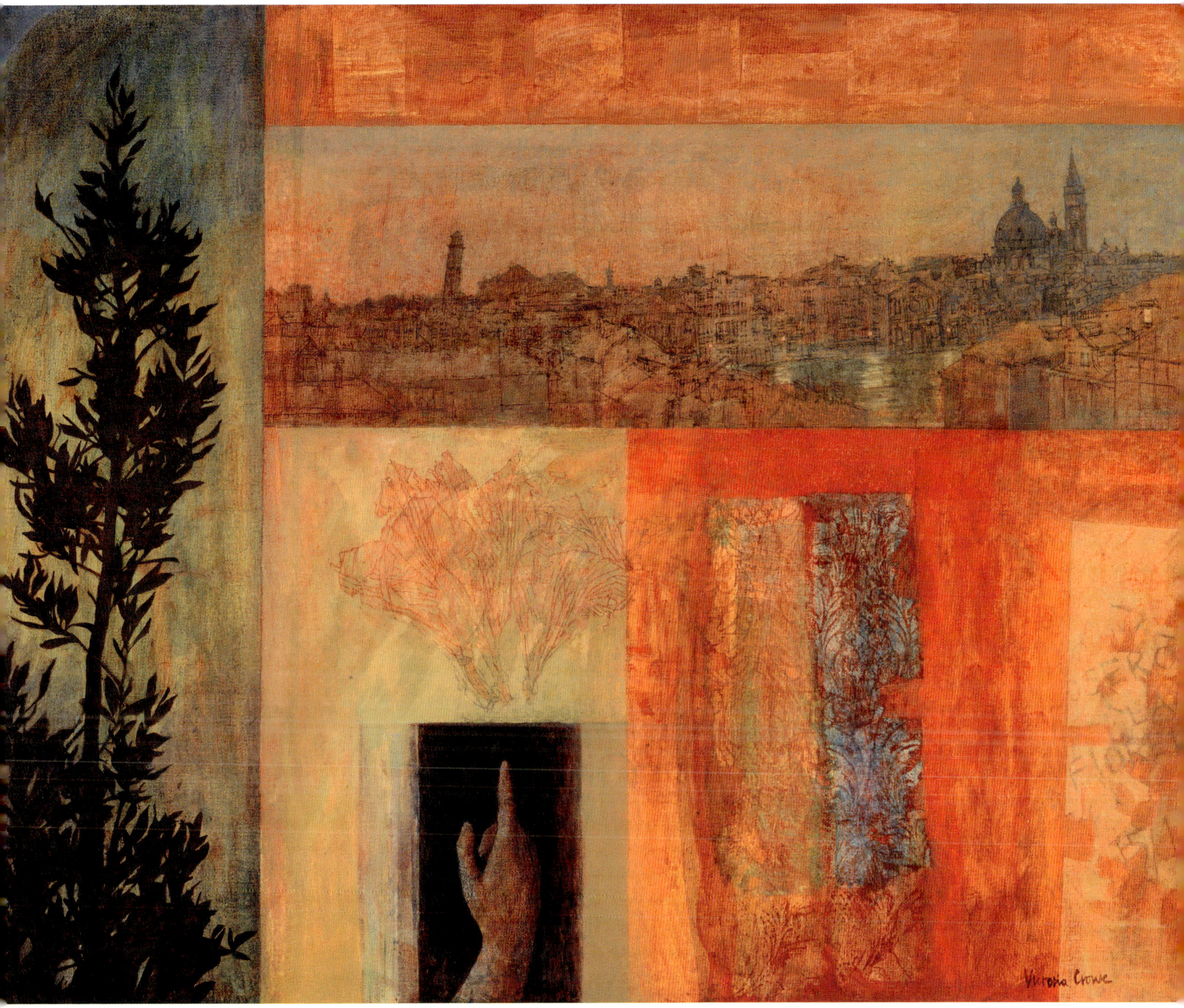

Tramonto

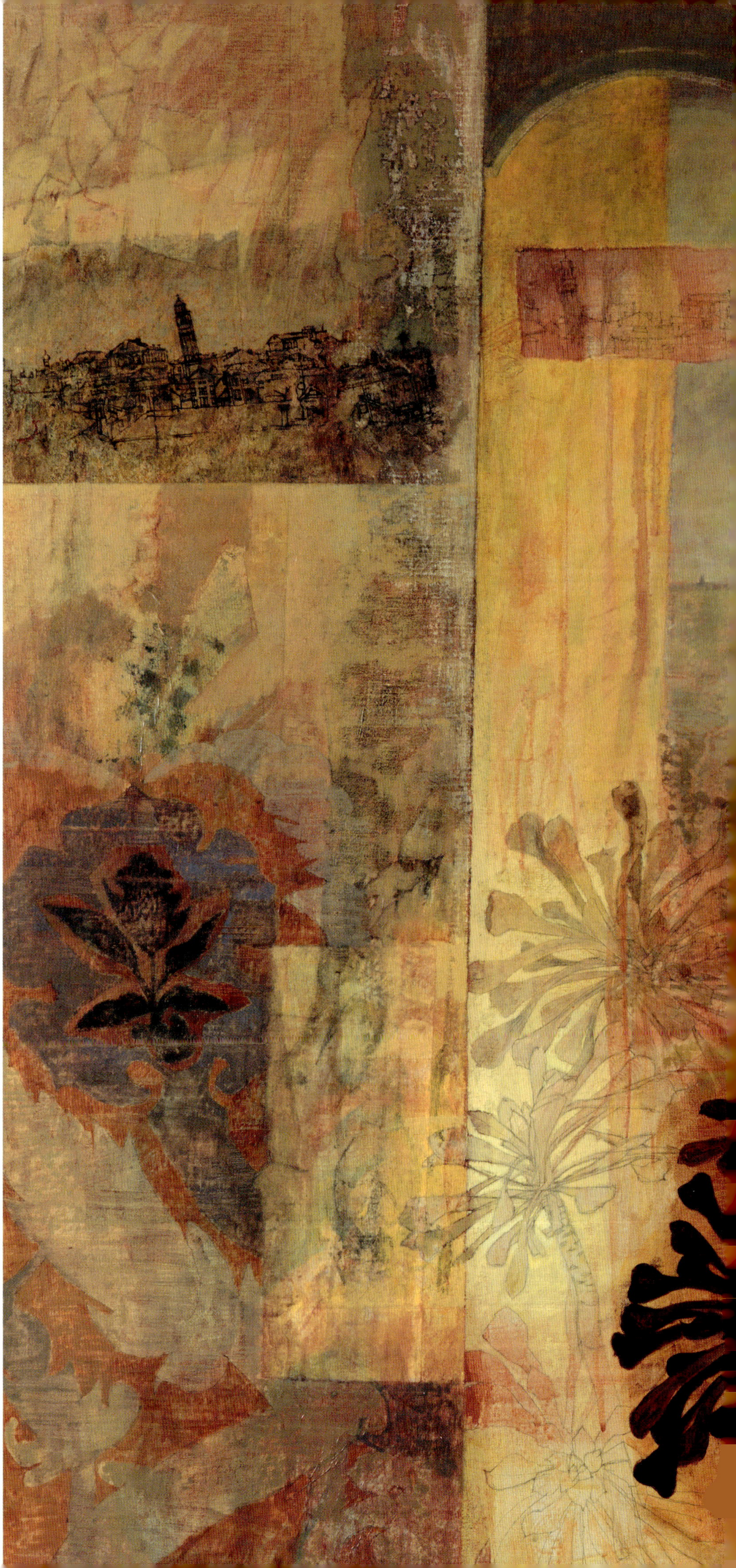

Studio Venice, Mirrored View

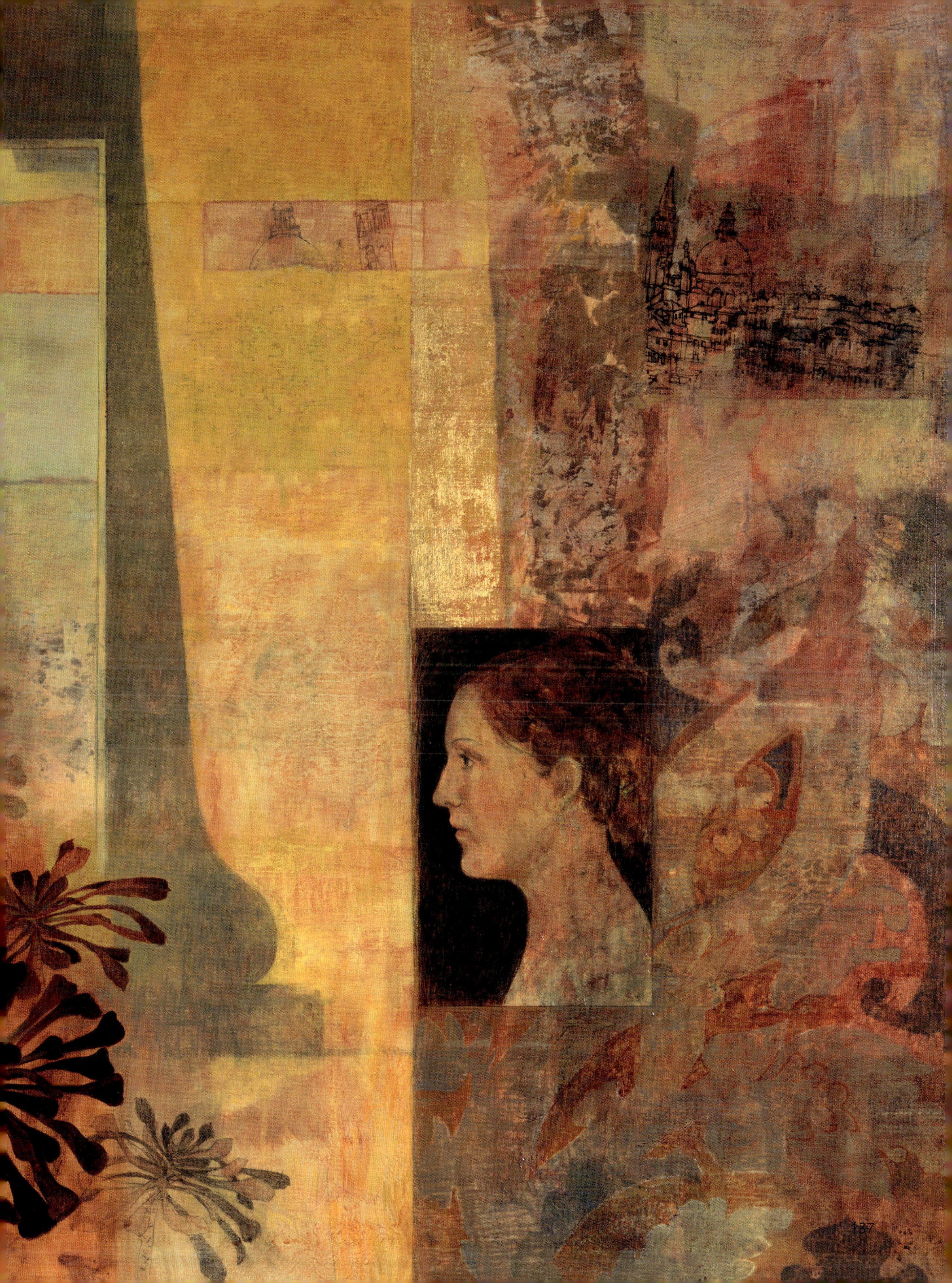

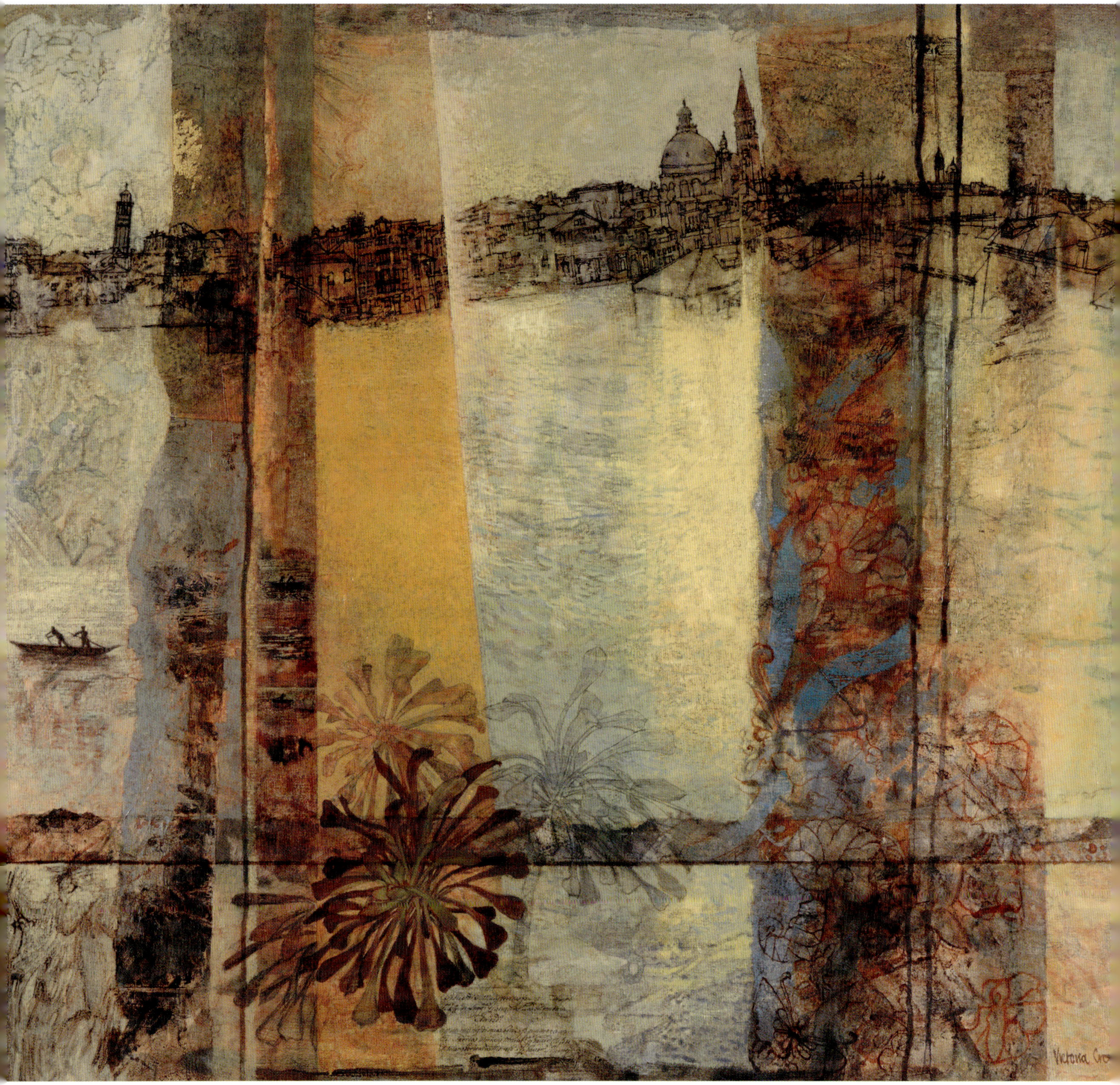

Morning, Reflections Across the Water

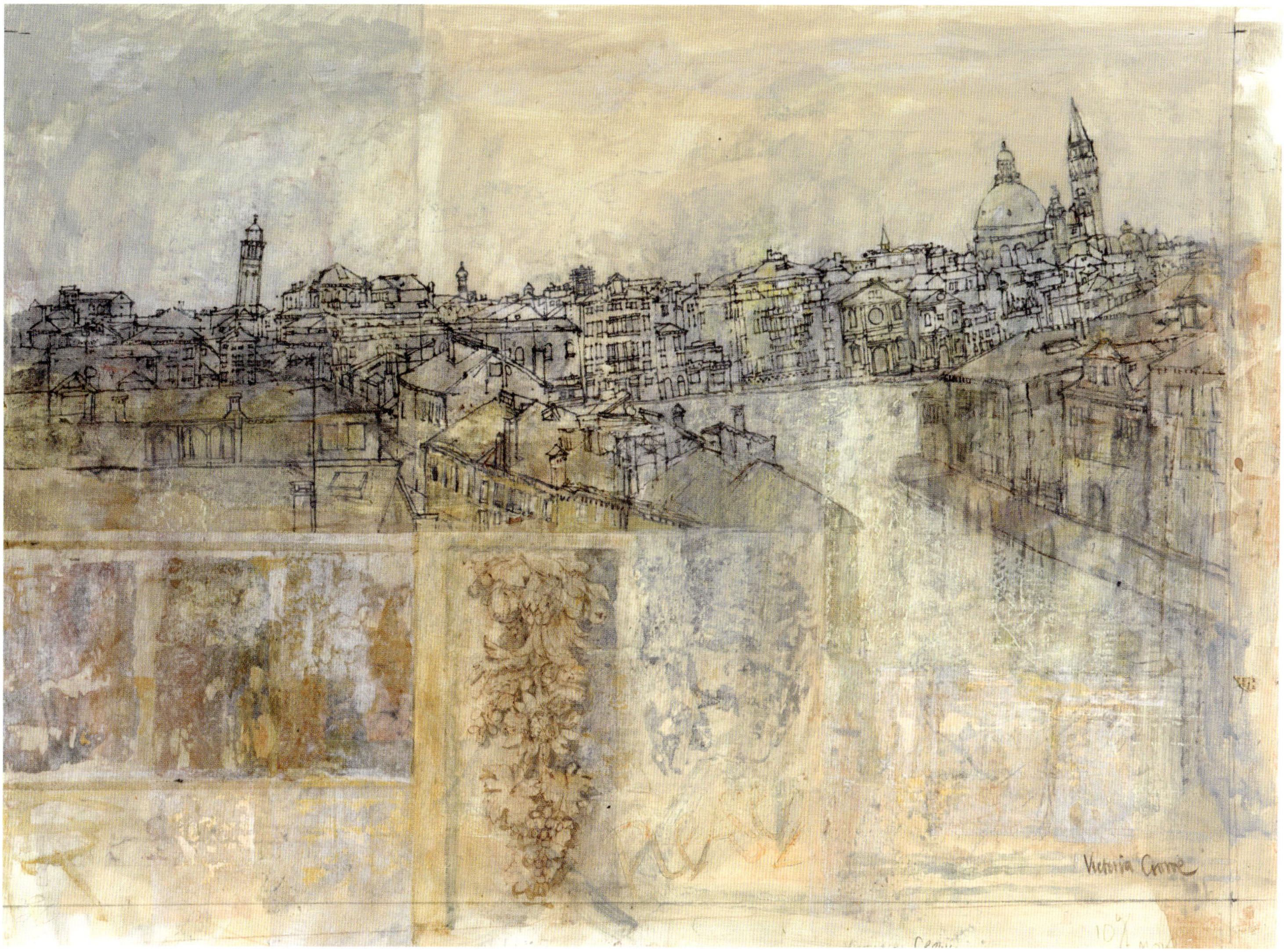

Thoughts on the City

Living on the Giudecca, we see the panorama of Venice, separated from us by the deep Giudecca canal. From the studio terrace, this vantage point is wonderful to draw from, but also to think about Venice, its history and artifacts. The distance from the very heart of the city seems to give one time to more fully reflect upon it. In a recent group of works I have used the skyline of the city as a kind of framework in which to refer to many other associations and memories of the city.

Victoria also began to broaden her Italian subject matter, however. The landscape at La Suvera near Siena, where she had been to stay a couple of times, appears in her drawings and in several paintings like *Dark Dog and Hillside*, *Landscape and Sentinel* and *Landscape – Duality*. The dogs that appear in these paintings, or in fact a lone dog in the two latter, appear, one black, the other white, in Piero's fresco of *Sigismondo Malatesta* in Rimini. She described them as guardians of the landscape, but in *Landscape – Duality* she also takes from Piero another idea. The dogs are set against two contrasted trees. These appear in Piero's *Resurrection*, bare and wintry to the left, green with spring to right, signifying the Resurrection as the renewal of life and Easter as the spring festival. By this symbol however, Piero, unconsciously no doubt, also links the Christian story to much older religions based on the year's cycle of renewal that had shaped its own calendar. The same two trees also appear on their own, one dark against red gold, the other almost flame-like against a dark landscape in *Holding the Heat of the Day*. Such memories of early Italian painting naturally drift into a landscape that is so reminiscent of it. A tall Annunciation lily migrates from a beautiful drawing of the flower itself to take its place in several pictures as a kind of mediator between the tangible world, the world of art and of things remembered. *Drawing Lilies*, a superb painting of different lilies against red gold, the central flower based on a magnificent drawing, looks back to 'Plant Memory' and the genesis of the exhibition is also referred to in *Still Life with Impermanence*. The herbarium specimen of *Sibbaldia Recumbens* that appears in David Ingram's portrait dominates the picture, but is transfigured as though in gold.

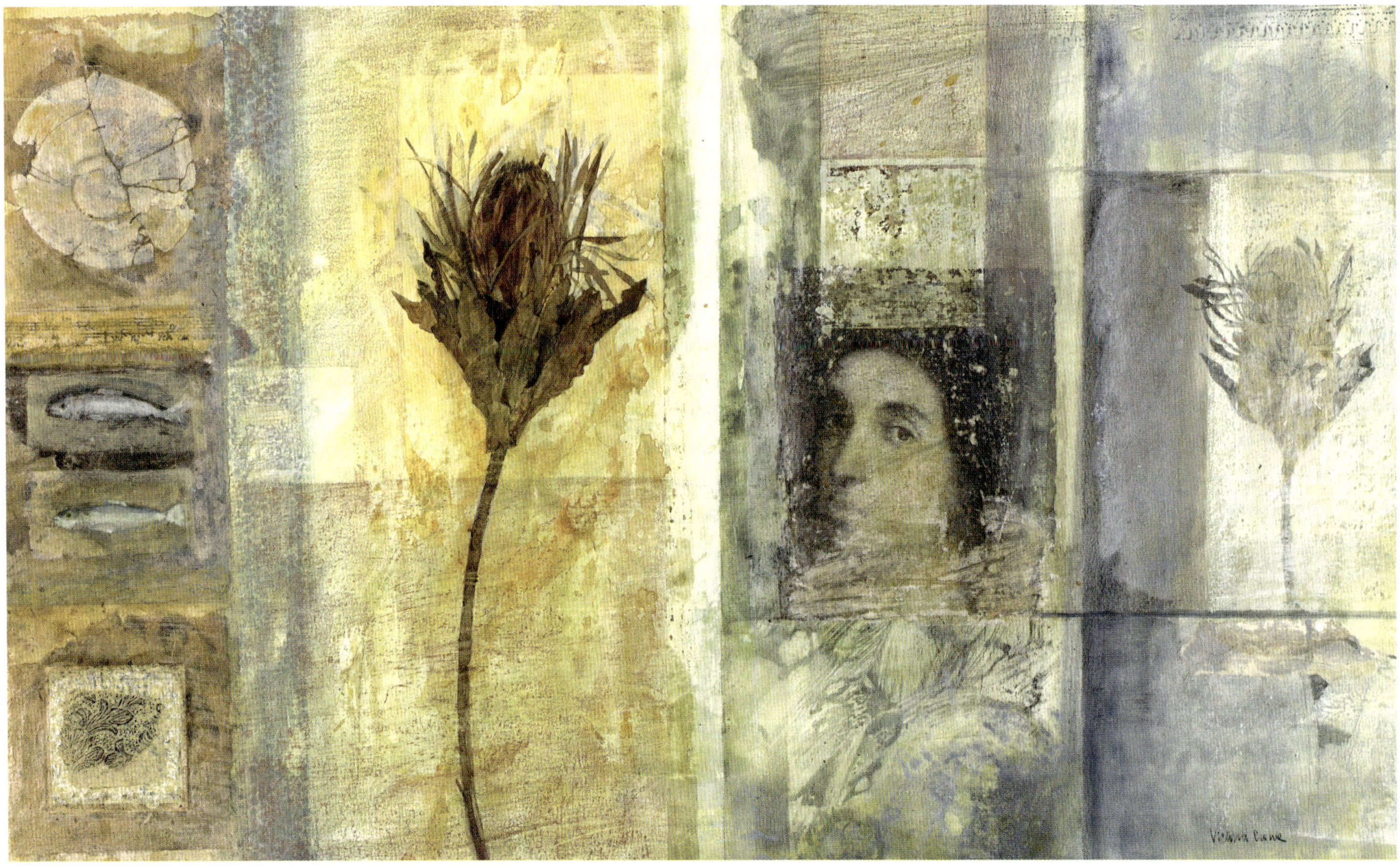

Reflected Contemplation

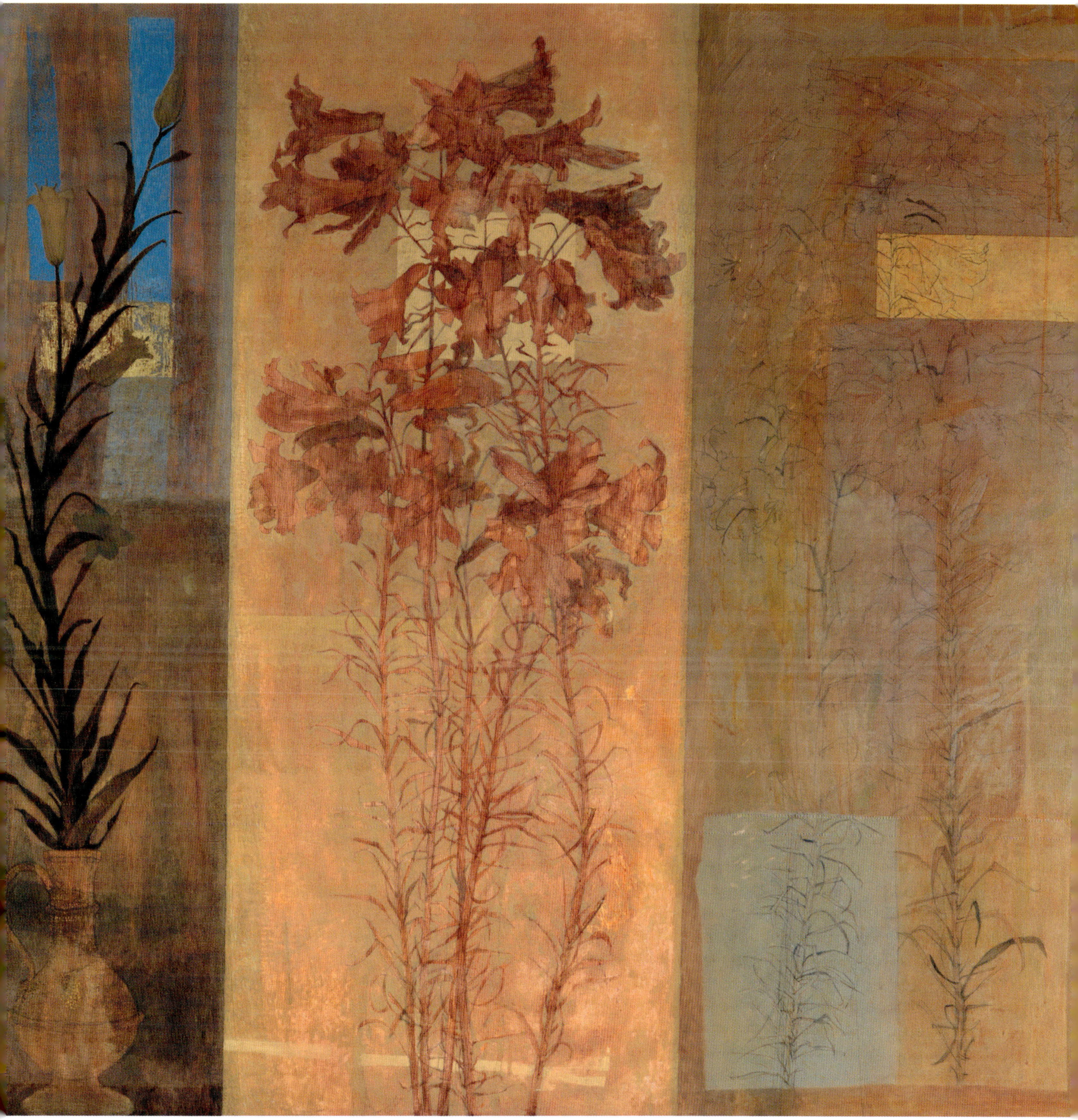

Drawing Lilies

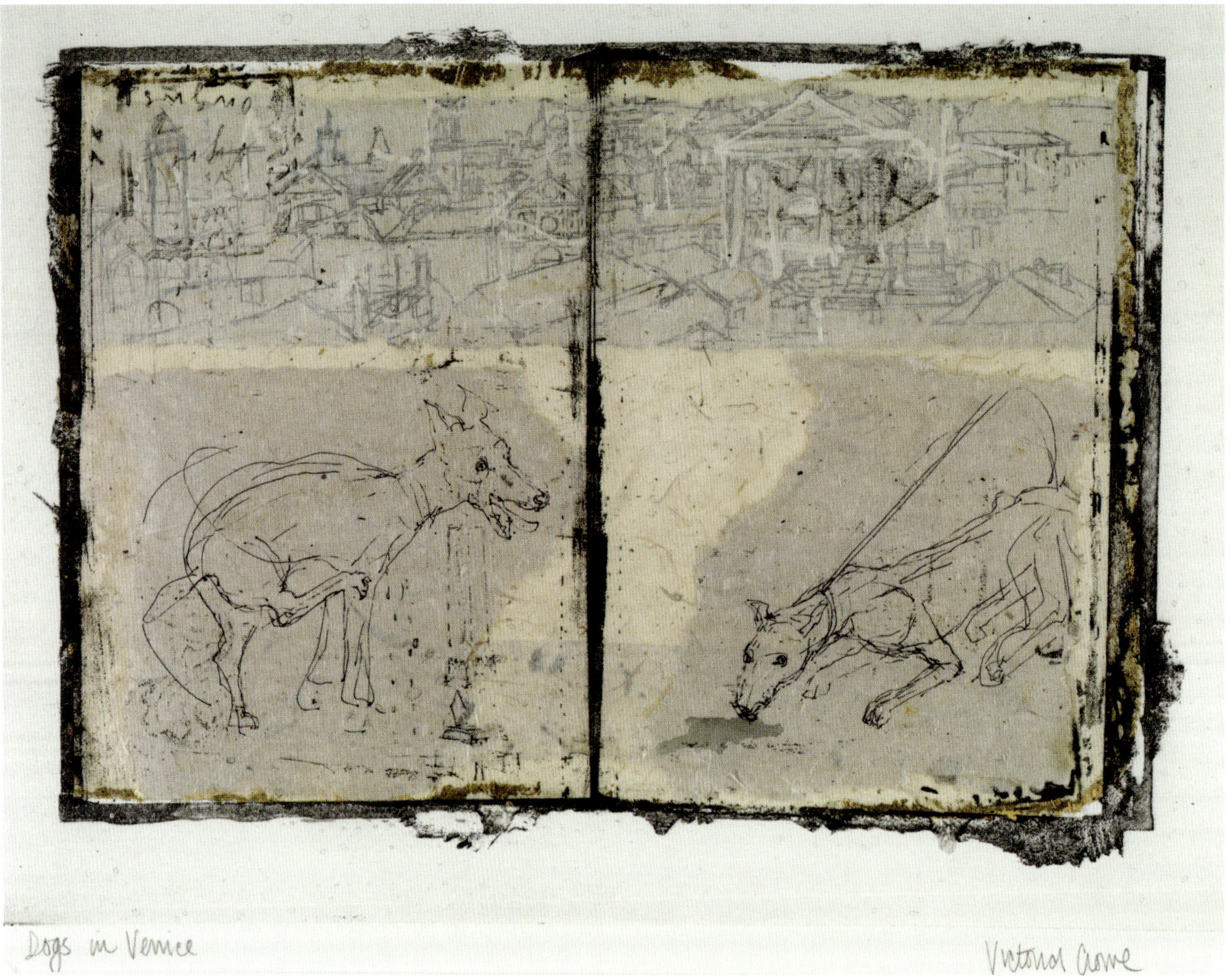
Dogs in Venice
Victoria Crowe

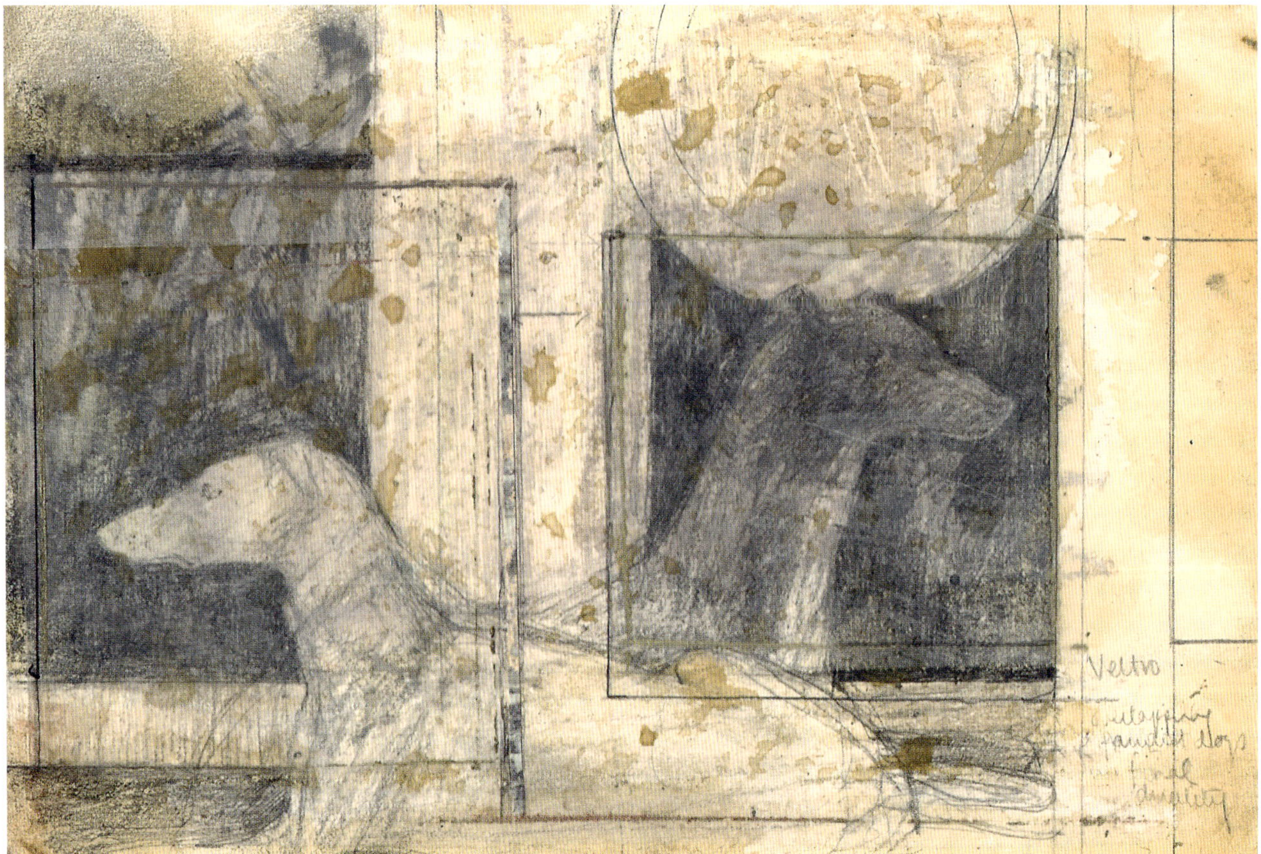
Veltro
Victoria Crowe

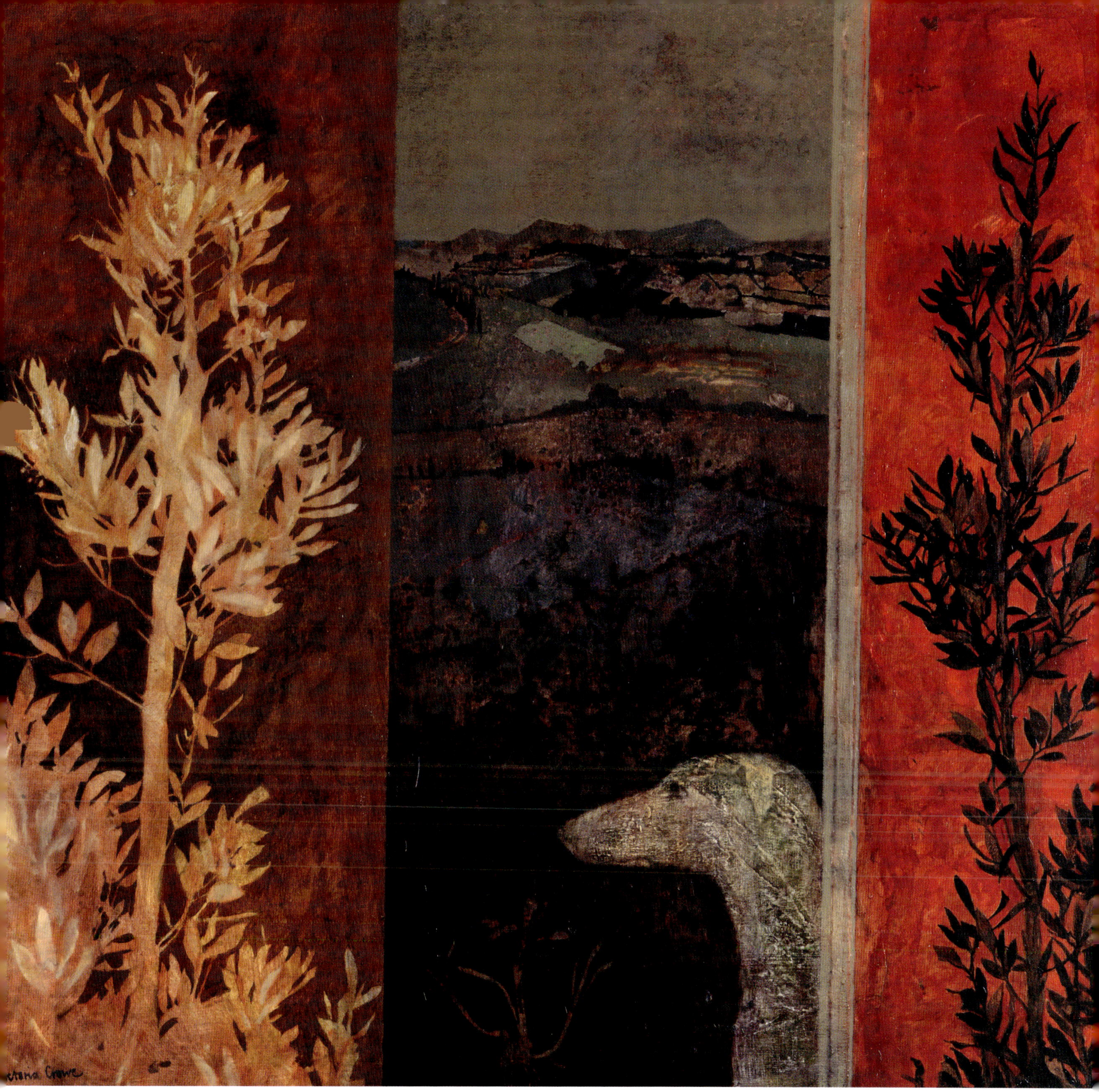

Landscape Sentinels

The estate of La Suvera, west of Siena, is rich in architecture and statuary. In an isolated part of the grounds I came upon a life-sized terracotta guard dog, ears docked, very fierce. This put me in mind of dogs and landscapes, but Piero's gentle greyhounds which inhabit my Italian landscapes are very different sentinels.

Dogs in Venice

Piero's Mysterious Dogs

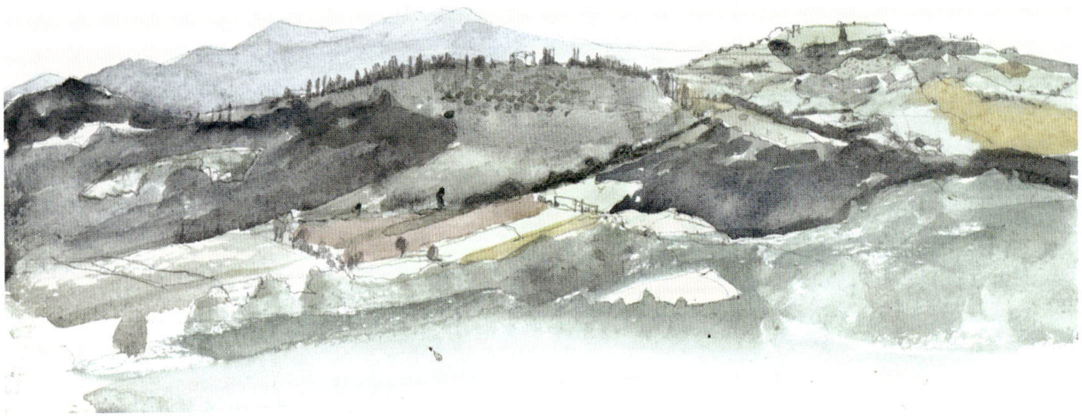

La Suvera, Landscape

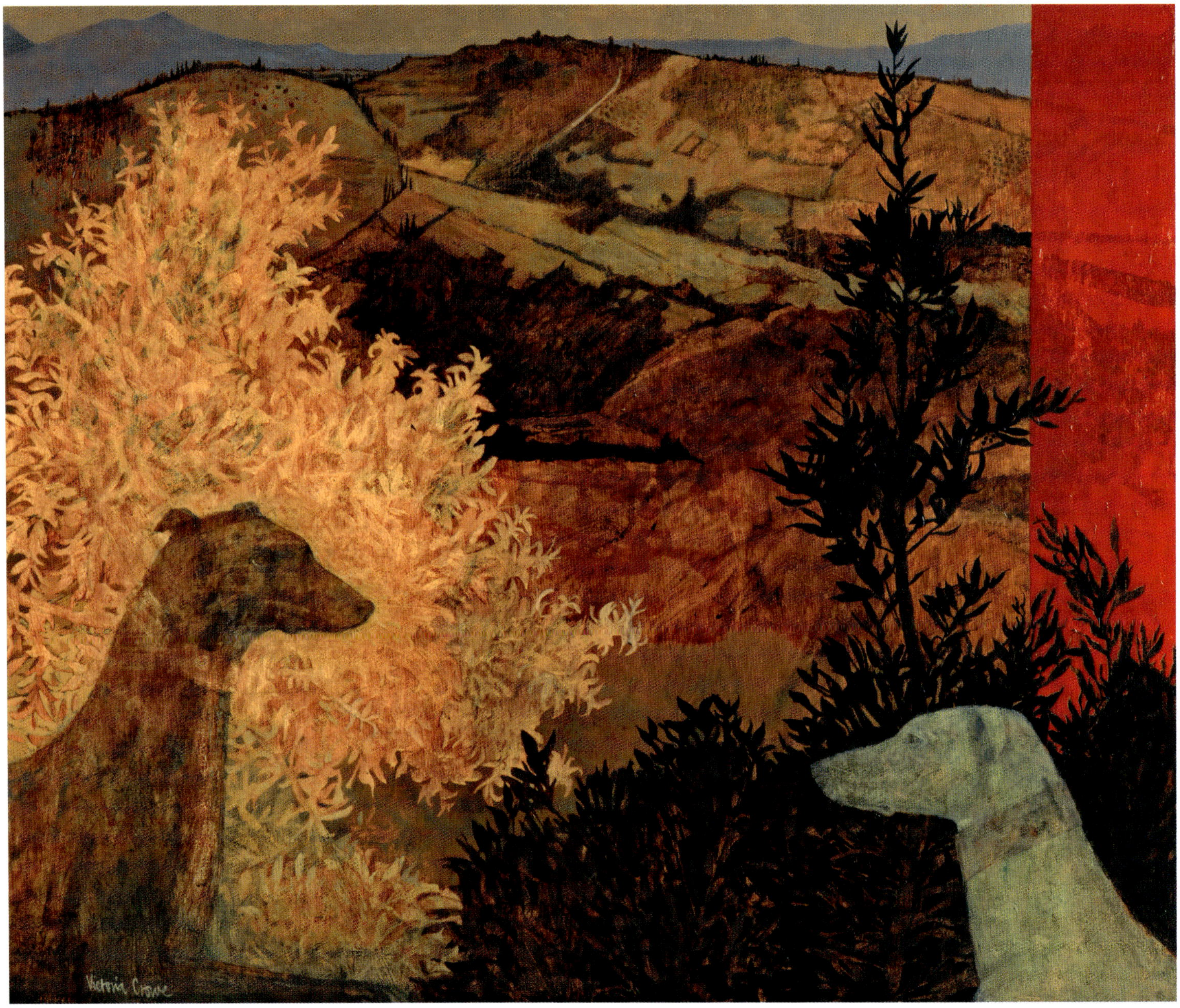

Landscape – Duality

Landscape and Sentinel, La Suvera

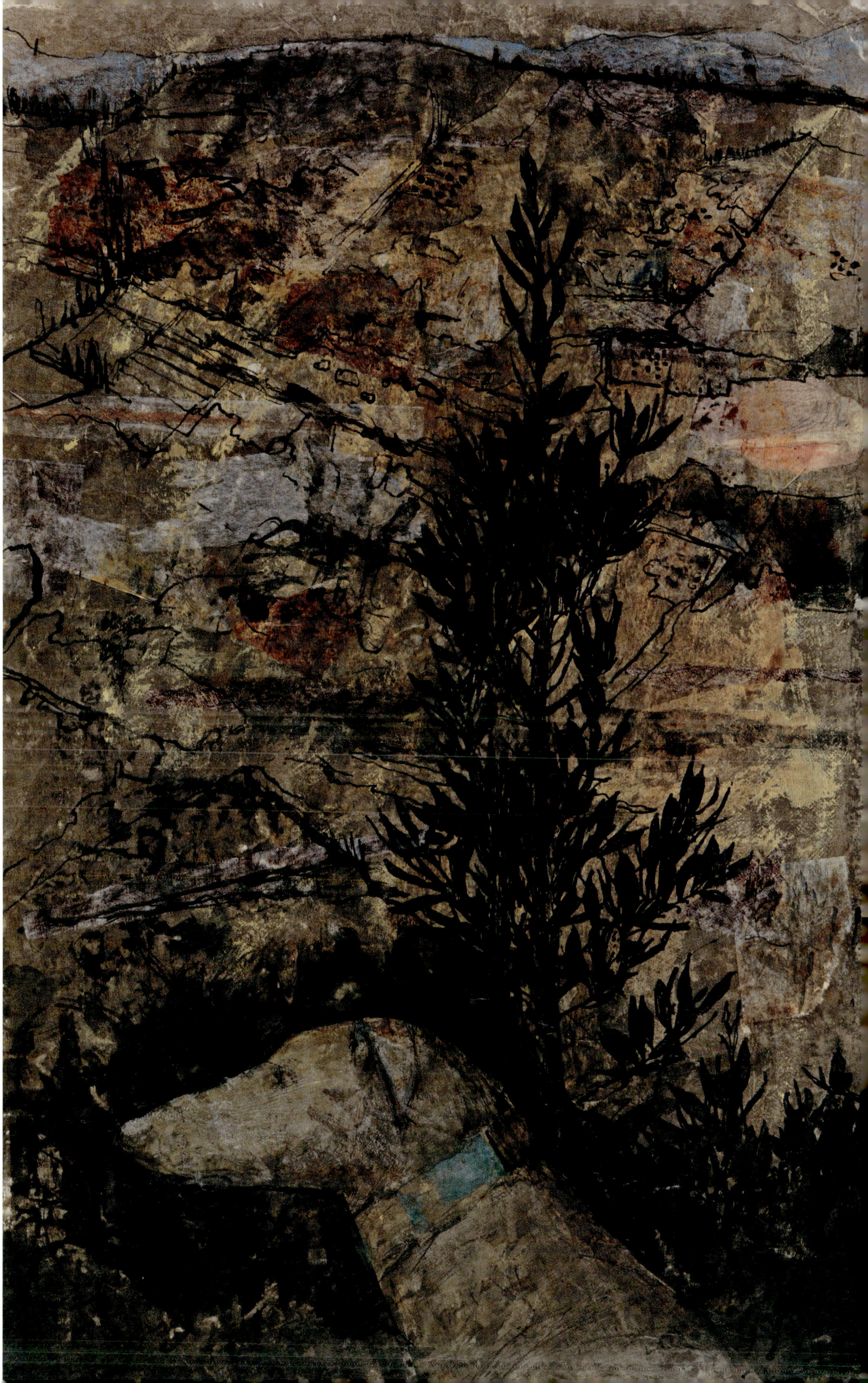

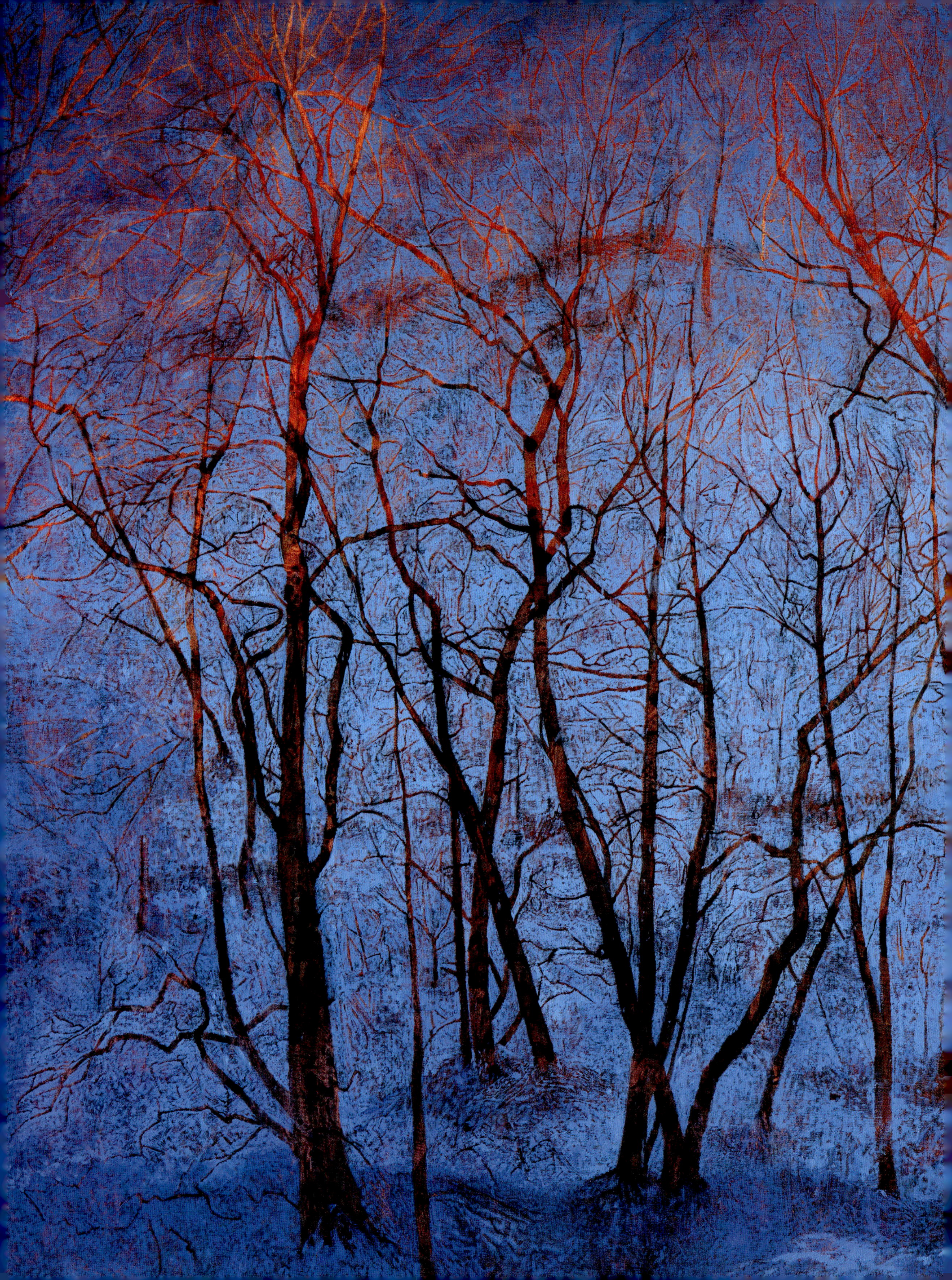

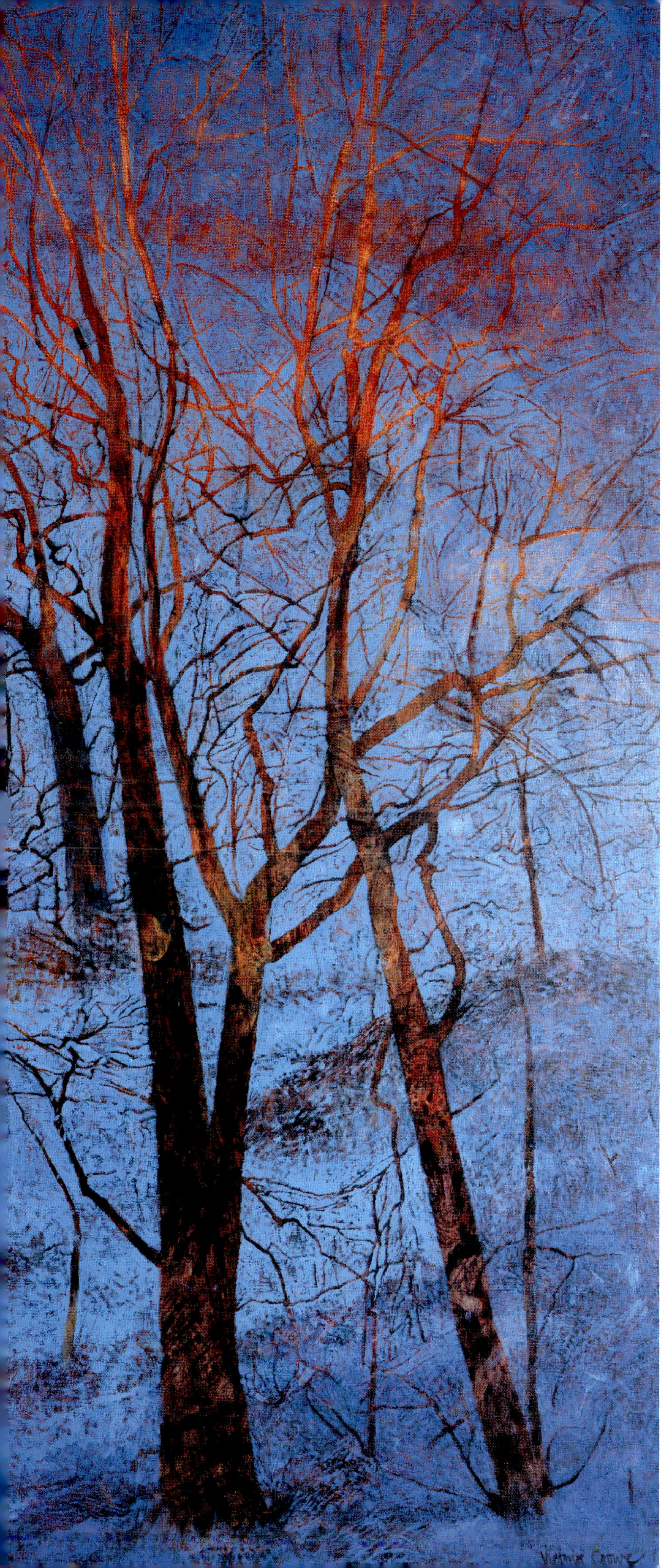

Blue Snow and Fiery Trees

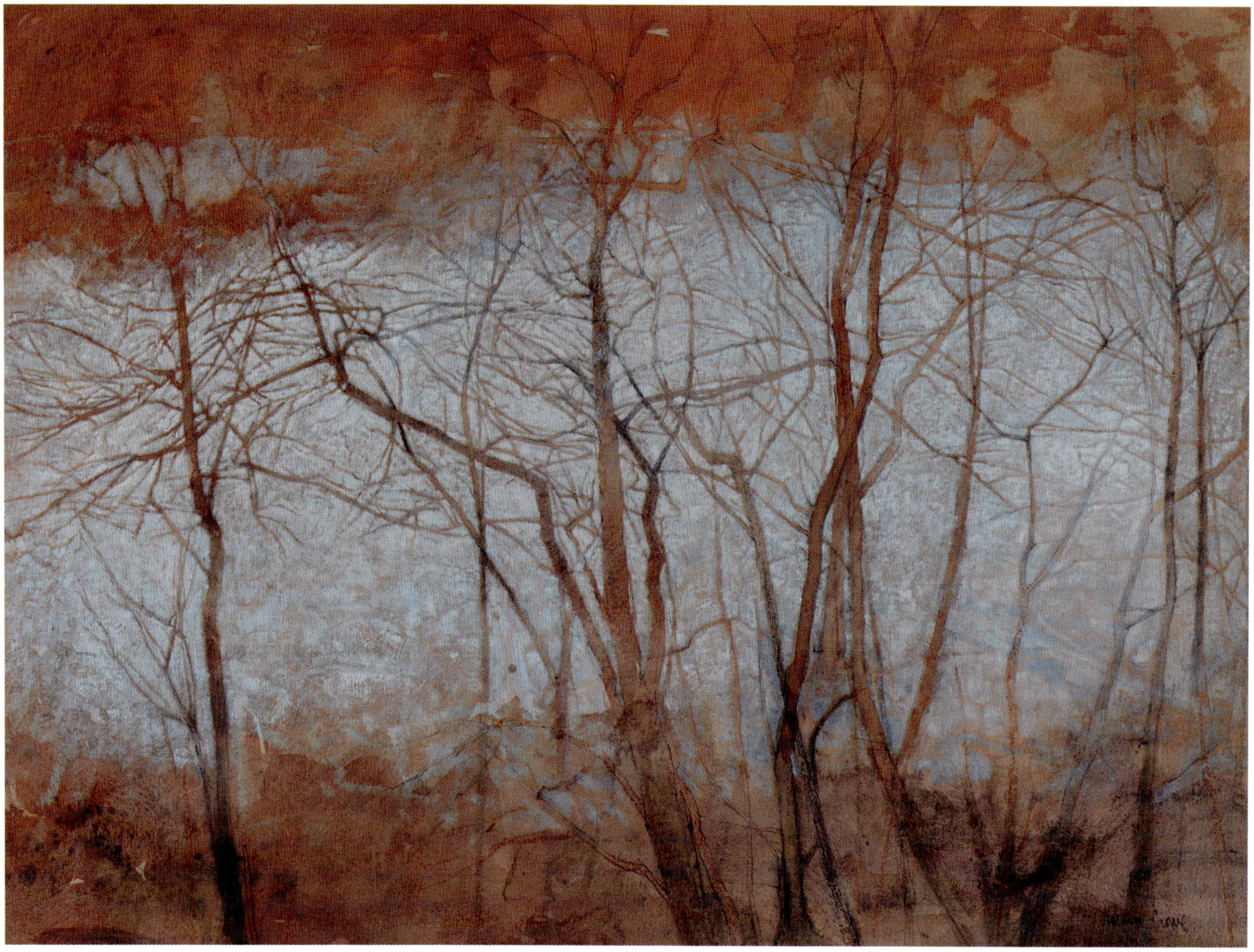

Tree Snow Study

During the two years since her Festival exhibition in 2010, Victoria's paintings of landscape have developed new resonances. The symbolism of the two trees in various paintings of 2010 reappears in a beautifully economical form in *Ice and Fire* and several other pictures inspired by a tree hung with ice seen against an evergreen, an image that also appears as a detail in *Events in the Garden*. Pictures like this and other winter landscapes like *Lying Snow, Winter Caveat, Snow Moment*, or *Snowlines* clearly echo the winter scenes of Victoria's earlier work. The latter picture, inspired by the hard winter of 2010, brings together scrapbook items, notes, her own sketches of winter scenes, some from years before, and a transfer from a stereoscopic photograph of men in bowler hats clearing snow a hundred years ago. This is a memory of a stereoscope that had belonged to her father and that she had known as a child. The background to the painting is the winter view of trees and the garden fence in West Linton, but the picture is not pinned down by its location. The collaged details extend it in time and explicitly in memory.

Winter Studio

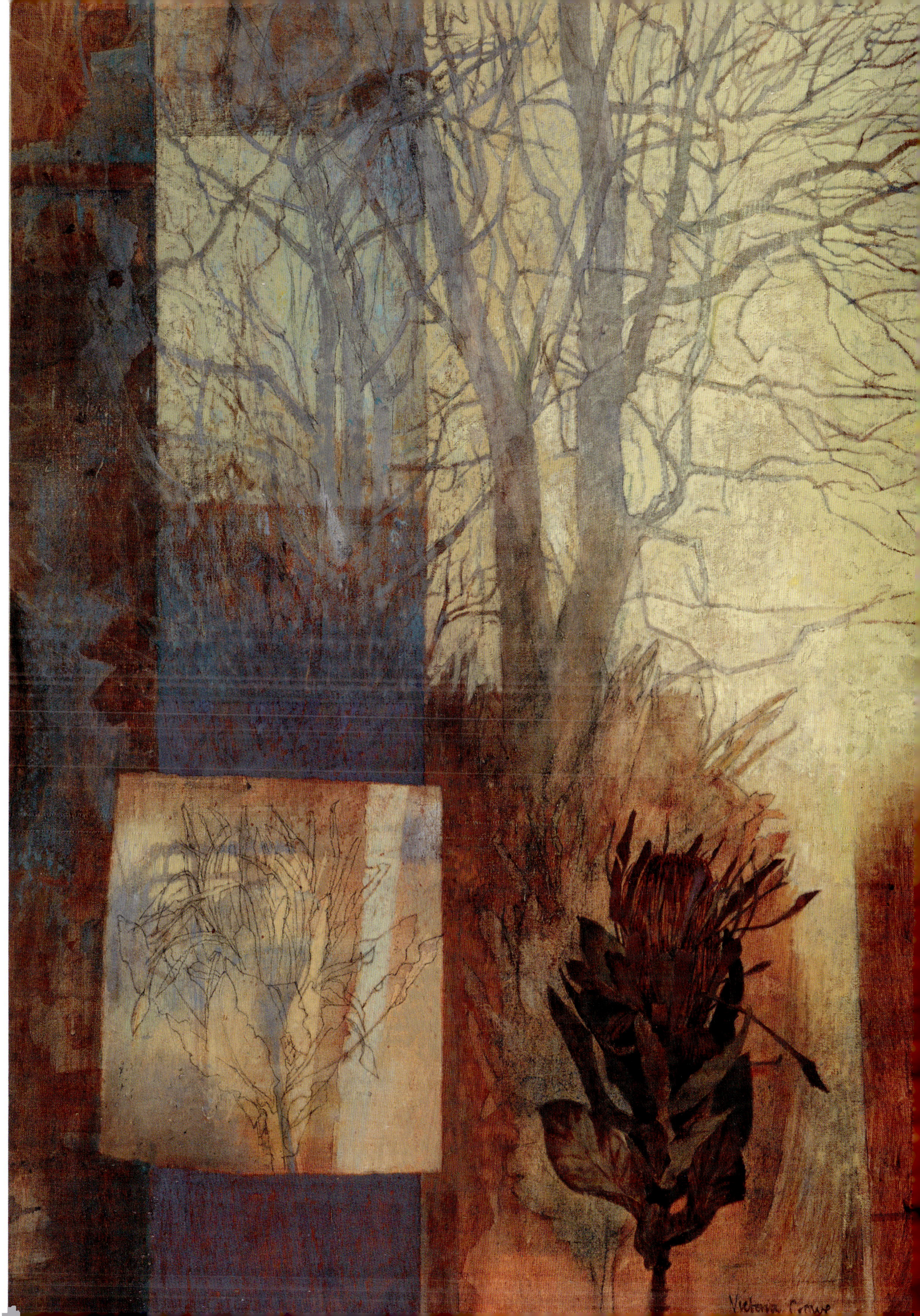
Victoria Crowe

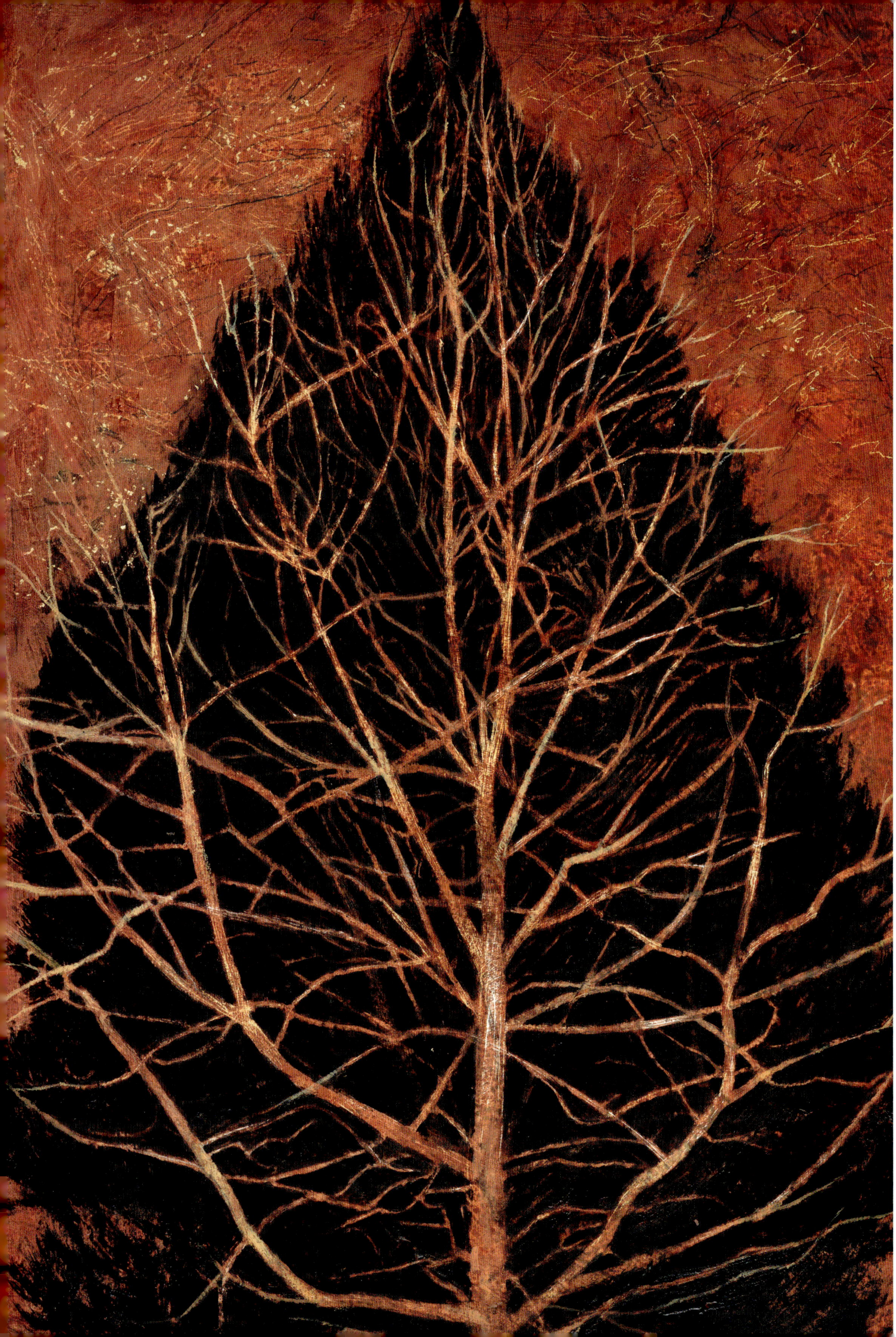

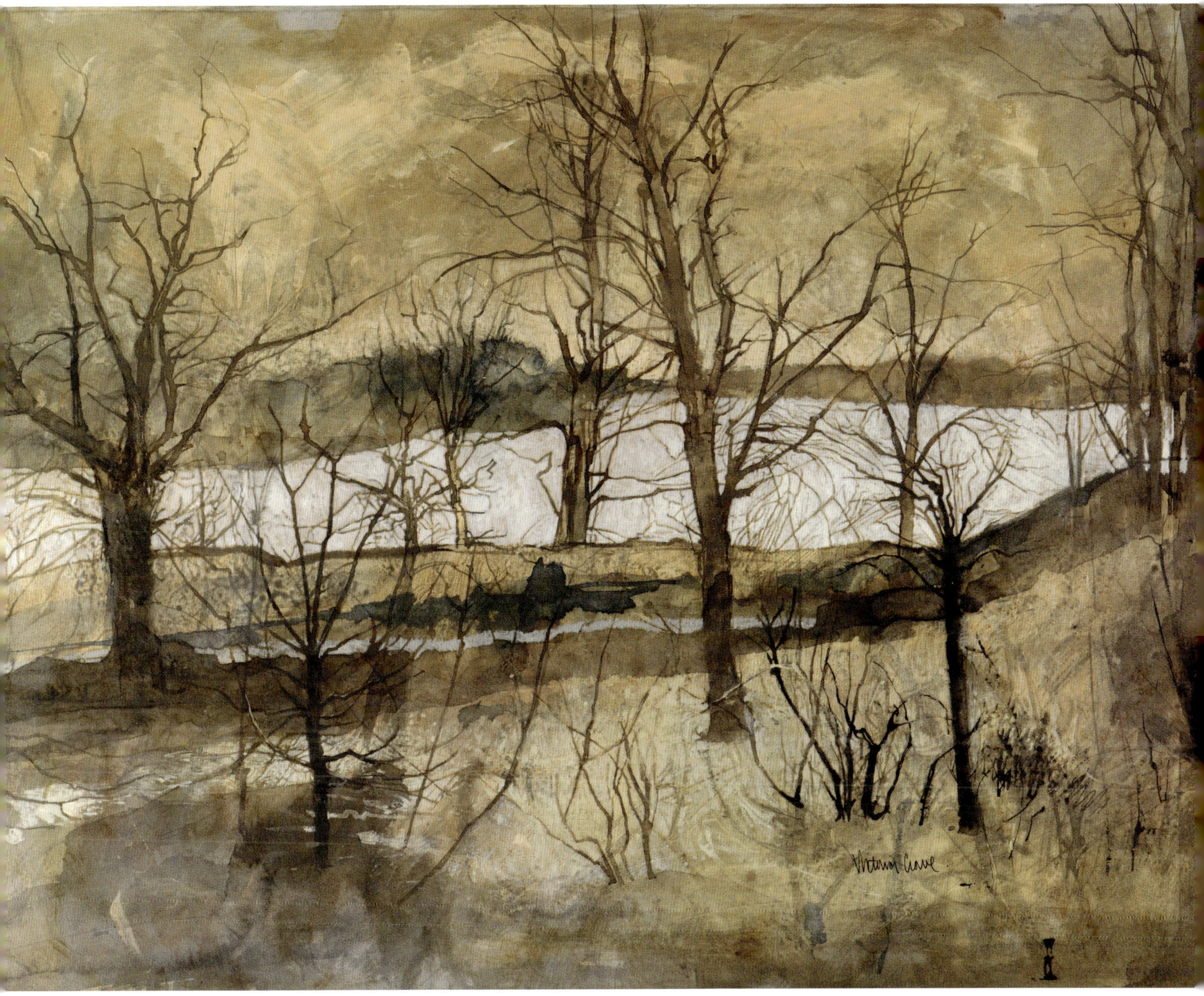

Lying Snow

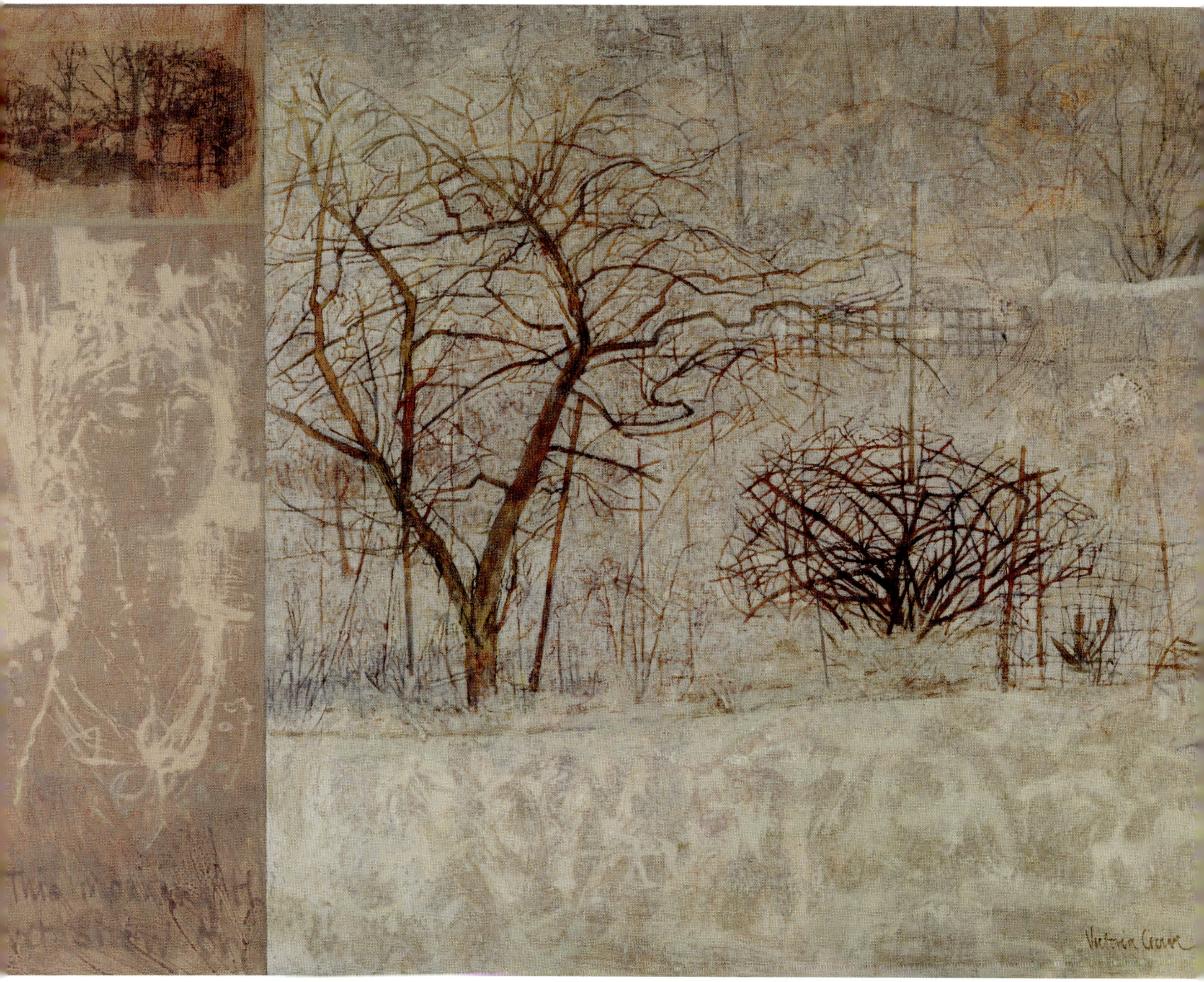

Rosa Proprina visits the Back Garden in Winter

The beautiful twisted hazel in the garden is a prominent feature in *Garden Room – A View from the Interior*, where it is seen against the snow through the multiple reflections in the windows of the conservatory that gives the picture its title. To the left a more distant tree is seen against the light of a winter sky filtered through a slatted blind. The Annunciation lily is there too in its role perhaps of mediator between the real and the imagined. The artist's own work is part of these memories, of course, and to make the link explicit Rosa Proprina revisits the scene and appears in several winter landscapes, one charmingly titled *Rosa Proprina visits the Back Garden in Winter*, Estella says it's frost. Estella is Mike and Victoria's grand-daughter.

Snow Moment

Visiting Cat and Two Snowmen

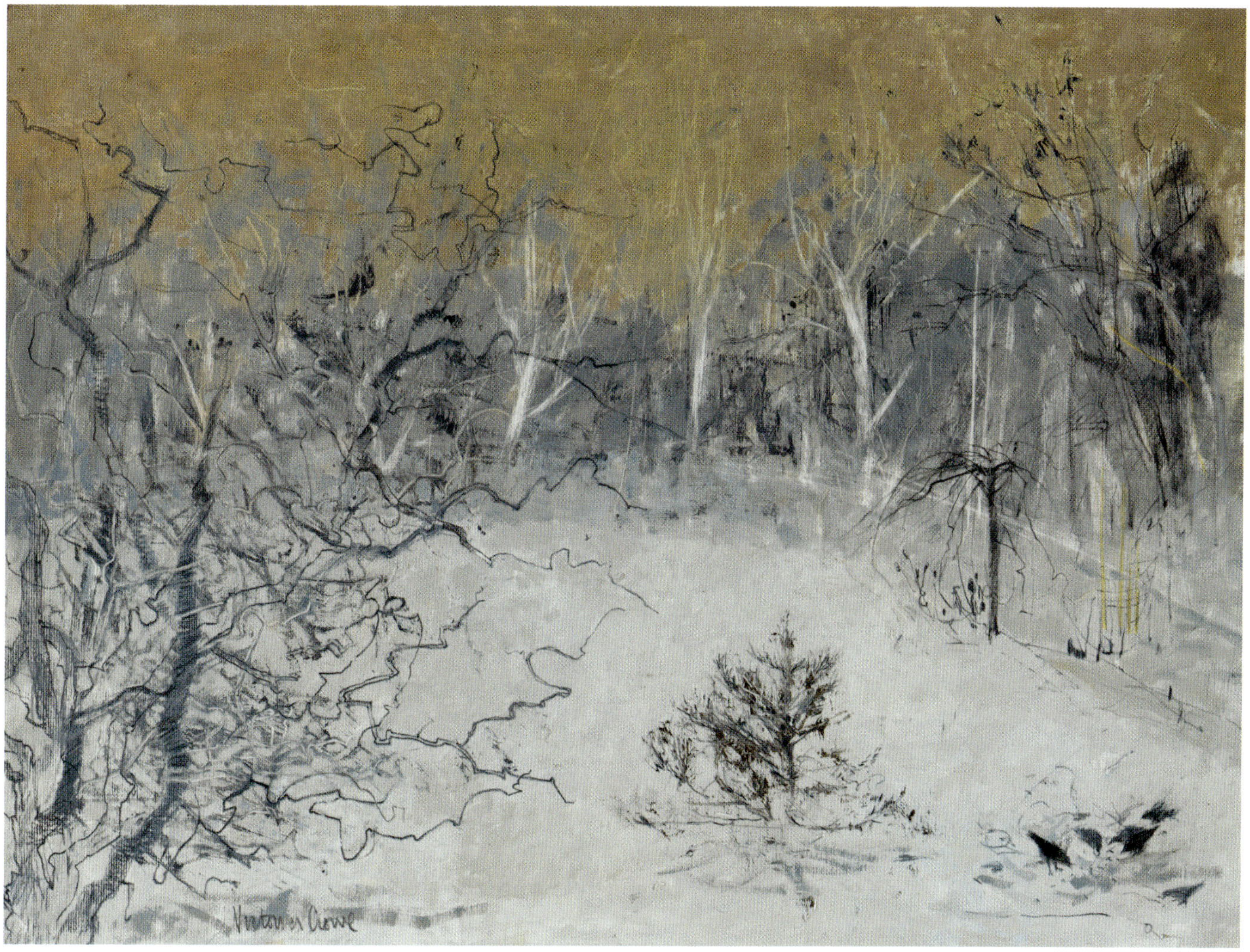

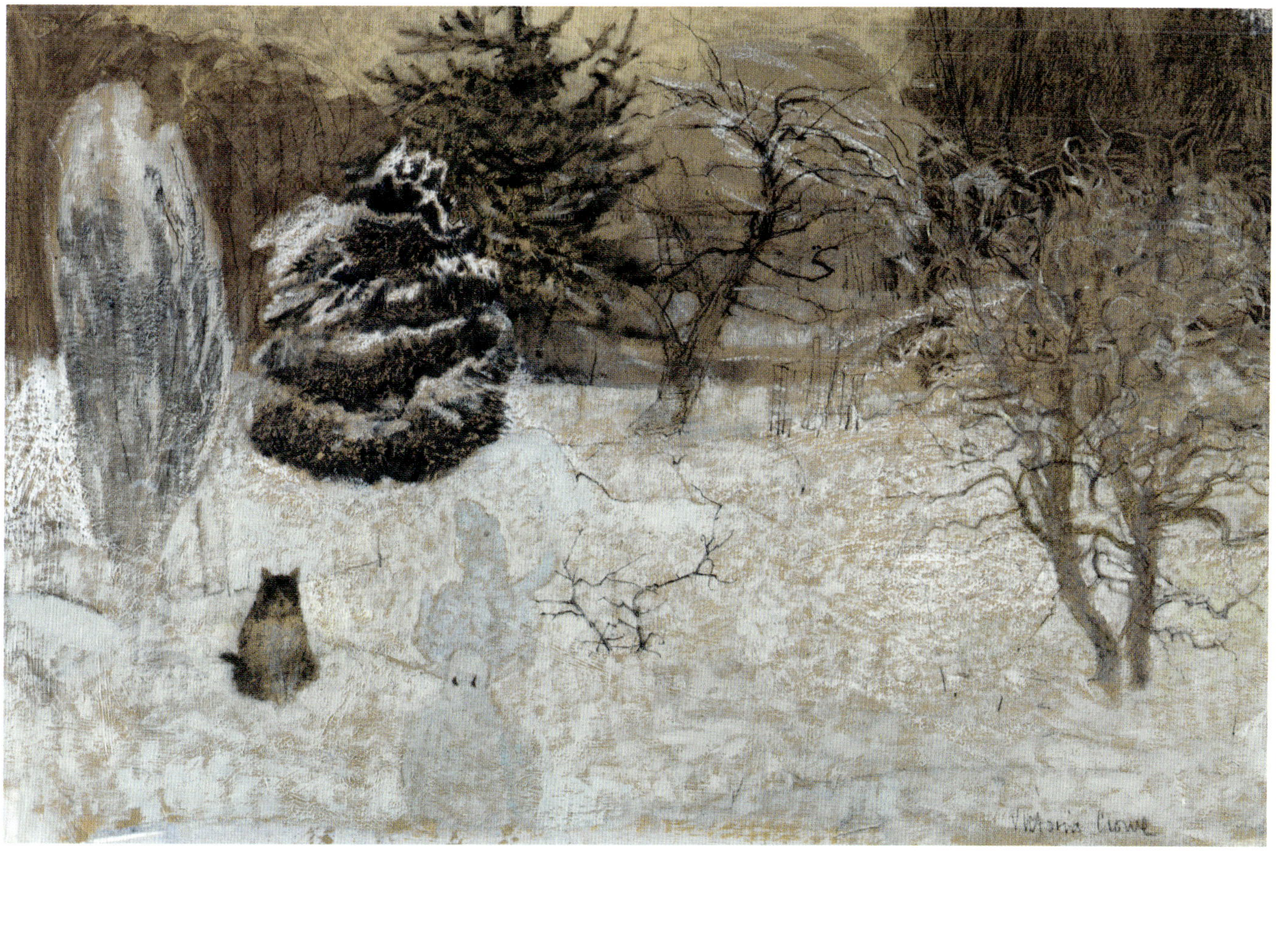

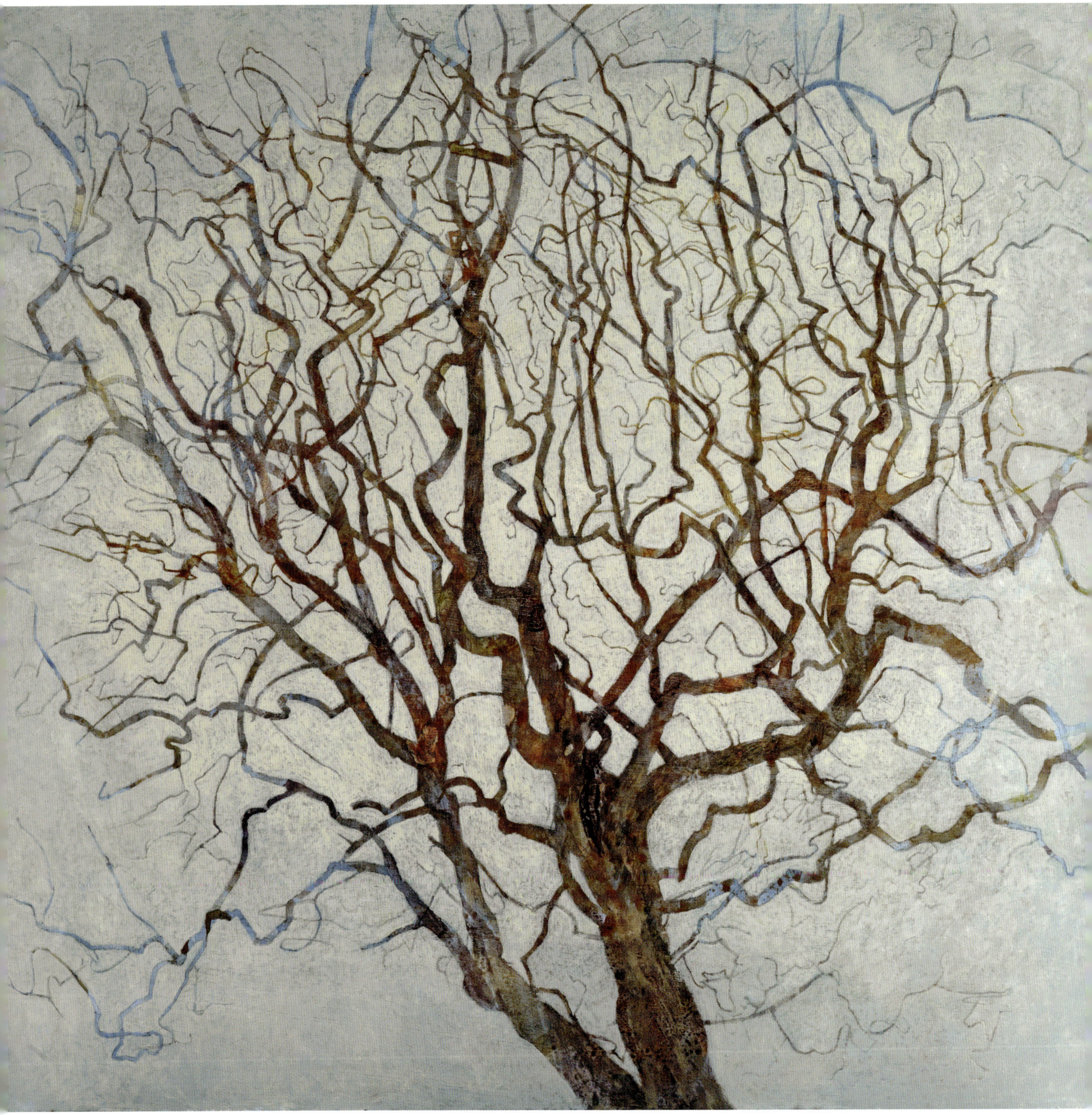

Numinous Tree

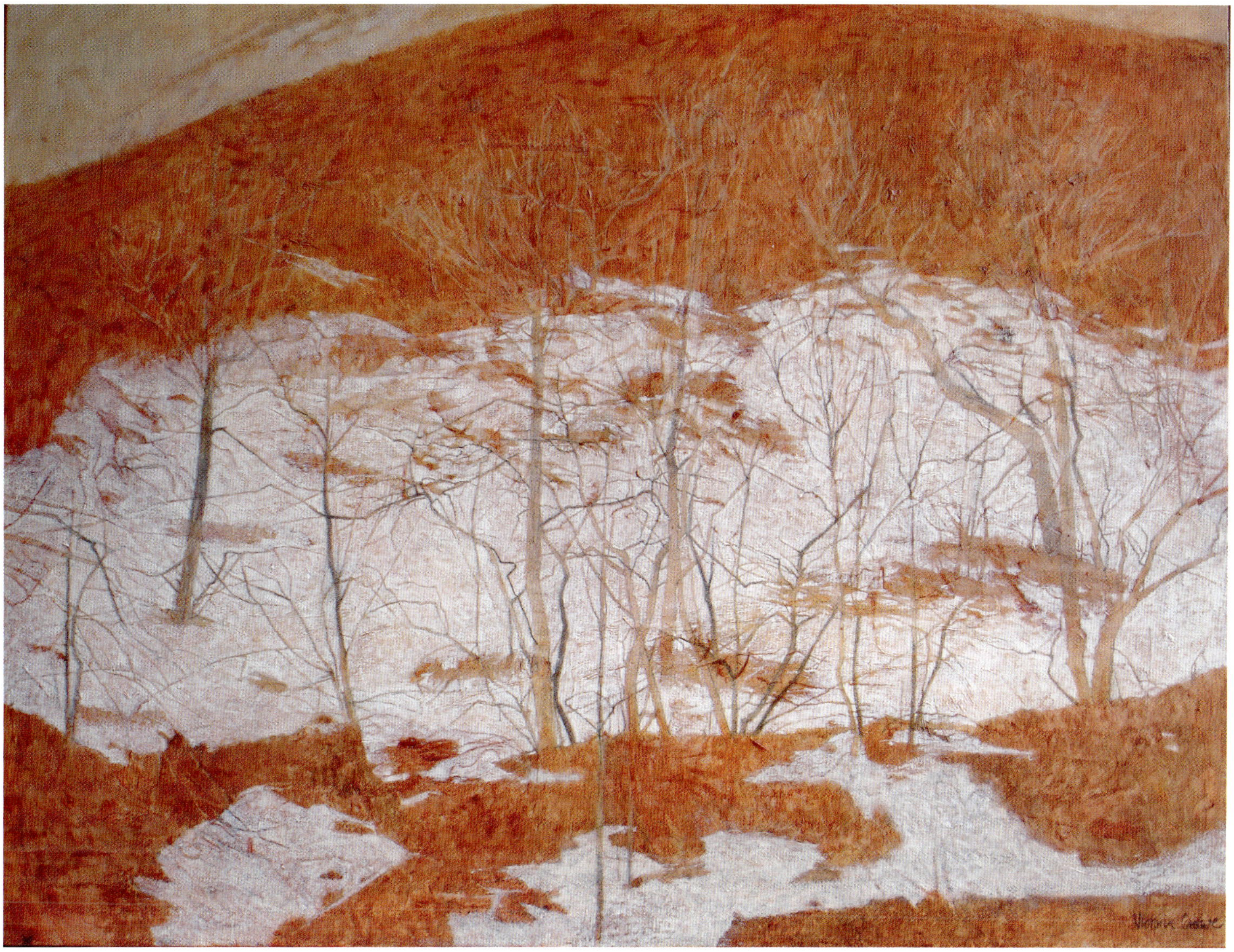

Shape of the Shadow

'Numinous', the *Oxford Dictionary* defines as 'having a strong religious or spiritual quality; indicating or suggesting the presence of a divinity.' Victoria uses the word again in the title of *Numinous Garden*, a painting of her twisted hazel tree against snow, dark in the immediate foreground, golden in the sun in the middle ground and blue in the distance closed by more scarlet trees. Once again the evening sun is touching them with pink and gold. Painted in 2010, *Shape of the Shadow* is a painting of trees that stand on a ridge above the green in West Linton. They catch the light of the setting sun when the river and green beneath are already in shadow. In the picture the hill itself is red with the light of the setting sun, and the trees are silhouetted against a patch of snow. A new departure, this was the first of several similar compositions painted over the next couple of years. One of the most striking is *Numinous Tree*. It is nothing but a bare tree against grey sky, but where once this would have been a painting in a minor key, now the tree is touched by the scarlet rays of the evening sun. The major key enters to suggest almost a moment of resurrection, certainly a promise of the year's turning. The title clearly proposes the picture is more than just a landscape.

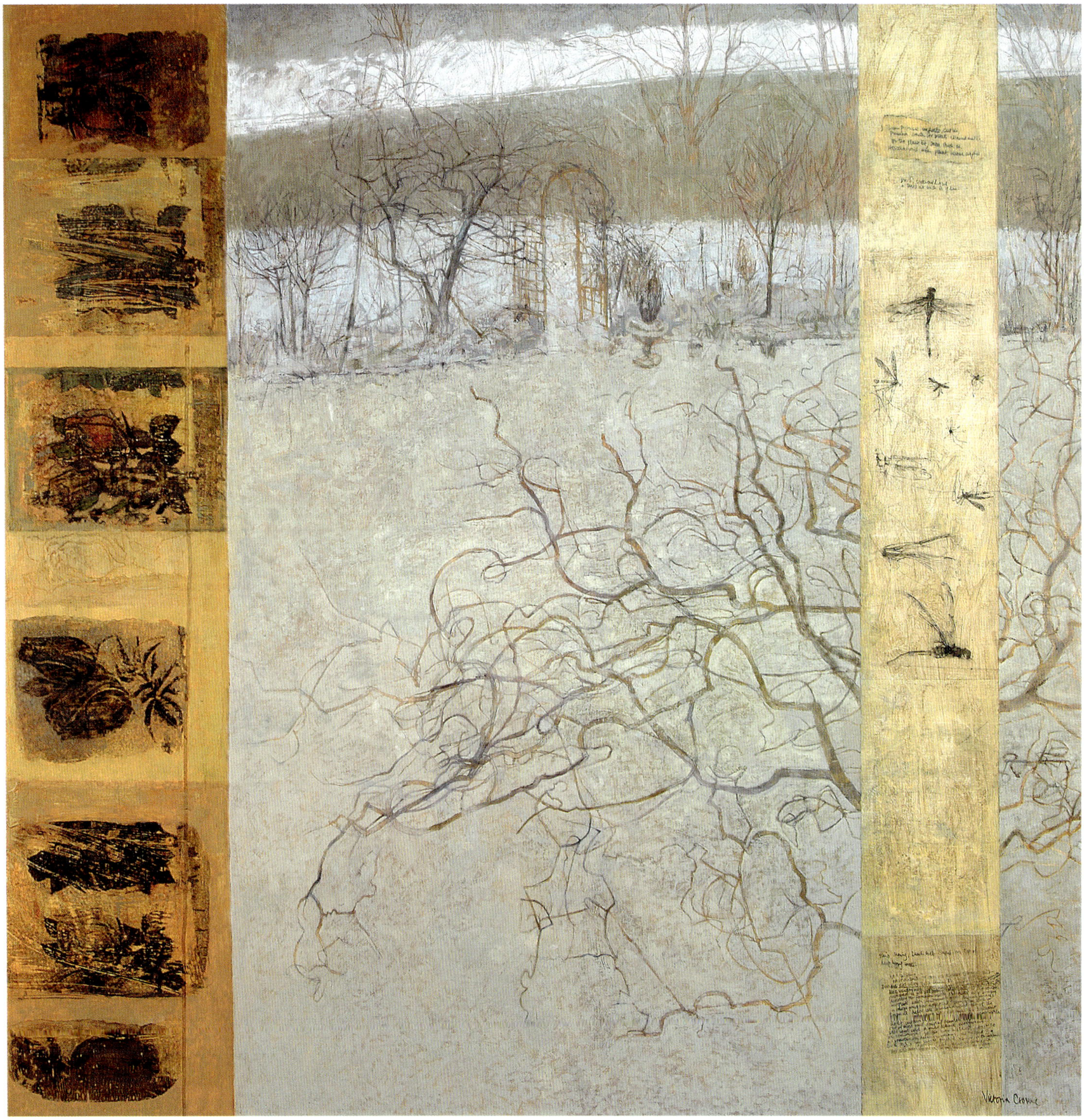

Winter Caveat

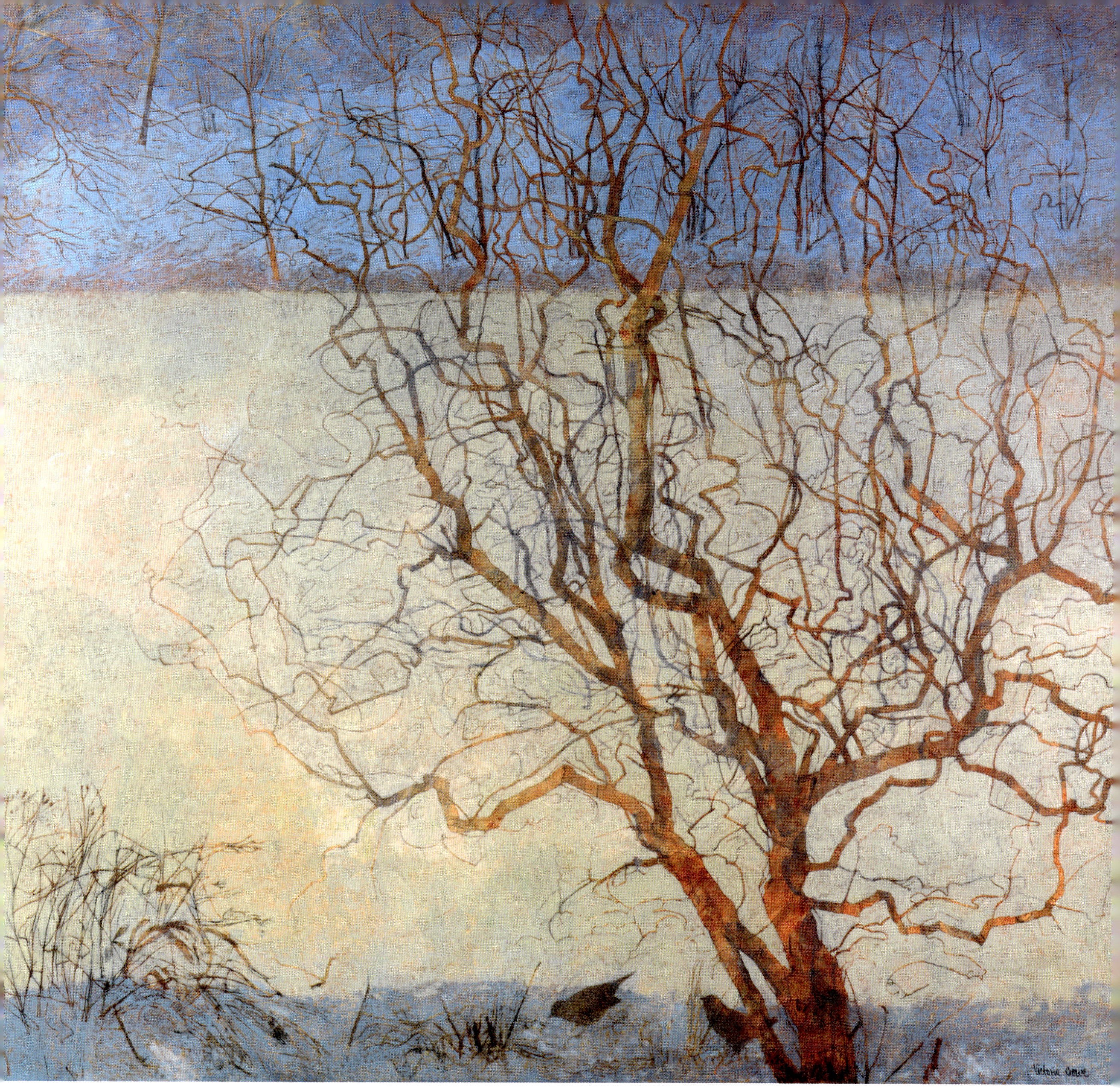

Numinous Garden

The most astonishing picture in this series, however, is *Blue Snow and Fiery Trees*. The trees alone are catching the sun's scarlet rays, but only in their upper branches. Already in shadow as the sun sets, their lower trunks are black and the snow beyond is blue in the approaching dusk. Equally striking though is *The Shortest Day*, a picture of the hazel tree seen against mist. There is light, but it almost seems to be coming from the tree itself. This is once again the still point of the turning year, but as the year is turning, so there is now the hope of the return of the light. These really are numinous pictures; they are spiritual landscapes. In the last lecture that he ever gave, Constable's advice to young painters was to quote *Ecclesiastes*: 'Remember now thy creator in the days of thy youth'.[1] Young or old, believer or unbeliever, you cannot do otherwise looking at pictures like this. Victoria has come a long way from transcribing Russian icons, but the ambition of her art is still the same. *Concerning the Spiritual in Art*, the words chosen by Wassily Kandinsky, like Rublev a Russian, for the title of his book might be used to describe its central preoccupation.

You have to look to Caspar David Friedrich to find landscapes that have such a powerful metaphysical presence although they seem at first so straightforward, or perhaps to Constable again. He also said, and both parts of the quotation have a bearing on Victoria Crowe's work, for in the first part he is talking about memory and association: 'Still I should paint my own places best; painting is with me but another word for feeling.'[2]

Duncan Macmillan, Edinburgh, 2012

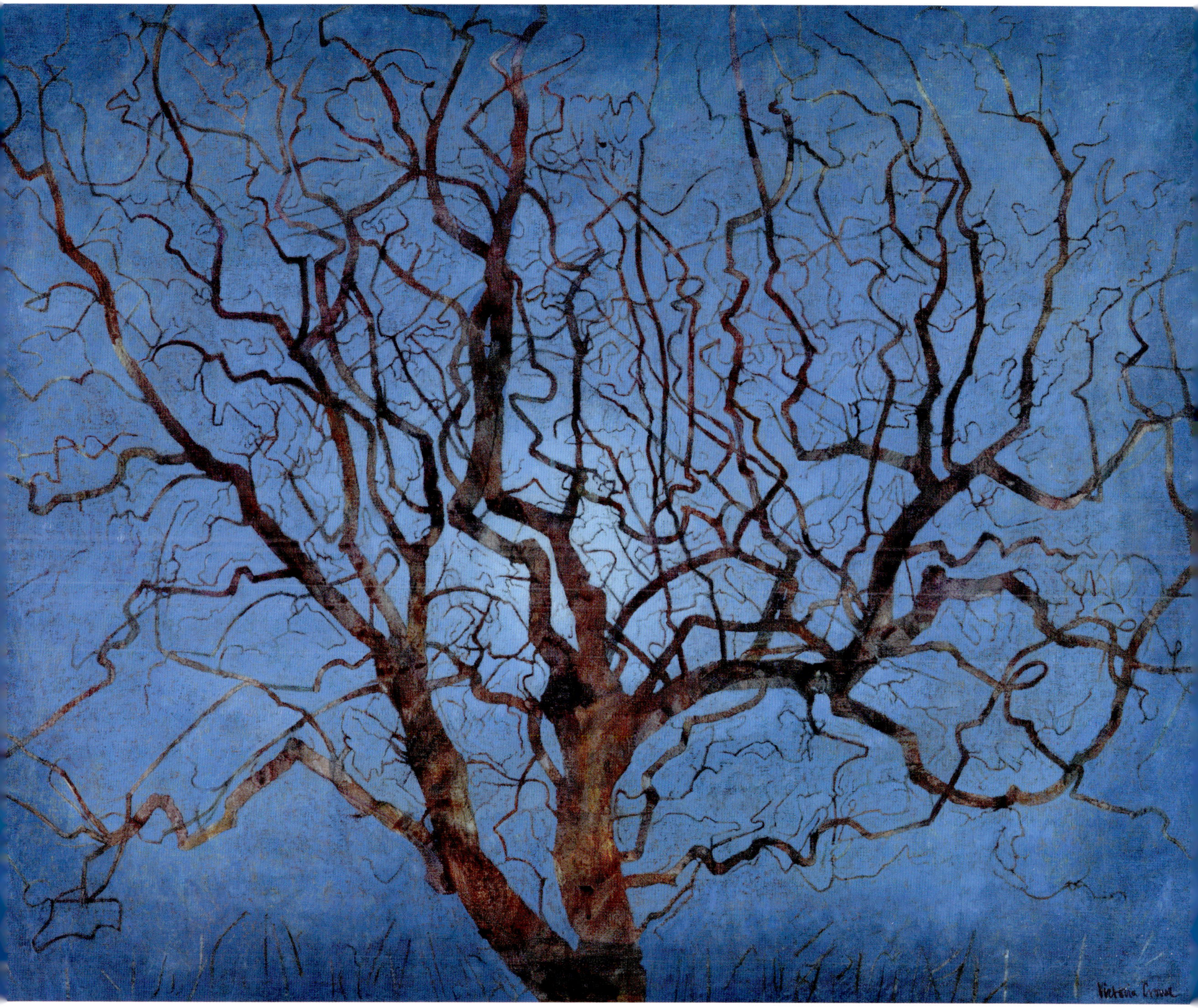

The Shortest Day

Recent Commissions

Tapestry

In 2008 I received a commission from the Duke of Buccleuch and Queensberry. This was woven for the regathering of 'A Shepherd's Life' at the Fleming Collection, London the following year. It was in keeping with the associations of Bowhill with Sir Walter Scott and James Hogg, the Ettrick shepherd, that the Duke chose one of these pictures for a tapestry. His choice was 'Two Views' from 1980-81. It shows Jenny through the window on the right feeding her sheep, while on the left hanging against the patterned wallpaper there is a photograph of her father. I think this link between the generations was one of the aspects that appealed to the Duke and his family. The tapestry, 4' by 8', was woven at the Dovecot Studios Edinburgh.

The success of this commission led the Dovecot Studios to undertake a second picture from the series, which is to be woven during 2012, the Year of Creative Scotland. 'Large Tree Group', one of the key images from the series 'A Shepherd's Life' is to be made using only undyed natural wool, including donations given by a variety of sources, from crofts to large estates. This limited palette of wools will recreate the wintry image of the Borders landscape and will relate back to Jenny Armstrong and to the importance of sheep farming in Scotland.

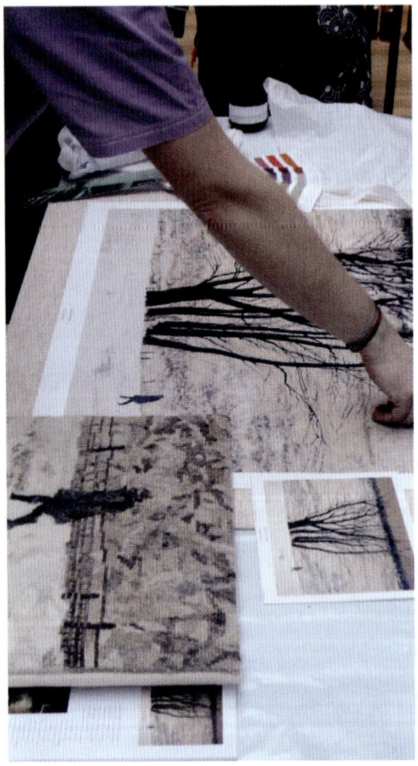

Discussing, Large Tree Group

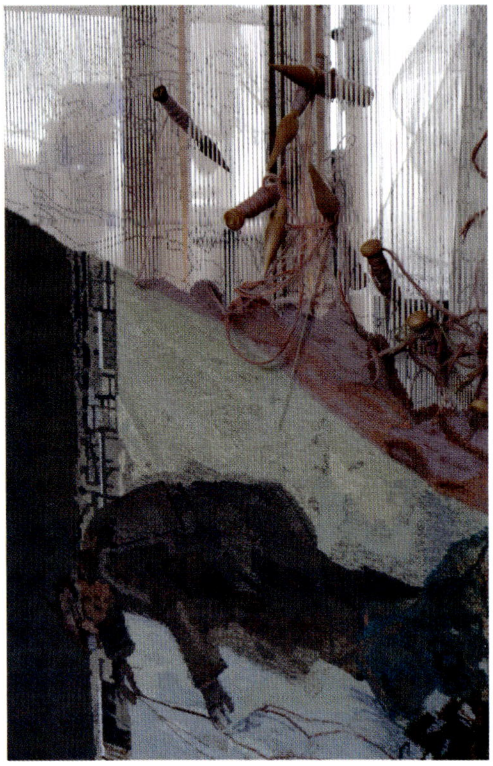

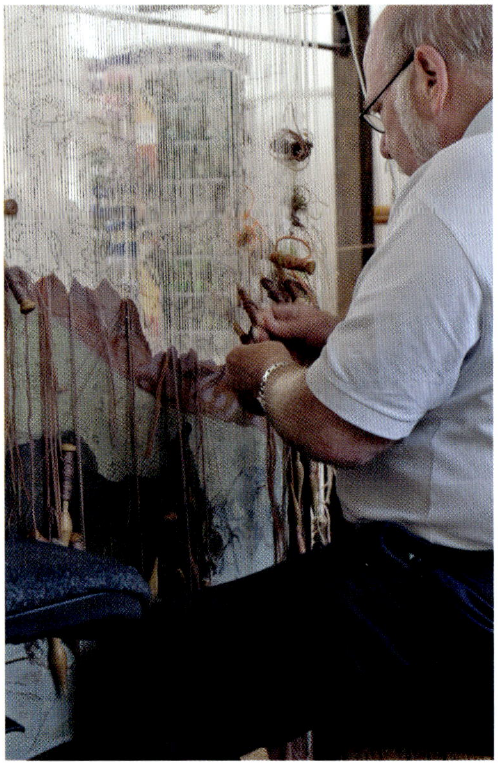

Weaving, Two Views

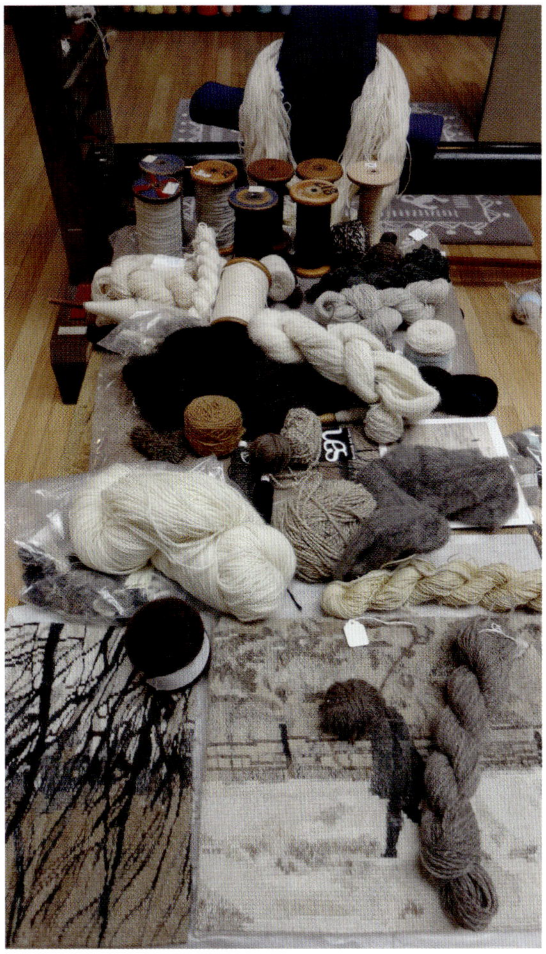

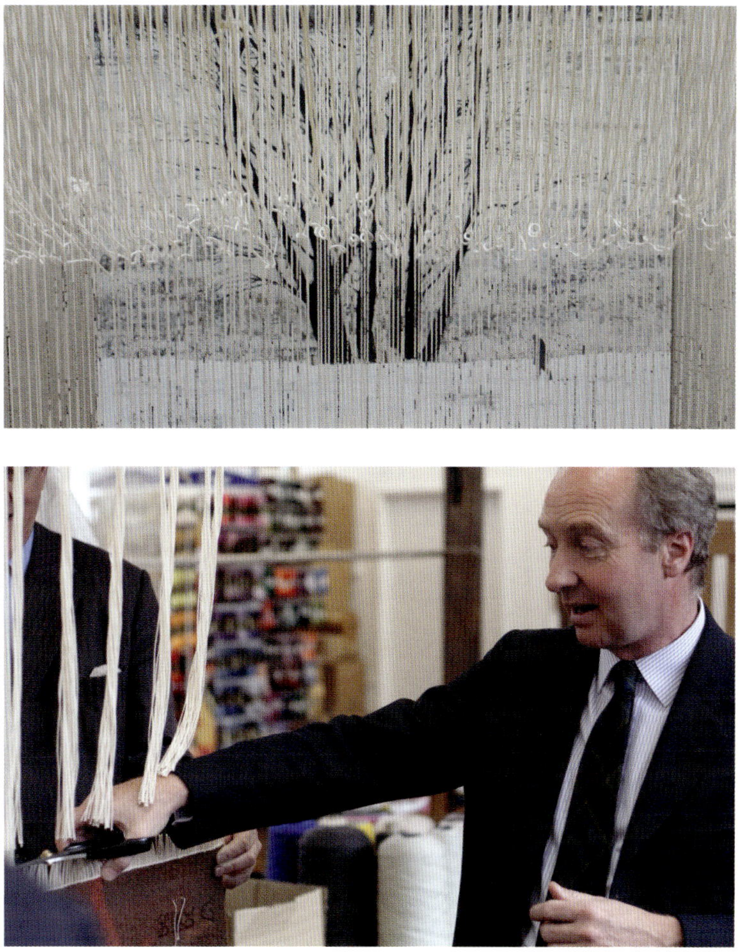

Tree Group, Studio views

The Duke of Buccleuch cutting off, Two Views

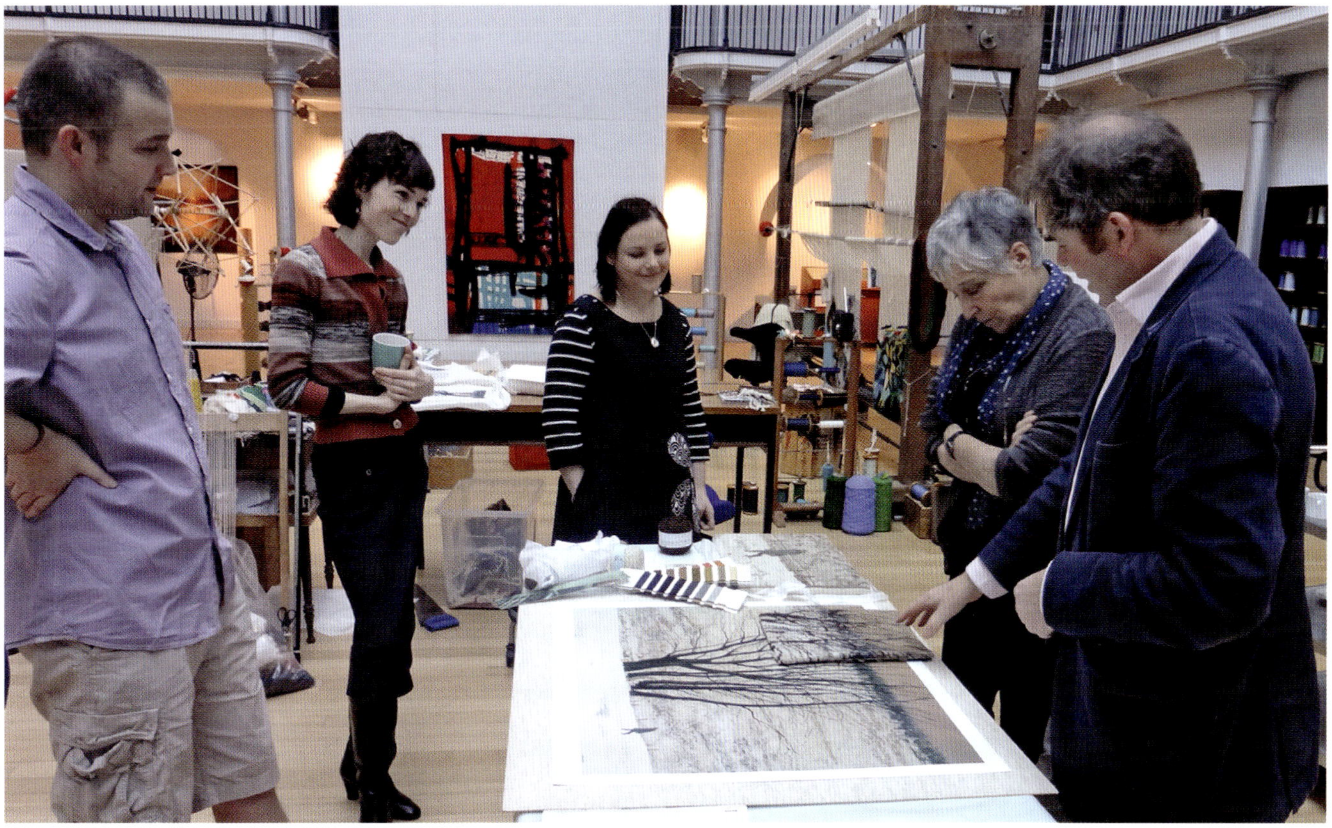

Selecting shades of undyed wools for Large Tree Group

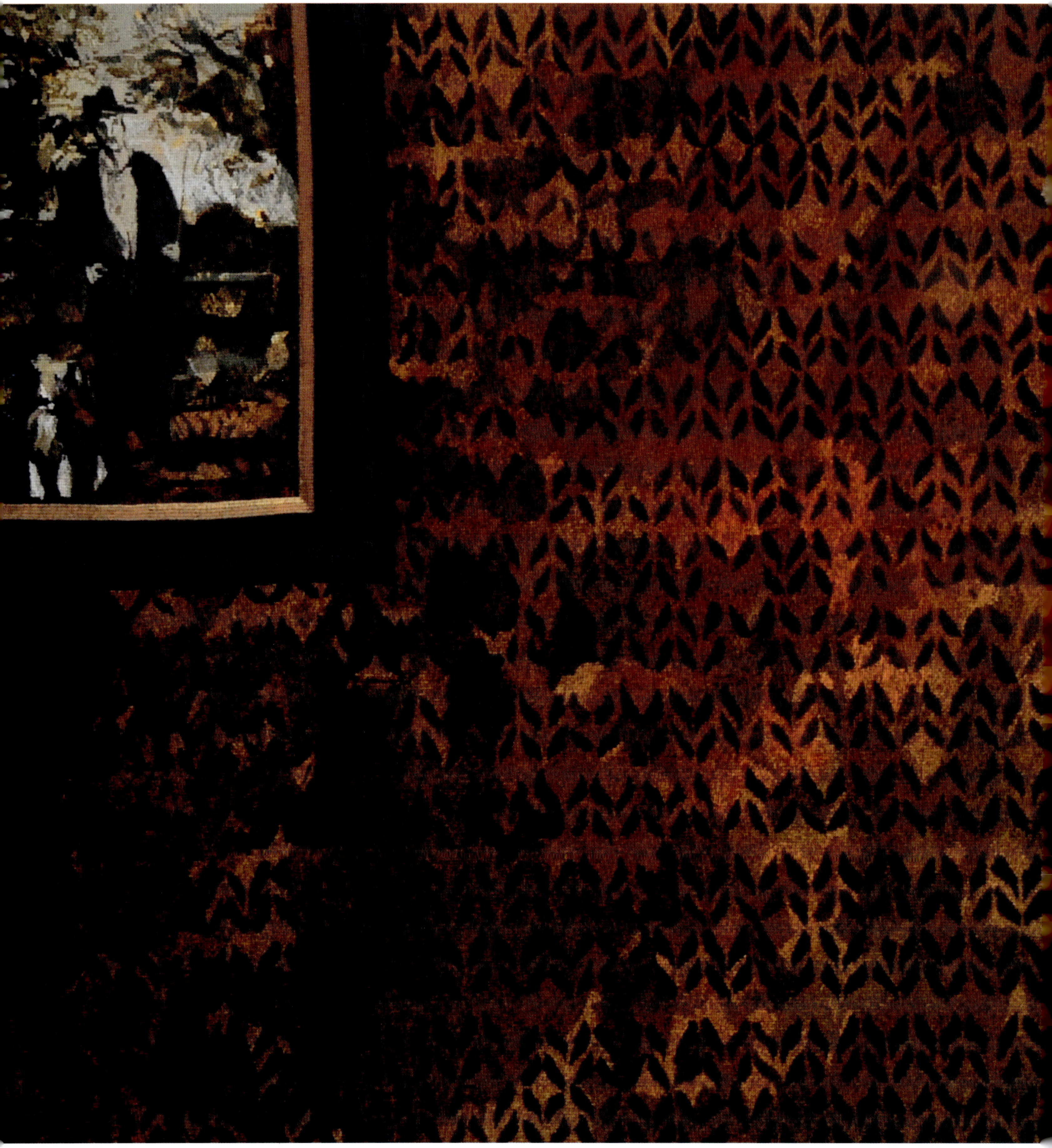

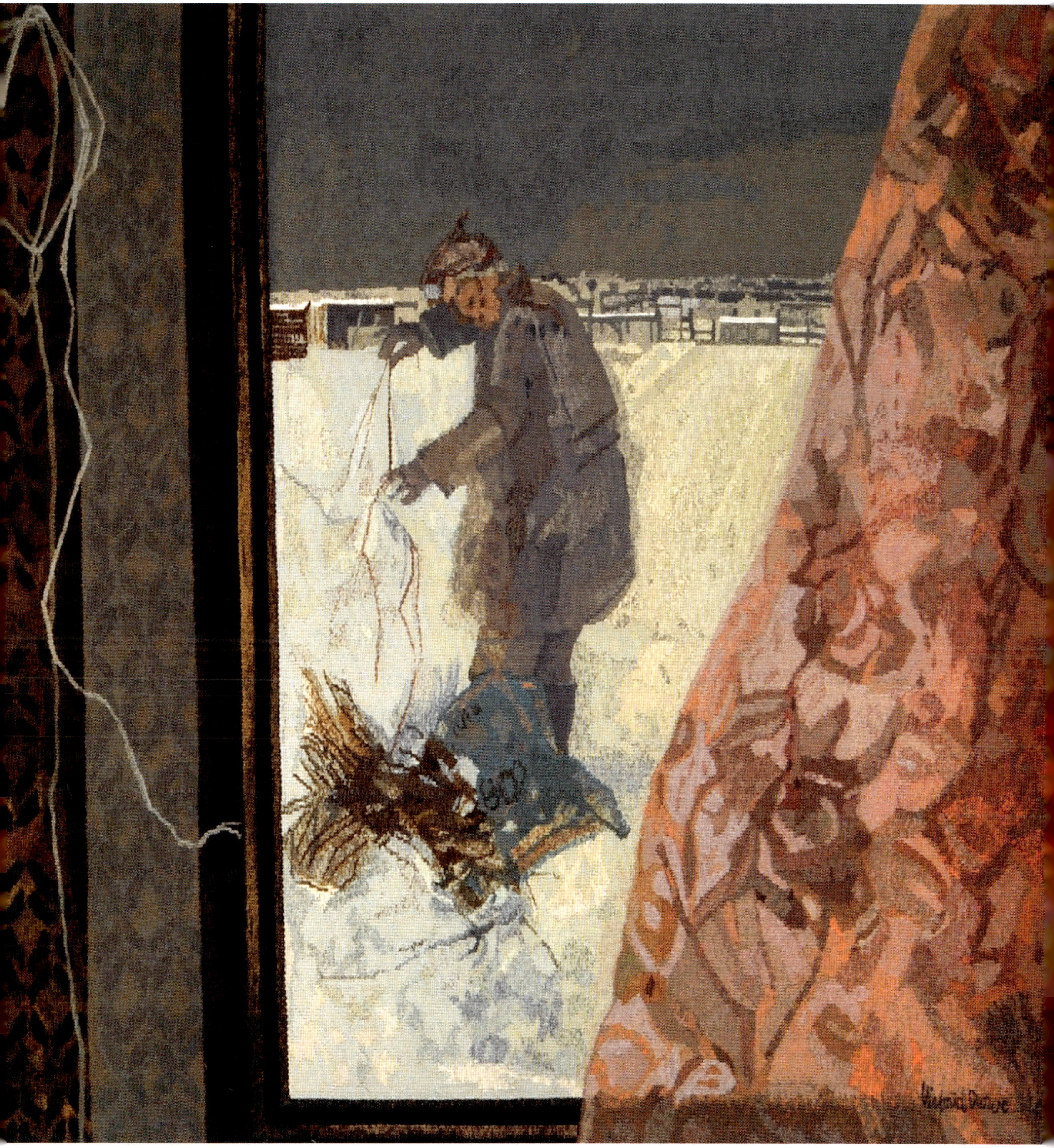

Two Views, Tapestry, woven in 2008

A House in the Borders

My Edingburgh Festival Exhibition of 2010 at the Scottish Gallery led to an unexpected commission to produce a suite of paintings for a country house in the Borders. This commission involved considerations of lighting, decoration and ornamentation which engaged Mike in the role of designer and overseer, in conjunction with plasterers, painters and decorators, electricians, a great lighting designer, master carpenters and flooring and glass specialists. The owner knew my work well and gave me the extraordinary briefs of "bringing the outside in", and "responding to the Italianate nature of the house". This was, of course, a joy to do and the project took over a year. The hard winter of 2010-2011 saw us snowed in for a couple of days while working there on the 'Events in the Garden' painting. The fascinating fernery with its tuffa walls, red glazing and frozen panes like ferns inspired 'Red Arcadia'.

Duncan Macmillan's words below describe the results.

The redesign and redecoration project involved turning what had been a dark, heavily decorated mill-owner's mansion into a house full of light and delicate decoration including not only Victoria's paintings, but some superb plaster relief ornaments, such as Thorwaldsen designs, commissioned by Mike from Grandisons, a historic firm in Peebles. Victoria's paintings include a number of earlier pictures including the *Changing Landscapes* triptych. However most were commissioned specifically for the house. These include *Forty Lilies for John*, a spectacular painting of a many-headed white lily against an old red damask from the Fortuny Museum. *Sentinel I* and *Sentinel II* are two Piero dogs, sitting as guardians at either side of a window while *Marriage Piece, Italian Landscape* is an overmantel. The central panel is a girl with Pre-Raphaelite hair. To her right and left are Italian landscapes behind a screen of roses and other flowers. These shift from direct observation to the formality of a *mille fleurs* tapestry from which a couple of rabbits have also strayed. This is perhaps an iconography suitable for a marriage, but the picture takes its name from its similarity in shape to an Italian marriage *cassone*. *Enigmatic View* is a small picture in similar mood with a fragment of Italian landscape, a hydrangea and a girl's head from Mantegna's fresco of the Gonzaga family in Mantua. She looks down into the picture with the same withdrawn reflective expression as Bellini's Magdalen. (It is an intriguing thought that Bellini was Mantegna's brother-in-law. They were linked by a woman, Bellini's sister Nicolasia.) *Events in the Garden* is inspired in part by the garden of the house and includes passages of its trees under snow, a running hare and Victorian photographs evoking the house's history. The project is ongoing but its inspired combination of painting and interior design is already unique in modern Scotland.

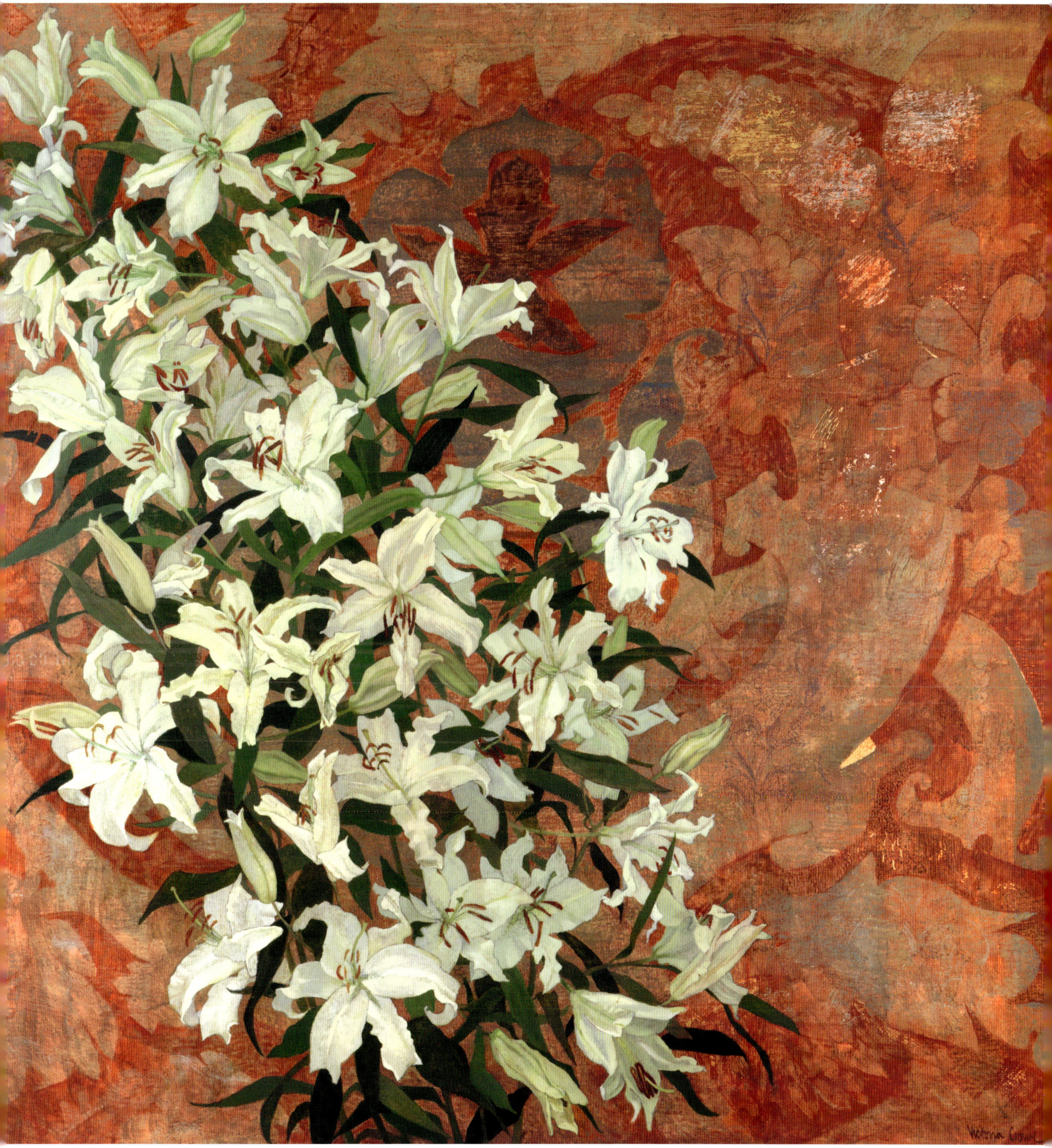

Forty Lilies for John

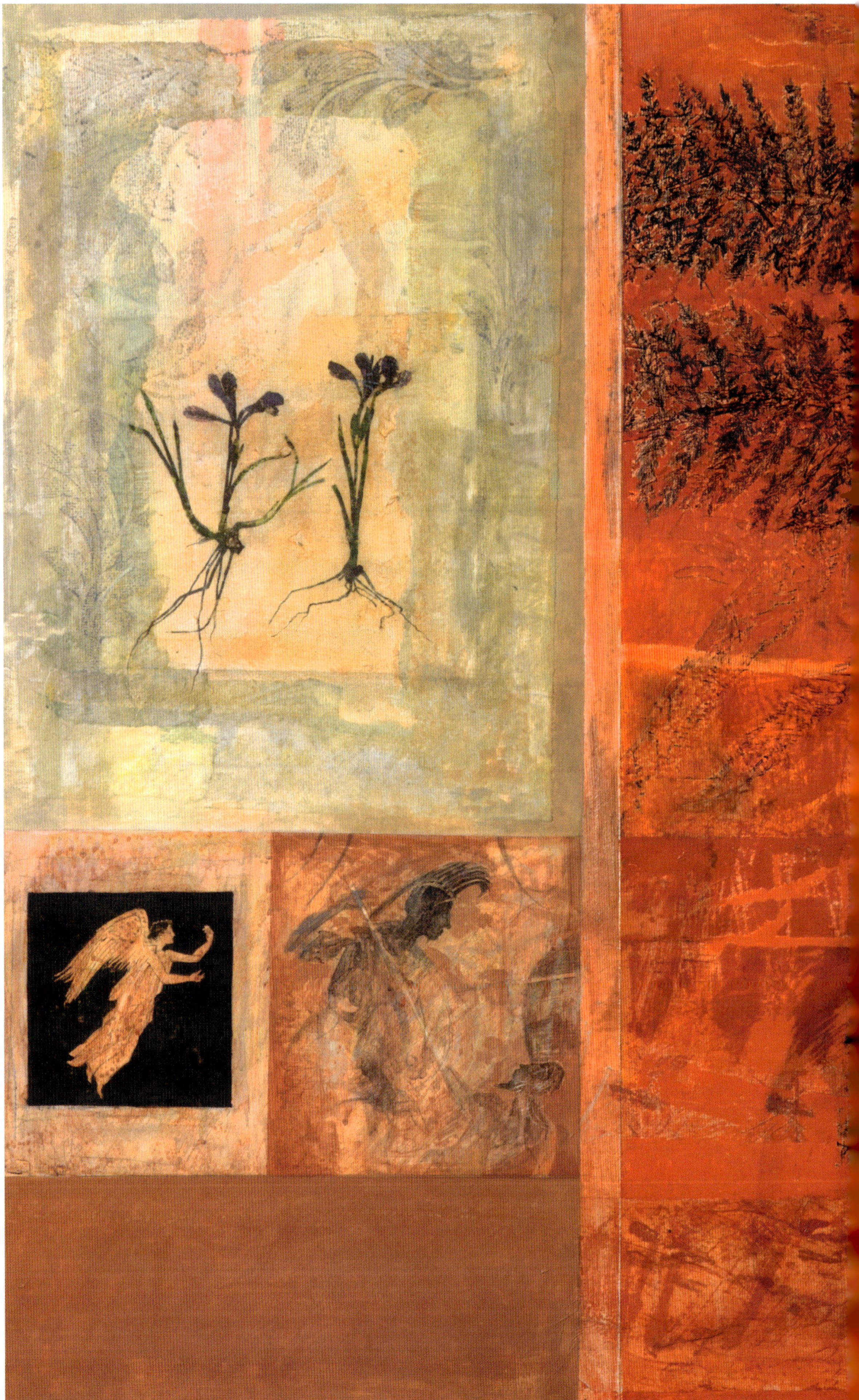

Red Arcadia

Overleaf:
Events in the Garden

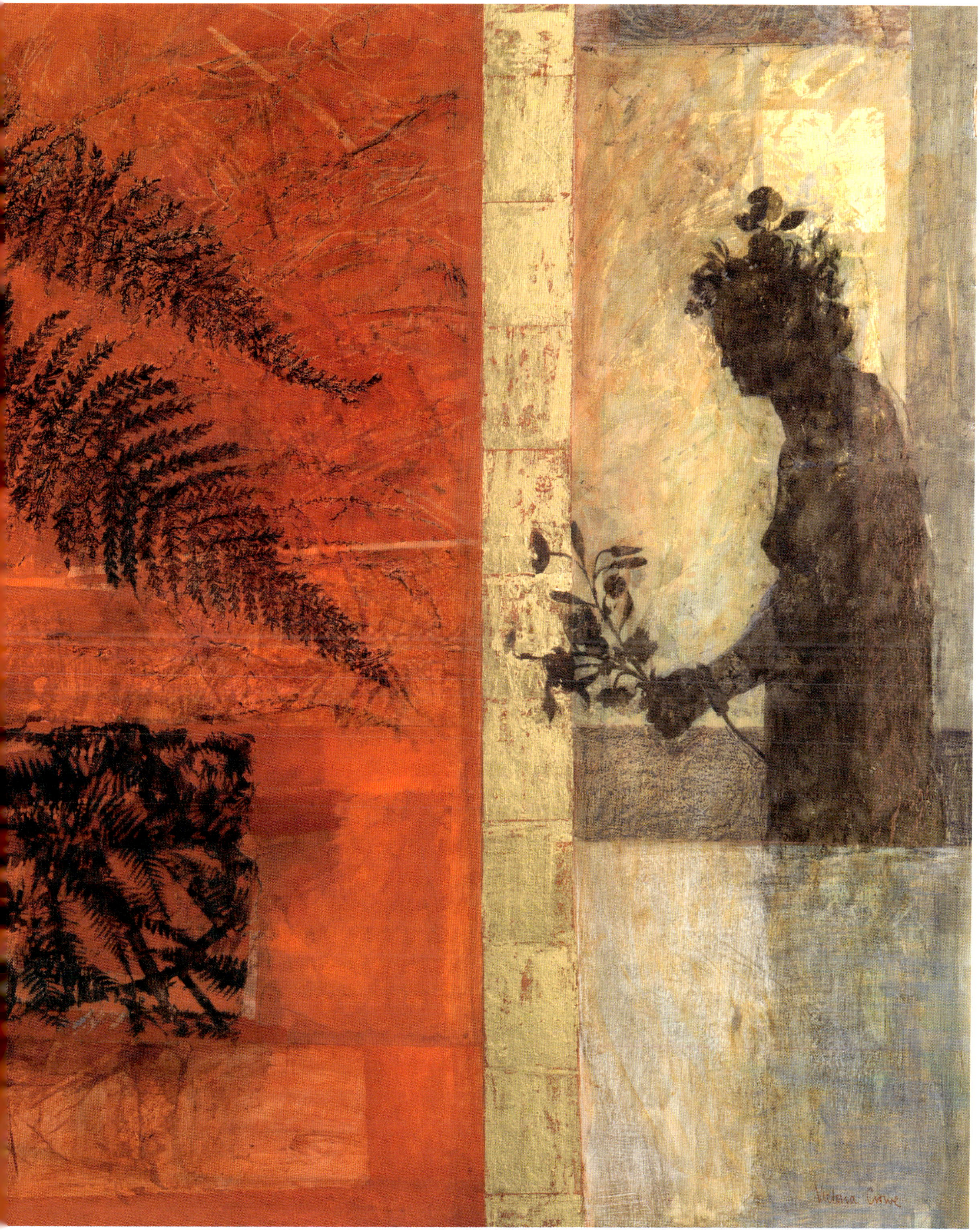

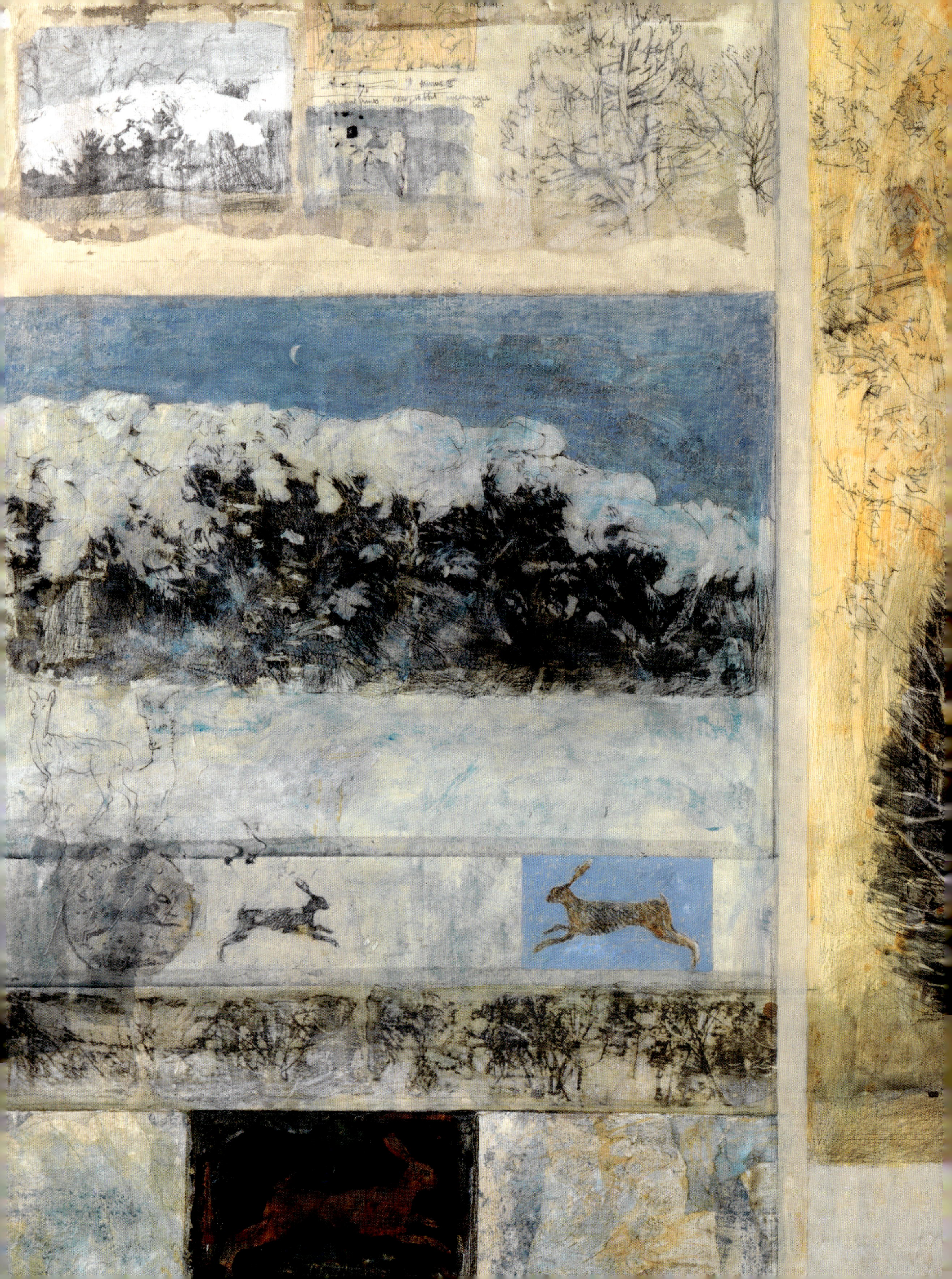

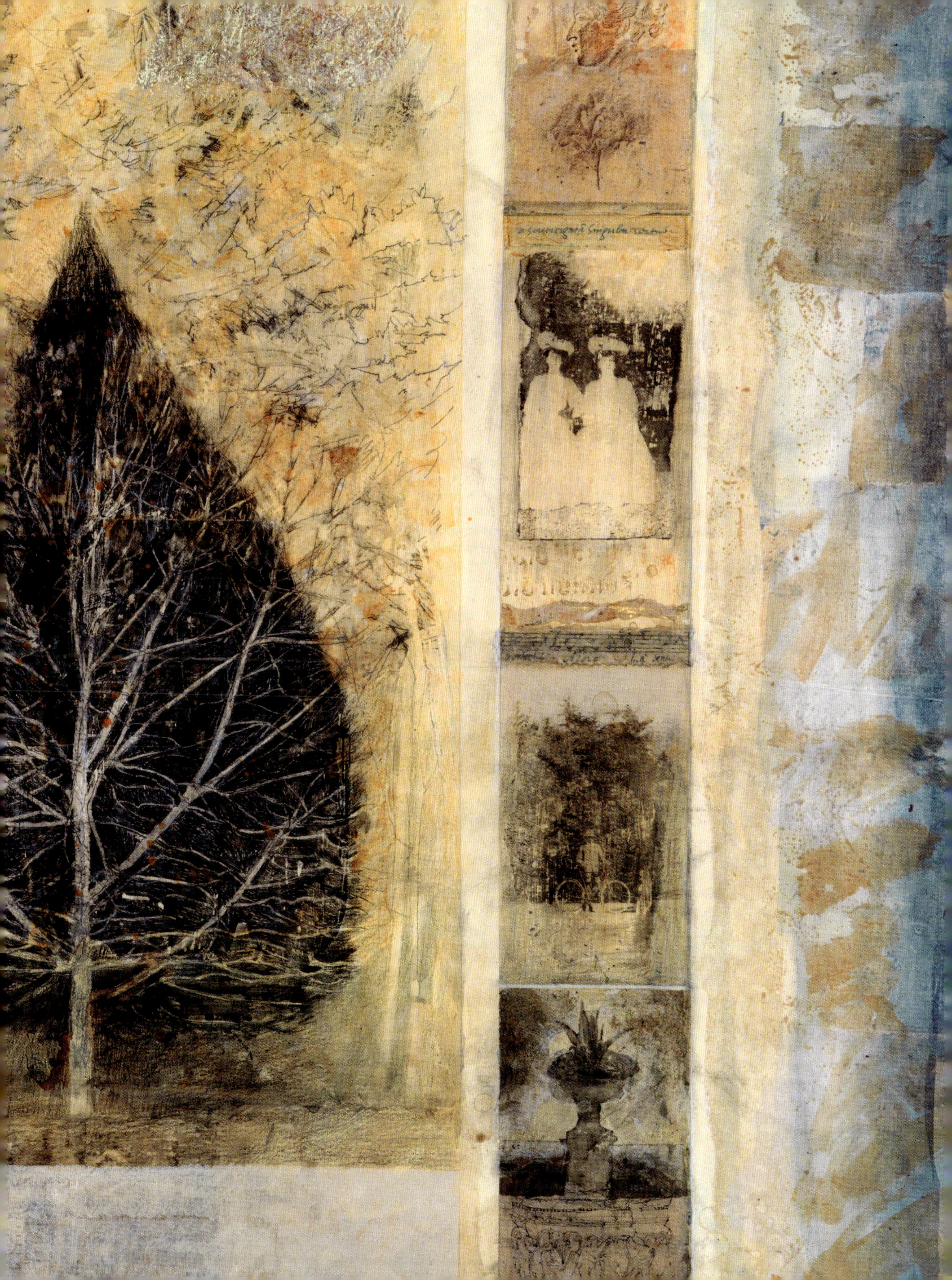

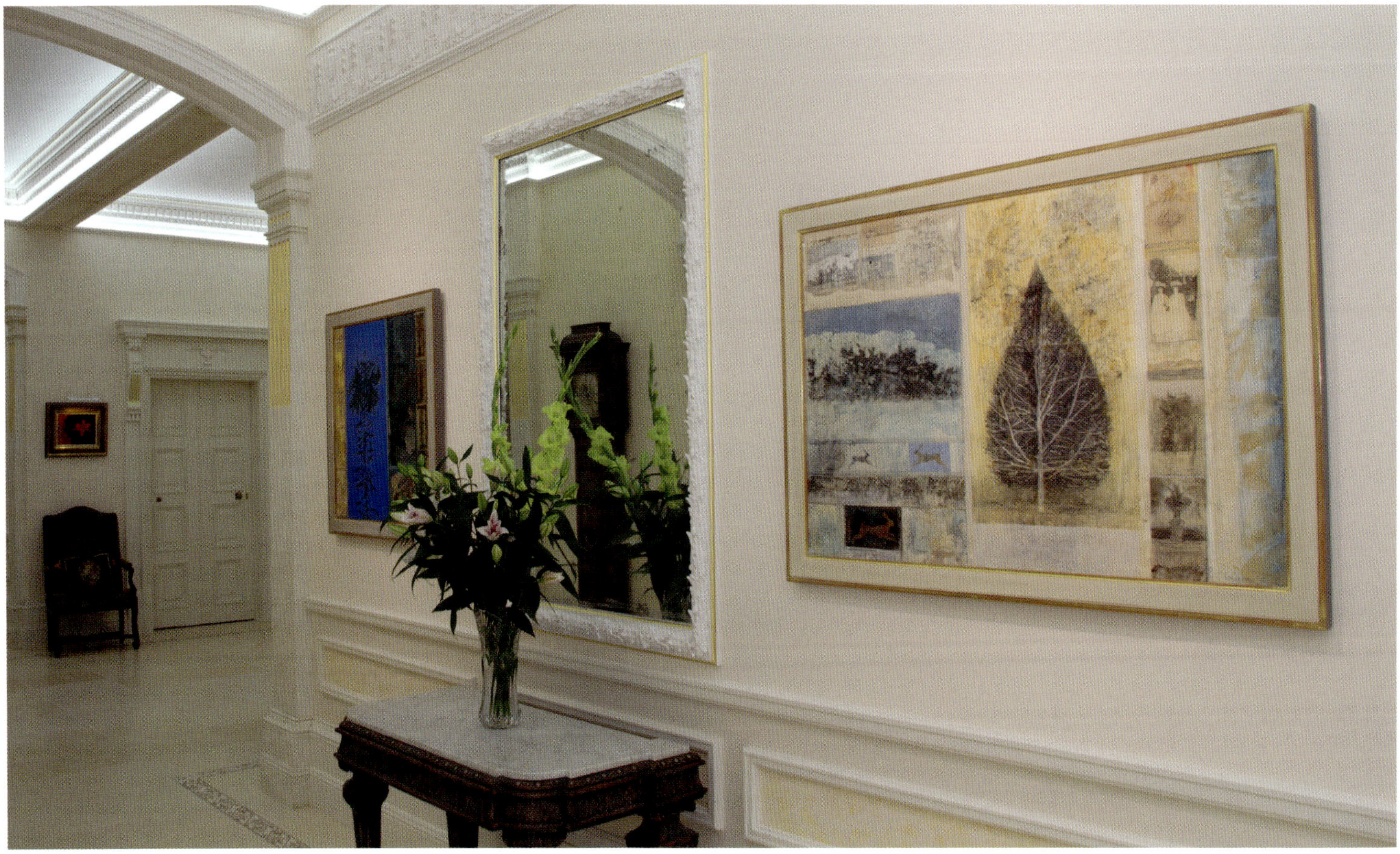

Installation of Events in the Garden

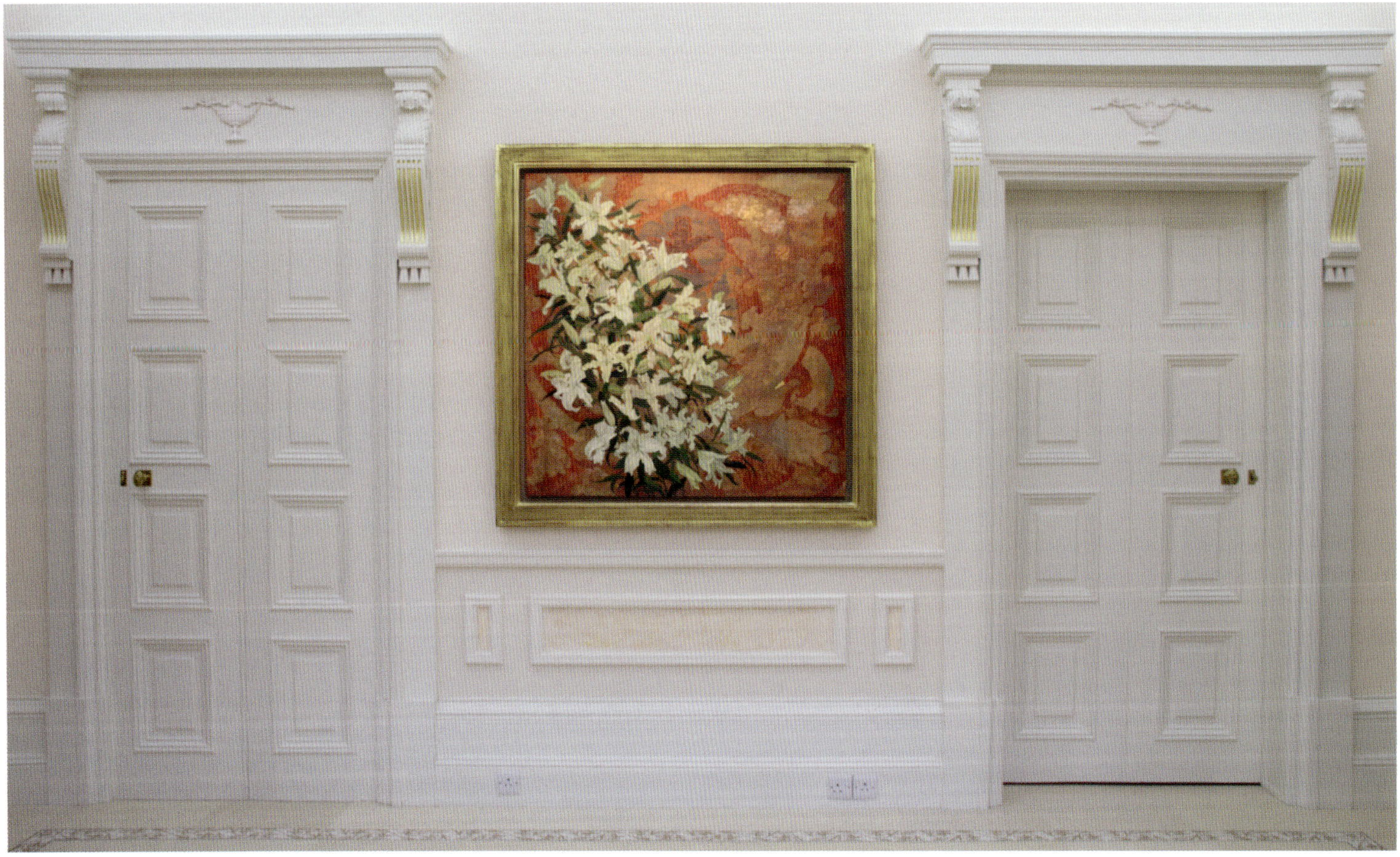

Installation of Forty Lilies for John

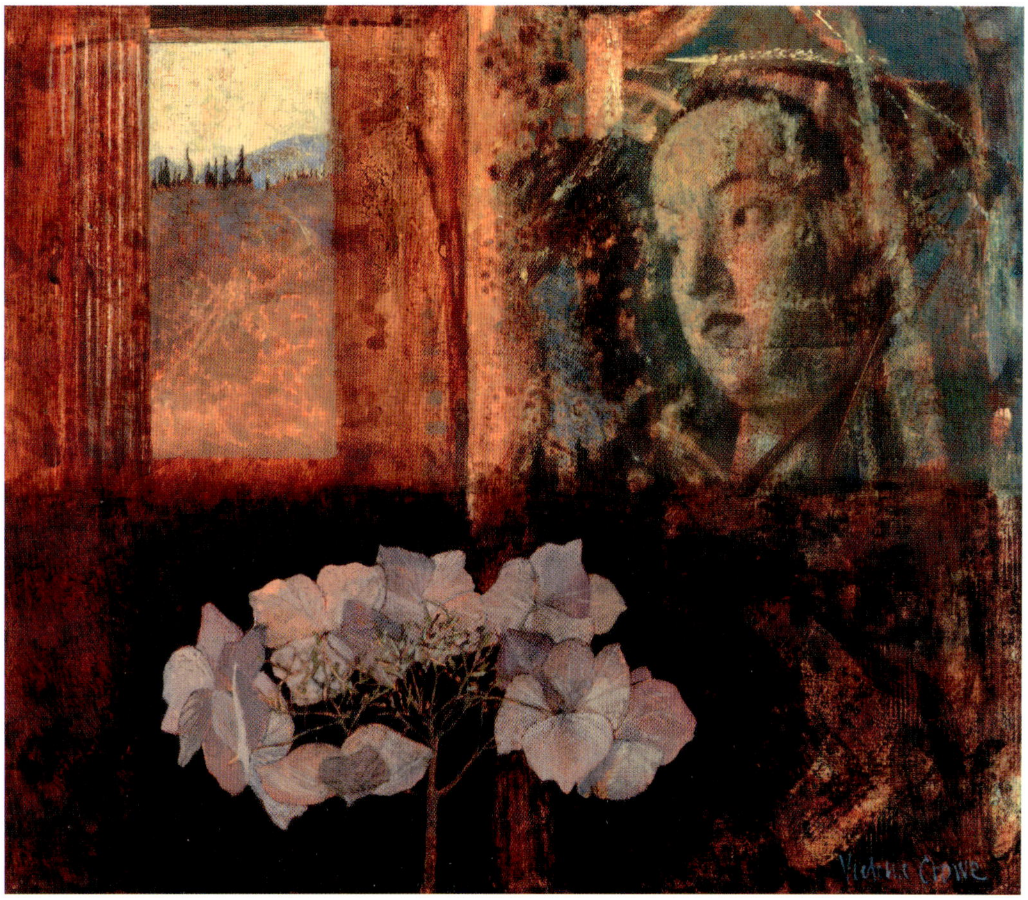

Enigmatic Head

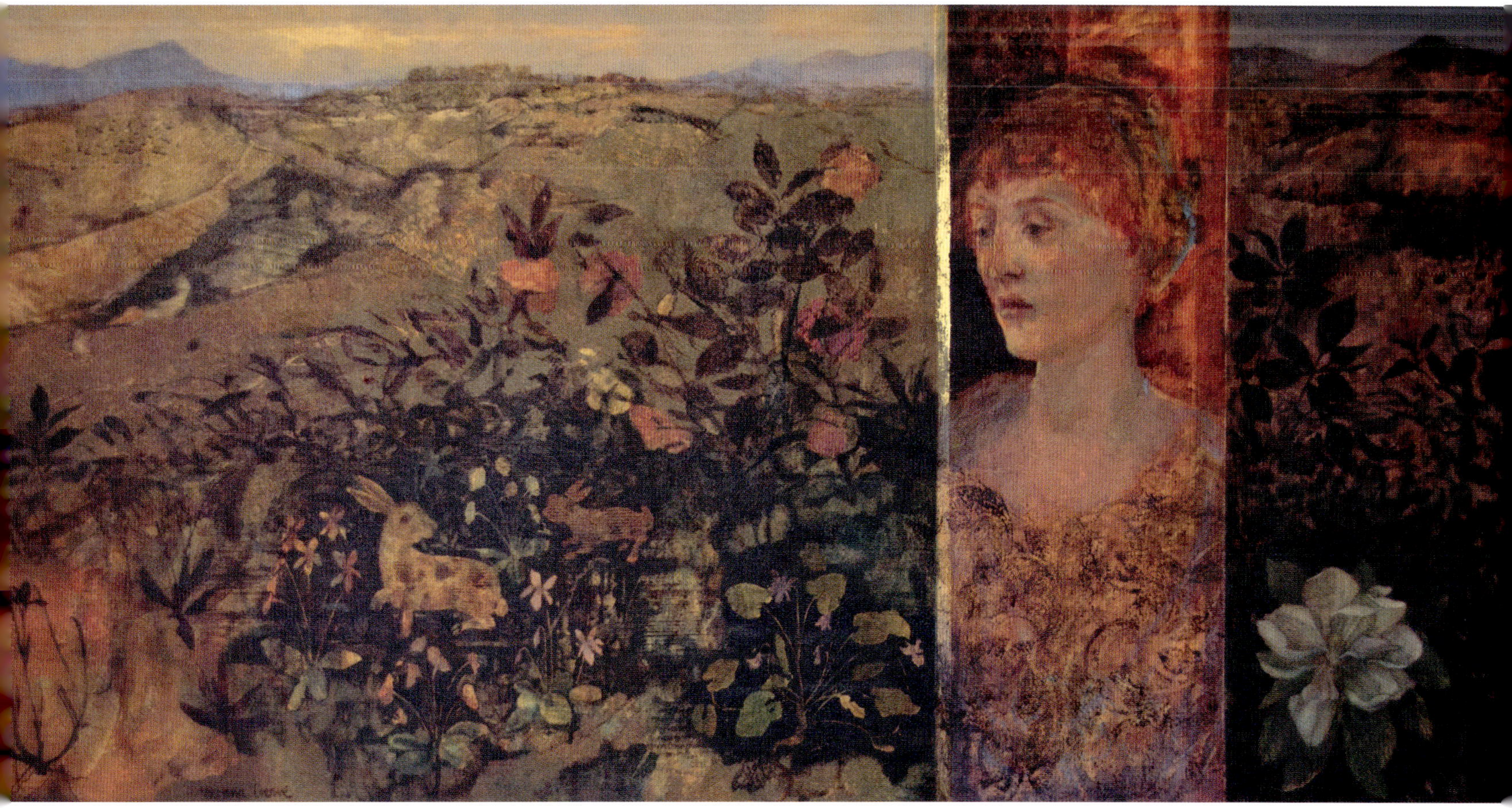

Marriage Piece, Italian Landscape

A House in Perthshire

'Paean', a major painting from 2011, was the result of a commission to respond to aspects of a house in Perthshire.

The room with the shifting light from the garden on two sides, changing through the seasons by the flowering of trellises and drawn blinds, had a very mysterious atmosphere. The composition of the painting suggested to me an altarpiece, with infinity (in the decoration on the plate) at its centre with the natural world beyond as a further focus. The hand on the left – actually that of the wife of the commissioner, above the blue agapanthus she grows – suggests some possible significance that I have not yet quite realised! The gesture reminds me of the Assisi fresco of St Francis blessing the birds. The table, although old and pitted, gave off the most extraordinary sheen, which acted as a luminous background and a secondary, reflective light source within the painting. After several visits, the objects within the work seemed to select themselves; the unexpected silver crocodile, the star trivet, the candle flames, the transparent plant forms on the glass ... the title of this work could just as well have been 'Alchemy'.

Victoria Crowe, West Linton, 2012

Paean

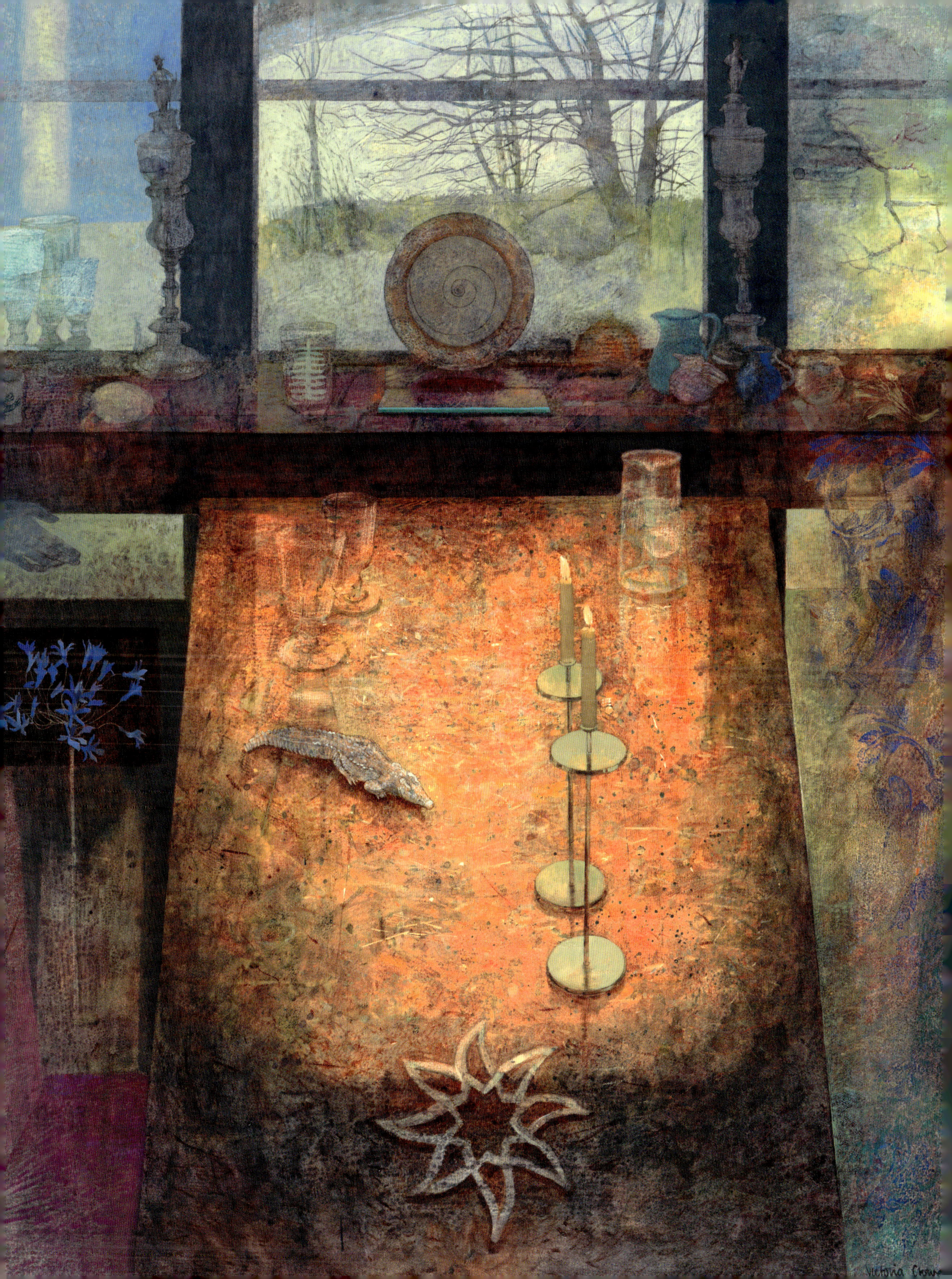

Chronology

1945	Born Kingston-upon-Thames, Surrey
1956-61	Ursuline Convent Grammar School, Wimbledon
1961-65	Kingston School of Art
1964	Visited Moscow and Leningrad via East Berlin and Warsaw with NUS
1965-68	Royal College of Art, London.
1967	Marries Michael Walton
1968	At RCA Postgraduate Degree show, invited by Robin Philipson and John Hunter to join the Painting School staff at Edinburgh College of Art on a one-year contract. Moved to Scotland, on the edge of the Pentland Hills.
1969-70	David Murray Landscape Award from RCA, taken in west coast of Scotland and Greece
1969	Scottish Arts Council Bursary
1970	Permanent part-time lecturing contract, ECA. Continuing until early retirement in 1998. Moved to Kittleyknowe. First meeting with Jenny Armstrong. Introduced by Robin Philipson to Bill Macaulay of the Scottish Gallery and began regular solo shows there which continue until the present day.
1971	VC and MW visit Leningrad, Moscow, Vladimir and Suzdal on an Art and Architecture exchange through Edinburgh University
1973	Son, Ben, born in April. Anne Redpath Award. Travel to Denmark, Sweden and Finland
1975	Scottish Arts Council bursary to work from the life model
1976	Daughter, Gemma, born in June
1981	*Glasgow Herald* painting prize-winner Scottish Arts Council Printmaking Bursary
1982	Elected member of The Royal Scottish Society of Painters in Watercolour
1983	Begins regular solo shows with the Thackeray Gallery, London until 2007
1987	Elected Associate of the Royal Scottish Academy Winner of the Daler/Rowney Prize for Watercolour, Royal Academy, London
1988	Hunting Group Major Award Winner
1991	Elected Associate of the Royal Watercolour Society Major Award winner (Chris Beetles Prize), Royal Watercolour Society Open Exhibition
1992	Sabbatical term from ECA. First visit to Italy, funded by Sir William Gilles bequest for travel and study, RSA. Invited by Artists for Nature Foundation to join a group of artists working on a conservation project in Poland.
1994	Invited by ANF to work on a conservation project in the Extremadura, Spain
1995	Son, Ben, dies of cancer
1997	Commissioned by Danish National Portrait Gallery to paint the Danish Resistance leader, Ole Lippmann for the 20th Century Collection of portraits at Frederiksborg Castle, Copenhagen. Invited by Glasgow Museums and Art Galleries to take part in the Tiger,Tiger project at Bandhavgarh National Park, India.
1998-99	Further study visits to Italy: Florence, Siena, Urbino, Perugia, Arezzo, Orvieto
1998	Early retirement from ECA
2000	Invited artist for shortlist of Jesus 2000 commission, Glasgow Museum and Art Gallery
2001	Began Visiting and working in Venice. Co-publication with Carol Robertson Graal press
2002	Benton Humfries Award, Discerning Eye, Mall Galleries, London
2003	Acquires a studio in Venice on the Giudecca
2004	Awarded OBE for Services to Art
2004-7	Sir William Gillies Award, Royal Scottish Academy, working on *Plant Memory*. Senior Visiting Scholar, St Catharine's College, Cambridge University. Artist's Book, *Inflorescence*, with Robert Adam, Graal press.
2008	Commission of tapestry, *Two Views*, Dovecot Studios, Edinburgh
2009	Awarded Doctor Honoris Causa (DHC) University of Aberdeen.
2010	Elected Fellow of The Royal Society of Edinburgh
2011/12	Commission for a major suite of paintings for a re-designed period house in the Scottish Borders
2012	Commission of tapestry, *Large Tree Group*, Dovecot Studios. Year of Creative Scotland Begins showing with Browse and Darby, London

The Artist lives and works in the Scottish Borders and Venice

Selected Solo Exhibitions

1970 The Scottish Gallery (Aitken Dott), Edinburgh
1973 The Scottish Gallery (Aitken Dott), Edinburgh
1977 The Scottish Gallery (Aitken Dott), Edinburgh
1982 The Scottish Gallery (Aitken Dott), Edinburgh
1983 Thackeray Gallery, London
1985 Thackeray Gallery, London
1986 Mercury Gallery, Edinburgh
1988 Abbot Hall, Kendal
From *Carlops to Corinth*, The Fine Art Society, Edinburgh and Glasgow
1989 Thackeray Gallery, London.
Border Connections, The Bruton Gallery, Somerset
1991 Thackeray Gallery, London
1993 The Bruton Gallery, Bath
1994 Thackeray Gallery, London
1995 The Scottish Gallery, Edinburgh
1997 Corrymella Scott Gallery, Newcastle upon Tyne
1998 The Scottish Gallery, Edinburgh
Accomplished Journeys, Bruton Gallery, Leeds
1999 Thackeray Gallery, London
A Shepherd's Life, paintings of Jenny Armstrong by Victoria Crowe, Scottish National Portrait Gallery, Edinburgh. Exhibition curated by the SNPG, touring Newcastle, Harrogate and Scotland 2001/02
2001 *Victoria Crowe – New Works*, Edinburgh Festival Exhibition, The Scottish Gallery
Thackeray Gallery, London
2002 Aldeburgh Festival Exhibition, Gallery 44 (Thackeray Gallery)
Bohun Gallery, Henley on Thames
2003 Alchemy, Drumcroon, Wigan Education Authority Arts Centre
Thackeray Gallery, London
2004 *Italian Sketchbook*, Works on Paper, Thackeray Gallery, London
The Scottish Gallery, Edinburgh
2005 *On Reflection*, Thackeray Gallery, London
2006 *Works on Paper – Landscapes from Italy and Scotland*, The Scottish Gallery, Edinburgh
2007 *Reflections on Venice*, Bohun Gallery, Henley on Thames
Thackeray Gallery, London
Plant Memory, Royal Scottish Academy, Edinburgh
2008 *Victoria Crowe – Recent Work*, Scottish Gallery, Edinburgh.
2009 *Overview: Paintings by Victoria Crowe*, Fine Art Society, London
A Shepherd's Life, paintings of Jenny Armstrong by Victoria Crowe, The Fleming Collection, London
2010 *Reflection – New Work*, Edinburgh Festival Exhibition, The Scottish Gallery, Edinburgh
Collected Journeys, The Bohun Gallery, Henley on Thames
2012 *Victoria Crowe, New Work*, Browse and Darby, Cork Street, London
Forthcoming: Works on Paper, The Scottish Gallery, Edinburgh, December
2014 Edinburgh Festival Exhibition, The Scottish Gallery, Edinburgh

Selected Group Exhibitions: Please see the artist's website for a detailed list
Portraits: Please see the dedicated section on the artist's website

Selected Public Collections

Bank of Scotland
Calderdale Museum and Art Gallery
Carnegie Dunfermline Trust
Contemporary Arts Society
Cornelian Asset Managers Ltd
Danish 20th Century Portrait Collection, Copenhagen
Department of Neuroscience, University of Edinburgh
District Council of Edinburgh
District Council of West Lothian
Edinburgh City Art Centre
Education Authority of Edinburgh
Education Authority of Inner London
Fleming-Wyfold Art Foundation
Glasgow Museums and Art Galleries
Harlow New Town Council
Heriot-Watt University
Highland Council
Inverness Museum and Art Gallery
Medical School, New Royal Infirmary, Edinburgh
Mercantile and General Reinsurance Company
McLean Gallery, Greenock
National Portrait Gallery, London

National Trust for Scotland
Newcastle University
Nuffield Foundation, Paintings in Hospitals (Scotland)
Palace of Westminster
Reader's Digest
Reading Museum and Art Gallery
Royal Academy, London
Royal Bank of Scotland
Royal College of Art, London
Royal College of Physicians, Edinburgh
Royal College of Surgeons of Edinburgh
Royal Scottish Academy
Scottish Arts Council
Scottish Life Insurance Company
Scottish Media Group
Scottish National Gallery of Modern Art
Scottish National Portrait Gallery
Smith Art Gallery, Stirling
St. Leonard's School, St. Andrews
The Boots Company
Trustee Savings Bank
University of Aberdeen
University of Cambridge
University of Dundee
University of Edinburgh
University of Glasgow
University of Oxford
University of St Andrews
Wigan Education Authority
William Bowmore Collection, Australia
Worshipful Company of Painter-Stainers

Selected Private Collections

HM The Queen
HRH The Duke of Edinburgh
HRH The Prince of Wales
Earl of Moray
Lady Cawdor
Earl Haig
Duke of Buccleuch
Duke of Devonshire

Media

1991 *Portrait of the Wild*, Grampian and STV, 1991 and 1998
1998 *The Usual Suspect*, BBC Radio Scotland
Look North, BBC Television
2000 *Johnnie Walker Show*, BBC Radio 2, Feb.
A Scottish Connection, BBC Radio Scotland, Feb.
2000 *Brian Morton*, BBC Radio Scotland, Feb. 2000
Landward, Arthur Anderson, BBC2, March 2000
2001 *Woman's Hour*, interview with Claudia Hammond
2007 *National Life Stories*, British Library Sound Archive, interviewed by Jenny Simmons

Selected Published Work on Victoria Crowe

Books

2000-08 *A Shepherd's Life*, NGS, Mary Taubman & Julie Lawson (ISBN 978-1-90327-802-4)
2001-08 *Painted Insights*, The Antique Collectors' Club (ISBN 978-1-85149-589-4)
2012 *Victoria Crowe*, Duncan Macmillan, The Antique Collectors' Club (ISBN 978-1-85149-714-0)

Solo Exhibition Catalogues

1994 Thackeray Gallery, text by Mary Taubman
1995 Scottish Gallery, text by Duncan Thomson
1997 Corrymella Scott Gallery, text by Mary Sara
1998 *Accomplished Journeys*, Bruton Gallery, text by Derek Hyatt
1999 Thackeray Gallery, text by Clare Henry
2001 *New Works*, Scottish Gallery Festival Exhibition, text by Iain Gale
2003 Thackeray Gallery, text by Victoria Crowe
2004 Scottish Gallery, text by Lynne Green
2005 *On Reflection*, Thackeray Gallery, text by Michael Walton
2007 *Plant Memory*, RSA, David Ingram/Victoria Crowe
2009 *Overview*, FAS, text by Patrick Bourne
2010 *Reflection – New Work*, Scottish Gallery, text by Duncan Macmillan

For a full CV, and detailed list of publications, articles, reviews and forthcoming exhibitions please see Victoria Crowe's website: www.victoria.crowe.com

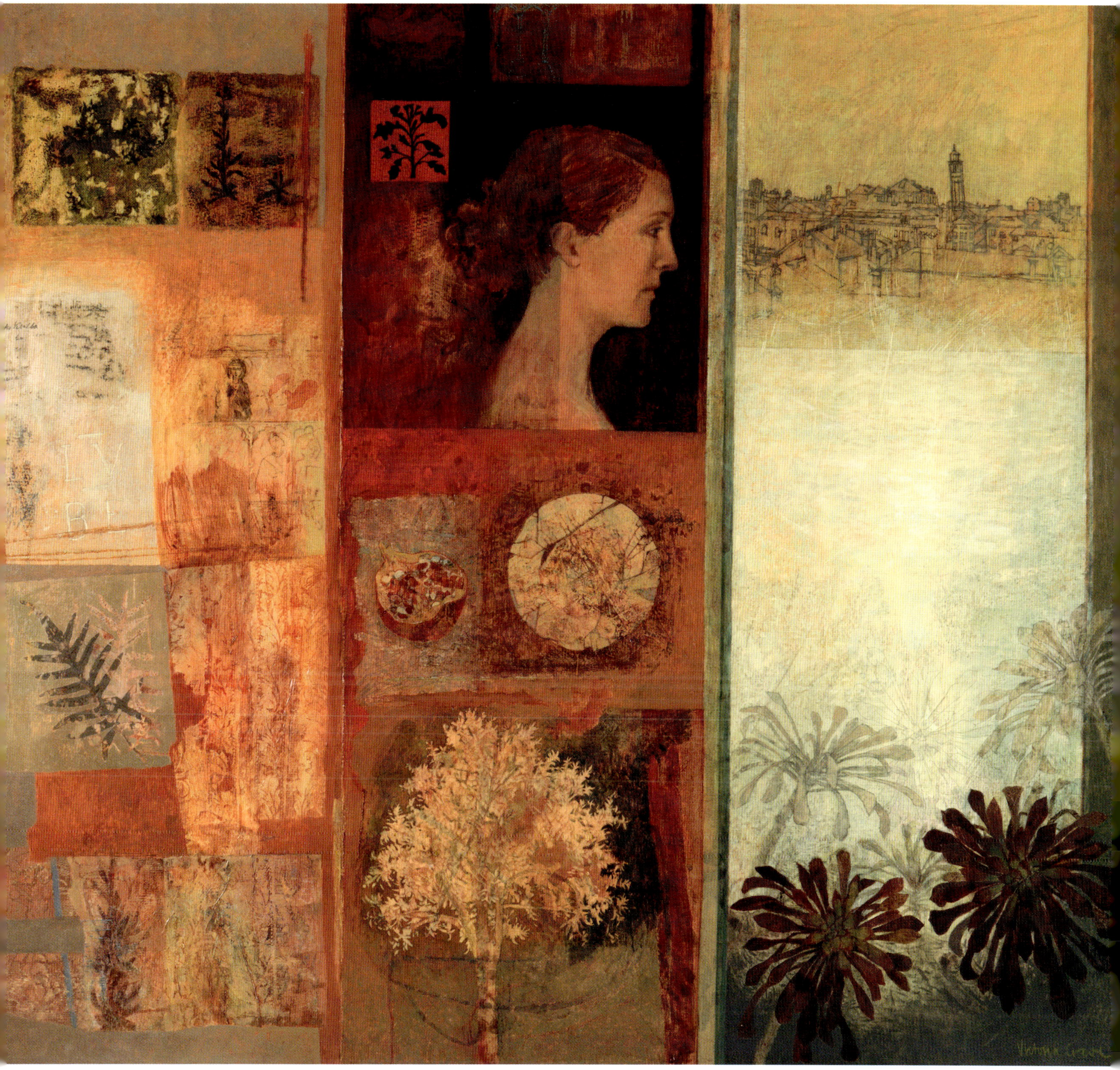

Known and Imagined World

List of Illustrations

For works of art which are mentioned in the text, yet not illustrated, please see *Painted Insights* (Antique Collector's Club, 2001/8) and the artist's website: www.victoriacrowe.com

Across the City; Cloister (p. 83)
2005. Mixed media, 21.6cm x 36.8cm
(8½in. x 14½in.)
Private Collection

Across the City; La Madonetta (p. 83)
2005. Mixed media, 21.6cm x 36.8cm
(8.5in. x 14½in.)
Private Collection

All That Remains, Padova (p. 96)
2004. Oil on linen, 101.5cm x 127cm
(40in. x 50in.)
Private Collection

Artefacts and Magical Texts (p. 86)
2001. Mixed media, 68.6cm x 99.1cm
(27in. x 39in.)
Private Collection

Asparagus and Sinners (p. 183)
2004. Oil on board, 39cm x 34cm
(15½in. x 13½in.)
Private Collection

Back Garden Monksview (p. 35)
1971. Oil on board, 71.1cm x 91.4cm
(28in. x 36in.)
Collection of the Artist

Back Garden Under Snow (p. 37)
1972-3. Oil on board, 91.4cm x 122cm
(36in. x 48in.)
Collection Tanya Westinghouse

Baler Twine (p. 41)
1978. Pencil and watercolour wash,
10.2cm x 17.8cm (4in. x 7in.)
Collection of the Artist

Being in Italy (p. 70)
1993-4. Oil, 7.6cm x 122cm (32in. x 48in.)
Private Collection

Black Icon (p. 29)
1971. Mixed media, 71.1cm x 91.4cm
(28in. x 36in.)
Private Collection

Blood of a Cat, a spread from
'Inflorescence' (p. 115)
2007. Mixed media, 21cm x 29.8cm
(8¼in. x 11¾in.)
Private Collection

Blue Snow and Fiery Trees (pp. 146-7)
2011. Oil on linen, 101.6cm x 127cm
(40in. x 50in.)
Collection of the Artist

Bouquet for a Warrior (p. 74)
1995. Oil on canvas, 101.6cm x 76.2cm
(40in. x 30in.)
Private Collection

Changing Landscapes, Triptych (pp. 54-5)
1983-4. Oil on canvas, each panel
61cm x 122cm (24in. x 48in.)
Private Collection

Circumspice – The Studio, Venice (p. 133)
2009-10. Oil on linen, 102cm x 127cm
(40⅛in. x 50in.)
Private Collection

Contemplating the Mysteries (p. 79)
1995. Oil on board, 35.6cm x 81.3cm
(14in. x 32in.)
Private Collection

Continuum (p. 126)
2010. Oil on panel, 71cm x 91cm
(28in. x 35 ⅞in.)
Private Collection

Contorta, Frost Sequence (endpapers)
2008, mixed media, 34.5cm x 104cm
(13⅝in. x 41in.)
Private Collection

December 25th (p. 50)
1981. Oil on board, 91.4cm x 71.1cm
(36in. x 28in.)
Collection Tanya Westinghouse

Deposition (p. 21)
1967-8. Oil on board, 61cm x 45cm
(24in. x 17¾in.)
Private Collection

Dialogue in San Sepulcro (p. 71)
1994. Oil on board with gold leaf,
35.6cm x 81.3cm (14in. x 32in.)
Destroyed by fire from a private collection

Do Not Disturb the Dreaming World (p. 81)
1995. Oil, 94.6cm x 109.2cm
(37¼in. x 43in.)
Private Collection

Dogs in Venice (p. 142)
2010. Mixed media, 27cm x 35cm
(10⅝in. x 13⅝in.)
Private Collection

Dominance of the Moon (p. 121)
2007-8. Oil on linen, 152.5cm x 152.5cm
(60in. x 60in.)
Private Collection

Dorsoduro Interior (p. 82)
1999. Mixed media, 57.2cm x 76.2cm
(22.5in. x 30in.)
Private Collection

Dr Winifred Rushforth (p. 62)
1982. 61cm x 71.1cm (24in. x 28in.)
Scottish National Portrait Gallery

Dr Winifred Rushforth, Lauder Road (p. 63)
1981-2. Oil on canvas, 63.5cm x
120.6cm (25in. x 47½in.)
City Art Centre, Edinburgh

Drawing for Back Garden Monksview,
(p. 34)
1970. Pencil and watercolour resist on
paper (mixed media), 24.1cm x 35.6cm
(9in. x 14in.)
Collection of the Artist

Drawing Lilies (p. 141)
2010. Oil on linen, 117cm x 122cm
(46⅛in. x 48in.)
Private Collection

Drawn from Italy (p. 83)
2001. Silkscreen, intaglio and chine collé,
38.1cm x 88.9cm (15in. x 35in.)
Private Collection

Echoed Landscape (p. 101)
2004. Oil on linen, 101.5cm x 91cm
(40in. x 35 ⅞in.)
Private Collection

Emma Tennant (p. 67)
1996. Oil on board, 60.8cm x 76.1cm
(23⅞in. x 30in.)
In the Devonshire Collection at Chatsworth

Enigmatic Head (p. 171)
2011. Oil on board, 25.4cm x 30.5cm
(10in. x 12in.)
Private Collection

Events in the Garden (pp. 168-9)
2010-11. Mixed media on museum
board, 81.3cm x 119.4cm (32in. x 47in.)
Private Collection

Florentine Winter (p. 98)
2004. Mixed media, 58.5cm x 100cm
(23in. x 39⅜in.)
Private Collection

Forty Lilies for John (p. 165)
2010-11. Oil on linen,
114.3cm x 121.9cm (45in. x 48in.)
Private Collection

Fragile Creatures (p. 97)
2005. Drawing and collage,
19.1cm x 21.6cm (7½in. x 8½in.)
Private Collection

Fragile Traces, Venice (p. 84)
1999. Mixed media, 24.1cm x 40.6cm
(9½in. 16in.)
Private Collection

Frost Pocket (p. 123)
2007. Oil on linen, 101.6cm x 101.6cm
(40in. x 40in.)
Private Collection

Frost Sequence (p. 122)
2007. Mixed media, 38.1cm x 109.9cm
(15in. x 43¼in.)
Private Collection

Garden, W6 (p. 19)
1967/8. Oil on board, 56.5cm x 69cm
(22¼in. 27⅛in.)
Private Collection

Garden Room – A View from the Interior
(pp. 128-9)
2009-10. Oil on linen, 102cm x 127cm
(40⅛in. x 50in.)
Private Collection

Greek Hillside I (p. 30)
1970. Ink and resist on hand-made paper,
16.5cm x 16.5cm (6½in. x 6½in.)
Collection of the Artist

Greek Hillside II (p. 30)
1970. Pencil and oil pastel on paper,
17.8cm x 22.9cm (7in. x 9in.)
Collection of the Artist

Greek Orthodox Interior (Paros), detail (p. 28)
1970. Mixed media, 35.6cm x 27.5cm
(14in. x 10 ⅞in.)
Calderdale Metropolitan Borough Council

Greek Sketch Book (p. 28)
1970. Pencil and watercolour,
22.9cm x 35.6cm (9in. x 14in.)
Collection of the Artist

Herbal Remedies (p. 116)
2006. Mixed media, approx 19.1cm x
24.1cm (7½in. x 9½in.)
Private Collection

Heroes and Villains (p. 69)
1991. Oil on board, 76.2cm x 109.2cm
(30in. x 43in.)
Collection of the Artist's Family

Hillside and Terrace, Tuscany (p. 97)
2006. Ink and wash on handmade paper,
35cm x 44cm (13¾in. x 17⅜in.)
Private Collection

Ice and Fire (p. 150)
2011. Oil on board, 38.1cm x 26.7cm
(15in. x 10½in.)
Collection of the Artist

Iconostasis Fragment (p. 28)
1973. Mixed media, 35.6cm x 30.5cm
(14in. x 12in.)
Private Collection

Induction Morning (p. 53)
1985-6. Watercolour, 45.7cm x 68.6cm
(18in. x 27in.)
Private Collection

Interior, Monk's Cottage (pp. 58-9)
1981. Oil on board, 91cm x 122cm
(35 ⅞in. x 48in.)
Calderdale Metropolitan Borough Council

Interior with Reflected Landscape (p. 127)
2007. Oil on board, 71.1cm x 66cm
(28in. x 26in.)
Private Collection

Into an Older Land (p. 94)
2006. Oil on linen, 101.6cm x 142.2cm
(40in. x 56in.)
Collection of the Royal Scottish Academy

Iris Albicans (detail) (p. 110)
2004. Watercolour study,
35.6cm x 25.4cm (14in. x 10in.)
Collection of the Artist

Iris Arenaria (detail) (p. 110)
2004. Watercolour study,
22.9cm x 22.9cm (9in. x 9in.)
Collection of the Artist

Isis Madonna (p. 117)
2006. Mixed media, approx 19.1cm x
24.1cm (7½in. x 9½in.)
Private Collection

Italian Reflections (p. 70)
1993. Oil on canvas, 73.5cm x 89cm
(29in. x 35in.)
City Art Centre, Edinburgh

Jenny at Home (p. 61)
1982. Watercolour, 49.5cm x 39.4cm
(19½in. x 15½in.)
Collection of the Artist

Jenny, Sheep and Dogs (p.45)
c.1975-6. Oil on paper, 30.5cm x 33cm
(12in. x 13in.)
Private Collection

Jenny's Fence Looking Towards Kittleyknowe
(p. 47)
1978. Pencil, crayon and watercolour on
paper, 39.4cm x 49.5cm (15½in. x 19½in.)
Collection of the Artist

Kathleen Raine (p. 65)
1986. Oil on board, 91.4cm x 71.1cm
(36in. x 28in.)
National Portrait Gallery, London

Kittleybrig, Winter (p. 42-3)
1979. Oil on board, 76.2cm x 91.4cm
(30in. x 36in.)
Private Collection

Known and Imagined World (p. 177)
2012. Oil on linen, 101.6cm x 127cm
(40in. x 50in.)
Collection of the Artist

La Suvera, Landscape (detail) (p. 144)
2009. Watercolour, 10.2cm x 20.4cm
(4in. x 8in.)
Collection of the Artist

Lamb and Lucifer (p. 74)
1994. Oil on board, 30.5cm x 35.6cm
(12in. x 14in.)
Private Collection

Landscape – Duality (p. 144)
2010. Oil on linen, 76cm x 91cm
(30in. x 35 ⅞in.)
Private Collection

Landscape Against the Light (p. 102)
2004. Oil on linen, 152cm x 152cm
(59 ⅞in. x 59 ⅞in.)
Private Collection

Landscape and Sentinel, La Suvera (p. 145)
2010. Mixed media, 49cm x 32 cm
(19¼in. x 12⅝in.)
Private Collection

Landscape at Silverburn I (p. 27)
1969. Mixed media and collage,
35.6cm x 55.9cm (14in. x 22in.)
Private Collection

Landscape on the Mirror's Surface (p. 103)
2004. Oil on linen, 101.5cm x 76cm
(40in. x 30in.)
Private Collection

Landscape Sentinels (p. 143)
2010. Oil on board, 71.1cm x 76.2cm
(28in. x 30in.)
Private Collection

Landscape with Figures and Dogs (p. 45)
c.1975-6. Oil on paper, 30.5cm x 33cm
(12in. x 13in.)
Private Collection

Large Tree Group (p. 39)
1975. Oil on board, 91.4cm x 101.6cm
(36in. x 40in.)
Private Collection

Last Portrait of Jenny Armstrong (p. 56)
1986-7. Oil on board, 122cm x 91.4cm
(48in. x 36in.)
City Art Centre, Edinburgh

Life Room, Kingston School of Art, The (p. 10)
1964. Drawing, 22.9cm x 17.8cm
(9in. x 7in.)
Collection of the Artist

Lilium Candidum I (p. 110)
2006. Mixed media, 38.1cm x 116.8cm
(15in. x 46in.)
Private Collection

Lilium Candidum II (p. 110)
2006. Mixed media, 38.1cm x 116.8cm
(15in. x 46in.)
Private Collection

Litany (pp. 118-9)
2007. Mixed media, 61cm x 81.3cm
(24in. x 32in.)
Private Collection

Lone Tree (p. 13)
1963. Oil on board, 49.5cm x 34.3cm
(19½in. x 13½in.)
Collection of the Artist

Luminous Winter (pp. 8-9)
2008. Mixed media, 38cm x 109.5cm
(15in. x 43in.)
Private Collection

Lying Snow (p. 151)
2010. Oil and mixed media on paper,
51cm x 71cm (20⅛in. x 28in.)
In the Devonshire Collection at Chatsworth

Madonna Lily (p. 111)
2007. Drawing on handmade Japanese
paper, 101.6cm x 50.8cm (40in. x 20in.)
Collection of the Artist

Marriage Piece, Italian Landscape (p. 171)
2011. Oil on linen, 61cm x 122cm
(24in. x 48in.)
Private Collection

Medieval Mind (p. 116)
2006. Mixed media, approx. 19.1cm x
24.1cm (7½in. x 9½in.)
Private Collection

Mellow Winter (p. 120)
2008. Oil on linen, 91.5cm x 71.5cm
(36in. x 28⅛in.)
Collection of Tanya Westinghouse

Midnight Garden (p. 77)
1996. Oil, 40.6cm x 50.8cm (16in. x 20in.)
Private Collection

Mirror of the South (p. 93)
2001. Oil on linen, 101.6cm x 127cm
(40in. x 50in.)
Private Collection

The Moment (pp. 90-1)
2004. Mixed media, 58.5cm x 100cm
(23in. x 36⅜in.)
Private Collection

Morning, Reflections Across the Water
(p. 138)
2012. Oil on linen, 91.4cm x 101.6cm
(36in. x 40in.)
Collection of the Artist

Myth and Message (p. 74)
1994. Oil on board, 30.5cm x 35.6cm
(12in. x 14in.)
Private Collection

Near Rialto (p. 88)
2004. Oil on linen, 76cm x 101.5cm
(30in. x 40in.)
Private Collection

Night of the Dragonfly (p. 76)
1996. Oil on board, 30.5cm x 40.6cm
(12in. x 16in.)
Private Collection

Night Travelling (p. 79)
1997. Charcol on handmade paper,
35.6cm x 78.7cm (14in. x 31in.)
Private Collection

November Window Reflecting (p. 78)
1996. Oil on board, 101.6cm x 122cm
(40in. x 48in.)
Private Collection

Numinous Garden (p. 157)
2011. Oil on linen, 114.3cm x 127cm
(45in. x 50in.)
Private Collection

Numinous Tree (p. 154)
2010. Oil on panel, 71cm x 76cm
(28in. x 30in.)
Private Collection

Observed Sequence (p. 114)
2005. Mixed media, 30.5cm x 101.6cm
(12in. x 40in.)
Private Collection

On Reflection (p. 100)
2005. Oil on linen, 23.6cm x 23.6cm
(60in. x 60in.)
Private Collection

On the Inside Looking Out (p. 49)
1977-8. Oil on board, 91.4cm x 122cm
(36in. x 48in.)
Collection Tanya Westinghouse

Outside Eden (p.117)
2006. Mixed media, approx. 19.1cm x
24.1cm (7½in. x 9½in.)
Private Collection

Paean (p. 173)
2010-11. Oil on linen, 127cm x 101.6cm
(50in. x 40in.)
Private Collection

Pale Nude (p. 11)
1964. Oil on board, 62cm x 76.2cm
(24½in. x 30in.)
Collection of the Artist

Pale Nude drawing (p. 10)
1964. 22.9cm x 17.8cm (9in. x 7in.)
Collection the Artist

Passionate Fruit (title page)
2003. Oil on board, 26.7cm x 21.6cm
(10½in. 8½in)
Collection of HRH The Prince of Wales

Pentland Hills at Marchwell (Winter) (p. 26)
1970. Ink resistance and body colour on
handmade paper, 33cm x 43.2cm
(13in. x 17in.)
Private Collection

Pentland Landscape (p. 26)
1970. Ink and mixed media on paper,
54.6cm x 74.9cm (21½in. x 29½in.)

Piazetta with Lily and Moon (p. 105)
2003-4. Oil on board, 91cm x 71cm
(35 ⅞in. x 30in.)
Private Collection

Piero's Mysterious Dogs (p. 142)
2010. Pencil and wash, 14cm x 20cm
(5½in. x 7⅝in.)
Private Collection

Pink Palazzo (p. 87)
2003. Oil on linen, 127cm x 127cm
(50in. x 50in.)
Collection of the Artist

Portrait of David Ingram (p. 108)
2003. Oil on linen, 127cm x 101.6cm
(50in. x 40in.)
Collection of St Catharine's College,
Cambridge University

Private View with Plastic Tulips (p. 60)
1978. Oil on board, 106.7cm x 86.4cm
(42in. x 34in.)
Collection of the Artist

R.D. Laing (p. 64)
1984. Oil on board, 91.4cm x 71.1cm
(36in. x 27in.)
Scottish National Portrait Gallery,
Edinburgh

Range and Semmit (p. 52)
1982. Oil on board, 91.4cm x 71.1cm
(36in. x 28in.)
Collection Tanya Westinghouse

Recovered Reflection (p. 95)
2003. Mixed media, 30.5cm x 19.1cm (12in. x 7½in.)
Private Collection

Red Arcadia (pp. 166-7)
2010-11. Mixed media, 81.3cm x 119.4cm (32in. x 47in.)
Private Collection

Reflected Contemplation (p. 140)
2008. Mixed media, 56.5cm x 94cm (22¼in. x 37in.)
Private Collection

Reflected Time (p. 92)
2003. Mixed media, 30.5cm x 49.5cm (12in. x 19½in.)
Private Collection

Reflected Sequence (p. 114)
2005. Mixed media, 30.5cm x 102.9cm (12in. x 40½in.)
Private Collection

Reflected Winter (p. 99)
2008. Oil on linen, 127cm x 101.5cm (50cm x 40in.)
Private Collection

Reflection on a Lost Empire (p. 131)
2010. Oil on linen, 117cm x 112cm (46⅛in. x 44⅛in.)
Private Collection

Rialto? (p. 132)
2010. Mixed media, 23cm x 30cm (9⅛in. x 11⅞in.)
Private Collection

Rosa Proprina and the Pentland Hills (pp. 24-5)
1970. Ink and mixed media on paper, 48.3cm x 76.2cm (19in. x 30in.)
Collection of the Artist

Rosa Proprina Visits the Back Garden in Winter (p. 152)
2012. Oil on linen, 76.2cm x 101.6cm (30in. x 40in.)
Collection of the Artist

The Rout of San Romano (pp. 32-3)
1970. Details not available.
Private Collection

Trees in Richmond Park (p. 12)
1964. Oil on board, 66cm x 78.7cm (26in. x 31in.)
Collection of the Artist

Trees in Richmond Park, study (p. 12)
1963. 14.6cm x 19.7cm (5¾in. x 7¾in.)
Collection of the Artist

Self portrait, sketch book studies (p. 15)
1963. 22.9cm x 35.6cm (9in. x 14in.)
Collection of the Artist

Self Portrait with Icon (p. 17)
1964-5. Oil on board, 76.2cm x 91.4cm (30in. x 36in.)
Private Collection

Sensual Processes (p. 89)
2003. Oil on board, 96.5cm x 109.2cm (38in. x 43in.)
Private Collection

Shape of the Shadow (p. 155)
2010. Oil on linen, 76cm x 102cm (30in. x 40⅛in.)
Private Collection

Sheep, Shepherdess and Harbour Craig (p. 46)
1975. Oil on board, 78.7cm x 99.1cm (31in. x 39in.)
Private Collection

The Shortest Day (p. 159)
2012. Oil on linen, 71.1cm x 91.4cm (28in. x 36in.)
Collection of the Artist

Sign and Symbol – Herbarium Pages (p. 113)
2005. Oil and mixed media on linen, 91.4cm x 71.1cm (36in. x 28in.)
Private Collection

Skyline, Venice (p. 134)
2011. Mixed media on handmade paper, 20.3cm x 29.2cm (8in. x 11½in.)
Collection of the Artist

Snow Moment (p. 153)
2009-10. Oil on paper, 32cm x 51cm (12⅝in. x 20⅛in.)
Private Collection

Snow Sky (p. 48)
1977. Oil on board, 91.4cm x 122cm (36in. x 48in.)
Private Collection

Snowlines (pp. 124-5)
2010. Oil and mixed media, 79cm x 119cm (31⅛in x 46 ⅞in.)
Private Collection

Snowbound Cottages (p. 40)
1977. Oil on board, 91.4cm x 122cm (36in. x 48in.)
Private Collection

St Basil's Cathedral, Moscow (p. 14)
1964. Oil on board, 72.4cm x 61cm (28½in. x 24in.)
Collection of the Artist

Stephanosis Ascending (p. 104)
2004. Oil on linen, 101.5cm x 91cm (40in. x 35 ⅞in.)
Private Collection

Studio Venice, Mirrored View (pp. 136-7)
2011. Oil on linen, 100.3cm x 127.6cm (39½in. x 50¼in.)
Collection of the Artist

Study for December 25th (p. 51)
1980-1. Watercolour on cartridge paper, 22.9cm x 27.9cm (9in. x 11in.)
Collection of the Artist

Study for Deposition I (p. 20)
1967-8. Pencil on Paper, 38.1cm x 28cm (15in. x 11in.)
Collection of the Artist

Study for Deposition II (p. 20)
1967-8. Pencil on Paper, 19.1cm x 14cm (7 ½in. x 5½in.)
Collection of the Artist

Study for Garden, W6 (p. 18)
1967-8. Pencil on paper, 27.9cm x 48.3cm (11in. x 19in.)
Collection of the Artist

Study for the portrait of R.D. Laing (p. 64)
1984. Mixed media on handmade paper, 50.8cm x 40.6cm (20in. x 16in.)
Collection of the Artist

Study of the Pentlands (p. 27)
1969. Mixed media and collage, 55cm x 75cm (21⅝in. x 29½in.)
Private Collection

Svetlana Stalin in a Hammock (p. 23)
1968. Oil on board, 71.1cm x 91.4cm (28in. x 36in.)
Collection Tanya Westinghouse

Thea Musgrave (p. 66)
2006. Oil on linen, 76.2cm x 91.4cm (30in. x 36in.)
Trustees of the National Galleries of Scotland 2006

Thoughts on the City (p. 139)
2012. Mixed media on museum board, 54cm x 79.4cm (21¼in. 31¼in.)
Collection of the Artist

Tom Wickham's Barns (p. 41)
1978-9. Mixed media on handmade paper, 36.8cm x 47cm (14½in. x 18½in.)
Private Collection

Tramonto (p. 135)
2012. Oil on line, 76.2cm x 101.6cm (30in. x 40in.)
Collection of the Artist

Travelling by Moonlight (p. 75)
1995. Oil on board, 95.25cm x 109.2cm (37½in. x 43in.)
Collection of the Artist

Tree Snow Study (p. 148)
2011. Oil on handmade paper,
52.1cm x 73.7cm (20½in. x 29in.)
Collection of the Artist

Two Views, Tapestry (pp. 162-3)
2008. Tapestry, 1.22 x 2.44m (4 x 8ft.)
© Victoria Crowe / Dovecot Studios
Collection of The Duke of Buccleuch and Queensberry

Venice Reflected (p. 130)
2009. Watercolour and mixed media,
8.7cm x 14.2cm (22in. x 36in.)
Private Collection

Visiting Cat and Two Snowmen (p. 153)
2010. Oil and mixed media,
32cm x 48cm (12⅝in. x 18 ⅞in.)
Private Collection

Walking and Thinking in Venice (p. 132)
2010. Mixed media, 29cm x 79cm
(11⅜in. x 31⅛in.)
Private Collection

Walking the Way of Time (pp. 106-7)
2003. Oil on linen, 76.2cm x 101.6cm
(30in. x 40in.)
Private Collection

While in Italy; Variation (p. 72)
1994. Silkscreen print and oil,
20.3cm x 55.9cm (8in. x 22in.)
Private Collection

While in Italy; Variation Braccio Reliquario, San Sebastiano (p. 72)
1994. Silkscreen print and oil,
20.3cm x 55.9cm (8in. x 22in.)
Private Collection

While in Venice (p. 85)
1998. Water-based silkscreen print,
58cm x 58cm (22⅞in. x 22⅞in.)
Private Collection

Winter Caveat (p. 156)
2010-11. Oil on linen, 127cm x 127cm
(50in. x 50in.)
Collection of the Artist

Winter at Kittleybrig (p. 38)
1974. Oil on board, 122cm x 91.4cm
(48in. x 36in.)
Private Collection

Winter Fuel (p. 52)
1985-6. Watercolour, 45.7cm x 68.6cm
(18in. x 27in.)
Collection of Dr and Mrs Lindsay Neil

Winter Sequence (p. 122)
2007. Mixed media, 39.4cm x 110.5cm
(15½in. x 43½in.)
Private Collection

Winter Studio (p. 149)
2010. Oil on linen laid on board,
76.2cm x 53.3cm (30in. x 21in.)
Collection of the Artist

Winter Walk (p. 44)
1977. Oil on canvas, 71.1cm x 91.4cm
(28in. x 36in.)
Private Collection

Within and Without (p. 73)
1993-4. Oil on board, 50.8cm x 61cm
(20in. x 24in.)
Private Collection

PHOTOGRAPHS

Discussing, *Large Tree Group* (p. 160)
Photo © Mike Walton

The Duke of Buccleuch and Queensbury cutting off, *Two Views* (p. 161)
Photo © Ken Gray

Installation of *Events in the Garden* (p. 170)
Photo © Ken Gray

Installation of *Forty Lilies for John* (p. 170)
Photo © Ken Gray

Large Tree Group, studio views (p. 161)
Photo © Mike Walton

Postgraduate Degree Show, RCA, 1968 (p. 22). © Mike Walton

R.D. Laing (p. 64)
1984. 25.4cm x 30.5cm (10in. x 12in.)
© Mike Walton

Selecting shades of undyed wool for *Large Tree Group* (p. 161)
Photo © Mike Walton

Victoria Crowe drinking Georgian champagne in Leningrad, 1971 (p. 31)

Victoria Crowe in her studio (frontispiece).
© Robin Scott

Weaving, *Two Views* (p. 160)
Photo © Ken Gray

Notes

Early Years
1. Recorded in an interview with Jenny Simmons for *Artists' Lives*, British Library (2007).
2. RCA Thesis, p. 6.
3. *Artists' Lives*

Scotland
1. *Artists' Lives*
2. *'à porter sans fléchir, sur leur gouttelette presque impalpable, l'édifice immense du souvenir.'* Marcel Proust, *Du Côté de chez Swann* (Paris 1954), p. 68.

Kittleyknowe
1. *A Shepherd's Life*, National Galleries of Scotland (2000 / 2008), p. 59.

Interiors
1. *Lycidas*, lines 39-41.

First Portraits
1.Dr. Winifred Rushforth Issue No. 1, *Sempervivum Magazine*, Sept–Dec, 1978.
2. *Artists' Lives*
3. *R.D.Laing: Creative Destroyer*, ed. Bob Mullen (London 1997), pp. 116-125.
4. Victoria Crowe and Michael Walton, *Painted Insights*, Antique Collector's Club, Woodbridge (2001 / 2009), p. 51.

West Linton
1. *Painted Insights*, p. 76.

Venice
1. Thackeray Gallery catalogue (2003).
2. Henri Bergson, *Matter and Memory* (London 1911) p. 303.
3. Thackeray Gallery (2003).

Plant Memories
1. *Quand lui, le chercheur, est tout ensemble le pays obscur où il doit chercher.* Proust, *Du Côté de Chez Swann*, p. 66.
2. Thackeray Gallery (2003) note on *Guardians of the Real World.*
3. *Victoria Crowe,* 'Plant Memory', RSA (Edinburgh 2007), p. 9.
4. 'Plant Memory', p. 29.
5. *Matter and Memory*, p. 319.

New Departures
1. Constable's last lecture, 25 July 1836, quoted by C.R. Leslie in *Memoirs of the Life of John Constable Esq. RA* (London 1845), p. 388.
2. Constable to to Rev. John Fisher, 23 October, 1821, quoted in Leslie, *Constable*, p.120.

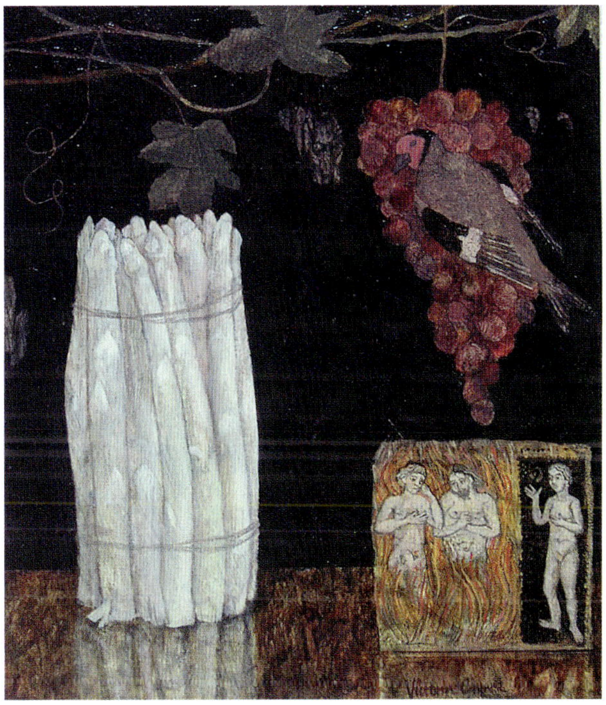